JABAL MUHAMMAD BUABEN

IMAGE *of the* PROPHET MUḤAMMAD *in the* WEST

A STUDY OF MUIR, MARGOLIOUTH AND WATT

The Islamic Foundation

ISBN 0 86037 260 X (HB)
ISBN 0 86037 261 8 (PB)

Published by
The Islamic Foundation,
Markfield Dawah Centre,
Ratby Lane, Markfield,
Leicester LE67 9RN,
United Kingdom

Quran House,
PO Box 30611,
Nairobi, Kenya

PMB 3193,
Kano, Nigeria

Printed in Great Britain by The Cromwell Press Ltd.
Broughton Gifford, Melksham, Wiltshire

Dedication

TO

My parents
the late Papa Bukr Kwesi Munkwaabo
and
the late Maame Hawa Adwoa Ketseaba
whose sweat and toil
took me to school.

Also to all scholars
who endeavour to project the truth.

Supplication

If I have written anything contrary to the true teachings of Islam as presented by the Holy Prophet Muḥammad (s.a.w.) or if there is anything which directly or indirectly denies the truth in God and His Messenger and His revealed Word, the Holy Qur'ān, I beg forgiveness from Him Who is *Al-Raḥmān, Al-Raḥīm* (the Merciful, the Compassionate).

بسم الله الرحمن الرحيم

Contents

Abbreviation of Journals Consulted

AHR	*American Historical Review*
AJISS	*American Journal of Islamic Social Sciences*
AQR	*Asiatic Quarterly Review*
AREA	*Arabica-Revue d'Etudes Arabes*
BO	*Bibliotheca Orientalis*
BSOAS	*Bulletin of the School of Oriental and African Studies*
BZAZ	*Beilage Zur Allgemeinen Zeitung*
CHR	*Catholic Historical Review*
CMI	*The Church Missionary Intelligencer*
CR	*Calcutta Review*
DI	*Der Islam*
HI	*Hamdard Islamicus*
HIS	*Humaniora Islamica*
HJ	*The Hibbert Journal*
HTR	*Hartford Theological Review*
IC	*Islamic Culture*
ICMR	*Islam and Christian-Muslim Relations*
IJISS	*International Journal of Islamic Social Sciences*
IJMES	*International Journal of Middle Eastern Studies*
IL	*Islamic Literature*
IMA	*Islam and the Modern Age*
IOQ	*Islamic Order Quarterly*
IOS	*Israel Oriental Studies*
IQ	*Islamic Quarterly*
IRM	*International Review of Mission*
IS	*Islamic Studies*

JASB	*Journal of the Asiatic Society of Bengal*
JBL	*Journal of Biblical Literature*
JESHO	*Journal of Economic and Social History of the Orient*
JIJ	*Journal of Jewish Studies*
JIS	*Journal of Islamic Studies*
JNES	*Journal of Near Eastern Studies*
JPHS	*Journal of the Pakistan Historical Society*
JQR	*Jewish Quarterly Review*
JRAS	*Journal of the Royal Asiatic Society*
JSS	*Journal of Semitic Studies*
MEH	*Medievalia et Humanistica*
MEJ	*Middle East Journal*
MLR	*Modern Language Review*
MW	*The Muslim World*
MWBR	*Muslim World Book Review*
NAR	*North American Review*
POC	*Proche Orient Chretien*
QR	*Quarterly Review*
RC	*Race and Class*
REI	*Revue des Etudes Islamiques*
RMES	*Review of Middle Eastern Studies*
RSO	*Rivista Degli Studi Orientali*
RT	*Revue Thomiste*
SI	*Studia Islamica*
SM	*Studia Missionalia*
TR	*Table Ronde*
URM	*Ultimate Reality and Meaning*
VOI	*Voice of Islam*
YIS	*Yale Italian Studies*

بسم الله الرحمن الرحيم

Foreword

Regrettably it was mostly in terms of serious religious differences and the resultant hostility that the West first learnt about Islam and Muslims. With the phenomenal rise and spread of Islam in the seventh century the West became all the more apprehensive about the new faith. Soon Islam appeared on the European scene itself in that it knocked at the European doors from the West, through Spain, in the Centre, from Sicily to southern Italy; in the East, into the Balkans and southern Russia. Perceiving Islam as a great threat the West, most notably the Church, resolved to arrest its spread by casting Islam in the role of a despicable and grossly repulsive enemy. This, in turn, fuelled the confrontation manifested in the Crusades (1096–1271). Although the Crusades helped, in a sense, in forging a variety of links between the two adversaries – ranging from an exchange of military techniques to food, dress and vocabulary – the relationship between the two great civilizations – Western and Islam – has been, on the whole, vitiated by misconception and hostility. To this day, regrettably, such hostility is still at work, prompting some influential writers of our times, namely Huntington and Fukuyama to prophesy a catastrophic 'clash of civilizations' in the near future. Against this backdrop, one readily recognizes the urgent and pressing need for developing a better understanding between the two civilizations and for improving human communications.

A study of *Sīrah*, or the biography of the Prophet Muḥammad (Allah's blessings and peace be upon him) may serve best as the starting point for gaining and promoting mutual understanding.

For *Sīrah* is central to grasping the meaning and message of Islam. Far from being a mere agent who faithfully transmitted what God asked him to impart as His final Messenger, Muḥammad (pbuh) stands out as a perfect embodiment of Islam itself. Through his words and deeds he exemplified at its best what Islam prescribes in theory. Moreover, his conduct represents a unique amalgam of the particular and the universal; the time-space specific and the eternal. God presents him in the Qur'ān as the model to be emulated by mankind of all times and all places: '(O Mankind!) You have indeed in the Messenger of God a perfect role model' (*al-Aḥzāb* 33: 21).

The eminent position *Sīrah* occupies in Islam was not lost on Western writers. From the earliest times down to this day numerous Western writers have produced works on *Sīrah*, a point amply borne out by Chapter One of the present book. It is quite obvious that the medieval writers on *Sīrah*, especially the Christian polemicists, became overawed by the spectacular success of Islam and ultimately developed an intense prejudice and hatred against the religion, in particular against its two fundamental sources – the Qur'ān and the *Sunnah*. They spent all their energies painting the darkest possible picture of Islam and the life of the Prophet. What is rather strange and in many respects unforgivable, is that modern scholars, who have a better understanding of Islam and are better trained in their discipline, have better access to original Islamic sources, occupy special chairs of Islamic Studies at well-known Western universities and have no excuse for showing ignorance in their writings, should indulge in polemical writings and repeat unpalatable statements about the Prophet and the fundamentals of Islam. It is rather unfortunate that the vulgar attack on Islam and invectives against the Prophet which was the hallmark of medieval writers, has now given way to a subtle technique of research and interpretation, and the open criticism of Islamic history and culture has now been clothed in the modern attire of objective study and the paraphernalia of academic discipline. This is amply borne out in the writings of many critics of Orientalism, such as A.L. Tibawi, Edward Said and others.

It is most gratifying to note that Jabal Muhammad Buaben, in the present research based on his doctoral thesis, has explored energetically and effectively the medieval legacy and the relevant aspects of Western writings on *Sīrah*. While focusing on the works of the three most influential British writers on *Sīrah* – William Muir, David S. Margoliouth and W.M. Watt, he brings out the historical background and roots of the negative image of the Prophet (pbuh) in the West. The section surveying major twentieth-century writings is especially illuminating in terms of both its wide coverage and its insightful critical study. Buaben has very clearly shown that despite their claim to have a better understanding of Islam and to show objectivity in their appreciation of Islamic teachings, the medieval portrayal of the life and mission of the Prophet has, by and large, survived in later times, especially in the period of enlightened scholarship. Professor Watt's insistence, for example, that the Qur'ān is a 'subdued revelation' and is not wholly true; that the report of the despatch of the Prophet's emissaries to the emperors of Byzantium and Persia is unreliable, in addition to casting doubt on many of the classical traditions, showing a special fascination with the concocted story of the 'Satanic Verses', attributing less credit to contemporary Islamic scholarship and relying on his own conjectures and, most outrageously, putting the Prophet in the category of Adolf Hitler in their creative imagination, among many others, are nothing but specimens of subjective scholarship, reminiscent of the bigotry and hatred shown by Christian polemicists in the medieval period.

Buaben's study, I am sure, will go a long way in equipping better the students of Islam in grasping the chequered history of relations between Islam and the West. It will also help dispel some common misconceptions, prevailing especially in the West, about the life and mission of the Prophet Muḥammad (pbuh) who, by any yardstick of greatness, was and remains to this day a perfect role model for the whole of mankind. Buaben deserves every credit for setting the record straight about this great man and his equally great achievements.

I am extremely grateful to my colleagues in the Foundation, in particular Dr. A.R. Kidwai, Dr. Ataullah Siddiqui, Mokrane Guezzou, Naiem Qaddoura, Sohail Nakhooda and Mr. E.R. Fox for going through the manuscript, giving their perceptive comments and suggestions and helping in the design and publication of the book. May Allah accept their humble effort and make it a source of objective and positive study of the life of the Prophet in the West.

Leicester
Rabīʿ al-Awwal 1417 H
August 1996 CE

Muhammad Manazir Ahsan
Director General

Preface

This is a study of the biographical works of three prominent British scholars on the Prophet Muḥammad (peace be upon him). Sir William Muir, David Samuel Margoliouth and William Montgomery Watt have been selected owing to the impact their works on Muḥammad have had upon both Muslims and non-Muslims in the English-speaking world.

One of the central issues investigated in this study is the medieval polemical image of the Prophet and its survival in our period of enlightened scholarship. The issue is of great significance in a world where the geo-political scene is very unpredictable despite the apparent desire in many quarters for Inter-Faith relations. If Inter-Faith relations are to have a positive effect, there is a need to excise from people's consciousness some of the medieval war psychosis propaganda which has created a caricature of Islam in the minds of many people. Mutual respect and trust are necessary.

In medieval times, Islam was painted as an enemy and Muḥammad (pbuh) had to take the brunt. In our modern era, there seems to be signs of a call for that painting to be retouched. It is the works of eminent scholars, such as those with which this study deals, that perhaps confirm some of the medieval stereotypes. The present study brings out this regrettable fact.

Scientific method creates avenues for a dispassionate study of a subject and contributes to a judicious application of sound academic principles. Our study upholds this and insists that since the world is now a global village, the need to know and understand each other increases daily but this can only be done if we are sincere, honest, and fair in our outlook towards each other.

The work is in two Parts with three Chapters in each Part.

Chapter One looks at the medieval European view of Muḥammad. This is done on the hypothesis that the current attitudes derive their roots from the medieval war-propaganda period.

In Chapter Two, the works of Sir William Muir are examined with special emphasis on his biographical work on Muḥammad.

Chapter Three looks at David Samuel Margoliouth and his main book on Muḥammad (pbuh).

Chapter Four is a survey of twentieth-century literature, and sets the context for a critique of William Montgomery Watt who forms the subject of Chapter Five.

It could be observed that there is a greater emphasis on Watt and it takes up a substantial portion of the work. This is inevitable, primarily because he is the only one of the three still alive and, being a prolific writer, there is more material on him than on Muir and Margoliouth. Therefore, we have allowed, in a sense, the material to dictate the length of the discussion.

For each of these three writers, their main books on *Sīrah* are painstakingly analyzed, identifying the major themes of each. Choice of theme is a good pointer to a scholar's methodology, therefore we have noted the issues which occupy their attention.

In some cases we have made observations on the lacuna and omissions which have been either deliberately or unwittingly left.

Although each chapter has a short Conclusion, Chapter Six offers an overall appraisal. In this final chapter, some observations are made on the study of religion in line with the norms of sound enlightened scholarship.

The apparent deliberate efforts of some scholars to denigrate Islam and Muslims, especially by recreating a medieval image of Muḥammad, does not help in fostering the trust we need for interacting with each other.

It is our hope that this study will, in a small way, contribute in awakening people to question the dominant Western opinions about Islam and Muslims, in general, and about Muḥammad in particular.

I would like to express my deepest gratitude to all those who, in one way or another, have helped me to bring this work to a conclusion after many nerve-racking years.

I thank Professor David Kerr who started the supervision with me, Dr. Jorgen S. Nielsen who took over and became more of a colleague, confidant and a father than a supervisor, and indeed all the staff of the CSIC, Birmingham who offered various support.

I wish to record the kind offer of a Teaching Fellowship at the CSIC which sustained me during the last lap. I would also like to acknowledge the generous assistance extended me by the Lembaga Bersekutu Pemegang Amānah Pengajian Tinggi Islam, Malaysia.

Further, I am particularly indebted to the Yayasān Amān Berhād, Malaysia, for facilitating my trip to and stay in Birmingham.

My employers, the International Islamic University, Malaysia also deserve my profound appreciation for agreeing to suspend my contract to enable me to travel to the UK to complete this study.

As for my wife and children, I have only the highest praise for the good humour and resilience with which they endured my vagaries and eccentricities during the long and gruelling years I spent on this work. I apologize for all that they have been through because of my perhaps selfish attempt to obtain a higher degree.

I am grateful to the Islamic Foundation, especially its Director General Dr. M.M. Ahsan, for their encouragement and for the bringing out of my study as a Foundation publication.

To all my friends both in the UK and Malaysia who continuously urged me on when the going became tough, I say Jazākumullāh Khairan Kathīrā.

July 1995 CE **Jabal Muhammad Buaben**

PART I

CHAPTER ONE

The Medieval European View of Muḥammad

Introduction

Medieval writers, even those who had access to material on Muḥammad, preferred subjective to objective material. This work seeks to examine whether this problem of choosing negative material instead of that which objective scholarship provides has survived. One of the central questions is: To what extent do modern Western writers on Muḥammad owe their attitude to the medieval legacy?

This chapter examines medieval times up to the seventeenth century, seeking to present a survey of ideas prevalent in the then European world about Islam and Muḥammad and how these came to affect the cultural and intellectual basis upon which many later Western scholars based their writings. This, we believe, will provide a proper critique of the later material on Muḥammad in the West.

In order to make amends in our endless search for that seemingly ideal 'objective scholarship', it is pertinent to look at the past to know where we went wrong. That, simply stated, is one of the main aims of the study of history. If we fail to recognize where we employed improper methodology in our study of a subject, then it will be difficult to arrive at sound conclusions. We will still be groping in the dark, merely restating what some people thought was worth recording.

Some of the questions we will grapple with are such as Waltz has asked: 'Why did the writers select some events as worthy of report and ignore others, and were their interpretations only personal or also representative of a considerable stratum or spectrum of society?'[1]

Our objective is also to show that medieval writers were very selective in their choice of material, while pointing out that there was no relationship of objectivity to material. By looking at the medieval age, we believe that we can tackle the issue better. It is this age, we are convinced, which gave a considerable impetus to later scholars in the West. It gave a 'communal opinion' to Norman Daniel's expression, which has survived for centuries.[2] The hegemonic European always identifies his civilization as advanced, and superior while the Oriental and other non-European civilizations are backward and inferior.[3] The West needs to sincerely question this inherent attitude. There must be an unlearning of this innate dominative mode.

Books from the West on Islam and Muḥammad constitute an important barometer of the intentional and unintentional philosophy of its people. If yet another layer of ill-informed stereotyping about Muslims and Islam is to be excised, a critique of the nature we have set out to produce is necessary. The 'them and us' approach that characterizes many a Western writer's approach is no longer tenable.

If our main objective in history is 'simply to show how it really was (*wie es eigentlich gewesen*)' as asserted by Von Ranke,[4] then we stand the risk of losing one of the most important assets of humanity – freedom of thought. This is because 'how it really was' tends to be the way earlier writers saw it. Barraclough notes that 'the history we read, though based on facts, is strictly speaking not factual at all, but a series of accepted judgements'.[5] It is with this in view that we look at the 'accepted judgements' of early Western writers which their progeny have depended upon when writing about Muḥammad. Antonie Wessels surmises that, 'The task of understanding anew what it means in modern times to say that God spoke to or through Muhammad, as we find reflected in the Qur'ān, lies in my opinion, still ahead.'[6] The concern expressed here can be remedied if Western scholarship reassesses itself and shakes off the remnants of the ill-informed medieval opinions about Muḥammad.

As Carr points out, it is an essential function of the student of history to master and understand the past 'as a key to understanding the present'.[7] The constant interplay of past and present is worthwhile and indeed necessary if we are to understand and make constructive progress in *Sīrah* scholarship in the West. The West needs to 'recreate' Muḥammad and this can best be done by looking at the past where the old image was moulded.[8] This is not to suggest that we do not intend touching on Muḥammad as a 'theological challenge' to the Western scholar. It is difficult to separate Muḥammad as a 'historical enigma' from a view of him as the 'theological enigma' that the West has to fully grasp and unravel. Without this theological challenge, Muḥammad would have been considered in the West as a mere historical personality but it seems it is this theological aspect which created much concern in the then establishment.

The Challenge of Islam and Attempts to Deal With It

Islam posed both a practical and theological challenge to the church in the Middle Ages. On the practical side, various options like crusade, conversion, coexistence and commercial exchange existed to deal with the problem. Theologically, Islam consistently called for answers to the multifarious questions it posed. Was it an indication of the prophesied eschatological era, another stage of Christian growth, a mere heresy, a separatist movement or a complete religion in its own right? Answers were difficult to come by.

The early vitality of Islam and the speed with which it achieved intellectual, social and economic momentum can hardly be rivalled in Western history. In terms of conquest, the picture was even more worrying, with Islam knocking at the doors of Germany after overrunning Byzantium and other states in its wake along the southern shores of the Mediterranean. Muḥammad could not simply be dismissed as 'a storm in a tea cup'. As Watt again writes: 'In deadly fear Christendom had to bolster confidence by placing the enemy in the most unfavourable light.'[9]

The medieval mind, with its tendency to portray the enemy as devilish and strange-looking, was set to work. *Non-sequitur* inferences formed the grounds upon which overdrawn generalizations were made which brought in their wake wrong judgements supposed to be historical facts. Character assassination became an honourable duty as long as it was against Muḥammad. The intellectual war against Muḥammad began in earnest. Daniel notes that '. . . the most probable explanation of what happened must be that Christians thought that whatever tended to harm the enemies of truth was likely itself to be true'.[10] Indeed, Guibert of Nogent admitted having no source for the work he produced on Muḥammad but he explained that, 'It is safe to speak evil of the one whose malignity exceeds whatever ill can be spoken of.'[11] Commenting on this, Southern writes: 'In a variety of forms, . . . this rule inspired a great deal of writing in the first half of the twelfth century.'[12] Later students in the West treated these as sacrosanct and immortalized them. The situation which bred the opinions which have survived was such that, 'Methodological acuity, reinvestigation and rigorous questioning are continually called for.'[13]

In order to incite maximum Christian hatred against Muḥammad and Islam, vile propaganda was initiated by the church authorities and taken up by others; for example: 'The anonymous author of the *Gesta Francorum* reported Corboran (Corborgha) as swearing "by Muhammad and all the gods" and his account was widely copied and served as a basis for the histories written by Robert, Baldric, Guibert and others who repeated its statements.'[14] This also formed the foundation for the charge of idolatry made against Muslims. A story circulating in the twelfth century claimed that Archbishop Thiemo of Salzburg was martyred in 1104 AD because he destroyed a Muslim idol. Even though Otto Freising, who displayed a fair knowledge of Islam, denied this idolatry charge and maintained that Muslims were strictly monotheistic while criticizing the martyrdom policy of certain Christians, the story is indicative of how the scholars' mentality worked. Against this background, the propensity to create more stories reviling Muḥammad and Islam could not be discounted.[15]

The Levels of Medieval Thinking About Muḥammad

We can perhaps best describe medieval thinking about Muḥammad and Islam in the form of three models. These are on a parallel with Southern's which divides the period into:

(a) Age of Ignorance.
(b) Age of Reason and Hope.
(c) The moment of vision.[16]

Our models are based on certain 'logical' conclusions the West made about Islam even though the premises they used were faulty and suited the kind of objective they wanted to achieve.

The first model consists of the assumption that there was no truth outside the church. Christianity was 'the truth' and the truth was God, therefore no truth (and hence God) lay outside Christianity. The only thing outside Christianity was the devil (the Anti-God) and therefore Islam was the work of the devil and Muḥammad was inspired by him. With this line of thinking there was nothing about Islam to be accepted. To them, Muḥammad was a false prophet.

The second model rests on the later medieval scholars' premise that revelation lay only in Christianity. Since the Qur'ān contained certain aspects of Judaic (Old Testament) and Christian (New Testament) teachings, it had some truth.

However, whatever truth it had was derivative and therefore not absolute. Even though this position is more positive than the first, it is still less appreciative of Islam as a true religion worthy of any spirituality of its own. At best, it contained paganistic and heretical teachings.

The third model is based on the study of Islam as a philosophical system. It was argued that there was some evidence of reason in Islam. Nicholas of Cusa suggested that philosophy contained revelation and therefore wherever there was philosophy there also existed revelation. However, it was argued, the philosophy of Islam was not independent but was recognized as wholly Greek. It was also seen as derivative.[17] Even though this represented an improvement on the second position and led to seventeenth and eighteenth-century enlightenment, the root of Islam – revelation, spirituality or divine origin – was, by implication, denied.

The main arguments against Muḥammad and Islam in medieval times were based on the Christian scripture and therefore nothing outside the scripture could be true. Whatever the Qur'ān said differently from the Bible, was regarded as wrong. Muslim morals were not seen as independent entities but as merely reinforcing or violating Christian ones. The absolute authority of the church and the scripture was such that reason or natural law was not a valid tool for examining any material especially that concerning Muḥammad. As late as 1889, S.W. Koelle maintained that 'the religion of Christ presents the standard by which all other religions have to be judged'.[18]

Some of the differences between Christianity and Islam, around which most arguments centred were, as presented by Norman Daniel: the nature of revelation (God's method of revealing Himself to man), the nature of revelation through Christ and the nature of revelation through Muḥammad; the characteristics of prophethood, the question of trinity and the incarnation of the spirit of God.[19] John of Damascus, who spearheaded the Christian onslaught, centred his argument on the nature of Godhead in Muslim thinking, setting it out in a document which came to be a reference book for Christian scholars.[20] He was bent on dismissing Muḥammad and what he saw as his invention – Islam. Nicetas of Byzantium in his polemical work argued that since, to him, the God of Islam did not accept the Christian doctrines, He could not possibly be true and Muḥammad was not a true prophet after all.[21] One of the greatest influences on medieval scholars' thinking on Muḥammad was the converted Jew Pedro de Alfonso whose *Dialogi*, written between 1106 and 1110, was entirely polemical.

The twelfth century saw the West taking seriously works on Islam and by the thirteenth and the mid-fourteenth centuries, there was a wide dissemination of literature on Muḥammad and Islam. Fables were then invented to discredit Muḥammad, some of them still popular today – for example the pathological theory. Muḥammad was portrayed as an epileptic who, whenever he had a seizure, explained to his wife Khadījah that an angel had come upon him. This and other legends gained currency and little thought was given as to their credibility. Guibert of Nogent, Waltherius, Alexandre du Pont, Sigebert of Gembloux, Ricoldo da Monte Croce and San Pedro, in medieval Christian times scholars of repute, used this theory in their work.[22] The theory has survived the ravages of time. Frank R. Freemon, a neurosurgeon of Nashville (USA) in a recent article, 'A Differential Diagnosis of the Inspirational Spells of Mohammed, the Prophet of Islam', gives a 'scientific' justification for it. He claims that the most reasonable explanation of Muḥammad's condition is '. . . psychomotor or complex partial seizures of temporal lobe epilepsy. . .', though, as he readily admits, the findings '. . . are unproven and forever unprovable'.[23]

Obviously the stories were meant to ridicule the Prophet Muḥammad and were not a conscious attempt at education though often both results were achieved. On the question of idolatry, the Crusades were fought with this whipped-up enthusiasm and emotion, that the Christians were fighting idolaters who had usurped the holy lands. The church used recruitment as an acid-test for true Christian belief and the propaganda was couched in the most appealing language. The Crusades were 'divinely backed holy wars' which offered absolution from sins. Those who could not serve at the war fronts induced death at Muslim hands to become martyrs. The Spanish Martyrs Movement was born principally of this.[24] Peter the Venerable, however, wrote that Muḥammad changed the Arabs, 'away from idolatry, yet not to one God, but . . . to the error of his own heresies'.[25]

Stories such as that of the dove which was trained by Muḥammad to pick grain from his ear to signify reception of revelation, and the bull with documents on its horns as revelation, were part of the machinery to destroy the credibility of the Prophet. Since their objective was to denigrate and not to appreciate, they spared no effort to achieve this. Pedro de Alfonso gave the three main criteria of a true prophet as '. . . probity of life, the presentation of miracles, and the constant truth in all his sayings'.[26] In all these respects, to him, Muḥammad did not measure up to the standard. The fact that the Qur'ān itself testified that Muḥammad was not a miracle worker gave them good reason for scorn. In medieval times, miracles constituted a symbol of divine authority and therefore it was unimaginable for a law-giving prophet to have no miracles to back him up. This was a favourite theme and gained much prominence in the eighteenth century. It was held up as a means to prove the authenticity of the Christian faith against that of Islam. John Locke stated that miracles were 'the credentials of a messenger delivering a divine religion'[27] therefore the revelation in Christianity was proved beyond reasonable doubt by the constant use of miracles by Jesus. Muḥammad was therefore scoffed at for implicitly, disproving his own authenticity. Richard Simon also wrote that, 'They who introduce a new religion ought to show some miracles.'[28] Since this conclusion had already been reached, the Christian apologists only needed to reinforce their case. They rejected the miracle of the *Isrā'* and *Mi'rāj* as not satisfying one of the cardinal criteria for sanctioning miracles – that of its public nature. They argued that a miracle must necessarily be performed in public and therefore the *Isrā'* and *Miʿrāj* was not admissible since it was a private event.

Humphrey Prideaux even rejected the whole issue of *Isrā'* and *Miʿrāj* as a fabrication merely to meet popular public demand and George Sale suggested it was invented merely to enhance the Prophet's reputation.[29] As for the point that the unique, inimitable nature of the Qur'ān should be an ultimate miracle in favour of Muḥammad, that was rejected on the grounds that, as Robert Jenkins put it, it was 'false, absurd and immoral'.[30] The few who were able to identify miracles in Muḥammad's life, which they could have used to rebut the arguments, rather turned the whole issue another way, accusing Muḥammad of being a magician. Henry Smith, in his *God's Arrow Against Atheists* contended that Muḥammad was 'thoroughly instructed in Satan's schoole, and well seine in Magicke'.[31] Logical reasoning was framed in such a way that room was left only for the Christian case. In the words of D.A. Pailin, the contention was: 'Mahomet claimed to bring messages from God; divine revelations are backed by miracles – the Bible shows this; Mahomet produced no trustworthy miracles; therefore his claim must be false.'[32]

Of course, miracles have their place in the Islamic tradition as authenticating evidence of prophethood. Islam recognizes the miracles of earlier prophets as valid but on the understanding that it is solely with the permission of God that they occur. If wondrous events were employed merely to fascinate people and so induce them to believe in one's mission, that might properly be categorized as magic instead. There is a natural propensity for man to believe in the marvellous as pointing to something which is true, hence the demand. Since miracles cannot be induced because they are wrought only with the permission of God, miracles *per se* do not prove the authenticity or otherwise of a prophet.

Muḥammad's detractors were not receptive to rational

arguments. The answers always had to agree with what they harboured in their subconscious.

The Prophet's sexual life also became a dominant area of attack because of the Medieval philosophical and theological notion that sex and holiness were incompatible. Reference was constantly made to Aristotle, who asserted that of all human senses, touch, especially when involved in sex, was the most bestial.[33] The large number of Muḥammad's wives caused opprobrium in the Christian West and the tradition attributed to him that he liked unguent women and prayer most was repeatedly referred to, sometimes omitting the prayer altogether.

Pailin cites Robert Jenkins, who saw Muḥammad as 'lustful, proud, fierce and cruel', while Jacob Bryant thought the Prophet was 'false, treacherous, blasphemous' and 'the bane of all happiness'.[34]

The issue of polygamy therefore became a favourite topic. The force of such arguments is seen in the work of William Muir as late as the last part of the nineteenth century. He wrote: 'By uniting himself to a second wife Muhammad made a serious movement away from Christianity, by the tenets and practice of which he must have known that polygamy was forbidden.'[35] The 'Christian' principle against polygamy seems to be a legacy from Western cultural thought rather than a clear Biblical doctrine.[36]

The apologists and polemicists failed to see Muḥammad's life as being in tune with the reality of human needs. They discussed the Prophet's marriages and criticized the permission for Muslims to marry more than one wife as if it was a religious duty. They were not prepared to listen to any explanation about the provision being an exception. Thomas Carlyle also gives a thought to the issue of the charge of profligacy against Muḥammad and points out that people completely overlook the fact that Muḥammad lived with Khadījah alone until her death and took other wives only after he had passed his prime.[37]

The Prophet's roots also became a centre of ridicule. The Arabian peninsula of his day was said to be peopled by pagan

Arabs and heretical Jews and Christians (Nestorians and Jacobites). The Arabs were described as 'rough, uneducated simple men easy to seduce and fleshy',[38] an image often supported by Muslims to show how the advent of Muḥammad changed the situation. The medieval scholars however used the material differently, contending that nothing good could come from such a society; an argument which is, of course, a theological as well as a historical fallacy. The Christian scriptures contain evidence that good, holy men and prophets arose from sinful nations. With so many Christian heretics around, nothing could be more appealing than to suggest that Muḥammad was actually taught by some of these; hence names like Bahīrah and Sergius were bandied about as being responsible for his 'heresy'.[39]

Interpretation of the revelation in *Daniel* 7: 23–5 pointed at Islam and Muḥammad as the king due to arise to subdue the kings of the existing empires – the Greek, the Frank and the Goth. Muḥammad was the Anti-Christ, a picture of the apocalyptic verses was seen in Islam and Muḥammad.[40] His tremendous successes were, at best, attributed to the devil but they failed to question how the devil could be so successful for so long. Questions like this would have disturbed the desired objective. Fra Fidenzio believed that Muḥammad used oppressive methods to achieve his aims and surrounded himself with evil men, thieves, plunderers, fugitives, murderers and such like ready to kill, plunder and liquidate every community that refused to follow him.[41] This charge of violence still exists in the West though a blind eye is turned to whatever Christianity perpetrated; that was, to them, obviously done to 'defend the truth'. The battle of Uḥud was used as classic evidence that Muḥammad had no divine guidance, as if Badr or any other battle was not fought at all.

Even the death of Muḥammad brought various theories, ranging from him eating a poisoned shoulder of lamb as held by San Pedro, Vitry, James of Acqui and others, the notion by Allan of Lille that Muḥammad was eaten by dogs, to probably the most widely circulated: his death at the hands of swine.

The latter was possibly suggested by Guibert of Nogent and even the corozoan texts repeated it. Gerald of Wales is referred to as maintaining that 'since he (Muhammad) taught uncleanness and shame, it was by pigs, which are considered unclean animals, that he was devoured'.[42]

The question then is why should the church fathers stoop so low, neglecting every possible ethical prudence in Christianity to maintain such views about Muḥammad and Islam, while well aware of the fact that they were mostly a pack of lies, farcical or wilful manipulation of material? Perhaps, due to their polemical method, material was not judged by its type and origin but by the way it could be arranged and presented. It was not the argumentative spirit found within it which was important but whether it could be twisted enough to fit the objective – intellectual war on Muḥammad.

The thirteenth-century English philosopher Roger Bacon saw war as a hopeless medium for defeating Islam and therefore preferred miracles and philosophy and since miracles no longer existed in the church, philosophical argument was the only option remaining. This led to the Council of Vienna in 1312 accepting the need to establish centres for Semitic languages in European cities. However this did not come about for more than 200 years and the old attitudes still survived.[43]

Between 1450 and 1460, resurgent Islam was the greatest problem for John of Segovia, Nicholas of Cusa, Jean Germain and Aeneas Silvius. John's concern was to prove that the Qur'ān was not the word of God but he admitted that the existing Christian material was not very helpful due to mistranslations.[44] Rejecting war and preaching, he suggested '*contraferentia*' a term sometimes translated as 'conference',[45] but in reality meaning 'confrontational dialogue', to convert Muslims.

To Nicholas of Cusa, the problem of Islam was that between Western and Nestorian Christianity since Muḥammad was nurtured by the latter. Jean Germain, however, stuck to the war option and called for resumption of the Crusades. The goals and the plans to achieve them differed but it seems that common sense and a certain amount of reason was preferred to speculation and useless xenophobia.

However, during the following centuries, writers merely continued with the tradition and even those who were supposed to be well informed could not distinguish authentic from false sources, showing a preference for the most mediocre. Daniel puts it succinctly: 'To read San Pedro and Ibn Ishaq side by side is to be given a striking lesson in the way the same material can be used in order to give totally different impressions.'[46] For example, after a lengthy discussion of the Bahīrah story, Shabo deduces that Muslims tell the story apologetically to prove Muḥammad's prophethood while Christians, with al-Kindī as a typical example, refer to the story to disprove exactly that and show Bahīrah as a heretical Nestorian. Here, it is used polemically. Yet again, the Nestorians, Shabo argues, used the story to secure themselves a place under Muslim rule since the parent church had excommunicated them.[47] Though this is not the place to discuss the validity or otherwise of any of these presumptions, they further illustrate how people with different objectives can manipulate the same material. The hidden agenda behind the writers' works was to prove that Muḥammad was merely human with no divine intervention in his life and therefore he could not be a prophet. Since the recipient of a divine message had to be totally different, aspects of his life which showed him as ordinary were but further proof of his falsity.[48]

The medieval Christians were faced with the enormous dilemma of Islam. It was winning souls and lands from the church and culminated in the Crusades, which they saw as against Muslim aggression. They marshalled every means to defend the church from a gradual waning of its power and influence and probably its demise. Therefore, when 'the menace' of Islam was no longer felt so acutely in Western Europe in the late eighteenth and nineteenth centuries, the tone against Muḥammad and Islam became less hostile.[49] However, despite changes in tone and methodology, the average Western scholar's view of Muḥammad has still not reached a level of satisfaction for Muslims and does not allow dispassionate academic study.

This is because a change in methodology *per se* does not necessarily entail a change in attitude. The human touch, the personal experience of Muslims and Muslim societies, is what most Western scholars miss to their cost.

Montgomery Watt concedes that although efforts have been initiated to change the distorted image of Muḥammad inherited by present Western scholars, opinions are so endemic that success is difficult to achieve.[50] It is precisely due to statements like these by eminent Western scholars that the need to re-examine the image of Muḥammad in the medieval age has become vital. If more and more people realize that much of the present Western material on Muḥammad carries reminiscences of that age when Western scholars and the church were obsessed with carving out a holy identity over and against Islam and so revelled in pure speculation, then major headway can be made towards balancing the scales and the real picture of Muḥammad, the Prophet of Islam, can emerge.

Though certain academics argue that the way Muslims see and regard Muḥammad should not necessarily be the same as others see or think about him, in matters of scholarship no methodology can be more dangerous than pure speculation and wilful distortion of material.

Western writers share certain basic presuppositions and students of Islam and Muḥammad need to examine these and expose those based on ill-informed sources and views. The roots lie in medieval times, so going back is worthwhile and indeed inevitable.[51]

In the following chapter, therefore, the work of William Muir on Muḥammad is examined.

Notes

1. J. Waltz, 'The Significance of the Voluntary Martyrs of Ninth Century Cordoba', *MW,* Vol. 60 (1970), pp.144–5.

2. N. Daniel, *Islam and the West – The Making of an Image* (1980, reprint); see Ch. 9.

3. E. Said, *Orientalism*, p.7.

4. E.H. Carr, *What is History?* (1985), p.8.

5. *Ibid.*, p.14.

6. A. Wessels, 'Modern Biographies of Muhammad in Arabic', *IC,* Vol. 49, No. 2 (1975), p.105.

7. Carr, *What is History?*, p.26.

8. Watt declares that Western scholars are '. . . the heirs of a deep-seated prejudice which goes back to the "war propaganda" of Medieval times'. W. Montgomery Watt, *What is Islam?* (1968), pp.1 and 2.

9. *Ibid.*

10. Daniel, *Islam and the West*, p.245.

11. R.W. Southern, *Western Views of Islam in the Middle Ages* (1962), p.31.

12. *Ibid.*, pp.31–2.

13. J.E. Royster, 'The Study of Muhammad: A Survey of Approaches from the Perspective of the History and Phenomenology of Religion', *MW,* 62 (1972), p.56.

14. D.C. Munro, 'The Western Attitude Towards Islam During the Period of the Crusades', *Speculum,* 6 (1931), p.332.

15. Discussing the relationship between Christendom and Islam in the Middle Ages, Helen Adolf, writes '. . . the barriers between the two worlds were formidable: differences of language and script, of race, climate, and manners of ideology, most of all – hence hot and cold war, which made it dangerous to sympathize – fear, hatred, prejudice, and an incredible amount of ignorance: the exact formula for an iron curtain'. Helen Adolf, 'Christendom and Islam in the Middle Ages: New Light on "Grail Stone" and "Hidden Host" ', *Speculum,* 32 (1957), p.105.

16. Southern, *Western Views, passim.*

17. J. Hopkins, *Nicholas of Cusa's Pace Fidei and Cribratio Alkorani (Translation and Analysis),* (1994), esp. the Prologue to the 'Cribratio Alkorani I', p.79 ff. And J.E. Biecher, 'Christian Humanism Confronts Islam: Sifting the Qur'ān with Nicholas of Cusa', *JECS,* 13 (1976), pp.1–14.

18. E. Royster Pike, *Mohammed – Prophet and the Religion of Islam* (1968), p.54.

19. Daniel, *Islam and the West*, p.1.

20. *Ibid.*, pp.3–4.

21. Daniel describes this work as '. . . less febrile but inclined to a niggling pettiness in a dialectical subtlety that one would suppose could convince nobody, least of all a Muslim', *ibid.*, p.5.

22. A comprehensive discussion of this theory is in Arthur Jeffery's article 'The Quest of the Historical Mohammed', *The Moslem World*, Vol. 26, No. 4 (October 1926), pp.335–6 in which the survival of the concept is discussed.

23. Article in *Epilepsia*, 17 (1976), pp.423–7. Syed Ahmad Khan in an exhaustive analysis, points out that Gibbon and Davenport traced it to the door of Greek superstition: Syed Ahmad Khan, *The Life of Muhammad and Subjects Subsidiary Thereto* (1979, reprint), pp.196–9.

24. Arnold describes the Martyrs as '. . . a fanatical party. . . which set itself openly and unprovokedly to insult the religion of Muslims and blaspheme their prophet, with the deliberate intention of incurring death by such misguided assertion of their Christian bigotry'. T.W. Arnold, *The Preaching of Islam* (1913), p.141. Arthur Jeffery, *op. cit.*, p.331. J. Waltz, 'The Significance of the Voluntary Martyrs of Ninth Century Cordoba', *op. cit.*

25. Daniel, *Islam and the West*, p.42.

26. *Ibid.*, p.68.

27. J. Locke, *A Discourse on Miracles* (1768), p.226.

28. D.A. Pailin, *Attitudes to Other Religions – Comparative Religion in Seventeenth and Eighteenth Century Britain* (1984), p.311, note 54.

29. *Ibid.*, note 58.

30. *Ibid.*, p.312, note 65.

31. *Ibid.*, p.311.

32. *Ibid.*, p.89.

33. Aristotle, *Ethics* iii.x.8.

34. Pailin, *Attitudes to Other Religions*, p.91.

35. W. Muir, *The Life of Mohammed from Original Sources* (1858–61), p.202. M. Cook, *Muhammad*, Past Master Series (1983), pp.49–50.

36. John Davenport has looked at this charge of polygamy and immorality in detail in his *An Apology for Mohammed and the Koran* (1869); see the 1975 Lahore reprint, pp.151–61.

37. T. Carlyle, *On Heroes, Hero Worship and the Heroic in History* (1849), p.53.

38. Daniel, *Islam and the West*, p.82.

39. See Nicholas of Cusa's opinion in J. Hopkins, *Nicholas of Cusa's Pace Fidei and Cribratio AlKorani*, p.79 ff.

40. Southern, *Western Views*, pp.23–4, and Arthur Jeffery, 'The Quest of the Historical Mohammed', *op. cit.*, pp.343–4.

41. Daniel, *Islam and the West*, p.92.

42. *Ibid.*, p.104. These stories may seem unimportant today but the damage done to the image of Muḥammad was such that remnants still remain. Southern, *Western Views*, pp.31–2.

43. Southern, *Western Views*, pp.72–3.

44. Munro speaks of Peter the Venerable's translation of the Qur'ān as '. . . unfortunately very inaccurate and full of errors; but it was the only one known in the West until the end of the seventeenth century'. Munro, 'The Western Attitude Towards Islam During the Period of the Crusades', *op. cit.*, p.337. Helen Adolf also confirms that 'most facts about Mohammad were known, through the Byzantine historians, through Peter the Venerable and his Koran translators in Toledo . . .'. Adolf, 'Christendom and Islam', *op. cit.*, p.105.

45. Southern, *Western Views*, pp.91–2. Also cited in Said, *Orientalism*, p.61.

46. Daniel, *Islam and the West*, p.237.

47. A.M. Shabo, 'An Evaluative Study of the Bahīra Story in the Muslim and Christian Traditions', unpublished MA Thesis, Dept. of Theology, University of Birmingham (UK), 1984.

48. *Ibid.*, p.245.

49. Rodinson makes a good analysis of many of these issues. See his *Europe and the Mystique of Islam* (1988), translated from the French by Roger Veinus; esp. pp.3–40.

50. W. Montgomery Watt, 'Western Historical Scholarship and the

Prophet of Islam', *Message of the Prophet,* a series of articles presented at the First International Congress on Seerat, Islamabad, 1976, pp.70–1. See also his *What is Islam?,* pp.1–2.

51. Trude Ehlert's article on 'Muhammad' in *The Encyclopaedia of Islam,* New Edition, Vol. VII, pp.360–87. Section 3 of the article deals with 'The Prophet's Image in Europe and the West'. The author also provides a very helpful list of Western sources on Muḥammad from the eighth to the nineteenth century.

CHAPTER TWO

Sir William Muir

Introduction

This is a critical review of Sir William Muir's *The Life of Mohammed from Original Sources,* which aims to assess his contribution to the development of the image of Muḥammad in Western scholarship. We chose Muir as our starting point in nineteenth-century Western scholarship primarily because his was the largest work undertaken during that century. Secondly, it was one of the first in English based on original Arabic sources.

Alfred Von Kramer accuses European scholars of not '. . . treating the history of Muhammad according to the principles of a sound enlightened criticism'.[1] He accuses them of hiding behind supposed unavailability of original source-material and so relying on Orientalist material of the modern age, discarding the ancient Arabic originals. Indeed, he says, in the West the reader on Muhammad '. . . prefers the wonderful tales of late compilers to the simple and manly style of an old Arabic chronicler'.[2]

The acceptability of Muir's work as the *sine qua non* source-book on Muḥammad in the West is evident from the way many later writers constantly refer to it. It was supposed to be a wide shift away from medieval polemics and hatred. For these reasons, it was widely acclaimed for its 'objectivity' by many who quickly acknowledged it as 'the standard presentment in English, of the career of the prophet of Islam'.[3]

Lyall describes it as full of 'excellences', 'systematic' and with 'sobriety of judgement', but admits that it '. . . is marked with a polemic character which necessarily renders it in some degree antipathetic to those who profess the religion of Muhammad'.[4]

Therefore, to trace if the medieval attitude to Muḥammad became a heritage for the West and lasted into the nineteenth and twentieth centuries, Muir's work cannot be overlooked. We will attempt to analyze critically his assessment of Muḥammad, locating evidence of fairness and objectivity whilst also noting indications of prejudice, bias, and other aspects of inappropriate scholarship. We will also note any traces of a medieval-style approach to Muḥammad. Some of the basic questions we may attempt to answer are:

(a) How far does Muir's explicit commitment to the Christian church and Christian mission as well as the British Raj influence his appraisal of Muḥammad's life?
(b) Has his Western orientation kept him in line with his medieval forefathers?
(c) How honest has Muir been in seeking to study the life of Muḥammad, a man whose image had previously been so maligned in the West?
(d) Moreover, has the fundamental change in methodology brought about any shift in attitude?

These, and many offshoots of these questions, will be discussed.

Muir's Methodology

Muir begins, in the Introduction to his book, with an exhaustive discussion of the main sources of material for Muḥammad's biography. He identifies legends, traditions and historical records as the three avenues through which the early biographers compiled their work. He points out that, 'Tradition and the rhapsodies of bards have, for their object actual or supposed events; but the impression of these events is liable to become distorted from the imperfection of the vehicle which conveys them'.[5] We share his observation with regard to the problems oral tradition is prone to be fraught with. However, he acknowledges that Muslim oral tradition is of a different standard from every other and believes that there is much authentic recorded material about Muḥammad through this medium.

At this point, we think it is apposite to cite Margoliouth's statement concerning this topic. He says:

> With us, the natural seat of a book is some material such as paper: It may or may not be committed to memory. With the Arab, the natural seat of a book is the memory: It may or may not be committed to writing. In the Qur'ān, there are indications that the seat of the book is regarded as the memory, notwithstanding the importance which is therein attached to writing.[6]

The philosophy behind Arab thinking is that the message written in the hearts and minds of men is difficult or impossible to remove. Though the generalities of the statement could be open to serious debate, the underlying basic assumption is there, that, to the Arabs, it is the safest and best means of recording and retaining material.

The genuine logical concern Muir expresses in his analysis of the traditions we cannot refute. There is good evidence that spurious traditions were perpetrated by probably not totally dishonest people in *stricto sensu* – but nevertheless by zealous people. The example of Bukhārī's method of collection, in which several thousand traditions were rejected, is a classic case in point.

Muir, in his endeavour to satisfy academic scholarship, subjects the early biographers to scrutiny, looking at each and his time of writing and the likely encumbrances affecting his work. The period of the 'Abbāsid Caliph al-Ma'mūn (198–218

AH) with its attendant theological problems was the very era of three great biographers, al-Wāqidī, Ibn Hishām, and al-Madā'inī. Ibn Isḥāq wrote under the Caliphate of the first two ʿAbbāsid rulers. The problems of the age might have had profound consequences for the material from which they compiled their work.

However, with this premise, Muir has a weapon to wield against any material that, to him, appears suspicious. After referring to the existence of *ḥadīth* criticism, he advises the European reader to be wary because the method was not rigorous and credible enough. Though he admits some 'guarantee of sincerity', he suspects that the floodgates of speculation, error, exaggeration and pure fiction were flung wide open.[7]

The enormous gravity of the problem of *ḥadīth* in academic scholarship is recognized by many scholars and indeed Muir highlights it. He recognizes the dilemma in the following words: 'The biographer of Muhammad continuously runs the risk of substituting for the realities of history some puerile fancy, or extravagant invention. In striving to avoid this danger, he is exposed to the opposite peril of rejecting as pious fabrication what may in reality be important historical fact.'[8]

Of course, owing to the particular interests of specific groups, be they believers or unbelievers, members of the Prophet's household or ordinary people outside his immediate family, close associates and others, an element of suspicion is almost always justified when dealing with material from them.

Because of this fundamental assumption, Muir reasons that unfavourable traditions against Muḥammad might be true because, he argues, they could not have survived if they were not. In fact, this is not a new view and scholars like Sprenger, Grimme, Weil, and later Goldziher and Schacht have used the same argument. Muir was certainly familiar with the works of some of these who were his contemporaries and predecessors.

Though Muir cautions against a universal application of this hypothesis, we see him treating it so. By the same contention of interest groups, unfavourable statements would likely have been the creations of later generations.

Muhammad Asad, reflecting on this question of authenticity of *ḥadīth,* writes:

> The fact that there were numberless spurious *ahadith* did not in the least escape the attention of the *Muhaddithun*, as European critics naively seem to suppose. On the contrary, the critical science of *hadith* was initiated by the necessity of discerning between authentic and spurious, . . . The existence, therefore, of false *ahadith* does not prove anything against the system of *hadith* as a whole – no more than a fanciful tale from the *Arabian Nights* could be regarded as an argument against the authenticity of any historical report of the corresponding period.[9]

After a fair amount of deliberation on the works of earlier biographers, Muir states that the works of Ibn Hishām, al-Wāqidī (from his scribe Ibn Saʿd), together with al-Ṭabarī form the tripod of original sources upon which any biography of Muḥammad could conveniently be based. He recognizes al-Bukhārī, Muslim and al-Tirmidhī as supportive authorities. Muir then advises the student of *Sīrah* to reject any other material outside these sources, thereby slamming the door in the face of other sources he does not favour.

One detects in Muir, a struggle to portray the falsity of Muḥammad's claims. In certain cases his language is bitter and could probably be interpreted as insulting. His thesis in the preliminary discussions that any story which puts Muḥammad in a bad light must be true and that which shows him in a good light is false or, at best, suspect, is directing him in his interpretation of the events in Muḥammad's life. Muir's intimation of Christianity as a 'purer faith'[10] in itself constrains him and is where certain aspects of his methodology are found wanting. He uses basic Western historical methodology which involves a very sceptical approach to history. This method, we believe, in the context of religion usually obfuscates the real identity of the subject under study. We see this in the works on the quest for the historical Jesus. Hamilton Gibb points out that Islam 'is an autonomous expression of religious thought and experience, which must be viewed in and through its own principles and standards'.[11]

Selected Themes

'Pre-Muhammadan' Makkah – Birth and Childhood of Muḥammad

Muir, as do many other Islamists, notes the enormous religious, social and political difficulties in Arabia which needed a solution. He is of the opinion that these problems were solved by Muḥammad through several tactics, including 'war' and 'plunder' which the 'wild Arabs' found irresistible.[12] He acknowledges, however, that Christianity and Judaism as they existed during the sixth and seventh centuries in Arabia could not tackle these problems. He writes: 'The material for a great change was here. But it required to be wrought; and Muhammad was the workman.'[13]

What Muir finds difficult to credit Muḥammad with is that the extraordinary skill, which he employed to solve the problems of the 'wild' people, came from outside himself. The old notion that Muḥammad borrowed most of his thoughts from Judaism and Christianity reappears in order to deny him any original spirituality in his mission.[14] This surviving idea in the West, of copying by Muḥammad, cannot be conclusively proved. The main question is, perhaps, that if the source of revelation is one and the same (that is God), what prevents God revealing to Muḥammad concepts similar to those that exist in earlier scriptures? Indeed the Qur'ān itself states, and Muslims believe, that the revelation vouchsafed to Muḥammad confirms the essence of the earlier ones.[15]

Muir subscribes to the pathological theory and that of auto-suggestion. He describes the event which occurred in Muḥammad's early childhood when he was living with Ḥalīmah as evidence of epileptic fits.[16] It is interesting to note that Muslim pious writings have explained this incident of the opening of Muḥammad's chest as cleansing of the heart by angels. There is indeed no authentic evidence that Muḥammad in his pre-prophetic life experienced anything that can be alluded to as fits.

Emile Dermenghem appropriately writes: 'Neurotics, false mystics and authentic visionaries present certain phenomena in common. The one is purely passive; the other active and creative. At the most we might say that the morbid tendency may facilitate trances which, in their turn, would increase the tendency. But one finds no traces, as it seems, of this pathological state in Mahomet.'[17]

Syed Ahmad Khan subjects this topic to a careful and exhaustive analysis.[18] He looks at the text of Ibn Hishām and points out that Muir has made a serious error of judgement and interpretation. The Arabic quotation and its English translation carry no mention of epileptic fits. The argument then centres on the Latin rendering of the Arabic text, giving Āminah's reaction when Muḥammad returned to her. Āminah was supposed to have asked: 'Ah, didst thou fear that he was under the influence of [an] evil spirit?'[19]

Pockocke in his Latin translation uses the expression 'hypochondrium contraxerit' during his work on parts of Abū al-Fidā's material in 1723. This expression, in Latin, suggests epilepsy or falling sickness.

In the original text of Ibn Hishām, the word which Muir misreads and misinterprets is *Uṣīb,* which in classical Arabic means simply 'afflicted' and does not imply epilepsy.[20]

Syed Ahmad Khan asks: 'When, then could such a notion have originated, and by whom was it encouraged and propagated?'[21] He gets the answer from Gibbon and Davenport who lay the origin of this interpretation at the door of Greek superstition.[22]

Even though Gibbon had debunked the idea and given the origin of the notion, Muir, who must have known Gibbon's works, uncritically accepts the ongoing tradition. Muir seems to have fallen prey to existing notions of misrepresented facts without checking their authenticity. The symptoms of epilepsy which medical evidence gives and the historical testimony of the robust health of Muḥammad stand in sharp contradiction and disprove the theory.

From Youth to Prophethood

Despite the epilepsy problem as Muir sees it, Muḥammad is described in the book as being, 'Endowed with a refined mind and delicate taste, reserved and meditative, he lived much within himself, and the ponderings of his heart no doubt supplied occupation for leisure hours spent by others of a lower stamp in rude sports and profligacy.'[23] Such a description does not fit an epileptic.

Muir does not dispute the possibility that Muḥammad might have met some monks on his journeys to Syria and might have discussed matters with them or listened to them, but he calls ridiculous and puerile the idea that he met Nestorius.[24] Perhaps his rejection of this idea is not because the two could not have met, but merely to fit his larger design to refute any suggestion that a certain monk of high status pronounced Muḥammad to be a prophet. Further, he reiterates that Christianity as it existed at that time in Syria and its environs was not pure and that if Muḥammad had encountered pure Christianity, he would have become a Christian.[25] He then continues: 'We may well mourn that the misnamed Catholicism of the empire thus grievously misled the mastermind of the age, and through him eventually so great a part of the eastern world.'[26]

Muḥammad's visitations to the Cave of Ḥirā' are reduced to events of self-contemplation and a period in which he '. . . would give vent to his agitation in wild rhapsodical language, enforced often with incoherent oaths, the counterpart of inward struggle after truth'.[27]

Due to his insistence on the auto-suggestion theory, Muir

finds it impossible to accept that the change in Muḥammad's life signified true prophethood. He remarks: 'How such aspirations developed into belief that the subject of them was divinely inspired, is a theme obscure and difficult.'[28]

Prophethood in Makkah

Throughout the volume, Muir appears sympathetic to the cause of Muḥammad at least in Makkah. However, he sticks to a purely psychological interpretation of Muḥammad's mission and sees him as not receiving messages from outside himself but that it was his subconscious which was at work. He grapples with the problem of reconciling this theory and the well-known fact of a divine presence behind Muḥammad's utterances. He argues:

> It is certain that the conception of the Almighty as the immediate source of his inspiration and author of his commission, soon took entire and undivided possession of his soul; and however coloured by the events and inducements of the day, or mingled with apparently incongruous motives and desires, retained a paramount influence until the hour of his death.[29]

There seems to be a contradiction here because it is strange that a prophet whose life was fully in the hands of Allah would lapse into a situation where he looks for secular ends only. This might cast considerable doubt on the whole question of divine guidance itself. Muir, however, unwittingly admits Muḥammad's sincerity. Observing the upright character of the earliest converts and the social standing of his close friends and members of his household, he writes, that these 'could not fail otherwise to have detected those discrepancies which ever more or less exist between the professions of the hypocritical deceiver abroad and his actions at home'.[30]

Again, he looks at Abū Ṭālib who, even though he did not embrace Islam, put his honour and even his life at stake in defence of Muḥammad. This could not have been out of mere family relationship, he agrees, and concludes: 'They afford at the same time strong proof of the sincerity of Muhammad. Abu Talib would not have acted thus for an interested deceiver; and he had ample means of scrutiny.'[31]

In these words, therefore, we detect Muir's rejection of the notion of Muḥammad being an impostor even though he does not state it and in fact later discussions tend to deny this.

Muir finds the incident of the so-called Satanic Verses interesting.[32] He sees the root of the problem in the troubled self of Muḥammad who finds it difficult to reconcile the *Ka'bah* as the House of God, used by the Makkans for their idols, and his message of one God. He contends that Muḥammad, in order to resolve the issue and win over the people to the worship of the one true God, had to make some compromises hence his statement implicitly accepting the power and efficacy of the idols. In view of Muir's earlier admission of Muḥammad's strong stand against idolatry, how he can now consciously revoke the whole basis of Muhammad's mission becomes a difficult task for him.

Syed Ahmad Khan, referring to seventeen sources, discusses this question in detail, analyzing the traditions upon which the story is founded.

For Muir, the incident is well supported by the traditions and here he refers to Ibn Hishām, Ibn Sa'd and al-Ṭabarī. However, after a thorough analysis of the traditions, Syed Ahmad Khan rejects as spurious the tradition upon which Muir and others have built their story.[33] He points out that the portion that was supposed to uphold the idols was an interpretation by one of the idolators who anticipated, judging from the way the passage had begun, that Muḥammad was going to rain insults on their gods. However, since the culprit was not found, the Muslims concluded that whoever did it did so at the instigation of Satan.[34]

Syed Ahmad Khan further argues that as the story gained

currency, it was referred to by certain scholars and, in the same way that some scholars have recorded spurious traditions, this one also found its way into the books. He then observes that, 'Sir William Muir's experience as a literary man of the first class, ought, most assuredly, to have taught him that mere assertions, unsupported by argument and by proofs, ever recoil to the destruction of the very purpose they were intended to subserve.'[35] Syed Ameer Ali, perhaps not unexpectedly, follows the same line of thinking.[36]

The subject of the *Miʿrāj* appears in the discussion. Muir dismisses this in a page and a half in a language that belittles the importance of the issue in Islam. He writes that when Muḥammad wanted to tell his people about the experience, he was advised not '. . . to expose himself to derision of the unbelievers. But he persisted. . . . As the story spread abroad, unbelievers scoffed and believers were staggered; some are even said to have gone back.'[37] This time he has no tradition to support this. He describes Muslim opinion about the issue as full of fanciful stories. To him, the insignificance or perhaps its falsity is seen from the fact that it is mentioned only in *Sūrah al-Isrā'* or *Banī Isrā'īl*.[38]

Muir's ridiculing of the incident seems to be further proof of his inconsistency and unfairness. If he believes in the transfiguration story in the life of Jesus and his bodily ascension and also that the Bible says Elijah was carried to heaven in chariots of fire, it is strange that he cannot accept Muḥammad's experience as a deep and authentic spiritual incident.[39]

From the psychology of religion we learn that the experience of Muḥammad in the *Miʿrāj* story is not ridiculous. It is a universal phenomenon in religious experience. By dismissing it the way he does, Muir shows a lack of familiarity with contemporary sciences of the nineteenth century. He is not up to date with the scientific thoughts of his day.

Even though William James' work *The Varieties of Religious Experience* was published in 1902, after Muir had written his work, it shows that enough scientific study of religion was in vogue during his time and he could have acquainted himself with it.

Syed Ahmad Khan also takes up this issue and analyzes various traditions under eighteen sections.[40] However, he rejects the idea existing among certain Westerners that the bodily ascension of Muḥammad is believed by all Muslims. He criticizes Prideaux for thinking that the *Miʿrāj* event is an article of faith.[41] The real issue, he points out, is that the event was spiritual and even its denial, especially the bodily interpretation, does not make a Muslim an apostate.[42] One would have expected a scholar like Muir to give much thought to this incident and to have discussed how even those who believe in it as a physical ascension of Muḥammad are not irrational after all.[43]

Muḥammad in Madīnah up to His Death

Though we have referred to Muir's criticism of Muḥammad in Makkah, it is his period in Madīnah which receives the bitterest censures. Many Western scholars who see Muḥammad as a prophet in Makkah see him differently in Madīnah. He usually becomes a mere secular head of state; indeed sometimes a despotic ruler.

For many Christian thinkers of the nineteenth century, including Muir, by establishing a worldly *Ummah* (community) in Madīnah, Muḥammad betrayed the office of prophethood. He is accused by Muir of having used revelation '. . . as a means of reaching secular ends, and even . . . of ministering to lower objects'.[44]

Nineteenth-century Christian piety set a sharp divide between religion and politics. Pietism with its stress on holy life and good works was perhaps part of Muir's philosophy. In this philosophy religion is made an exclusively private affair with state and religion completely divorced.

We read in Muir's life history that he was reluctant to use his official position as governor and an official of the church to

Christianize. Is this an indicator of pietism? However, when faced with the Indian Mutiny in 1857, he was prepared to use the imperial army to quell the revolt. He thought it was just. In fact, Clinton Bennet points out that Muir used his official position for Christian missionary ends.[45]

Muir, a perfect child of his Western culture, finds it impossible to penetrate Muḥammad's cultural and religious environment. He reopens the old chapter on Muḥammad's inability to perform miracles to prove his authenticity. He writes: '. . . the prophets of old were upheld (as we may suppose) by the prevailing consciousness of divine inspiration, and strengthened by the palpable demonstrations of miraculous power; while with the Arabian, his recollection of former doubts, and confessed inability to work any miracle, may at times have cast across him a shadow of uncertainty'.[46]

R.B. Smith states that '. . . the most miraculous thing about Muhammad is, that he never claimed the power of working miracles'.[47] He continues, on the same page, that he is firmly convinced that Christians will one day uphold the prophethood of Muḥammad.

Leitner also remarks: '. . . if self-sacrifice, honesty of purpose, unwavering belief in one's mission, a marvellous insight into existing wrong or error, and the perception and use of the best means for their removal, are among the outward and visible signs of inspiration, the mission of Muhammad was inspired'.[48]

We see Muir's charge as a restatement of the earlier strong Christian contention that miracles constitute an essential factor in the proof of authentic prophethood. St. Thomas Aquinas held a similar opinion and laid this charge against Muḥammad.[49] Of course, miracles have their place in the Islamic tradition as authenticating evidence of prophethood. Islam recognizes the miracles of earlier prophets as valid but on the understanding that it is solely with the permission of God that prophets work miracles. In the examples of Prophets Ṣāliḥ, Ibrāhīm, Mūsā and 'Īsā, God worked miracles to support them.

The question of Muḥammad's sexuality, especially in terms

of polygamy, constitutes another major theme of interest for the West and for Muir. He writes: 'By uniting himself to a second wife Muhammad made a serious movement away from Christianity by the tenets and practice of which he must have known that polygamy was forbidden.'[50] Muir is applying a questionable 'Christian' yardstick to Muḥammad and he even overlooks the fact that Muḥammad took wives when he was over fifty. At that age, there seems a lot of sense in the argument that Muḥammad married many of his wives for various reasons other than his sexual appetite.

From the eleventh chapter, we find Muir moving further away from fairness in his study. He gives a hint as to how he is going to deal with the rest of Muḥammad's life by saying that the reader is to see '. . . more stirring scenes'.[51] He charges Muḥammad with nurturing in his heart hostility against the Quraysh and that he just wanted a fertile ground to translate that hatred into action. To him, Madīnah offered that fertile ground. Muir does not seem to share the general opinion that Muḥammad did not leave Makkah for Madīnah primarily to re-arm himself against the stiff Makkan opposition and persecution but rather for the sake of peace. He was to save his people from possible extermination and also prevent further turmoil in the Makkan society.

The various expeditions which, to Muir and many others like him, were engineered by Muḥammad against the 'innocent' Qurayshī caravans are also discussed. They form a substantial part of a larger plan to castigate Muḥammad in Madīnah. In each of them, Muḥammad appears as the aggressor. Muir's judgement usually appears one-sided. For example, he cannot find anything worthwhile in the instructions Muḥammad gave to the leader of the Nakhlah expedition, ʿAbdullāh ibn Jahsh, to comment upon as to his character.

Muir discusses the main wars extensively, portraying Muḥammad as engendering a 'savage spirit' and slaughtering innocent people in cold blood.[52] On the battle of Badr, for example, he presents Muḥammad as starting the war but suggests that it is reasonable to assume that with the agreements made with the Madīnan delegation at ʿAqabah and taking into account the apprehension he had of attack from Makkah, Muḥammad would not have wanted to 'stir the beehive'. Muir even suggests that the defeat of the Makkan army at Badr might have boosted the morale of the Muslims in Madīnah. It can be argued that the morale boost could only have been realistic if the war was a morally justifiable one as is generally believed. It was for the repulsion of aggression and that was why the Muslims achieved such high spiritual elation.

Muir's own reference to the treatment given to some of the prisoners of war from Badr seems to contradict the charge of cruelty against Muḥammad. In fact, he does not reflect on this. He writes that when it comes to war, Muslims have no compunction. The whole discussion is tilted in favour of Muḥammad's opponents who are pictured as victims.[53]

The case of the Banū Qaynuqāʿ and their subsequent expulsion is related in a tone which excites emotions. Muir portrays Muḥammad as callous and inhuman in refusing the pleas of ʿAbdullāh ibn Ubayy.[54] It does not show the same Muḥammad who freed prisoners. The same fervour is seen in the description of the so-called 'secret assassinations'. A typical example is that of Kaʿb ibn al-Ashraf whose death, Muir says, is one of the 'dastardly acts of cruelty which darkens the pages of the Prophet's life'.[55] In his narrative, he indicates that the instigation, assent and the go-ahead were all given by Muḥammad. However, he states that he is '. . . far from asserting that every detail in the . . . narrative, either of instigation by Muhammad or of deception by the assassin, is beyond question'.[56] The way he treats the stories about these killings seems to fit his thesis that any story of immense disadvantage to Muḥammad must be true. He is even able to find a tradition to support his assertion that some Muslims were murmuring their dissent at the Prophet's behaviour.[57]

His comparison of Christianity and Islam in the use of violence is unfortunate and shows the bad methodology of comparing the ideal in one religion with real occurrences in the society of the other. If the behaviour of Christians is to be judged in a *tu quoque* fashion, we see that history contains several episodes of wars against the idolaters. The stories about the fall of Jericho, the Amalekites, the Amorites, and Jebusites alone point to the fact that different periods look at things differently and hence one cannot censure the Children of Israel for 'causing' these events.[58] Carlyle even reminds us that, 'Charlemagne's conversion of the Saxons was not by preaching.'[59]

Miller also makes a similar statement concerning violence and concludes that Christianity is perhaps more guilty.[60] Syed Ahmad Khan criticizes Muir's imputation of violence against Muḥammad[61] and Ameer Ali points out that certain issues taken by Muir as the grounds for criticism of Muḥammad do not exist in authorities such as Ibn Hishām, al-Ṭabarī, Ibn al-Athīr and Abū al-Fidā'. He opines that where they do exist, they are either apocryphal or the interpretation put on them is completely false.[62] It is perhaps necessary to note here that the classical texts do not have the problems we have today concerning such issues because they are not using nineteenth-century liberal idealism as a criterion.

On the Banū Naḍīr, Muir doubts the events which led to their expulsion, arguing that no trace of it exists in the Qur'ān. With his scholarly capability, Muir should have realized that the Qur'ān is not primarily a history book. Therefore the best place to see this is in the Traditions but, standing by his principle, the story would put Muḥammad in a good light and therefore it cannot be true.

Perhaps the issue giving the critics the best opportunity to attack Muḥammad is that of the Banū Qurayẓah. Muir, not unexpectedly, spends much time on it. He rejects the argument of a pact between Muḥammad and the Jews of Madīnah and therefore seems to propose that they were justified in taking whatever action they saw fit. He agrees with Sprenger that the experience at the battle of Uḥud when the Jews' help was declined and the incidents of the two expulsions, made the

Banū Qurayẓah a disinterested party in the Khandaq skirmishes. It is, however, not unreasonable to argue that knowing what happened to the Banū Naḍīr and the Banū Qaynuqāʿ, and the fact that they themselves had been prevented from fighting at Uḥud, the Banū Qurayẓah would have become so incensed that they would see their future lying only in the rooting-out of the Muslims from Madīnah. With the event of Uḥud fresh in their minds, they were under no illusions that helping the Quraysh would enable them to achieve the desired results. Muir's description of the executions is characteristic of the medieval era.[63]

By the rejection of any collaboration between the Banū Qurayẓah and the Quraysh, Muir, following Sprenger and others, lays the foundation for seeing the case as barbaric, inhuman and Muḥammad himself as not worthy of the noble office of prophethood. This is perhaps why he is silent on the document dubbed the 'Constitution of Madīnah'. By omitting it, there is no basis for Muḥammad accusing the Banū Qurayẓah of breaking a pact or being guilty of treachery even if the theory of plotting were to be accepted.

Curiously, Muir then recognizes that the behaviour of the Banū Qurayẓah was traitorous and demanded 'a severe retribution', but he objects to what took place, saying it '. . . cannot be recognized otherwise than as an act of monstrous cruelty'.[64] In *Mahomet and Islam* he admits again that the Banū Qurayẓah merited severe chastisement for joining 'the enemy at so critical a moment' even though he calls the punishment a 'barbarous deed which cannot be justified by any reason of political necessity'.[65] Muir's position on this matter wavers a lot. After arguing that the Banū Qurayẓah remained a disinterested party in the Khandaq siege, he now recognizes that they plotted to join the enemy camp. Even granting that the punishment meted out was exactly as Muir describes, he does not share a suggestion that it indicates a firm implementation of justice.

Cherāgh ʿAlī even looks at the situation on the basis of international law and though it may look a bit far-fetched for a seventh-century society, since this seems to be the very category Muir is thinking in, Cherāgh ʿAlī's method is acceptable. He points out that the crime was high treason against a besieged city and hence the perpetrators deserved to die. They were not killed merely for being prisoners of war, he argues. He doubts the authority upon which Muir rests his analysis and referring to Ibn Sayyid al-Nās, Abu'l Muʿtamar Sulaimān and Syed Ameer Ali, rejects the numbers usually quoted as executed and referred to also by Muir, as grossly exaggerated to suit people's interests.[66]

Ameer Ali, after discussing the matter writes: 'We must in sentiment or pity, overlook the stern question of justice and culpability. We must bear in mind the crimes of which they were guilty, – their treachery, their open hostility, their defection from an alliance to which they were bound by every sacred tie.'[67] He concludes that the judgement was in '. . . perfect consonance with the laws of war, as then understood by nations of the world . . . these people brought their fate upon themselves'.[68]

Barakat Ahmad re-examines the whole issue of the relationship between Muḥammad and the Jews and seems to bring in a completely new phase. He writes: 'Intergroup relations, especially when religion is also involved, are full of conflict and suffering. Martyrology feeds the myth and prejudice adds bitterness to the legend. Political expediency and biased scholarship invest the legend with the status of history. The account of Muhammad's relation with the Jews of the Hijaz is one of such legends.'[69] He introduces a new dimension into the episode, doubting the details of events as presented in many history books and in Muir's work for that matter. After closely examining the *Sīrah* of Ibn Isḥāq, and noting the *isnād* carefully, he realizes that out of 304, only nine were Jews or Jewish converts and the subjects they reported on do not refer to the 'heinous and atrocious killing' of the Jews as we often hear.

Ahmad also notes that Jewish scholars do not mention the case of the Banū Qurayẓah's extermination and this is most unusual because the Jews do not usually forget their adversities.[70] He points out that Samuel Usque, who is described as a '. . . deft painter of Jewish suffering [who] caused the long procession of Jewish history to file past the tearful eyes of his contemporaries in all its sublime and glory and abysmal tragedy', did not refer to the story of the Banū Qurayẓah.[71]

We are not assuming that because Jewish writers did not refer to it, this means the event did not happen. We cite Ahmad here merely to show that a whole new look could be taken at the issue.

The event at Ḥudaibiyyah is then touched on by Muir but with no examination of what it tells us about Muḥammad's character. After the previous narration about Muḥammad as inhuman, revengeful, warlike and bloodthirsty, here we have Muḥammad accepting some unthinkable amendments to an already 'insulting' pact with his arch enemies who are now virtually helpless at his feet.

Muir, in narrating the incident comments that the foundation is suspicious and though it might have occurred, it is highly coloured. We suspect that because this is another opportunity for us to see a reasonable, diplomatic, calm, just and sincere Muḥammad, Muir doubts its authenticity. He applies his theory of 'disadvantageous tradition' as a law.[72]

In fact, this theory needs an in-depth investigation because it could even be that what Muir and his colleagues might view as disadvantageous using nineteenth-century Victorian criteria may not have been regarded as so by the seventh- to eighth-century transmitters. Hence, the method again implies anachronism. It might even be possible to turn the concept around and say that the type of tradition transmitted might be an indicator of what seventh- to eighth-century transmitters considered advantageous, which might give a very different value system from that applied by Muir. A deeper discussion of this theory is however beyond the immediate concern of this work.

Attention now shifts back to expeditions. The description of the way Kinānah, the chief of Khaybar, was killed after the conquest, is couched in language reminiscent of the medieval period where the sole objective was to portray Muḥammad as evil as possible.[73] Muḥammad's humane attitude towards the poor and the needy is given only passing mention, usually in a sentence or two. For example, after stressing Muḥammad's allocation of state property to his own household, and part to the army, Muir remarks that 'the poor were also not forgotten'.[74]

We realize that if Muir gives much prominence to the concern for the poor, the needy and the like, it will contradict the uncaring image of Muḥammad he has constructed. On Muḥammad's return to Makkah for the lesser pilgrimage (*'Umrah*) according to the terms of Ḥudaibiyyah, Muir is silent.

That Muḥammad accepted to leave Makkah without even celebrating his wedding feast (after his marriage to Maymūnah) tells us much about him. However, these details would be favourable and Muir generally resents that. If the Prophet were heartless, of dubious character and always ready to fabricate revelations to satisfy his personal desires, he could have used one of these avenues to prolong his stay in Makkah at least until the consummation of his marriage.

Muir is set on seeing Muḥammad as a different man in Madīnah. On the triumphant entry into Makkah, there is no discussion as to the lessons we can learn about Muḥammad from the event.

Lane-Poole points out that Muḥammad surprised all his critics who were expecting blood in the streets now that his old, bitterest enemies stood impotent before him.[75]

It might be argued that Muḥammad, because his entry had received no definable opposition, spared his opponents. But even that would have told us something about his character. The mean, violent and cruel Muḥammad is now ordering his soldiers not to cause any harm.[76] If he were by nature implacable and vindictive as he is portrayed, it would have made no difference between showing mercy when there is no opposition and being harsh when resisted. Muir, however, admits that Muḥammad's magnanimity on this occasion was admirable but, in order to counter any reference to accepting his exemplary morality, he is quick to add that Muḥammad acted as he did for strategic reasons. He says: 'It was indeed for his own interest to forgive the past, and cast into oblivion its slights and injuries.'[77] In many cases, Muḥammad's strategic skills are given prominence for the wrong reasons. The argument is basically to show him as not only clever but also sly.

Conclusion

The last chapter of the book is devoted specifically to an appraisal of the person and character of Muḥammad in a thematic form in the light of the discussions in the preceding chapters.

Lyall writes about Muir's work: '. . . It can scarcely be doubted that the author always strives to be just and fair: anyone who has read the thirty-seventh chapter, dealing with the character of the prophet, must be convinced of this.'[78] This statement does not seem convincing because the average assessment of the book does not produce such a picture.

Muir makes some fair comments about Muḥammad's personal appearance, faithfulness, moderation, and magnanimity. It may also be true that he acknowledges Muḥammad's deep conviction of divine guidance, steadfastness, determination and honesty in Makkah and his strong denunciation of polytheism and idolatry. However, his censures regarding the Prophet as cruel, crafty, deceptive, voluptuous, sexually profligate, inconsistent, as fabricating revelations, and the fact that his prophethood attenuated into worldly and evil affairs, counteract any fair comments.

Again, Lyall's remarks cannot be objective. If the thirty-seventh chapter alone is what the book has to show of Muir's impartiality then it is very inadequate in the light of the size of the book. From the way the arguments are constructed, it is difficult to see Muir balancing his thesis.

Muir's main themes of emphasis are the falsity of Muḥammad's prophethood, faking of revelations to justify evil acts, violence, sexuality, immorality and the like. No disinterested reader is likely to disagree that the book is founded very much on *parti pris*. Certainly issues like the Charter of Madīnah, treatment of the poor, the needy and prisoners of war and slaves, patience towards his adversaries in Madīnah, his meekness towards people, the event at Ḥudaibiyyah and the peaceful entry into Makkah, deserve far more attention than Muir gives them. Furthermore, to refuse to accept the authenticity of Muḥammad's immense religious experience is a major shortcoming in Muir's work. To portray Muḥammad as a world hero or ruler, misses his real personality entirely.

The assessment of Muḥammad on Christian principles is a very inapposite methodology to use in academic scholarship. Sometimes the very language Muir uses seems vulgar and this does not show the book in a good light academically.

Syed Ahmad Khan points out that the fact that Muir undertook the study at the instigation of Rev. Karl Pfander, alone caused him to strive under a heavy dose of prejudice, bias, and Christian polemics, all of which show up in his work.[79] He criticizes Muir's attitude to the *ḥadīth* and maintains that by using the strictly suspicious method, Muir prejudiced the outcome of his study.[80]

Higgins accuses certain Christian scholars of writing so negatively about Muḥammad that even though they were learned and '. . . indeed ought to have been above such conduct, . . . (their) zeal in this case actually destroyed their senses of right and wrong, and as it should seem, taken away from them the use of their understanding'.[81]

We suspect this might be true of William Muir as well. His high academic calibre would normally have prevented him from making such prejudiced interpretations. In the opinion of Barakat Ahmad and Syed Ahmad, Muir's uncritical reliance on al-Wāqidī's material reduces the status of the work.[82]

Earle H. Waugh discusses the problems the Western writer

encounters in dealing with Muḥammad. He sees the Prophet as a 'paradigmatic figure' who has to be tackled along several lines before an appreciable assessment can be made of him.[83]

Muir had the original sources before him, much as a blacksmith with a piece of iron in front of him; however, he has made a hoe instead of a cutlass. His defectiveness is not that he could not read the Arabic but in insisting that he reads it in a particular way.

Certain intellectual attitudes in the Middle Ages towards Muḥammad have crystallized into patterns of thought and have been echoed for millennia and worn smooth by generations of Western scholars both historians and theologians. However much Muir has tried to divest himself of the old heritage, traces, too evident to overlook as insignificant, remain.

Notes

1. A. Von Kramer (ed.), *History of Muhammad's Campaigns by Aboo Abdallah Mohammad Omar Al-Waqidy* (1856), p.1.

2. *Ibid.*, p.2.

3. C.J. Lyall, 'Obituary of Sir William Muir', *JRAS* (1905), p.876.

4. *Ibid.*, p.877.

5. W. Muir, *The Life of Mohammed from Original Sources* (1858–61), p.xiii.

6. D.S. Margoliouth, *Lectures on Arab Historians* (1930), Lecture 1, p.3.

7. Muir, *The Life*, pp.xliii–iv.

8. *Ibid.*, p.xlviii.

9. Muhammad Asad, *Islam at the Crossroads* (1975), pp.127–8.

10. Muir, *The Life*, p.li.

11. H.A.R. Gibb, *Mohammedanism* (1949), p.vi.

12. Muir, *The Life*, p.xciv.

13. *Ibid.*, p.xcviii.

14. *Ibid.*, p.xcvii and pp.197–203. Also *The Sources of Islam*, a Persian treatise by the Rev. W. St. Clair-Tisdall (1901), esp. Chs. 3 and 4.

15. For example, see the Qur'ān 2: 41, 89, 97; 3: 3; 4: 47; 5: 48; and *passim.*

16. Muir, *The Life*, pp.6–7.

17. Emile Dermenghem, *The Life of Mahomet* (1930), trans. by Arabella Yorke, pp.251–2.

18. Syed Ahmad Khan, *The Life of Muhammad and Subjects Subsidiary Thereto* (1979), Reproduction, p.196.

19. *Ibid.*, p.196.

20. E.W. Lane, *An Arabic Lexicon* (1980), p.1739 ff. esp. p.1740. Here, there is a detailed analysis of the word with the general notion being 'affliction' or 'calamity'.

21. Khan, *The Life*, p.196.

22. *Ibid.*, pp.198–9. See also Gibbon, *The Decline and Fall of the Roman Empire* (1923), Vol. 5, p.373.

23. Muir, *The Life*, pp.19–20.

24. Nestorius died about 451 AD, about 120 years before the birth of Muḥammad.

25. Muir, *The Life*, p.21.

26. *Ibid.*, p.22.

27. *Ibid.*, p.38.

28. *Ibid.*

29. *Ibid.*, p.47.

30. *Ibid.*, p.55.

31. *Ibid.*, p.106.

32. *Ibid.*, pp.80–6.

33. Khan, *The Life*, pp.317–32.

34. *Ibid.*, pp.328–9.

35. *Ibid.*, p.332.

36. *A Critical Examination of the Life and Teachings of Muhammad* (1873), p.87.

37. Muir, *The Life*, pp.121–2.

38. *Ibid.*, p.126.

39. Ameer Ali, in *A Critical Examination*, p.59, poses a similar question and wonders why Christians who believe in the bodily ascension of Jesus and the case of Elijah feel the Muslim belief is less rational or improbable. See the Bible, *2 Kings* 2: 11, *Matthew* 17: 1 ff. and *Acts* 1: 11.

40. Khan, *The Life*, p.344 ff.

41. *Ibid.*, p.347.

42. *Ibid.*, p.372. We need to note here, however, that the subject of acceptance of the bodily journey is a touchy one and cannot be dismissed as easily as Syed Ahmad Khan does here. He was known not to be particularly disposed to accepting the miraculous and we suspect this is behind his reasoning. The issue has much to do with obedience to the Prophet.

43. Antonie Wessels offers a detailed and serious discussion of Haykal's interpretation of this subject, referring to several Muslim and Western opinions. See his *A Modern Arabic Biography of Muhammad: A Critical Study of Muhammad Husayn Haykal's Hayat Muhammad* (1972); see pp.64–7; 81–4; 213–47. See also Widengren, *Muhammad, the Apostle of God and His Ascension* (King and Saviour V), (1955), esp. Ch. V where the Qur'ānic evidence and various writings on the *Miʿrāj* are discussed.

44. Muir, *The Life*, pp.53–4.

45. C. Bennet, *Victorian Images of Islam* (1992), p.14; see also Ch. 5.

46. Muir, *The Life*, p.126.

47. R.B. Smith, *Muhammed and Muhammedanism* (1874), p.340.

48. G.W. Leitner, *Muhammadanism* (1889), p.4.

49. James Waltz, 'Muhammad and Islam in St. Thomas Aquinas', *MW*, Vol. 66, No. 2 (1976), pp.81–95. See also Daniel, *Islam and the West*, pp.73–7.

50. Muir, *The Life*, p.202.

51. *Ibid.*

52. *Ibid.*, p.227 ff.

53. *Ibid.*, pp.233–4.

54. *Ibid.*, pp.241–2.

55. *Ibid.*, p.245.

56. *Ibid.*, p.248.

57. *Ibid.*, note on pp.248–9.

58. J. Davenport, *An Apology for Mohammed and the Koran* (1869), pp.135–44. See also the Bible, *Joshua* 6: 10, *1 Samuel* 15, *Judges* 1: 21.

59. T. Carlyle, 'The Hero as a Prophet: Mahomet in Islam', in *On Heroes, Hero Worship and the Heroic in History* (1849), p.61.

60. W.A. Miller, 'A Note on Islam and the West', *Theology*, Vol. 84, No. 697 (January 1981), p.37. He points out that Christianity is perhaps more guilty.

61. Khan, *The Life*, pp.432–7.

62. *A Critical Examination*, p.82, see note.

63. Muir, *The Life*, p.316 ff.

64. *Ibid.*, p.322.

65. W. Muir, *Mahomet and Islam: A Sketch of the Prophet's Life from Original Sources and a Brief Outline of His Religion* (1884), p.151.

66. Cherāgh 'Alī, *A Critical Examination of the Popular Jihād* (1885), pp.87–91.

67. *A Critical Examination*, p.111.

68. *Ibid.*, p.112.

69. Barakat Ahmad, *Muhammad and the Jews – A Re-examination* (1979), p.ix.

70. *Ibid.*, p.24.

71. *Ibid.*

72. Muir, *The Life*, Ch. 19.

73. *Ibid.*, pp.376–8.

74. *Ibid.*, p.380.

75. S. Lane-Poole, *Selection from the Qur'an and Hadith* (1882), (1975 reprint), pp.28–9.

76. Muir, *The Life*, p.411.

77. *Ibid.*

78. See his 'Obituary of Sir William Muir', *JRAS* (1905), p.876.

79. Khan, *The Life*, pp.xviii–xix; Lyall also makes an observation like this; see note 2 to his obituary article.

80. *Ibid.*, p.299.

81. Abu Fazl (ed.), *Mr. Godfrey Higgins' Apology for Mohamed* (1929), A Verbatim Reprint, edited with Introduction, critical notes, Appendices, and a chapter on Islam, p.11.

82. Barakat Ahmad, *Muhammad and the Jews* (1979), pp.18–19, and Syed Ahmad Khan, *The Life*, pp.xiv and 304.

83. See his article 'The Popular Muhammad: Models in the Interpretation of an Islamic Paradigm', in R.C. Martin (ed.), *Approaches to Islam in Religious Studies* (1985), pp.41–54, esp. pp.42–3.

CHAPTER THREE

David Samuel Margoliouth

Introduction

After Muir's work in the second half of the nineteenth century, there was very little new English material on Muḥammad in the West. The few works that did appear were essentially repetitions of what might be called the 'Muir theories'.

Though, over the course of almost half a century (1861–1905) one would expect new developments in the field of methodology and in the growth of general scholarship and comparative religion in particular, it seems that the only scholar to enter the arena with a new work was David Samuel Margoliouth. It is because of this, together with Margoliouth's academic standing, that we investigate this scholar's work on Muḥammad.

Though Margoliouth wrote extensively on Islam, the book which gives a definitive biographical study and critique of Muḥammad is his *Mohammed and the Rise of Islam.*[1] This work, Margoliouth's *magnum opus*, received acclaim from Western reviewers while Muslims have largely been suspicious of its value as an academic work.

Margoliouth's Intellectual Biography

David Samuel Margoliouth was born in London on 17 October 1858 and died on 22 March 1940, aged 81. He was the only son of Ezekiel Margoliouth and Sarah Iglitzki. The father, formerly a rabbi, became an Anglican missionary to the Jews. His father's uncle, Moses Margoliouth (1818–81),[2] was himself a Jewish convert to Christianity who was well known for his expertise in Biblical and Oriental studies; he served in his later years as vicar in Little Linford in Buckinghamshire.[3] David S. Margoliouth was therefore a Jew by descent and a product of Jewish converts to Christianity. He was born of a strong Anglican missionary background.

Margoliouth was exceptionally bright and crowned his efforts with first-class honours at New College, Oxford. He assumed the Laudian Chair of Arabic at the University of Oxford in 1889 and held this position until about 1937 when he retired due to failing health. Ordained in 1899, he was soon to become famous as an eloquent and brilliant, if somewhat unorthodox, preacher. He liked to travel and undertook lecturing tours to India and also spent some time in Iraq.

Gilbert Murray asserts rather extravagantly that Margoliouth '. . . built up a reputation of knowing Islamic things better than the Moslems themselves . . .'[4] The author of this biographical piece further says: 'At the time of his death, Margoliouth had among the Islamic peoples of the East, and indeed among the Oriental scholars in Europe, "an almost legendary reputation".'[5]

Margoliouth won a number of academic scholarships in extensive and diverse fields such as Arabic, Greek, Hebrew, Latin, Sanskrit, Syriac and Turkish. His expertise in Arabic literature is testified to by the statement in *The Dictionary of National Biography*: 'Unlike most scholars he was a brilliant linguist, and although somewhat silent in English, he became full of conversation when addressed in Arabic or Turkish.'[6] Margoliouth's natural endowment in the academic field perhaps caused him to become somewhat arrogant. An incident is reported of a critique of some of his theories on ancient Greek literature. His reply to his critic was in the form of an elaborate display of his genius.[7]

As an Oriental scholar, Margoliouth wrote extensively on almost every subject. He handled intricate areas in Arabic literature with ease. His book *Mohammed and the Rise of Islam* (1905) together with his *Mohammedanism* (1911) and the Hibbert Lectures of 1913 entitled *The Early Development of Mohammedanism*, brought him recognition as an able scholar of Islam and one whose works set the standard in their fields.[8] He was, however, also seen as controversial by some scholars. His works, as Murray points out, with '. . . their ironical tone sometimes infuriated his Muslim readers'.[9]

In 1925, in an article published in *The Journal of the Royal Asiatic Society*, Margoliouth poured scorn on the authenticity of pre-Islamic Arabian poetry, the first time a scholar of his calibre had raised such a question.[10] He wrote:

> If on the question whether Arabic versification goes back to immemorial antiquity or is later than the Qur'an it seems wisest to suspend judgement, the reason lies in the bewildering character of the evidence that is before us. We are on safe ground when we are dealing with inscriptions; and the Qur'an can be trusted for the condition of the Arabs to whom it was communicated in the Prophet's time. But for the history of Arabic verse we have to go to other authorities, who for the most part treat of times and conditions for which they themselves had no experience, and whose training had caused them to assume much that necessarily misled them. In judging their statements we can carry scepticism too far, but we may be too credulous.[11]

Margoliouth had a photographic memory which was a tremendous boon for his enormous and ambitious efforts. Gilbert Murray writes: 'It was in editing and translating Arabic texts, that Margoliouth's scholarship found its most congenial field. His prodigious memory, which carried without effort the fruits of his vast range of reading in many languages, was an unequalled instrument for his task.'[12]

Margoliouth was on the Council of the Royal Asiatic Society from 1905, became its director in 1927 and was president from 1934 to 1937. In 1928, he was awarded a Gold Medal for his excellent services to the Society. He became president of the Eastern Question Association in 1910 and chairman of the governing council of Warneford Hospital for Mental Diseases at Headington, Oxford. He became a fellow of the British Academy in 1915 and it was under its auspices that he delivered the Schweich Lectures for 1921 on *The Relations Between Arabs and the Israelites Prior to the Rise of Islam.*[13] Margoliouth's adeptness in his field brought him fellowships of the German Oriental Society in 1934 and the American Oriental Society in 1937. He is described as having an almost emotional and extreme attachment to orthodoxy and being sceptical of all things that were against what he held to be the truth. He had much love and sympathy for the Jews and their cause.

In concluding his article in the *Dictionary of National Biography*, Murray points out that Margoliouth '. . . was certainly a man of most massive learning and great ingenuity. In problems of literature his judgement seems often to have been unbalanced, a fault which was more conspicuous because he never "played for safety" or took refuge in vagueness'.[14]

One might be tempted to think that perhaps Margoliouth was so self-confident that he never thought of making mistakes. While it is advisable in scholarship while writing to create a 'safety net' because man being the fallible creature he is, can, if unintentionally, make mistakes, it could also be argued that such 'safety nets' are created by scholars who possibly do not have full confidence in themselves. Margoliouth perhaps deemed himself completely and absolutely confident with the material in his field. Murray adds that Margoliouth '. . . had an immense memory. He was never slipshod, never unprepared. No scholar of his generation left so deep and permanent a mark on Oriental studies'.[15]

In an obituary, Arthur Jeffery pays Margoliouth a glowing tribute, placing him in the group of specialists in the field of Islamic Studies in the West, alongside celebrated non-English writers such as Antoine Isaac Baron, Silvestre de Sacy, Heinrich Leberecht Fleischer, Theodor Nöldeke, Ignaz Goldziher and Reinhardt Dozy.[16]

Margoliouth's reputation as a linguistic prodigy and his towering status was widely acknowledged by contemporary scholars. Arthur Jeffery states that he '. . . had few rivals in his knowledge of Persian, Turkish, Armenian and Syriac, as well as being an Hebraist'.[17] This, in addition to his great competence in Greek and Latin, made him '. . . the foremost Arabist in Europe'.[18]

Margoliouth opened the door to academic excellence with his thesis entitled *Analecta Orientalia Ad Poeticam Aristoteleam* published in 1888. In this field of Greek Classics, he followed up, in 1911, with *The Poetics of Aristotle* and thirteen years later with *The Homer of Aristotle.* It was in the last work that he advanced arguments on chronograms, a controversial subject in the academic world at the time.[19] He cultivated an early interest in the Islamic Near East and it is suggested that he took up the study of Hindustani merely to have a springboard for the study of Islam in the Indian subcontinent.[20]

Like his uncle Moses Margoliouth, he wrote extensively on Biblical scholarship, mainly articles for dictionaries, encyclopaedias and eminent academic journals. He also wrote on Armenian and Syriac intellectualism. Arthur Jeffery's obituary says: 'He was very conservative in Biblical studies, and somewhat unduly suspicious of critical work on the Old Testament, even producing a little book, now almost forgotten, *Outlines of a Defence of the Biblical Revelation.*'[21]

However, Margoliouth made his greatest impact in the world of intellectual excellence through Arabic and Islamic Studies. In addition to the works already mentioned, he also wrote *Letters of Abū al-ʿAlā'* in 1898 and single-handedly edited Yāqūt's *Dictionary of Learned Men,* a work of seven volumes, between 1907 and 1931. Also, in 1922, he worked with H.F. Amedroz, editing the six volumes of Miskawayh's *Eclipse of the Abbasid Caliphate.*

Reputed to be a gifted Arabic papyrologist, in 1893 Margoliouth wrote a book on the Bodleian Library Arabic

Papyri and did the same, in 1933, for the papyri material held in the John Rylands Library in Manchester.

We would not do justice to Margoliouth's erudition if we made it appear that he was a reclusive scholar who wrote for a select academic club; he served the general public as well. His work *Cairo, Jerusalem and Damascus*, published in London in 1907, is a fine testimony to this.[22] In 1939, a year before he passed away, he published another piece on Muḥammad in the series *What Did They Teach?* and this was also meant for public consumption.

Arthur Jeffery notes that though Margoliouth passed away at the ripe age of 81, '. . . Islamic Studies will ever be poorer for the loss of those projects . . .'[23] which would not see the light of day due to his demise. His writing and unyielding efforts in unearthing new evidence in classical works was highly appreciated. It is not surprising therefore that the eulogy ends by asking whether some monumental work might be produced to the glory of '. . . a great and painstaking scholar, whose influence over successive generations of students has been very great, and whose views, even if not always acceptable, were always stimulating and deserving of consideration?'[24]

Margoliouth's competence and excellence in his field is continuously attested to by scholars. A reviewer of his presentation at the Schweich Lectures writes:

> As a whole, the subject of the lectures requires a wide range of knowledge for its adequate treatment. No one could be more peculiarly well qualified to deal with it than Professor Margoliouth. He shows himself as much at home in philology, epigraphy, and Hebrew literature as he is in Arabic poetry and pre-Islamic history. He collects the latest results of modern researches, and all his facts are supported by reference where necessary. His clear arrangement and valuable and interesting comment make the lectures good reading.[25]

Frank Hugh Foster, whose article on the question of 'Islam as a heresy' received comments and rebuttal by Margoliouth,[26] replied in a short note justifying his arguments in the earlier article. However, despite the contention between the two, Foster pays tribute to his critic's academic acumen. He writes: 'I am prepared to accept Professor Margoliouth's authority upon this subject. He is an eminent Arabic scholar, one of the first now living, among whom our own MacDonald is to be numbered. I do not regard myself as belonging to that class at all.'[27]

Eliot Howard's review of Margoliouth's *Mohammed and the Rise of Islam* contains an instructive statement which adds to the numerous attestations to Margoliouth as a man of prowess in the domain of Islamic Studies. He states: 'This book is of importance owing to the perfect knowledge of Arabic possessed by the writer. He is able to collect his materials at first hand, and, whether he is dealing with the Koran or with the numerous Muslim writers whom he quotes, we have confidence that he knows his subject thoroughly.'[28]

The *New Encyclopaedia Britannica* says that Margoliouth's '. . . pioneer efforts in Islamic Studies won him a near legendary reputation among Islamic peoples and Oriental scholars of Europe'.[29] He was said to be regarded in Baghdād as '. . . more knowledgeable on Islamic matters than most Arab scholars'.[30] Inayatullah, writing in the 'Personalia' column of *Islamic Culture* on 'Three British Orientalists', is very critical of Margoliouth but at the same time he acknowledges his eminence, describing him as a man of unique, unquestionable scholarship in Islam.[31]

His Book on the Prophet

We believe we have justified our choice of Margoliouth's *Mohammed and the Rise of Islam* as the book which underscores Margoliouth's views on the life of Muḥammad. The book, which has thirteen chapters each of which is expertly treated within the context of English Orientalist writing, begins with an analysis of the roots of Muḥammad in pre-Islamic Arabia. The argument then develops through the Prophet's early life, how Islam evolved secretly, became open, analysis of the *Hijrah* event, the first battle and the fluctuating progress of the nascent religion. The panorama continues with the confrontation with the Jewish communities, a subject Margoliouth deals with in a rather melodramatic way for reasons which we will come to later. He then looks at Muḥammad's re-entry into Makkah and ends with Muḥammad's last moments. In the Preface, he discusses writers on Muḥammad, both Muslim and non-Muslim, and considers Sir Walter Raleigh's *The Life and Death of Mahomet,* published in 1637, the most famous of the biographies. However, he states that, 'The palm of eloquence and historical insight may well be awarded to Gibbon.'[32]

His Sources

Though the work of Abū al-Fidā' on Muḥammad was a major source of reference in Gibbon's time, Margoliouth says that the nineteenth-century scholars had to go beyond Abū al-Fidā' to the original Muslim sources since Abū al-Fidā' was such a late authority.[33] After lauding earlier scholars such as Weil, de Perceval, Wüstenfeld, Sprenger and Muir for their skills in bringing some of these original sources to light, Margoliouth points out defects in Muir's and Sprenger's works even though he still considers them as classical.[34] Muir's work is described as '. . . written with confusedly Christian bias', while Sprenger's is said to be '. . . defaced by some slipshod scholarship and untrustworthy archaeology'.[35]

The initial impression is that Margoliouth's work will stand out from the crowd and will not get caught in the same snares that the earlier scholars he criticizes were caught in. He relies heavily on the *musnad* of Aḥmad ibn Ḥanbal and the *Tafsīr* of al-Ṭabarī, and others such as the *Iṣābah* or dictionary of individuals who had personal knowledge of Muḥammad, compiled by Ibn Ḥajar.[36]

The works of ʿAmr ibn Baḥr, called *Al-Jāḥiẓ*, which was a polygraph, is also mentioned as being important. About these works Margoliouth remarks that, 'Though not dealing directly with Mohammed, they contain many an allusion which it is possible to utilize.'[37]

Referring to the traditions (*aḥādīth*), which he considers ahistorical and forged, Margoliouth writes: 'The number of motives leading to the fabrication of traditions was so great that the historian is in constant danger of employing as veracious records that were deliberate fictions.'[38] He then adds that, 'I can only hope that I have displayed greater credulity than my predecessors',[39] assuring the reader of his commitment to fair scholarship. He categorically states that the book '. . . does not aim at being either an apology or an indictment'.[40] This statement is put to the test in the analysis which follows shortly.

He considers that Syed Ameer Ali's work is the greatest apologetic work on Muḥammad while Muir's falls within the domain of an indictment.[41] He claims that while other works seek to prove the superiority or otherwise of Islam *vis-à-vis* another religion, his work does not follow that course. He asserts that he has freed himself from all these prejudices.[42] These are very positive statements and coming from a scholar of Margoliouth's eminence, the student should, under normal circumstances, have no qualms about the material he has set himself to read. Margoliouth sets his ideas into context by discussing pre-Islamic Arabian history and Arabia in the period of Muḥammad's advent. He writes that, 'Religious fanaticism was introduced by Islam, as an addition to the dangers of the country; otherwise Arabia of the twentieth century is similar to the Arabia of the sixth.'[43]

After praising the pre-Islamic Arab's wisdom, pride, strength, courage, piety and fidelity as expressed by some scholars, Margoliouth then seems to suggest that these values are illusory. He considers the Old Testament as being the source of Arab genealogical wisdom and asserts that many of the claims by them are not true historical facts, with fanciful ideas finding their way into the general corpus. He states that '. . . the steps which connected the individual with the founder of the clan, and those whereby the clan was deduced from the tribe, represents a theory, rarely a genuine tradition; and instances are not wanting of both persons and clans being artificially grafted on tribes with which they had no physical connection'.[44]

Margoliouth disputes the ancient antiquity of Makkah, saying that Muslims have given the city this status because of theological speculation. He argues that a '. . . more sober tradition placed the building of the first house at Meccah only a few generations before Mohammed's time, this act being ascribed to a member of the tribe Sahm, whose name was variously given as Su'aid, son of Sahm and Sa'd son of 'Amr'.[45]

It could be argued that Margoliouth, in these arguments against the genealogical consciousness of the Arabs and the antiquity of Makkah, is laying a foundation for some profound arguments against a large chunk of the superstructure of Islam. We foresee here preparation of the ground for rejecting the *aḥādīth*, a subject he has already touched on.[46]

He begins his critical approach by pointing to the evidence that exists to support the fact that the ancient Arabs worshipped stones. He therefore concludes that the Black Stone connected with the *Ka'bah* has been '. . . thought to be the real god of the Meccans'.[47] He speculates on the origin of Allah, saying: 'It seems possible that Allah, really a male deity, of which al-Lat was the female, identified by Mohammed with the object of monotheistic adoration, was the tribal god of the Kuraish; and indeed in lines which may possibly be pre-Islamic the Kuraish are called Allah's family.'[48]

In his use of Muslim sources, Margoliouth is sceptical. In his article on Muḥammad in the *Encyclopaedia of Religion and Ethics* he plays down the authenticity of almost every classical Muslim writer.[49] He refers to Ibn Isḥāq's work, which he says is not extant but the main parts exist in the works of Ibn Hishām and al-Ṭabarī. He then asserts that:

> Its author was in communication with eminent members of the prophet's family, but is said to have been a man of indifferent morals, besides being a Shiite and a Qadari (believer in the freedom of will); he employed versifiers to compose poems to be put into the mouths of the personages

> who figure in his narrative, and his credibility was otherwise impugned.[50]

He takes little interest in the works of Mūsā b.ʿUqbah, al-Wāqidī and his secretary Ibn Saʿd and the collections of Aḥmad ibn Ḥanbal. He describes these works as not of enough historical utility. However, he settles for Ibn Isḥāq, assigning the main reasons for his preference. He sees Ibn Isḥāq as being conscious of events in chronological order, and keeping out supernatural or metaphysical issues. Thirdly, he says, 'The character which the narrator ascribes to his prophet, is on the whole exceedingly repulsive.'[51] This, he argues, is indicative of Ibn Isḥāq's independence of mind, resisting all forms of influence from society or those in authority as happened to many scholars of the day.

In a sermon at St. Aldate's Church, Oxford, on the occasion of the Oxford Church Missionary Association meeting on 11 February 1900, Margoliouth emotively attacks Muḥammad and Islam. He castigates Muslim scholars for attributing edifying fables to the Prophet, attempting to portray him as an ethical man.[52]

One can appreciate the circumstances in which Margoliouth was speaking. To an audience of the Church Missionary Association, he probably felt he had to say these things. However, it could be argued that with his position and eminence in the circle of élite scholars of Islamic Studies, one would have expected less vituperation. It seems that Margoliouth's mistrust of Muslim scholars is deeply embedded in his subconscious, probably due to his dual Jewish and Christian backgrounds.

Selected Themes

The Pathological Theory

Margoliouth's choice of themes is reflected in the way he almost immediately discusses the age-old issue of Muḥammad being an epileptic.

The subject has been dealt with in previous chapters on

medieval scholarship and in the analysis of Muir's work. However, its recurrence here seems to support our earlier contention that many of the medieval theories about Muḥammad had a strong impact on the academic scene and defied all changes in scholarship to survive. Margoliouth writes that '. . . the notion current among Christian writers that he was subject to epilepsy finds curious confirmation in the notices recorded of his experiences during the process of revelation the importance of which is not lessened by the probability that the symptoms were often artificially produced'.[53]

After describing Muḥammad's experiences when receiving revelations as recorded by certain scholars, he mentions two instances only in which the fits, he believes, were not personally induced. He gives the case of his fainting at the battle of Badr and the occasion when he passed out when being bled after fasting. Margoliouth however admits that '. . . some of the signs of severe epilepsy – biting of the tongue, dropping what is in the hand, and gradual degeneration of the brain power – were wanting'.[54]

There is a further hint of the pathological theory when Margoliouth discusses the children born to Muḥammad and Khadījah. He notes, correctly, that the sons died in infancy but adds that the girls were sickly and, after pointing out that the longest surviving daughter never reached her fortieth birthday, concludes that '. . . some who understand medicine have drawn their inferences about the father'.[55]

There is an innuendo here that Muḥammad was a weakling, Margoliouth perhaps attributing this to his belief that Muḥammad was a pathological case. This is the most rational explanation for his implication. However, Muḥammad's robust health is attested to by the difficult duties he had to shoulder as a leader under intense persecution and pressure in Makkah and the even more arduous tasks he had to undertake in Madīnah. There is no hint anywhere that Muḥammad's health was substantially impaired to merit such an opinion. By not providing any support for that reasoning and showing which medical experts thought

Muḥammad's health was feeble, Margoliouth overlooks a crucial principle in academic scholarship – supporting an argument with sound, authentic evidence.

Margoliouth returns to the subject of epilepsy in the third chapter. He states: 'We have already seen reason for believing that Mohammed at sometime had epileptic fits; whence the phenomena accompanying such a fit may have suggested a form which could afterwards be artificially reproduced.'[56]

In his article on Muḥammad in the *Encyclopaedia of Religion and Ethics,* he gives some conflicting signals with regard to this theory. He refers to the opinions of Sprenger and other scholars who wrote on the theme but doubts whether the so-called 'fits' were real. Despite his earlier reference in his biographical work on Muḥammad, as mentioned earlier, he finds it strange that the reality defies the theory. He looks at Muḥammad's acknowledged pleasant personality and casts doubt on the authenticity of the theory. He writes:

> It is clear that he was a man of great physical strength, since his life as *tyrant* [emphasis ours] of Medina was spent in constant military expeditions, added to the cares of a rapidly increasing community, of which he was at once priest, legislator, ruler and judge. Yet we never hear of his breaking down under the strain. The 'fits' seem to have been experienced only when they were required for the delivery of the revelations, and in no case to have interfered with his activities.[57]

From this statement one might think that Margoliouth rejects the theory. He does not. He ends up restating his initial line of thinking, that the 'fits' were actually induced. It could be that there is a hidden agenda to this reasoning. Even though he might be convinced that such a malady had a negative effect on the physique of the person, with Muḥammad, he had to deny this because the thesis does not fit the reality. Muḥammad was too healthy to be an epileptic.

Secondly, one could argue that he persued the issue of inducement because it offers an opportunity to criticize the revelations as being simulated and therefore fake. This then raises the question of Muḥammad's personality as a whole.

Revelation of the Holy Qur'ān

We have reasoned, from Margoliouth's analysis of Muḥammad's health, that he has a particular view of the Muslim Scripture. He brings back the old theory that the Qur'ān was Muḥammad's own creation. He comments on the Qur'ānic style and deduces that '. . . the tradesman Prophet could not keep free of metaphors taken from his business'.[58]

The Qur'ān's elaborate teachings in the conduct of fair business, to Margoliouth, is a sure indication that Muḥammad had a hand in its composition. He takes up certain Qur'ānic verses and forces upon them interpretations which could serve the object of sanctioning his reasoning. He writes that Muḥammad, 'At one time . . . commanded his followers to make an offering to the poor before they addressed him, but this had to be rescinded.'[59] This is his interpretation of the passage in *Sūrah al-Mujādalah*. The passage reads:

> O you who believe! When you consult the Prophet in private, spend something in charity before your private consultation. That will be best for you, and most conducive to purify (of conduct). But if you find not (the wherewithal) God is oft-Forgiving, Most Merciful. Is it that you are afraid of spending sums in charity before your private consultation (with him)? If, then, you do not do so, and God forgives you, then (at least) establish regular prayer; practise regular charity; and obey God and His Prophet. And God is well-acquainted with all that you do.[60]

The impression created by Margoliouth's assertion is that Muḥammad had to 'withdraw' the statement because it was too demanding on the people. However, from the Qur'ān itself, as quoted above, there is no suggestion of the statement being 'rescinded'. As with many other Qur'ānic statements of such nature, allowance is made for the possibility of people not being able to perform the particular action recommended. This is why it is normally argued that the Qur'ān deals with realistic issues of human life, allowing for human frailties, and does not base its arguments or injunctions on speculative and abstract theories.

Yusuf Ali explains in his notes on the passage in question that human nature might make some people a bit selfish and want to monopolize the Prophet's time with their individual private concerns. This was thus recognition of such weakness and the charity was meant to expiate for this. It was a way of teaching people to purify their motives. However, in the same vein, the injunction is not put in such a way as to scare people away from the Prophet altogether. Consequently, God's magnanimity is open to those who might not be able to offer charity. At the same time, the situation is almost foolproof in that since God's forgiveness is not guaranteed, one has to rely on one's own conscience.

Margoliouth's perception of the Qur'ān is seen again when he discusses revelations in Madīnah. He says that Muḥammad never allowed even his Companions to see the 'roots' of his revelations.[61] He refers to some scribe who '. . . is said to have gone back to paganism by observing that the prophet allowed him to write whatever he chose'.[62] It is unfortunate that Margoliouth, despite his scholarly knowledge should find in the Qur'ānic text interpretations which are not there. But it ties in with the low esteem he had for the Qur'ān as a revealed book and Muḥammad as its recipient.

In his article on Muḥammad in the *Encyclopaedia of Religion and Ethics*, Margoliouth does not see the Qur'ān in a positive light. He says: '. . . the Qur'an is on many grounds ill-suited for a basis of jurisprudence. It is imperfect, self contradictory, and destitute in order'.[63]

In some cases he is so incensed and bent on disproving the authenticity of the Qur'ān that he uses language which leaves much to be desired. He describes some of the Qur'ānic legislation as savage and stupid and mentions an instance when Muḥammad, on his death bed, attempted to formulate a new code of law for the community.[64] He comments that '. . . to those who supposed that they had in the Qur'an the actual word of God this utterance not unnaturally seemed delirious'.[65]

He asserts that it was the advent of European laws which came to save the imperfections and inadequacies of the Qur'ānic codes. Until such time, Margoliouth continues, Muslims were not able to work out any sound law.[66]

Looking at Qur'ānic philosophy, Margoliouth doubts any firm theological foundations and even claims that the Prophet's '. . . theory of the deity is, on the whole, naively anthropomorphic; the Allah of the Qur'an has been compared to a magnified Oriental despot'.[67] His reasoning is that Allah is made to be served by angels with Jibrīl sending communications to Muḥammad while other angels are sent to help him in his wars. These, to him, are all earthly things and best refer to human conditions.

He does not see the Qur'ān addressing metaphysical issues. He writes: 'The resurrection of the body is thought of as one of bodily pains and pleasures; hence metaphysical questions concerning the soul are scarcely touched [upon].'[68] This is a curious observation by an acclaimed scholar of Arabic who was reputed to have known Islam even better than the Muslims themselves. A casual look at *Sūrah al-Fajr* will show that the Qur'ān deals with the soul in the Hereafter. The Qur'ān says:

> (To the righteous soul will be said) 'O (thou) soul in (complete) rest and satisfaction! Come back thou to thy Lord, well pleased (thyself) and well-pleasing unto Him! Enter thou, then among My devotees! Yes, enter you My Heaven![69]

Metaphysical questions have always been vigorously addressed by Muslim scholars – theologians and philosophers alike – and we would have expected that as an eminent scholar of Islam, Margoliouth would have been familiar with the works of al-Kindī, Ibn ʿArabī, Ibn Sīnā, Ibn Rushd, al-Fārābī, and al-Ghazālī.[70]

Prophethood

Margoliouth looks at Muḥammad's prophetic mission and argues that the situation at that time impressed upon him the need for a prophet to fill the vacuum among the Arabs and be on an equal footing with the Jews, Christians, Magians and Sabeans who all had leaders. He further reasons that with the name of the Christian and Jewish God being identical to that of the Qurayshi 'god', Muḥammad saw the opportunity to proclaim himself as a prophet and leader. Margoliouth thus sees the greatness in Muḥammad as stemming from two things: the fact that he was able to draw '. . . the inference, and of his ability to render that knowledge effective'.[71] Muḥammad, to him therefore, is great mainly because he is a seeker who has realized the object of his search.

He continues, that the claim by Muslims that Arabia at the time of Muḥammad's advent was in dire need of a prophet, as well as the story of events in the ruler of Persia's court at the birth of Muḥammad, '. . . may be dismissed as *Vaticinium Post Eventum*'.[72] Looking at the Makkan society, the way they went into battle with vigour and enthusiasm, he sees the Makkans enjoying life exceedingly and concludes that they were not in need of a prophet.

The reasoning here is rather strange. If we accept that the need for a spiritual guide has much to do with the presumed 'here and now' philosophy that physical temporal pleasures usually offer, even though the Makkans seemed quite content with life and in high spirits, there was an emptiness in them which needed to be filled. The way that those who embraced the nascent faith, resolved to stand by their new-found way of life and never give in to blackmail, threats and persecution, even on pain of death, seems to belie Margoliouth's opinion.

Further, Jaʿfar ibn Abī Ṭālib's speech at the court of al-Najāshī in Abyssinia regarding the Muslims' lifestyle, does not seem to suggest a pure, satisfying existence.[73]

Margoliouth's image of Muḥammad as a prophet never seems to go beyond the level of the implausible. He writes that even though he had some impressive qualities, '. . . the process of revelation was so suspicious that one of the scribes employed to take down the effusions became convinced that it was imposture and discarded Islam in consequence'.[74]

The issue of Muḥammad's imposture is an 'old wives tale' which has existed since medieval times. Margoliouth rebuffs some of these medieval ideas but keeps those which suit his thesis. He rejects the story of Muḥammad training pigeons to pick grain from his ear, interpreting this as evidence of God revealing a message to him. He cites Thomas Carlyle as one of those who pour scorn on such fanciful ideas and points out that nothing in the Muslim sources even remotely suggests this.[75]

Nevertheless, he ridicules Muḥammad's behaviour as sometimes showing evidence of theatrical effects. He gives examples of Muḥammad allegedly claiming not to find a seat in an empty room because all were occupied by angels and turning his face away from a corpse because two *houris* had come to tend the dead man – their husband. He adds that Muḥammad sometimes made his followers believe they had seen Jibrīl. When he comes across scholarly opinion to the effect that Muḥammad's honesty and sincerity were sufficient to convince people of his prophethood, Margoliouth retorts with an alleged research finding. He refers to one F. Podmore, who carried out research on the history of spiritualism, the findings of which '. . . cast great doubt on the proposition that an honourable man would not mystify his followers; and also make it appear that the conviction produced by the performances of a medium is often not shaken by the clearest exposure'.[76]

Margoliouth discounts the historicity of the visit to Waraqah ibn Naufal by Khadījah and Muḥammad in which he was said to have confirmed the authenticity of Muḥammad's experience in the Cave of Ḥirā'. He argues on the premise that Waraqah '. . . figures no further in the narrative'.[77]

Charles J. Lyall, in response to Margoliouth's earlier article purporting to explain the origins of the words 'Ḥanīf' and 'Muslim', rebuffs Margoliouth's arguments as untenable.[78] In his analysis Lyall gives a list of the *Ḥunafā'* at that time and Waraqah ibn Naufal tops the list. He then states that, 'Warakah became a Christian and died in that faith during the fatrah or interval which elapsed between the first revelation to Muhammad (chap. xcvi of the Kuran) and that which followed it.'[79]

Waraqah is said to have died very early in Muḥammad's prophetic career.[80] One wonders whether he needed to feature further in the narratives. The fact that he does not feature in later narratives *per se* does not make him a mythical figure or cast doubt on the authenticity of earlier events he is connected with.

Margoliouth portrays Muḥammad as a sly man who always has intelligent answers, purporting that they are from the Divine. For example, in discussing Khadījah's conversion, he argues that '. . . maternal grief over her dead sons would enter into the process of conversion'.[81] To a question allegedly posed by Khadījah as to the fate of their deceased children, Muḥammad's reply came in the form of a revelation which, to Margoliouth, means she believed then that her children would be in eternal bliss and so she submitted.[82] Margoliouth calls this, 'A brilliant answer; . . .'[83] thereby further suggesting Muḥammad's deep personal role in the framing of the Qur'ānic message. The reasoning here looks ahistorical and strange since Khadījah, with her affection and love for Muḥammad, her husband, would not have needed such emotional pressure to believe in it as a genuine religious experience.

Again, available narratives say that Muḥammad, after his first terrifying experience in the Cave of Ḥirā', was almost immediately taken by Khadījah to see the scripturally-learned

Waraqah. The latter's reassurance and Khadījah's own early commitment leave little room for speculation about an emotional conversion. Khadījah would not have come back from that meeting and quizzed Muḥammad again before believing in him as having received a Divine message. All these arguments, no matter how implausible they might be, are calculated to achieve the objective of denying the authenticity of Muḥammad's Divine Mission.

Superstition and Idolatry

Margoliouth, despite all that he had read about Islam, sees Muḥammad as superstitious and even idolatrous. He accuses him of always acting in accordance with what he felt were good omens. He asserts that 'of the superstitions of the Arabs, which differ slightly, if at all, from those of other races, he would seem to have imbibed a fair share'.[84]

He also accuses the Prophet of believing in charms and even advocating the Lord's Prayer as an antidote against diseases and misfortunes. Margoliouth claims that Muḥammad taught his people to use it the way the Christians did.[85]

Muḥammad is further charged with engaging in idolatrous rites and Margoliouth even claims that, 'The names of some of the children shows that their parents when they named them were idolaters.'[86] The names of the Prophet's children are given as al-Qāsim, Zaynab, Ruqayyah, Umm Kulthūm, Fāṭimah, Ṭayyib ('Abdullāh) Ṭāhīr and Ibrāhīm. Except Ibrāhīm, who was born to Māriyah, the Copt, all were the children of Khadījah. From the above names, Margoliouth's deduction does not seem to have any basis since there are no indications of idolatry. Of course, it used to be an earlier Arabian practice to name children after one of the deities then kept in the *Ka'bah*, but none of the names given to the Prophet's children bore any resemblance to the names of deities.

Further, Margoliouth's reasoning goes against formidable evidence of the Prophet's practice in those days concerning the giving of names, a tradition which survives till this day. The Prophet changed the names of all those who embraced Islam if their names smacked of idolatry, pride, immorality and other evils.[87] One would, therefore, have expected Margoliouth to argue otherwise than the way he does. He further claims that Muḥammad and Khadījah '. . . performed some domestic rite in honour of one of the goddesses each night before retiring'.[88]

Again, quoting from J. Wellhausen's *Reste Arabischen Heidentums* (Berlin, 1897), Margoliouth asserts that Muḥammad '. . . confessed to having at one time sacrificed a grey sheep to al-'Uzzā – and probably did so more than once, since after his mission, he used to slaughter sheep for sacrifice with his own hands'.[89] Margoliouth also refers to a story in which it is alleged that the Prophet once invited Zayd b. 'Amr, the famous monotheist of Makkah, to partake in a meal prepared with meat offered to idols. Zayd, the story goes, refused to eat and, according to Margoliouth, that also turned Muḥammad against such food.

Throughout the history of Muḥammad, the most dominant theme has been his inexorable stand against idolatry. The anger of the Quraysh directed at the Prophet, and even his clan, was precisely because of this. When the Qurayshī chiefs appealed to Abū Ṭālib, asking him to try to stop Muḥammad's activities, the central issue was the Prophet's unyielding stand against idolatry. Their plea stated, among other things, that, 'Your nephew slanders our gods, calls our ancestors to have been misguided and looks upon us as fools . . .'[90] The Prophet's famous and instructive answer leaves no room for doubt about his principles as a man of genuine intense spirituality.[91]

In prophetic history, Ibrāhīm is known to have been an ardent iconoclast and Muḥammad is normally considered to be the closest to Ibrāhīm in that respect. As Ibrāhīm destroyed the idols of his relatives, and Mūsā showed his fury against the Israelites for worshipping the golden calf, Muḥammad waged an unflinching war against idolatry. The best example is that of the re-entry into Makkah. As Ismā'īl Rājī al-Fārūqī puts it:

'The Prophet destroyed the idols of the Kaʿbah and commanded his Companions to destroy all idols wherever they might be. After they destroyed the idols' physical existence, the Muslims launched a campaign against the very mention of idols and sought to wipe them out from history, literature, and indeed, from consciousness itself.'[92]

Margoliouth's examples seem to suggest that the Prophet might have grown out of idolatrous practices in later years. However, there is no sustainable evidence that even in his youthful days he engaged in idolatry. ʿAbd al-Raḥmān ʿAzzām points out that Muḥammad, in his youth, '. . . shared in the duties and rights of his society – except that he manifested from early years a revulsion to the worship of idols. Once when he was besought to act in the name of the gods al-Lāt and al-ʿUzzā, he replied with the startling answer, "Do not ask me anything for the sake of these idols. I have never hated anything more".'[93] Margoliouth also refers to the Prophet's practice of kissing the Black Stone as further evidence of his idolatry. However at this point he goes too far in rejecting even the fundamentals of religious practice as far as Islam is concerned.

As a scholar of Islam, armed with expert knowledge in the scriptural languages of almost all major religions, one would have expected Margoliouth to be aware of symbolism as an underlying factor in the expression of religious experience. From his Jewish ancestry, and his Christian commitment, almost certainly he would have defended to the hilt the daily practices of Christians using the same symbolism argument. One, therefore, cannot help but wonder why in the case of Muḥammad, Margoliouth's scholarship always becomes slanted.

In his day, even Islam's worst enemies were ready to accept that the basic problem they had with Islam was its stand on idolatry and some of their ancient practices which the Prophet vehemently criticized and repeatedly called for their abandonment. Margoliouth seems to be reading some unknown material or at best his interpretation of what he reads does not conform with even that of the avowed enemies of Islam.

The 'Satanic Verses'

A scholar's perception of a particular subject is usually shown by his choice of themes. In Margoliouth's case, following his earlier themes, this puts him into a particular group who almost always denigrate Islam. It is not necessarily the discussion of the theme itself but how it is done.

Margoliouth advances some rather strange arguments to support his belief in the story. He says that living in Abyssinia, under the patronage of the Negus, the Muslims had become a threat to the Makkans. Therefore the Quraysh, fearing that the Abyssinians might attempt another invasion of Makkah to compensate for the one in about 570 CE which failed, decided to entreat the Muslims to return. He then reasons: 'On the other hand the Prophet was probably aware that such an invasion would be a doubtful advantage to himself, since the Abyssinians would conquer, if at all, for themselves. Let Mohammed make some reasonable concession to Al-Lat and Al-'Uzza, and Allah's prophet would be recognized. This was in effect what happened.'[94]

It is astonishing how such reasoning could be arrived at. To argue that the Prophet compromised with the idolatrous beliefs of the Makkans in order to ward off an assumed Abyssinian attack appears too silly to be reasonable. It even suggests that Muḥammad knew what the Makkans were thinking. The argument also suggests that Muḥammad was very concerned about his personal status in Makkah and indeed in Arabia since, as the statement seems to imply, he did not want the Abyssinians to conquer Makkah and himself be left with nothing.

Margoliouth then tells the story, with some relish, of the incident which is said to have brought about the Satanic Verses, making it appear that the whole affair was stage-managed. He says that, after that, 'The ban on the Hashimites was withdrawn; the Abyssinian refugees returned.'[95] To him, there was nothing wrong if the story were true. He argues rather emotionally that, 'The compromise, which to us appears wise and statesmanly, was regarded as the most discreditable episode in the prophet's career, and in the chief editions of his biography it is suppressed.' He adds that, 'In the edition which preserves it Mohammed is represented as returning to Monotheism the same day.'[96]

One interesting thing is that the eagerness with which Margoliouth discusses the issue is not new. It is his attitude measured against his standing in respected scholarly circles which is surprising. Even in those versions of the story which tell of the event inducing a return of refugees, it is stated that only some of them returned. Here, Margoliouth's version makes it appear as if the story was so widely believed that all the refugees returned.

It is not surprising that Margoliouth does not find anything wrong with the version of the story which portrays Muḥammad as lapsing into idolatry. After all, from the earlier discussions, his image of Muḥammad as a prophet is that of a crafty, brilliant man who is so intelligent that he gives pragmatic responses. He is a shrewd impostor who is quickly able to take any circulating idea and mould it into another shape and incorporate it into a book in which he plays the main role in its composition while attributing it to a Divine source. Muḥammad, being a sort of precursor to Joseph Smith of the Mormons, to Margoliouth, it was not unusual for him to have 'compromised' on such a cardinal principle of his religion.[97]

Margoliouth tacitly admits that his version of the story is not the same as that provided by the major authentic 'chief' biographical sources. With his acclaimed scholarly aptitude, he could have stated why he preferred an inferior authority in such a crucial argument. By saying that the major authentic and reliable sources 'suppress' the story, he pronounces a verdict impugning the reliability of these scholars. Again, he does not give his reasons for taking such a position.

The story has survived the ages and we have dealt with it in our earlier discussions.[98] Perhaps the only addendum we can make here is that if 'Umar's conversion induced so much fear amongst Muḥammad's Makkan opponents, as Margoliouth says, then it does not stand to reason that the Prophet tried such a damaging concession. Margoliouth attaches so much importance to the story, he devotes five pages to it (pp.170–4), one of the main themes receiving the greatest attention.

Borrowing

The next theme concerns the originality of the Prophet's message. The arguments here seem to have flowed from earlier ones on the revelation and prophethood. The line of reasoning seems to be basically that, if Muḥammad was an impostor and the Qur'ān was his own composition, then whatever looks acceptable in it must have come from somewhere else. In the period, with many Jews around and at least some Christians, he must have 'stolen' the ideas from their Scriptures. Now, Muslims say that Muḥammad was not learned enough to have been able to read either Greek or Hebrew. Granted that this is true, he must have either been taught by someone or heard stories from the Jews and Christians.

One could argue that Margoliouth looks at the theme with this in mind. Hence, he starts by looking for that obscure teacher and finds him in the person of Waraqah. He then, without evidence, perpetuates the myth. He writes: '. . . Warakah, son of Naufal, cousin of Khadijah, is likely to have had much to do with the beginnings of Islam. He is credited with having translated the Gospel, or part of one, into Arabic; it was probably the Gospel of the Nativity, and was afterwards useful to the prophet.'[99] He carries this speculative trend further – that Muḥammad learnt from Jewish travellers and others he met, and this accounts for the Jewish tones heard in parts of the Qur'ān. From this assumption, he reasons that since parts of the Qur'ān '. . . afterwards contained a number of phrases which even his intimate associates at Meccah did not understand . . .',[100] the supposition cannot be doubted.

He then catalogues a series of such expressions which, in his opinion, were 'borrowed' from Arabian Jews and Christians.[101] He then adds: '. . . a biblical scholar would have easily been able to tell the source: Mohammed probably heard them in the conversation of his pious friends and automatically adopted them'.[102]

He admits that Muḥammad had no formal education nor much of the rote learning which was a characteristic of Arab society. However, he sees him as a man of such astuteness that nothing that he heard or saw escaped him.[103] He portrays him as a highly intelligent person with a brilliant receptive memory who, even when passing two Jews, Jabra and Yasar reading their scriptures, is able to pick up a few stories and incorporate them into 'his Qur'ān'. He then asserts that Biblical similarities in the Qur'ān were '. . . likely to have been all picked up by listening when services or Bible readings were going on'.[104]

Returning to the theory of Muḥammad being an epileptic, Margoliouth suggests that Muḥammad faked the events. He argues that, following the *modus operandi* of the old Kāhin or the modern medium, Muḥammad induced his strange behaviour and claimed he was receiving messages from God even though he was merely recounting what he had heard from others on his travels. Themes like 'the worship of one God', 'the day of judgement', and 'the torment of hell fire', Margoliouth argues, were commonly used by Christian preachers. He is also of the opinion that the style of the Qur'ān is typically Arabian which, he says, Muḥammad had no choice but to copy.

Margoliouth then sinks to a new low in his interpretation of the various postures in *ṣalāh*. He argues that the *qiyām* is Jewish, *sujūd* Christian and the *julūs* a combination of both. He sees *Sūrah al-Fātiḥah* as modelled on the *Paternoster* and says that the teaching of ritual purification before prayer existed in South Arabian communities long before Muḥammad. Nevertheless, he is of the opinion that Muslim *ṣalāh* possesses the character of a military drill.[105]

In his article on the concepts 'Muslim' and 'Ḥanīf', Margoliouth lays a strong foundation for this borrowing theory. His whole paper comes down to the fact that Musaylimah was the actual originator of the concepts 'Muslim' and 'Ḥanīf' and the Prophet took these from him. He reasons that from the very beginning much of Muḥammad's theological thinking owed its origin to Musaylimah and even the *sūrahs* of the Qur'ān were modelled on Musaylimah's. He states that the Quraysh used to ridicule the Prophet as being under the tutelage of Musaylimah. Margoliouth accepts this to be '. . . a fairly correct account of the facts, if we suppose Musaylimah's surahs to have been the earliest Arabic literature connected with monotheism, on which Mohammed modelled his early surahs; . . .'[106]

Referring to Hirschfeld and others who held similar views about the 'borrowing' theory, he concludes that at a later stage in the development of his religion, Muḥammad:

> . . . found it expedient to desert Musaylimah for the Old and New Testaments and the sayings of the Jewish fathers. I fear that (he continues) in any question of literary ownership there must be a presumption against Mohammed, for in cases where we know his sources he indignantly denies the use of them; hence, where we do not know them quite certainly, there is a suspicion that he is the imitator rather than the imitated.[107]

Charles Lyall rebuts Margoliouth's argument as historically and even etymologically untenable. He argues that Margoliouth's supposition would mean that:

> Musailimah's teaching should, for a considerable time before the appearance of Muhammad, have attained such a celebrity and extension in the Arabian Peninsula that, although the tribe to which he belonged had its settlements in al-Yamamah, . . . the ideas embodied in it had made their way across to the Western Hijaz and Tihamah, and these left in current use these words of religious import, without any trace surviving in the memory of men of their real origin.[108]

He then questions the rationale for Musaylimah waiting some nine or ten years after the *Hijrah* (9 or 10 AH) before posing a challenge to Muḥammad if the 'original ideas' were his and 'stolen'. Historically, Lyall points out, only two poets of the Banū Hudhayl were known to have used the concept Ḥanīf in their poetical literature during Muḥammad's time. He names these as Sakhr al-Ghayy and Abū Dhu'ayb. Sakhr, he says, was most probably a pagan, while Abū Dhu'ayb was a Muslim born in 622 CE.[109]

He cites Wellhausen, pointing out that the deputation of Ḥunafā' which paid a courtesy call on Muḥammad were Christians and had the institution of priesthood.[110] Lyall then deduces that, 'With Christianity in possession, before the appearance of Musailimah as a prophet, it is difficult to believe that he was the discoverer of the "religion of Abraham" and the propagator of the religious movement represented by the Hanifs.'[111] He subjects to critical linguistic analysis the words 'Ḥanīf' and 'Muslim' and rejects Margoliouth's reasoning as '. . . a very singular example of extravagant conjecture'.[112]

Margoliouth's charge of 'borrowing' is restated in his article on Muḥammad in the *Encyclopaedia of Religion and Ethics*. Here, he says, the Qur'ānic connection of the *Ka'bah* with Ibrāhīm is false and there was a lot of accommodation as far as Jewish and pagan values were concerned and sometimes Muḥammad disguised his borrowing with some '. . . serious modifications'.[113]

Despite all this, Margoliouth rejects any idea of Islam being close to Christianity. When Foster, in an article, suggests that Islam might be called a 'Christian heresy', Margoliouth spurns the idea, arguing that at best it could be closer to Judaism at least in its earlier stages.[114] However, Foster has to submit to Margoliouth's acclaimed, immense knowledge.[115]

On the issue of Muḥammad eavesdropping and incorporating what he heard in the Qur'ān, Margoliouth admits that it is controversial.[116] Looking at the Bible and the Qur'ān, he seems to have a problem sustaining his idea that Muḥammad was taught by someone. He points out some dissimilarities between the two scriptures and agrees that, 'This phenomenon almost disposes of the theory of a mentor, for no mentor could be so ignorant of the Bible.'[117] Nevertheless he sticks to it, implying that he believes in it. Touching on the narrative of Moses in the Qur'ān, he is of the opinion that, 'Further conversation led him to find out rather more of the history of Moses, which he worked up into his peculiar style, and repeatedly told; . . .'[118]

To Margoliouth, therefore, any teaching of Islam which contained views already in existence portrays how crafty Muḥammad was in plagiarizing Jewish, Christian and even pagan ideas when they suited his cause. His basic argument is that such stories were so common that '. . . it required no Christian interposition to reproduce'.[119] Though Margoliouth is apparently silent on the implications of these 'thefts' and 'borrowings' on the general reputation of the Prophet, the most logically discernible inference is the negative one.

It is quite logical for the themes of Muḥammad's preaching to have followed the common subjects of earlier preachers. This, in itself, does not necessarily mean that he copied from or reproduced what he heard from the Jews and Christians. It defies any reasonable explanation why, if Muḥammad just reproduced what he heard, the Qur'ān reserves its strongest denunciation for the most important doctrine of Christianity – the Trinity. This is the strongest indication of Muḥammad's independent mindedness.

The argument that only heretical Christians lived in that area at that time is highly contentious and might even be said to be indicative of arrogant spirituality on the part of its perpetrators. Foster suggests that the type of Christian ideas Muḥammad received were from the Gnostics, thereby 'pardoning' him for his obvious 'ignorance' of central doctrines.[120] In fact, Margoliouth shares a similar view, that the Christians in those days were not that committed and in many cases not very different from the heathen.[121]

Further, Robertson's analysis of 'Christianity from the Second Century to the Rise of Mohammedanism' lists a host of alleged

Arabian Christian practices during Muḥammad's time which were a parody of genuine Christian life.[122]

Whatever, some of the differences between the basics of Christianity and what one reads in the Qur'ān are too diverse to attribute them to even the worst Christian. In a situation where the people had priests and other institutions of the Church, it is going too far to imply that all these differences arose from the garbled Christianity of that time.

The most disturbing point in this whole deduction of 'borrowing' is not so much that it charges Muḥammad with lack of originality in his prophetic career, but the implicit suggestion that whoever introduces a 'new' faith must present teachings completely dissimilar to existing ones. In the Muslim view, the whole purpose of God sending prophets to mankind has always been to continue reminding people to observe earlier Divine teachings.[123] Therefore, if God is One, then His message must invariably be one even though the mode or tone of it might differ from one epoch to another. There is therefore not much to choose between prophets *qua* prophets. For this very reason, the Qur'ān makes it absolutely clear that believing in all God's prophets is the essence of Islam. One's faith is questionable if one picks and chooses among the prophets.[124]

It therefore stands to reason that God speaks to prophet 'x' and reveals the same issue to prophet 'y', albeit with some variations. If such variations are so serious that they amount to a completely different message, it could be argued that a thorough check has to be made of the form in which the old version has existed over the years.[125]

Morality

Muḥammad's personal probity is called into serious doubt by Margoliouth. After discussing the moral precepts introduced by Muḥammad, he sees '. . . no evidence that the Moslems were either in personal or altruistic morality better than the pagans'.[126] However, he then contradicts himself by admitting that, 'There can be no doubt, however, that the liability to persecution under which the Moslems suffered led to a more stringent morality on their part than they had previously practised; . . .'[127]

Margoliouth calls Muḥammad the 'head of a robber community whose teachings included lying and treachery'.[128] He also accuses him of being a 'cattle thief' whose activities were acceptable to the tribesmen who themselves followed basic instincts. His contempt for Muḥammad becomes more apparent as he describes events which took place in Makkah when the Prophet and his followers re-entered the city in about 630 CE (8 AH). He refers to some pictures which were effaced and then says: '. . . whom or what they represented we know only on Mohammed's authority, which we are not inclined to trust; . . .'[129]

Though Margoliouth agrees that the Prophet spared all his enemies in Makkah, something was needed to explain the 'strange' behaviour of a man who he has described as 'robber-chief', 'cattle-thief' and untrustworthy. He finds the rationale that it was because the Prophet was not content with Makkah under his control. It was 'self-gratification' more than mere clemency which actually led to that behaviour, he suggests.[130]

He further advances the rather strange opinion that Muḥammad instituted *zakāh* just to make up the shortfall in the state treasury since the Jews he used to 'rob' were no longer available, 'having all been either massacred or despoiled'.[131]

Zakāh or even voluntary *ṣadaqah* has been part of the Islamic faith from its very inception. In fact, *zakāh* is next only to *ṣalāh* as a principle of *īmān*. In many places in the Qur'ān the two are mentioned together, the former following the latter. The institution of *zakāh* was established in the Makkan period as the Qur'ānic references indicate.[132] It is therefore strange that Margoliouth talks of Madīnan issues in the Makkan period. At least, historically, this is erroneous.

Margoliouth further portrays Muḥammad as being more interested in material wealth and booty than anything else. He claims that the Prophet intended to keep all of the booty, purporting to do so on behalf of God, but due to some inducement, he agreed to keep only a fifth.[133] However, he leaves the reader in the dark as to the source of his information and on whose inducement Muḥammad capitulated. Granting that there is any truth in this version of things, if Muḥammad was that greedy and wanted to keep all of the booty, it would have taken more than human conviction for him to give up as much as eighty per cent. Unless, of course, Margoliouth accepts that Muḥammad, at least in this particular case, received genuine Divine intervention, it would be difficult to prove what prevailed upon Muḥammad. But how can Margoliouth accept that Muḥammad received the Divine word after all that he has said about his prophetic career? He therefore concludes that the best possible explanation is that the fifth compares well with that enjoyed by pre-Islamic sovereigns – even though at a fourth theirs was a bit higher.[134]

Margoliouth then returns to the story of Muḥammad's re-entry into Makkah and seems to distrust any account that reflects favourably upon Muḥammad[135] but at the same time admits that, 'If Mohammed took anything from Meccah, he gave it more.'[136] From the pages following this statement, one reads his meaning of what Muḥammad gave to Makkah, the whole suggesting Muḥammad's materialistic motives. It reinforces Margoliouth's earlier reasoning of a lack of genuine spirituality in Muḥammad's teaching and of his whole life being fraught with immoral undertones.[137]

In his article on Muḥammad in the *Encyclopaedia of Religion and Ethics*, supposedly relying on the work of Ibn Isḥāq, Margoliouth concludes that, 'The stories of his successes . . . indicate a complete absence of moral scruple; but they also show a combination of patience, courage, and caution, ability to seize opportunities, and distrust of loyalty when not backed by interest, . . .'[138]

Margoliouth is more caustic in his sermon on 'The Failure of Islam'. He says:

> That career, to those who care to read the original authorities, represents one which has few equals in its atrocity: to suppose that God could have directly employed such a servant as that is to blaspheme . . . The mischief that is done by such a man as the founder of Islam being made a pattern of conduct is incalculable.[139]

The tone of this statement is not very different from the 'war propaganda' period of medieval times. Its survival in Margoliouth is a serious indictment on his scholarship.

Sexuality / Sensuality

This has been a favourite theme for Western scholars in biographies of the Prophet. Norman Daniel in *Islam and the West – The Making of an Image* gives a detailed account of some of the medieval charges of Muḥammad's sexuality and how these have come to survive the ages even into the period of so-called enlightened scholarship or objective research.[140] Margoliouth follows some of these images.

In order to establish a good foundation for his reasoning, Margoliouth, relying on the Talmud, says that in the field of sexual passion, nine parts were given to the Arabs and one part to the rest of mankind.[141]

He starts on a comparatively sympathetic note, disputing the usual charge by European scholars as to the motives for the Prophet's multiple marriages. He rejects the charge of blind passion, arguing that they were '. . . mainly dictated by motives of a less coarse kind'.[142] He mentions three basic reasons: political alliance, cementing of relationships and the strong desire for a son.[143] He acknowledges the Prophet's remarkable temperance during his marriage to Khadījah, but only because he was awaiting '. . . the favourable moment before putting any plan into execution'.[144]

Margoliouth's interpretation seems to suggest that Muḥammad's restraint was merely a ploy in order to unleash his real self at the opportune time. He presents the traditional narrative of the Qurayshī attractions offered to Muḥammad through his uncle Abū Ṭālib to dissuade him from his mission, which the Prophet declined, as legends not worthy of credence.[145] He does not explain fully why he disbelieves the account, offering only a rather feeble statement that, 'After the part of divine ambassador had been acted for ten years with very considerable success it could not well be given up.'[146] However, an 'impostor' like Muḥammad with no well-grounded principles, as Margoliouth's earlier discussions seem to suggest, could easily have given up his vocation when such an incredible enticement was offered.

Margoliouth takes up the marriage of ʿĀ'ishah and describes her as someone whose malevolent nature caused many problems for the Prophet in his household. He explains that this was the reason the Prophet resorted to drawing lots in order to find out who would be travelling with him on a particular journey.[147]

These interpretations form a prelude to the 'Necklace Affair', thus indirectly preparing the reader for Margoliouth's version of the story. After briefly relating the story, he writes: 'Why evil should have been thought of what seems to us a perfectly natural occurrence we know not, but we must remember that the Moslem mind had by this time been somewhat tainted by licentiousness, whence any meeting between persons of different sex gave rise to sinister rumours.'[148]

The discussion takes up four pages, which is indicative of how important it is to Margoliouth's cause. He describes ʿĀ'ishah as a '. . . blooming girl who claimed premiership in the harem, the pert minx, as others called her, who made so many victims of her laziness and her caprices, who even made the prophet feel that he was her father's debtor'.[149] He does not offer any justification for this attack and the portrayal of Muḥammad as clinging to a woman of such nature. From what we know of ʿĀ'ishah's character from Muslim sources, which Margoliouth of course would spurn, this opinion is untenable.

Margoliouth goes on to make the claim that when people

detected Muḥammad's weakness, which he believes was sex, women '. . . from various parts of Arabia or the husbands of fair and fruitful women offered to hand them over to the prophet . . .'[150] He continues: '. . . and indeed at Medinah, whenever a woman became a widow, her relations would not find her a husband before asking whether the prophet wanted her'.[151]

Again, on the presentation of Māriyah the Copt to Muḥammad, Margoliouth taunts: '. . . concubines would have been a suitable present for Achilles, but how come the Alexandrian to know that they were equally suitable for the founder of a new religion?'[152] Margoliouth attributes no understanding to the Prophet's sexual relationship except that he was licentious and the so-called teaching of unlimited concubinage was a reflection of Muḥammad's own preference.[153]

We read of the narrative concerning the marriage feast of Maymūnah, the Prophet's last wife, when the Makkans refused the Prophet permission to celebrate the marriage because he had been allowed to remain in the city for only three more days. Margoliouth is silent on the implications of this on the Prophet's character. He does not even mention Maymūnah's name in the historical setting in which she appears – the first *'Umrah*.[154]

Violence

Accusations of violence have been at the root of almost all attacks on Islam as a genuine faith and Muḥammad as a recipient of Divine revelation. Norman Daniel devotes a whole chapter to it, cataloguing a series of events which show, as his title indicates, 'The Place of Violence and Power in the Attack on Islam'.[155] This subculture had a considerable influence on William Muir and even Margoliouth could not escape it. In an opening discussion on the theme, he says that Muḥammad was so intemperate that '. . . his temper in debate was not easily controlled, and he was apt to give violent and insulting answers to questioners'.[156]

Margoliouth's reasoning is strange considering the amount of material available on Muḥammad's self-comportment.

Violence was certainly not a general characteristic of Muḥammad. Nobody can dispute, for example, that Jesus was violent in the way he chased out the gamblers and traders from the Temple in Jerusalem.[157] As far as language is concerned, Muḥammad was never known to have used foul expressions.

A statement attributed to ʿAlī, one of those closest to the Prophet, says: 'He was predisposed to refrain from unseemly language, curses and revilings and deeds shameful; in no wise he said or did anything improper; he never raised his voice in a market place, . . .'[158] Unfortunately, Margoliouth describes such statements as mere propaganda. However, though the original sources he claims to depend upon contain evidence of this, his interpretation is different. If the Prophet's character had been as depicted by Margoliouth, then his reputation as testified to by those closest to him would have been irreparably damaged.

Margoliouth presents a questionable interpretation of a passage in *Sūrah al-Anʿām*. The text reads: 'When you see men engaged in vain discourse about Our Signs, turn away from them unless they turn to a different theme. If Satan ever makes you forget, then after recollection, do not sit in the company of those who do wrong.'[159] Margoliouth interprets this to mean that the Prophet was asked to avoid discussing issues with the unbelievers. However, simple reflection suggests that the Qur'ān is referring to insulting, useless, time-wasting ridiculing of the truth; the type of irresponsible debate the enemies of Islam might try to initiate merely to deride Islam.

Margoliouth further argues that the sovereign power enjoyed by Muḥammad created what he sees as tyranny. He writes: 'Let one man be given absolute and uncontrolled authority in a community, a number of parasites are sure to arise, ready to plunge into any sort of mire in the hope of gaining a smile from their master.'[160]

When Asmā' bint Marwān, a leading member of the taunting group was executed for plotting to murder the Prophet, Margoliouth acknowledges that, 'Since . . . she had deliberately incited the people of Medinah to a murderous attack on the prophet, her execution would not have been an inexcusably ruthless measure, judged by any standards; and it must not be forgotten that satire was a far more effective weapon in Arabia than elsewhere; . . .'[161] Immediately after this, however, he writes: 'The employment of the assassin where the executioner might reasonably have been employed is what excites horror.'[162] He then mentions in the footnote that both Sprenger and Muir condemn such incidents as inhuman.

Interest in the incident is further sustained by Margoliouth arguing that the fact that only the satirist suffered punishment, showed a remarkable improvement on the existing practice in which whole families or tribes of culprits had to brace themselves for reprisals. However, he shows his disdain for stories that are in favour of Muḥammad by doubting whether '. . . verses ascribed to Asma be genuine . . .'[163]

Attention now shifts to an anecdote concerning ʿAlī and Ḥamzah. Ḥamzah, while drunk, was said to have killed two camels belonging to ʿAlī. These camels were supposed to be required for a trading arrangement that ʿAlī had struck with the Banū Qaynuqāʿ. The incident, according to Margoliouth, was a big embarrassment to the Prophet. Admitting problems in getting authorities for some details of his story, he then adds that, 'A few more steps we must ourselves supply.'[164] The details he supplies conclude that the Muslims were ordered to attack the Jews to compensate for ʿAlī's loss as a result of Ḥamzah's insobriety. Thus, he continues, prohibition of wine, which was to destroy one of the main areas of trading by the Jews, offered itself as a plausible alternative and hence a revelation was brought.[165] Without offering any other explanation other than making the Prophet and his close relatives appear in a bad light – Ḥamzah drunk, ʿAlī irritated and the Prophet annoyed – Margoliouth concludes with the Muslims attacking the Jews.

One cannot think of any other reason why Margoliouth thinks that this kind of reasoning should be accepted as sound. With the Banū Qaynuqāʿ, ʿAlī's trading partners having kept their part of the agreement by loading the camels, how could Muḥammad, hitherto described as a shrewd man who always acted for his own political advantage, act like that?

Margoliouth shows much interest in the story of Kaʿb ibn al-Ashraf of the Banū Naḍīr who ostensibly tried to arrange for an attack on Makkah. Muḥammad is said to have expressed the wish that Kaʿb should be slain and this was carried out in the dead of night when he was allegedly invited out by five young men led by Muḥammad ibn Maslamah.[166] Margoliouth relates another version of the story, which he says, '. . . increases the horror by making two of the assassins Kaʿb's foster-brothers, . . .'[167] and questions how Madīnans became foster-brothers to a Jew. He does not realize that this could come about through *ta'ākhī*.[168]

Furthermore, Mahīsah, a Khazrajite, was supposed to have killed a Jew called Ibn Subainah following a declaration by Muḥammad that Jews were outlawed, '. . . giving any Moslem who found one the right to kill him'.[169] A brother of Mahīsah is said to have been so impressed by the loftiness of Islam because of that killing that he accepted Islam. Perhaps, sensing the improbability of the way much of the arguments are going, Margoliouth seeks to ameliorate the situation. He concludes with a statement that, 'Without fresh orders from the prophet, the Jews could not have continued to remain in Medinah.'[170]

The chapter discussing the prelude to the capitulation of Makkah begins with an accusation that the Prophet was out for revenge and the conquest of more territories now that his mortal enemies in Madīnah were no longer a problem. He mentions the expedition to the Banū Lihyān and claims that, in a '. . . demonstration of force . . .', the Prophet marched towards Makkah with 200 people to intimidate the people.[171] The Khaybar event, to Margoliouth, was a signal to the whole world that it was in danger of being engulfed by Islam. He launches perhaps his bitterest attack yet on Muḥammad, accusing him of living '. . . by robbery and brigandage . . .'[172] He argues that there was no reasonable justification for the expedition to Khaybar except '. . . because there was booty to be acquired there, and the plea for attacking it was that its inhabitants were not Moslems'.[173] He claims that in fact the sole objective of the Khaybar expedition led by ʿAlī was to force the people there to accept Islam.

Margoliouth continues that the Prophet now abandoned his toleration of the Jews and other people and became infused with a passion for bloodthirsty assaults on communities that had not accepted Islam. He compares what he sees as the Prophet's zeal for dominating the world with that of Alexander and Napoleon.[174]

In his sermon at St. Aldate's Church, Margoliouth again assails Muḥammad with preaching a violent faith. He says: 'Those passions which religion is so much concerned with restraining are constantly let loose. There is nothing incongruous about the association of religious leadership with rapine and violence to those whose ideas have been formed on the life of the prophet of Islam.'[175]

Margoliouth raises the much debunked theory that the so-called violence of Islam has been the secret of its success. He writes: 'The fact of primary importance in the rise of Islam is that the movement became considerable only when its originator was able to draw the sword and handle it successfully.'[176] He further claims that Muḥammad '. . . organizes assassinations and wholesale massacres. His career as tyrant of Medina is that of a robber chief, whose political economy consists in securing and dividing plunder, the distribution of the latter being at times carried out on principles which fail to satisfy his followers' ideas of justice'.[177]

Throughout the discussions, Margoliouth gives no consideration to the self-defensive acts by Muḥammad and his followers to protect their persons and the nascent Islam. And this despite what the Qur'ān teaches about freedom of religion, and documented evidence of the Prophet's advice to preachers of Islam to present the message and allow people to decide for themselves.[178] At the time of Margoliouth's writing, Cherāgh ʿAlī's work on the *Jihād* could well have been on the market and with his position in the field of Islamic Studies, Margoliouth should have been aware of it. In this work, Cherāgh ʿAlī argues *in extenso* that the wars fought by Muḥammad were generally defensive and he did not violate Qur'ānic injunctions on aggression and compulsion in conversion.[179]

Bribery

This theme continues the general discussion about the image of Muḥammad and how repugnant his teachings were. The general deduction is that because of the nature of the man and his religion, bribery was resorted to failing which, of course, force was used in the religion's propagation.

In our earlier analysis we mentioned how Margoliouth interprets Khadījah's commitment to her husband's faith. He accuses Muḥammad of resorting to an emotional psychological influence on a woman who was distressed at having lost her children.[180] He then takes the conversion of ʿUthmān ibn ʿAffān and advances an argument that he also accepted Islam because Muḥammad 'bribed' him with his daughter Ruqayyah. Abū Bakr was supposed to have brokered the deal. Margoliouth presents the story in such a way that it appears as if Muḥammad agreed to the deal after just a few seconds' briefing by Abū Bakr when the latter had already obtained a commitment from ʿUthmān. He writes that while Abū Bakr and ʿUthmān were discussing the issue, 'Mohammed presently passed by. Abu Bakr whispered something into his ear and the affair was arranged. Othman became a believer and Rukayyah became his wife.'[181]

Margoliouth, however, then seems to contradict his own theory by writing immediately after this that it was the slaves, the underprivileged and the poor and the needy in society who were readily converted. But ʿUthmān ibn ʿAffān, as Margoliouth himself admits, was a cloth merchant and also a moneylender. He was not the sort of person who would have succumbed to the 'religion of the poor, the needy, the underprivileged and the slaves' if material and other worldly gains were the main attractions. Definitely, something more than marriage to Ruqayyah would have been the main inducement for ʿUthmān's conversion for Muḥammad made appeals centred on other-worldly gains rather than those of the here and now.

Margoliouth claims that, 'When men were asked what first led them to Mohammed, they were apt to give fantastic answers; perhaps they had forgotten the real motive or preferred to conceal it.'[182] Margoliouth does not attribute any other reason for people's acceptance of Islam than material gains. It is very difficult, if not impossible, for anyone other than the convert to rationalize as to why he converted. Religious experience is a personal matter which is often difficult for even the one involved to explain. Margoliouth should have been aware of this. It would appear obvious that the concern expressed over stories like this is basically because they carry an underlying tone of Muḥammad being materialist, sensual, and fraudulent, offering mundane baits to attract people to Islam.

Margoliouth is more forthright in writing: '. . . the religion which is embraced for sordid motives is often retained for honourable reasons; and early observers found that among the most sincere believers in Islam were persons who had been lured into it by bribes'.[183]

On the fall of Makkah, Margoliouth faces an enigma. For the Muḥammad he portrays as savage and vengeful with all those he dislikes, is offering a complete amnesty. However, he wriggles out of the dilemma by pointing out that, 'Our wonder is not that Mohammed easily took Meccah . . . , but that he had to conciliate so many of his old opponents with bribes.'[184]

Margoliouth concludes his deliberation on this theme with a reflection on the distribution of the spoils of war after the encounter at Ḥunayn. He charges that in the exercise, those opponents of Muḥammad who had not become Muslims were offered bribes of camels to embrace Islam. He views the alleged explanation given by the Prophet, that the new converts needed to be confirmed in their new-found belief, as nothing but an admission of bribery.[185] Nevertheless, he admits that, 'The motives which dictated this strange policy are hard to fathom: ill-gotten gains are consumed too quickly for us to suppose he had hoped to win the permanent gratitude of his former enemies by such bribes . . .'[186]

This statement puts the charge of bribery in doubt. Force and bribery turn people's heads not their hearts. The conviction to become Muslims must have been deeply reflected upon and, with all the difficulties the Muslims were experiencing in those early days, they must have made conscious efforts to embrace Islam knowing very well the kind of risks to which they were exposing themselves and their families.

Margoliouth's interpretation of these events though ingenious is not a truthful depiction. We do not know for how long Muḥammad would have continued to 'bribe' his followers in order for them to remain Muslims. Margoliouth does not deem it necessary to consider this.

The Madīnan Charter

Touching on the Madīnan Charter, Margoliouth, following Wellhausen, does not dispute its authenticity but doubts its importance as quoted in the later disputes. He does not believe that a mere 'treaty' such as that of Madīnah, carried the force of law to be referred to when judging the behaviour of people. He finds it difficult to understand why the Prophet produced such a document and not a Divine revelation.

The reasoning here goes back to the recurring argument that the revelations were the Prophet's own to which he had given the cloak of 'the Word of God'. Margoliouth, however, admits that '. . . the prophet displayed so much caution that he was perhaps unwilling to put into the mouth of God concessions the withdrawal of which he may have contemplated from the first'.[187]

Admitting that the Charter was meant to effect better relations among the various groups in the city, he briefly mentions some of the injunctions, especially the one regarding joint security efforts.

Hence, an important document, often regarded as the very

first written constitution and indicative of Muḥammad's diplomatic prowess, is summarily dismissed.[188] Margoliouth seems to look for 'juicy' themes which afford him the best opportunity for criticism.

The Jewish Question

A reader of Margoliouth on the above theme has to take an important factor into consideration – his Jewishness. Even though both his father and uncle converted to Christianity, and he himself grew up a Christian, his natural Jewish attachment and sympathies remained. Despite this, his stature in academia was such that one would have expected him to have outgrown some of the petty considerations that are found in his works. However, some of them are too unguarded to escape notice.

He begins his discussion on the Jews by referring to the incident of the bursting of the Ma'rib dam, and the consequent dispersal of tribes around Yathrib. The Jewish tribes, who were wealthy, had problems with some of the local tribes. He mentions a Khazrajite, Mālik ibn ʿAjlān who killed many Jews.

On why the Madīnan tribes approached Muḥammad and accepted him as their leader, Margoliouth argues that they did so in order to pre-empt the Jews who, they supposed, might also want him as their leader. He says the Khazrajites had been defeated in a battle by the combined efforts of the Jews and the Aws. The Khazrajites therefore speculated that since the Jews talked of a Messiah who would come and fight for them, and since their own assessment of what they heard of Muḥammad suggested he was like the expected one, they thought it wise to accept him before the Jews did.

He says that the Jews also thought it was their God who helped them to win the war of Buʿāth against the Banū Khazraj. Hence, the attraction of securing the help of the 'Jewish God' as well, because Muḥammad had proclaimed himself to have been sent by the same God.

Margoliouth further explains the background history, that

the Jews were initially happy with Islam because some of the basic teachings were akin to what they themselves believed in. Examples are given as: the Unity of God, hatred of idols, the doctrine of resurrection of the dead and the fact that the Muslims prayed towards Jerusalem. Margoliouth's tone then changes and he dwells on the subject of Muḥammad's alleged attempt to appease the Jews so that they would recognize him as the expected prophet. He then writes: 'If the Old and New Testaments are trustworthy, even prophets who could produce the most authentic credentials had little chance with the Jews; hence Mohammed, who had none that the Jews would recognize, had no chance with them.'[189]

Margoliouth is perhaps more forthright here, denying the essence of Muḥammad's authenticity because he did not possess the expected 'credentials'. The authenticity or not of Muḥammad's prophethood did not rest with the Jews, but the issue is clear: to Margoliouth, his Jewish bias tells him that anyone not sanctioned by the Jews could not be genuine. If we take this for granted, we might have a problem with Jesus Christ as well.

The argument then moves on, to the relationship with the Jews. Here, Margoliouth mentions some of the attempts supposed to have been made by the Jews to undermine the Prophet's mission. This, according to him, was primarily because they were envious that, 'Mohammed's power had been won by his use of their Bible; of which he had not a beginner's knowledge as compared with them.'[190] He claims that it was the Jews who passed on information about prophets, angels, revelation and other things with Muḥammad himself depending upon Jewish sources.

He then criticizes them for pouring scorn on some of Muḥammad's teachings, even though their own scripture, the Old Testament, did not vary much from these. He recalls how the Jews were furious when the Prophet ordered the stoning of an adulterer, even though their own scripture teaches the same punishment.

Again, he criticizes the Jews for ignoring Muḥammad when he referred to the Qur'ānic expression, 'Who will lend God a good loan,' while from the Old Testament, he cites: 'Men are advised to "lend unto the Lord".'[191] Furthermore, he writes: 'The Jews . . . professed disgust at a prophet whose concern was his harem – though their studies in the Old Testament should have shown them that this was not incongruous.'[192]

It is obvious that Margoliouth's brief shift of emphasis is to prepare for more scathing criticism of Muḥammad especially in his relationship with the Jews. He suggests a reason for Muḥammad's 'hostility' towards the Jews. He writes: '. . . doubtless the prophet's ultimate determination to destroy the Jews was due to his secret knowledge of matters on which he claimed authority'.[193] Unfortunately, we are not informed of the secrets the Prophet had access to and because of which he wanted the Jews exterminated. There is no reason to believe that the Prophet was hostile towards the Jews because of his personal ambitions. Possibly, the only reason to think like this would be because of the Qur'ānic critique of what it sees as attempts to distort the earlier revealed scriptures.

Margoliouth next turns to the arrival of the *Muhājirūn* at Yathrib and focuses on the pressure that the sudden increase in the population put on the facilities in the city. He then rationalizes the 'envy' of the Muslims, directed against the Jews who were relatively wealthy. Then, looking for the easiest way out, Muḥammad is again characterized as the leader of brigands seeking to level up the standard of living.[194]

With regard to some of the changes introduced by the Prophet, especially the change of *qiblah* from Jerusalem to the *Kaʿbah*, Margoliouth sees this as the clearest evidence yet that Muḥammad was bent on destroying the Jews. He even claims that the Jews offered to acknowledge the Prophet's mission if he would revert to Jerusalem as his *qiblah*.[195] He then criticizes the Jews for missing the opportunity to sever relations with Muḥammad. Instead, because of some phobia, they made the offer about the *qiblah* which Muḥammad resolutely refused. He writes: 'Had the Jews not been afraid of him, they would never have made it; had they any plan, any resolution, any courage, they would have utilized this period of failure and ignominy to crush him.'[196] The tone of the statement shows where Margoliouth's sympathies lie.

He spends a considerable time cataloguing Muḥammad's policies, which he thinks denote an anti-Jewish bias, and makes a deduction that these were the reason for the clashes with the Jews.[197]

The ninth chapter of Margoliouth's book carries the title 'The Destruction of the Jews' and this is indicative of its contents. He analyzes, one by one, the cases of the three Jewish tribes. He begins with the story of Muslim preachers sent to the tribes of ʿAdal and Karah, who were murdered by tribesmen even though the Muslims were sent to the tribes at their own request. He remarks that: 'With the followers of a sect who, as has been seen, practised treachery whenever it was deemed advisable, we cannot sympathise when they suffer from a similar crime . . .'[198] Here, Margoliouth judges as appropriate the suffering endured by Muḥammad and his people. If it had been the other way round, would he have immediately described it as barbarity and treachery? We detect a lack of consistency in the application of his principle. Margoliouth then catalogues a series of assassinations which, he claims, were carried out on the orders of Muḥammad.

Events leading to the expulsion of the Banū Naḍīr are discussed next and Margoliouth disputes the recorded version of the story, that the Banū Naḍīr plotted to murder Muḥammad. He asserts that it was a figment of the Prophet's imagination since he always believed that the Jews wanted to kill him.[199] When the expulsion order was passed, ʿAbdullāh ibn Ubayy advised them to resist but their fellow Jewish tribesmen – the Banū Qurayẓah – refused to help them. Margoliouth refers to this refusal and says: 'This act of cowardice prepares us to feel less sympathy with them for the fate that afterwards befell them.'[200] If 'killing' or 'barbarous' acts were in principle wrong, then Margoliouth should have sympathized with or at least understood the Banū Qurayẓah's refusal. However, one suspects that due to his own bias against Muḥammad and his people, for the Banū Qurayẓah to refuse their brethren help in fighting the Muslims became an offence and accounts for his lack of sympathy.

Margoliouth's line of thinking is also clear in the way he sometimes punctuates his statements with doubtful remarks, especially when the Jewish question is under discussion. The following are some examples: 'We know not with what truth . . .' The story is full of 'Mythical embellishment . . . we know not, having no Jewish account of the matter . . . if the number be correctly given . . . The accounts given (by his antecedents) are so fabulous that we cannot quote them here.'[201] Margoliouth uses these expressions only when the situation favours the Muslims. When the circumstances favour the Jews, he does not demand to see a Muslim account and does not even for argument's sake, raise the possibility of the Muslims fabricating stories to gain sympathy. He, on the authority of al-Wāqidī, agrees that the Jews had signed a secret treaty with the Quraysh to thwart Muḥammad's efforts in every way and this led to the siege of Makkah.[202]

Margoliouth relates the story of the Banū Qurayẓah and their fate in great detail, looking at the alternatives open to Muḥammad. He concludes that 'their fate, horrible as it was, does not surprise us. If they had not succeeded in harming him, they had manifested the will to do so'.[203] He then cautions the reader to assess the verdict on the Qurayẓah against the milieu of Arabia. There is some fairness here but, sadly, this is not widely evident in the work. Muḥammad, and the Muslims, are judged according to late nineteenth-century Western liberal Christian principles and with a Jewish bias.

Margoliouth then returns to his previous line of discussion, accusing Muḥammad of harbouring a theoretical love for the Jews whilst exhibiting a practical hatred for them. He suggests that the Prophet was 'jealous' of the Jews' position as 'the chosen people of God' yet prayed for their recognition. He became bitter when such recognition did not materialize. He writes: 'The change from a basis of reason to a basis of force had taken place gradually, but now was finally achieved.'[204] He mentions the death of Sallām ibn Abī al-Ḥuqayq, supposedly one of the organizers of the plot against the Muslims. He claims that '. . . five cut-throats went with the prophet's blessing to murder him in his bed'.[205] He pictures Muḥammad as not being satisfied after 'the mass slaughter', still persuing one man to his bed to murder him. Referring to opinions that the Muslims were helped by Divine intervention at the siege, he remarks that, 'Whether Mohammed, who resorted so readily to the aid of the assassin's dagger, believed in these supernatural allies, we know not.'[206] He could at least have assumed that Muḥammad believed that they were helped by angels. This claim is not new. There have been assertions that the Muslims had not been alone since the battle of Badr. By this remark, Margoliouth seems to suggest that Muḥammad's mission was such a fake that he could not even have believed that Divine help was available to him. In a rather contentious assertion, he writes that, 'Each time the prophet had failed, or scored an incomplete success, he compensated for it by an attack on the Jews, . . .'[207]

He deduces that Khaybar was taken because of events at Ḥudaibiyyah. It is beyond explanation why Margoliouth regards the Ḥudaibiyyah treaty as a failure for Muḥammad. All major discussions regarding the treaty conclude that it was a major diplomatic *coup* which ended in manifest success for the Prophet and his followers.[208]

Touching on the letter the Prophet sent to Emperor Heraclius, Margoliouth claims that mention of Muḥammad's name caused panic among people and even the emperor was terrified. He claims that if it were not for fear of the reaction from his people, the emperor would have accepted Islam. Assuming that his version of the story is correct, Margoliouth explains that it was not strange because Heraclius himself had massacred Jews before. Hence, he continues, when the emperor heard '. . . of a prophet in Arabia who had slaughtered six hundred Jews in one day; who, having ruined their settlements at Medinah, had just brought desolation on their greatest and most flourishing colony, killing the men and making the women concubines . . .',[209] he might have thought of him as a useful ally. He sees Muqauqis, who treated the Prophet's letter with respect, in the same light, asserting that Muqauqis might have given such a favourable response because Muḥammad, the emperor had been told, had exterminated a large number of Jews.[210]

The Christians

The Christians do not receive as much space and concern as the Jews, especially in his *Mohammed*. However, as a Christian himself Margoliouth often uses the yardstick of that faith in his assessment of the Prophet. This is perhaps for two main reasons. Firstly, because of his Jewish background he had more time for the Jews than the Christians. History shows that Jewish consciousness lingers on whether the person remains in Judaism or not. Secondly, confrontations between the Prophet and the Jews far outnumber those with Christians and therefore there is not enough 'ammunition' here with which to attack the Prophet.

The main discussion centres around the alleged incorporation of Christian ideas into the Qur'ān. Margoliouth opens the deliberations by claiming that despite the massive 'theological or scriptural plagiarism', the cardinal doctrine of Christianity – the Divinity of Jesus – came in for heavy criticism from the Prophet. He claims that the doctrine became the sticking point in Muḥammad's relations with the Christians and hence offered an excuse in which they '. . . might with impunity be plundered'.[211]

Margoliouth, however, fails to consider why Muḥammad 'borrowed' so much from Christianity but ignored the most important. Is it that he was also so bent on destroying them that he had to have an excuse? The historicity of this is difficult to rationalize but this is what Margoliouth's statements appear to suggest. Except where he had to protect or defend the fragile faith, and of course his own person, there is no evidence of

Muḥammad wilfully, without any cogent rationale, setting out to destroy the Christians or other tribes. Yet, Margoliouth continues to portray the Prophet as being '. . . bent on oppressing or exterminating'[212] Jews and Christians.

He takes up the visit to the Prophet of the Christian delegation from Najrān. Mentioning the deliberations on the nature of Christ they had with the Prophet, Margoliouth derides the Prophet's statements claiming that he merely recollected the speech of Jaʿfar ibn Abī Ṭālib at the court of al-Najāshī. He says the Prophet highlighted those details that he knew the Christians would dislike.[213]

He refers to the challenge of imprecation which, the sources say, the Christians declined. Margoliouth doubts the veracity of the story. He argues that the Christians refused to take up the challenge because, knowing how 'violent' the Prophet was, he '. . . would merely have to send some legions to Najran with orders to destroy the persons on whom destruction had been invoked, and the truth of his doctrine would be demonstrated'.[214] This again casts doubt on Muḥammad's prophethood, because the suggestion is that he would fake an attack on the Christians merely to justify his status. Margoliouth does not mention how the Christians were treated nor that the Prophet even allowed them to hold their service in the mosque. Again, he does not explain why Muḥammad did not attack the Christians at Najrān long before they sent a delegation to Madīnah if he was that aggressive and had vowed to destroy the Christians and Jews.[215]

In his article 'Is Islam a Christian Heresy?' as a rejoinder to an article by F.H. Foster, Margoliouth's main thesis is that Muḥammad's teachings were so devoid of the principal doctrines of Christianity that they could not even be considered.[216]

In his sermon at St. Aldate's Church, Margoliouth accuses Muslims of trying to shape the Prophet's life along the same lines as that of Jesus. He writes: 'If the founder of Christianity provides a model for imitation, the founder of Islam must perforce do as much; hence it has to be shown that his life was the most perfect ever lived.'[217] In a scathing attack, he speaks to his church colleagues in a language which depicts what one might rightly describe as deep hatred for the Prophet. He says:

> The social and domestic evils which the very name of Islam calls up cannot be rebuked or deplored without reflecting on the prophet's career, and without openly contradicting the so-called Word of God and the consensus of the most authorised teachers. Sin loses much of its venom if it be acknowledged to be sin, if it be open defiance of God's law; but when it claims to be what God has enjoined, and millions believe it, then, indeed, Satan has triumphed.[218]

Here Margoliouth sounds more like the son of a Christian minister and professor of a Christian University establishment than an academic. Nevertheless, it gives us a better picture about his perception of Muḥammad and his ministry.

The Ḥudaibiyyah Treaty

Margoliouth gives more coverage to the Ḥudaibiyyah Treaty than most of his contemporaries. However, one might argue that he does so for the wrong reasons. He is of the opinion that the trip to Makkah in *c.* 627 CE (*c.* 6 AH) was a mere pretext. He claims that Muḥammad actually wanted to capture Makkah and that is why he '. . . approached it by a circuitous route, known to few, . . .'[219] and arrived at Ḥudaibiyyah where he was confronted by the Makkan army. This is untenable because all the available sources explain the mood in which the Prophet and his followers arrived at Ḥudaibiyyah. The Prophet had already ordered them not to carry arms apart from the sword which every Arab man carried on a journey. They also had with them animals intended for sacrifice. Furthermore, the Prophet was in the garb for pilgrimage. As for the party's diversion from the normal route, this was to avoid the army of

Khālid b. Walīd who had been sent as an advance party by the Makkans to halt the Prophet's march.[220]

Margoliouth continues: 'If however, the idea of storming Meccah had to be given up, the pretence of the pilgrimage still remained; and also he was not unwilling to impress the Meccans with a sense of his might, wealth, and the reverence and awe which he inspired.'[221] However, he does not explain why the Prophet refused to show his awe-inspiring personality in order to instil more fear into the people who were then at his mercy.

He describes the details of the agreement signed with the Makkans and writes: 'He certainly submitted to humiliation, since though his followers slaughtered their camels, and shaved their heads, they could only by straining words be said to have entered the sacred precincts safely.'[222]

Margoliouth explains, correctly, that some of the Muslims, especially 'Umar ibn al-Khaṭṭāb, considered events so degrading that they openly showed their displeasure. However, he conjectures that Muḥammad, knowing these people well, used the expected raid on Khaybar as an allurement to keep them in check.[223]

He recognizes that the Makkans had an advantage over the Muslims as far as the terms of the agreement on the whole were concerned. Despite the compromises the Prophet had to make, the clause regarding extradition of renegades weighed heavily in favour of the Quraysh. Margoliouth acknowledges the fact that the Prophet stood by the treaty and returned to the Quraysh some Makkans who wanted to go to Madīnah.

However, he does not comment on the implications of this as far as the Prophet's character is concerned. The powerful 'bloodletting tyrant', the 'robber chief', the man whose moral senses do not waver when he is ordering the murder of innocent civilians, is accepting such 'humiliating treatment'.[224] Presumably the matter was left at that because a deeper reflection on it would have turned Margoliouth's basic thesis on its head. Scholars who have analyzed this 'humiliating treaty' have indeed recognized the Prophet's immense prudence. While his Companions were more concerned with what they saw as an immediate opportunity, Muḥammad was looking to the future, and perceived that the end result bore good news. Indeed, this was confirmed by Divine intimation.[225]

Ibn Khaldūn writes:

> And there was never a victory . . . greater than this victory; for, as Az-Zuhri says, when it was war the people did not meet, but when the truce came and war laid down its burdens and people felt safe one with another, then they met and indulged in conversation and discussion. And no man spoke of Al-Islam to another but the latter espoused it, so that these entered Al-Islam in those two years (i.e. between Al-Hudaybiyyah and the breaking of the truce by the Quraysh) as many as all those who had entered it before, or more.[226]

Haykal also affirms the true nature of the treaty. He points out: 'There was . . . no reason to doubt that the Ḥudaybiyah Treaty was a victory for the Muslims. History has shown that this pact was the product of profound political wisdom and far-sightedness and that it brought about consequences of great advantage to Islam and indeed to Arabia as a whole.'[227]

Muḥammad's Letters

Margoliouth takes a look at the letters the Prophet sent to various world leaders. He considers these invitations to be a proclamation of a programme of world conquest.[228] How Margoliouth comes to this conclusion is difficult to fathom. The tone of the letters (a subject we shall return to presently) does not suggest any desire to colonize the world.

The letters were a sequel to the Ḥudaibiyyah Treaty, which Margoliouth considers a humiliation. Islam, by its very nature, is meant to be offered to all people and therefore the Prophet was bound, by the nature of his mission, to invite these élites of the society to it.[229]

Starting with the letter sent to Muqauqis, supposedly the Coptic Patriarch and the Governor of Egypt, Margoliouth publishes a photograph of the original text and translates it without comment.[230]

The next letter mentioned is the one sent to Heraclius the Caesar who, Margoliouth suggests, treated the letter with respect because he was pleased the Prophet had massacred the Jews.[231] In connection with this, Margoliouth doubts the story about Abū Sufyān being summoned by the emperor to explain the circumstances of his kinsman Muḥammad's claim to prophethood. Though he admits that it is possible for Abū Sufyān to have been in Syria and be called into the presence of the emperor, he is of the opinion that knowing the problems the Quraysh had encountered with Muḥammad, Abū Sufyān would rather have sought the king's help to destroy Muḥammad and Islam.

Though Margoliouth's thinking is quite valid, and he claims that Abū Sufyān would have liked to bring down Muḥammad, we must take into consideration the period we are dealing with.[232] This was around 627–28 CE and by this time Muḥammad had achieved a stability which, Abū Sufyān knew very well, would have been almost impossible to change.

The Chosroes (Khusro Parvez) of Persia is mentioned next and that he treated the Prophet's letter with contempt. He died not long after this incident. Margoliouth does not accept the version of the narrative that when the Prophet was informed of how Chosroes had treated his letter, he prophesied the death of the king. He suggests instead that the Prophet had an efficient intelligence network, implying that he might have heard of the king's death before making the statement.[233] However, he does not explain the time-lapse between the delivery of the letter and when the emissaries who were supposed to arrest the Prophet, reached Madīnah. We read that the Prophet's prediction of the destruction of Chosroes and his kingdom came soon after a report reached him about the contemptuous way in which his letter was received. The emperor himself sent a note to Badhan, the Governor of Yemen, who in turn sent envoys to Madīnah to arrest Muḥammad. Taking into account the conditions in those days, it was probably several weeks before Badhan's envoys reached Madīnah. Therefore, Margoliouth's contention that Muḥammad must have known of Chosroes' death before making the curses, is not tenable.[234]

What is surprising is his failure to discuss the contents of the letters and what they tell us about the nature of the Prophet. The standard format of the letters is very clear: the Prophet was inviting (calling) people to Islam in accordance with the Divine dictates.[235] Nothing in any of the letters gives cause to speculate that the Prophet was interested in world domination.

A closer look at the letters provides a general pattern as follows:

1. Introduction: Praises to Allah; indicating the origin of the letter and its addressee.
2. Greetings to the addressee.
3. Invitation to Islam, indicating that it is for the addressee's own good. Sometimes, followed by a short theological statement, especially on Jesus and Mary.
4. The consequences of rejecting the invitation: the responsibility the ruler owes to his people and the fact that in the Hereafter he would be answerable to God for all the sins of his subjects.
5. Conclusion: the recipient to bear witness that he (the Prophet) has done his duty by inviting him.[236]

Muḥammad's Personality

Under this theme must be acknowledged Margoliouth's positive remarks in respect of the Prophet's personality. However, his comments are overshadowed by the bulk of material, which can fairly be described as designed to destroy Muḥammad. Nevertheless, fairness and indeed the requirements of basic academic scholarship do not permit these comments to be ignored.

Margoliouth recognizes Muḥammad's affectionate disposition and how he demonstrated this openly in his family life. This is also reflected in the way he treated his attendant, and later adopted son, Zayd. His general behaviour towards children, Margoliouth agrees, was commendable.[237]

Referring to *aḥādīth* sources, Margoliouth discusses the deprivations that sometimes the Prophet and his family had to endure. He writes: 'It must be admitted that the prophet shared the full misery of his followers: and indeed as he refused to employ the Alms for his private needs, he had no source of revenue.'[238] Continuing the discussion, he says: 'Hence, when casual and private generosity failed, he was content to starve.'[239]

He touches on those homeless Companions who spent most of their time around the Prophet's mosque and confirms that, 'When presents of food were sent to the Prophet, he would share it with (them).'[240] These Companions, dubbed *Ahl al-Ṣuffah* (People of the shed, bench), were very poor and did not have accommodation. With this comment, Margoliouth paints a more refreshing picture of Muḥammad. He gives a piquant description of events at the battle of Ḥunayn and accepts the sincerity and integrity of the Muslim historians.[241]

Again, he acknowledges Muḥammad's honesty when he cites the case where the Prophet borrowed money from ʿAbdullāh ibn Abī Rabīʿah. He points out that this loan was '. . . honesty repaid'.[242]

Despite the fact that he had earlier suggested that the Prophet imposed taxes on the Jews to replenish the state treasury, he now agrees as to the object of the *jizyah*. He points out that the alms were to be used in charity to look after the poor and were not for the Prophet's private use. The *jizyah*, he affirms, was payment for services rendered, these largely involving protection.[243] He seems to accept Muḥammad's moral probity when stating that the Prophet was above material aggrandizement.[244] He also depicts Muḥammad as a fair and firm administrator. Margoliouth points out that when his kith and kin requested special favours, Muḥammad '. . . did not readily grant such requests, and appears in no case to have injured his administration by nepotism; nor did he allow his relatives to interfere with the course of justice'.[245]

He remarks about 'Ā'ishah, who he had maligned so much in earlier pages:[246] '. . . from the time of her emergence from childhood till her death at the age of sixty-six, she exhibited a degree of ability and unscrupulousness which should earn her a place beside Agrippinas and Elizabeths of history'.[247]

Margoliouth increasingly uses a softer language, stating of Muḥammad: 'The occasions . . . on which he had to punish were exceedingly rare . . .'[248] Curiously, he accepts that, 'The recognition of his prophetic claim was to the end a sort of incense whose perfume never staled.'[249]

He touches on the Prophet's generosity to all creatures and mentions the incident where the Prophet, on learning that an ant-hill had been set afire, ordered the fire to be extinguished.[250]

Discussing the Prophet's teachings, he commends the numerous positive changes introduced into that decadent society. He praises Muḥammad's instructions banning infanticide and superstitious beliefs, and admits that Islam won much greater liberty for women.[251] On the treatment of slaves, he says that '. . . manumission was also declared by him to be an act of piety, and many an offence might be expiated by the setting free of a neck'.[252]

Margoliouth's article on Muḥammad in the *Encyclopaedia of Religion and Ethics* also offers a slightly different attitude even though, compared with the bulk of the article, this pales into insignificance. For example, on the moral reforms brought about by Muḥammad, he says:

> With the institution of private property and the acquisition of wealth he found no fault, and he deprecated extravagance in almsgiving as in other matters. The quality of personal courage he rated very high, and, though he often inspired it by the promise of paradise, it is clear that his followers were largely persons who required no such stimulus to make them brave.[253]

What can we make of such an apparent contradiction? Perhaps Margoliouth sees Muḥammad as having 'matured', especially as many of his 'sober' remarks cover the latter part of the Prophet's life.

It is also logical to presume that maybe Margoliouth, a European, is trying to be seen as 'playing fair'. Perhaps he recognizes that his whole credibility is at stake and therefore he needs to tone down his vitriolic assessment of Muḥammad.

Muḥammad-Joseph Smith Parallelism

Gibb, in his *Mohammedanism*, discusses the frantic attempts by Western scholars to somehow unravel the 'mystery' surrounding Islam and 'fill in the gaps' that they consider exist. He states:

> Consequently, there are almost as many theories about Mohammed as there are biographies. He has, for example, been portrayed as an epileptic, as a social agitator, as a proto-Mormon. All such *extreme subjective* views are generally repudiated by the main body of scholars, yet it remains almost impossible to avoid importing some subjective element into any account of his life and work.[254]

It is with this comment in mind that we examine Margoliouth's use of such a theory. He sees Muḥammad as a sort of Joseph Smith, the founder of Mormonism (The Church of Jesus Christ of the Latter Day Saints). He compares Muḥammad's regular visits to the Cave of Ḥirā' in the practice of *Taḥannuth* and Joseph Smith's wanderings in the forest, and deduces that both claimed angelic visitations.[255] Again, he likens Smith's claim to the access he had to some hidden tablets written in a '. . . language which he only could translate "by the Grace of God" ',[256] to the Qur'ānic revelations from the 'Preserved Tablet'.[257]

These assertions are very strange. Smith's wanderings in the forest do not compare with the established, well-ordered practice of the Arabian society at the time. Furthermore, Muḥammad never claimed that he was reading from a Sacred Tablet, the script of which he alone could read, understand and interpret. The revelation was in Arabic so there were no secrets. In fact, the Qur'ān says it was revealed in Arabic so that its first recipients would have no problem relating to it.[258] It is therefore surprising that Muḥammad should be seen as a sort of 'precursor' for Joseph Smith at least on this account.

Margoliouth alleges that Muḥammad claimed he was '. . . permitted only occasionally access to the guarded tablet',[259] and remarks that this reasoning is better than that of Joseph Smith who claimed to read directly and, by implication, constantly from his tablet. One wonders where Margoliouth got his information from. Muḥammad is not on record in any of the known sources as having claimed a periodic glimpse of the *Lawḥ Maḥfūẓ*. He is always said to have 'received' and 'heard' from a tablet and 'receiving' or 'hearing' a message either directly or indirectly belong to two incomparable categories.[260]

The Qur'ānic challenge to the disbelievers to produce a *sūrah* like that found in the revealed word[261] is likened to an alleged attempt by William E. McLellin, a follower of Joseph Smith, who failed to write a work like the Mormon scripture.[262] Even the *Hijrah* of the Prophet is seen as replicated by Joseph Smith, when the Mormons moved from New York to Ohio and from there to Missouri and finally settled in Utah. He says that the Muslim situation is similar to that of the Mormons who, '. . . vexed and persecuted, fled to a new land and started a now thriving colony'.[263]

Margoliouth's methodology has been described by Snouck Hurgronje as a polemical tactic called 'Crypto-Mohamedanism'. Hurgronje argued that the Roman Catholic Church used to vilify the Protestants by comparing their doctrines to those of Islam.[264]

This theory was further developed by Rev. E.D. Howe who, in his *The History of Mormonism*, used it against the Mormons.

He described Joseph Smith as an ignorant prophet and a disciple of '. . . the great prince of deceivers, Muhammed'.[265] This theory was in vogue in the United States of America in the early nineteenth century, until 1861 when Richard Burton allegedly shifted the theory to Europe.[266] He is thus described as the first agent of this transplant. Arnold H. Green assumes that, 'It was perhaps via Burton that the comparison came to the attention of a less adventurist, more bookish Orientalist: D.S. Margoliouth of the University of London.'[267]

Margoliouth, the eminent scholar, should have realized the superficial nature and the ulterior motives of such an argument, and this does not augur well for serious academic work. On the other hand, it could be said that Margoliouth could have been trying to show his grasp of the phenomenology of religion, at the time a new field of study.

Conclusion

From the foregoing discussion, it can safely be concluded, by looking at Margoliouth's own stated aims in the book, what he has been able to achieve. He seems to agree with the perception that the greater the antiquity of material, the more likelihood of reliability.[268]

He gives an account of Muḥammad with reference to Ibn Isḥāq. He sees him undoubtedly as a great figure. However, as a Christian, he examines the Prophet through a Christian lens and so doubts the genuineness of his prophethood. Perhaps his position is not very different from that of Thomas Carlyle who saw the Prophet only as a hero.[269] The Oxford ethos demanded a particular style and, therefore, Margoliouth probably had to observe the rules of the game.

Margoliouth's style is fundamentally different from that of Muir. This is probably because Muir was an Imperial officer and, due to the authority of that office, this allowed him to be more blunt. Though Margoliouth uses more sources than Muir, he still approaches these sources with a mind wedded to the polemical tradition. The use of Muslim sources *per se* does not guarantee a shift in his biased attitude. It appears that he has failed to function critically in a disciplined way. This is not to question his use of sources but rather his interpretation.

The rather confessional posture he displays in some of his remarks, especially in *Mohammed*, his article in the *Encyclopaedia of Religion and Ethics* and his sermon at St. Aldate's Church, Oxford, raises a few questions about his ability as a scholar. His prejudicial treatment is often seen in his imaginative reconstruction of events when his sources do not provide adequate information. Quite often, he makes personal judgements on Muslim beliefs and not by force of rationality or academic reflection. For example, he mentions the story in which ʿUmar was supposed to have expressed his unhappiness when the Prophet prayed over the body of ʿAbdullāh ibn Ubayy. Shortly after this event a revelation banned praying for unbelievers. Margoliouth writes: 'To Omar, the coincidence did not apparently suggest the remotest suspicion; to us the revelation appears to have been nothing more than a formal adoption of a suggestion of Omar which the prophet supposed to represent public opinion.'[270]

In his characterization of Muḥammad and his followers as bloodletting people, Margoliouth comments on the death of ʿAmr ibn al-Ḥaḍramī, saying, 'ʿAmr, son of Al-Haḍrami (the man of Haḍramaut), was the first of the *millions* to be slaughtered in the name of Allah and his Prophet.'[271] What kind of conjecture puts the people killed in confrontations with Islam into millions?

In his attempt to understand the reasons for the resounding defeat the Quraysh suffered at the hands of the Muslims he supposes, among others, that the Muslims had experience of military drill because of their form of prayer (*ṣalāh*). He also adds that the Makkans did not want to shed the blood of their own kinsmen on the other side of the divide.[272]

Eliot Howard, in his review of *Mohammed*, is perhaps right when, after going through Margoliouth's images of Muḥammad, he remarks: 'This is not a very pleasant picture of a great religious leader; and, without venturing to dispute Professor Margoliouth's scholarship, we may venture to doubt whether the author (sic) of the earlier surahs of the Koran was as coldly selfish at the beginning of his course as he appears to have become under the pressure of circumstances.'[273] In a rather harsh comment in *The Comrade*, a Muslim paper in Calcutta at the dawn of the twentieth century, Howard sees Margoliouth's work on Muḥammad as '. . . far more dangerous . . .' than that of Muir which is openly characterized by its Christian prejudices. He goes on: 'Professor Margoliouth has hidden, though not always successfully, a worse Christian bias than Sir William Muir's, and in the praise of the hero has sought to kill the prophet. There is an insidious undercurrent running throughout the book, and the virus is skilfully mixed in every page.'[274]

In fact, Margoliouth's conjecture about a pathological theory tends to display something of a medieval heritage. As Norman Daniel points out, this conjecture probably started with Mark of Toledo, who described Muḥammad's mood at the time he received the revelations and concluded that it might be an epileptic seizure. Daniel then remarks: 'This account could not more closely or faithfully record the Muslim idea of how Muhammad received the revelations. The author's intention is likely to have been to provide information, and so to assist Christian Controversialists to prepare polemic which would be based on authentic and Muslim sources.'[275]

One would have expected Margoliouth to depend on conclusively proven ideas. However, the way he uses his sources is criticized by Shiblī Nuʿmānī who, though he acknowledges Margoliouth's scholarly aptitude, writes:

> Margoliouth has read every letter of the six huge volumes of *Musnad* of Imam Ahmad Ibn Hanbal . . . but in the entire history of the world there is not another book containing as much falsehood, accusation, misrepresentation and prejudice as his work on the life of the prophet. If he

> can claim any success it is that he has by his ingenuity changed the more simple and ordinary events, which have no trace of evil about them into something ugly.[276]

On Margoliouth's claim that the Prophet and his family used to practise idolatry and even named his children after idols, Nuʿmānī investigates his source and finds that in the *isnād* offered in Bukhārī's *Ta'rīkh al-Ṣaghīr* the first figure is Ismāʿīl b. Abī Uways who was considered not very trustworthy. Nuʿmānī states that: 'It has been conclusively proved that the prophet had begun to denounce idolatry even before his call to prophethood, and used to tell those persons in whom he had confidence to abstain from idolatrous practices.'[277]

Margoliouth, relying on Nöldeke, doubts whether the address given by Jaʿfar at the court of al-Najāshī can be accepted as genuine because Abyssinians and Arabs needed interpretation in their conversation.[278] However, Nuʿmānī emphasizes that the Abyssinians could understand Arabic. He points out that the Ethiopian language and Arabic had a close affinity. And, he adds, interpreters at the court of kings was a normal feature in those days.[279] This then leaves the question as to why Margoliouth of all people, the polyglot, could have overlooked this simple fact and deny the authenticity of Jaʿfar's speech.

Inayatullah, in his analysis of three British Orientalists – Deninson Ross, H.A.R. Gibb and D.S. Margoliouth – is also critical of Margoliouth. He pays tribute to his acclaimed scholarship but writes: 'While his erudition is certainly beyond all reproach and the series of his learned works have for several decades shed lustre on British Orientalist scholarship, we feel constrained to observe that his writings on Islam are, unfortunately, marred by a strong bias and have, in consequence, been regarded with distrust in the Muslim East.'[280] Margoliouth's constant comparison of Joseph Smith of the Mormons with Muḥammad, is poor judgement on his part because this has been used as a propaganda ploy by polemicists in the past.[281] His use of the theory is probably because of his background.

As an ordained minister of the Anglican Church he was, perhaps, upholding the position among certain Christians that revelation reached its culmination with the advent of Jesus Christ. For them, it is unacceptable to claim any revelation after Christ. Joseph Smith's claim to reception of revelation could therefore be nothing but an imposture. Since there has already been suggestions that certain aspects of Islam resemble those of Mormonism, Margoliouth readily falls for these theories.

Nevertheless, despite the fact that comparison of the historical experiences of both Muḥammad and Smith is possible, as could be done with any other claimant to prophethood, the plausibility of this in scholarly work leaves much to be desired.

We know that Margoliouth was a controversialist.[282] He has lived up to this characterization and has provided an account of Muḥammad laced with a mass of contentious opinions which, some might conclude, have impugned his scholarly aptitude.

Notes

1. *Mohammed and the Rise of Islam* (New York and London: G.P. Putnam, The Knickerbocker Press, 1905).

2. *Encyclopaedia Judaica*, Vol. 11 (Jerusalem: Ketter Publishing House Ltd., 1971), pp.966–7. Other dates given are 1820–81. See: Isidore Singer (ed.), *The Jewish Encyclopaedia*, Vol. 8 (1904), p.330. Also Leslie Stephen and Sir Sidney Lee (eds.), *The Dictionary of National Biography – From the Earliest Times to 1900*, Vol. 12 (1921–22), p.1044.

3. *The Dictionary of National Biography*, Vol. 12, *ibid.*, lists thirteen major works to his credit.

4. L.G. Wickham Legg (ed.), *The Dictionary of National Biography 1931–1940* (1949), (hereinafter cited as *DNB*), p.597.

5. *Ibid.*

6. *Ibid.*, p.598.

7. *Ibid.* One of his critics was said to have pointed out by some other arguments that his work on the *Iliad* and the *Odyssey* of Homer were not unique; he became enraged. Murray says: '. . . he retorted by producing not

merely "signatures" by anagram but also dates in the first three couplets of various tragedies'. He continues: 'It is difficult to know how far he was serious in these exercises of ingenuity. In another controversy, he took pains to try and justify his claim that the Egyptian papyri with information of Jewish settlement in Egypt as early as the 5th and even 6th century BC were phonies.' Murray also points out that despite the fact that only a few people agreed with him, 'his critics seemed silenced because he raised some complex questions which could not be answered'.

8. See his *Mohammedanism* (1911) and *The Early Development of Mohammedanism* (Hibbert Lectures), (London: Williams & Norgate, 1914).

9. *DNB*, p.599.

10. 'The Origins of Arabic Poetry', *JRAS*, Vol. 57 (1925), pp.417–49.

11. *Ibid.*, p.449.

12. *DNB*, p.599.

13. Published for the British Academy by Humphrey Milford (London: Oxford University Press, 1924).

14. *DNB*, p.599.

15. *Ibid.*

16. A. Jeffery, 'David Samuel Margoliouth', *MW*, Vol. 30, No. 3 (July 1940), p.295.

17. *Ibid.*

18. *Ibid.*

19. *Ibid.*, pp.295–6 and *DNB*, p.598. The feat which baffled his contemporaries was that he was able to reorganize the lines of the Greek Tragedies without tampering with the real substance and in each case he obtained a grammatically and metrically logical arrangement with sound meaning. His detractors, he accused, could not produce solid grounds for their objection. Margoliouth was in a class of his own.

20. Jeffery, 'David Samuel Margoliouth', p.296.

21. *Ibid.*

22. *Ibid.*, p.297.

23. *Ibid.*

24. *Ibid.*, p.298.

25. *JRAS*, Vol. 57 (1925), pp.153–4 under 'Review of Arabic Subjects'.

26. Margoliouth, 'Is Islam a Christian Heresy?', *MW*, Vol. 23, No. 1 (January 1933), pp.6–15. For Foster's article, see *MW*, Vol. 22, No. 2 (April 1932), pp.126–33. Foster's main line of reasoning is that Islam has too many Christian ideas, even though many of them are 'misrepresented' to be seen as closer to any religion other than Christianity. He enumerates some issues, including the status given to Jesus, which Judaism would never do, the belief in the return of Jesus at the end of time, the belief in the final judgement (which has less emphasis in Judaism) and the Qur'ānic idea of Jesus' death which he considers as a Gnostic influence. He also cites the reference in the Qur'ān about Jesus as an infant, making clay birds and making them have life and also Jesus speaking from the cradle. He claims that these ideas came from a document entitled 'Arabic Gospel of the Infancy of the Saviour', which he thought Muḥammad probably read. He then laments that Muḥammad '. . . thus became a heretic before he had ever become Orthodox' (see p.130 of the article). Margoliouth's rejection of the argument is straightforward, that Islam could not be a Christian sect.

27. Foster, 'Reply to Professor Margoliouth's Article, January 1933', *MW*, Vol. 23, No. 2 (April 1933), p.198.

28. *CMI*, Vol. 57 (July 1906), p.545.

29. *The New Encyclopaedia Britannica*, Micropedia, Vol. VI (Chicago and London: Helen Hemingway Benton, 1974), p.615.

30. *Ibid.*

31. *IC*, Vol. 11, No. 4 (October 1937), pp.535–6.

32. Margoliouth, *Mohammed*, p.iii.

33. *Ibid.* (Abū al-Fidā', d. *c.* 722 AH/1322 CE).

34. *Ibid.*, p.iv.

35. *Ibid.*

36. Calcutta 1853–94, 4 vols., see *ibid.*, p.v.

37. *Mohammed*, p.v.

38. *Ibid.*, p.vi.

39. *Ibid.*

40. *Ibid.*, p.vii.

41. Syed Ameer Ali, *The Spirit of Islam* (London, 1896, Calcutta, 1902). William Muir, *The Life of Mohammed* (1861).

42. *Mohammed*, p.vii.

43. *Ibid.*, p.2.

44. *Ibid.*, p.5.

45. *Ibid.*, p.7.

46. See note 38 above.

47. Margoliouth, *Mohammed*, p.8.

48. *Ibid.*, p.19.

49. See James Hastings (ed.), *Encyclopaedia of Religion and Ethics* (hereinafter cited as *ERE*), Vol. 8 (1915), pp.871–80.

50. *Ibid.*, p.872.

51. *Ibid.*, p.873.

52. *CMI*, Vol. 51 (1900), pp.241–8.

53. Margoliouth, *Mohammed*, pp.45–66.

54. *Ibid.*, p.46.

55. *Ibid.*, p.69.

56. *Ibid.*, pp.85–6.

57. *ERE*, pp.874–5.

58. Margoliouth, *Mohammed*, p.69.

59. *Ibid.*, p.216.

60. *Sūrah al-Mujādalah* 58: 12–13, Abdullah Yusuf Ali's translation.

61. Margoliouth, *Mohammed*, p.217.

62. *Ibid.*, pp.217–18.

63. *ERE*, p.877.

64. *Ibid.*

65. *Ibid.*

66. *Ibid.*

67. *Ibid.*

68. *Ibid.*

69. *Sūrah al-Fajr* 89: 27–30. See also *Sūrah al-Shams* 91: 7–10 and the Qur'ān *passim.*

70. For further insight into this subject, see contemporary works like: Muḥammad Iqbāl, *Six Lectures on the Reconstruction of Religious Thought in Islam* (1982 reprint), esp. Lecture IV on 'The Human Ego – His Immortality and Freedom'; Abdel Haleem Mahmud, *The Creed of Islam* (1978), esp. Ch. V on 'The Resurrection'; Fazlur Rahman, *Major Themes of the Qur'an* (1980), esp. Ch. Two on 'Man as an Individual' and Ch. Six on 'Eschatology'.

71. Margoliouth, *Mohammed*, p.74.

72. *Ibid.*, p.76. *'Vaticinium Post Eventum'* means literally 'prophecy after the event', i.e. 'an afterthought'.

73. For Jaʿfar's speech, see Shiblī Nuʿmānī, *Sīrat an-Nabī*, Parts II and III, translated into English by Fazlur Rahman (Karachi: Pakistan Historical Society, 1970), pp.220–1. Jaʿfar, among other things, said: 'O King, we were an ignorant people, who worshipped idols, at the (flesh of the) dead bodies, indulged in adultery and other evil practices, maltreated our neighbours, oppressed each other, and the strong among us destroyed the weak . . .'

74. *Mohammed*, p.89. See also note 61 where he makes the same observation in his article on Muḥammad in the *ERE.*

75. Some of these issues have been dealt with in the earlier parts of this work. Norman Daniel says there were '. . . of a dove whom Muhammad, or a wicked teacher of Muhammad, trained to eat grain or corn from the prophet's ear, to simulate the Holy Ghost; or of a bull, or calf, or camel, similarly trained to come at his call, bearing the Book of the Law bound in its horns'. See Norman Daniel, *Islam and the West – The Making of an Image*, Revised Edition (Oxford: Oneworld, 1993), p.52. See also pp.15, 31, 60–1, 257, 261–2 and 266.

76. Margoliouth, *Mohammed*, pp.88–9.

77. *Ibid.*, p.92.

78. Margoliouth, 'On the Origin and Import of the Names Muslim

and Hanīf', *JRAS*, Vol. 35 (July 1903), pp.467–93; and Lyall, 'The Words "Hanif" and "Muslim" ', *JRAS*, Vol. 35 (1903), pp.771–84.

79. *Ibid.*, p.772.

80. *The Shorter Encyclopaedia of Islam* (Leiden: E.J. Brill, 1953), p.651.

81. Margoliouth, *Mohammed*, p.93.

82. *Sūrah al-Ṭūr* 52: 21.

83. Margoliouth, *Mohammed*, p.93.

84. *Ibid.*, p.61.

85. *Ibid.*, pp.62–3. Margoliouth refers to the work of J.M. Robertson, *A Short History of Christianity* (1902). Robertson, in Part II of his book, under the general title 'Christianity from the Second Century and the Rise of Mohammedanism', discusses some rites and ceremonies over time. He writes:

> The sign of the cross was now constantly used in the same spirit, being held potent against physical and spiritual evil alike, insofar as any such distinction was drawn. But diseases were commonly regarded as the work of the evil spirits, and medical science was generally disowned, the preferred treatment being exorcism. A baptized person might further use the Lord's Prayer with its appeal against the Evil One – a privilege denied to the Cathechumen or seeker for membership (p.125).

86. Margoliouth, *Mohammed*, pp.69–70.

87. A.R.I. Doi, *Nigerian Muslim Names – Their Meaning and Significance* (1978). See Ch. One where the author discusses the importance of good names in Islam.

88. *Mohammed*, p.70.

89. *Ibid.*

90. Shiblī Nuʿmānī, *Sīrat an-Nabī*, p.204. See also: Ibn Hishām, *al-Sīrah al-Nabawiyyah*, Vol.1 pp.265–6; Muḥammad Husayn Haykal, *The Life of Muḥammad*, translated by Ismāʿīl R.A. al-Fārūqī (1976), pp.87–90; A. Guillaume, *The Life of Muhammad – Translation of Ibn Isḥāq's Sīrat Rasūl Allāh* (Karachi: Oxford University Press, 1978), pp.118–19; Abūl Ḥasan ʿAlī Nadwī, *Muhammad Rasulallah* (1982), pp.112–13.

91. The Prophet replied to his uncle's emotional appeal thus: 'By Allah, I will not desist from performing my duties, even if these people place the

sun in my one hand and the moon in the other. Either God will (make me) fulfill this mission or I will lay down my life for this (cause).' See Shiblī Nu'mānī, *op. cit.*, p.205.

92. See his translation of Haykal's *The Life of Muhammad*, pp.19–20.

93. *The Eternal Message of Muhammad*, translated from the Arabic by Caesar E. Farah. A Mentor Book (1965), p.29.

94. Margoliouth, *Mohammed*, p.170.

95. *Ibid.*, p.171.

96. *Ibid.* Rather than being suppressed in the major works on the Prophet's biography, Ibn Hishām, Ibn Sa'd and al-Ṭabarī all refer to the story. These are usually recognized as prominent works and Margoliouth himself mentions these in his introductory remarks to his books.

97. See p.106 ff. for a discussion of the equation of Muḥammad to Joseph Smith – the founder of Mormonism.

98. See the chapter on Sir William Muir. See also T.B. Irving, 'The Rushdie Confrontation – A Clash in Values', *IO*, 3rd Quarter, Vol. 2, No. 3 (1989), pp.43–51.

99. Margoliouth, *Mohammed*, p.42.

100. *Ibid.*, p.59.

101. *Ibid.*, pp.60–1. He gives examples as: 'tasting of death', 'to bring from darkness to light', 'to pervert the straight way of God', 'the trumpet shall be blown', 'to roll up the heavens as a scroll is rolled up', etc.

102. *Ibid.*

103. *Ibid.*, p.59.

104. *Ibid.*, p.107. See also p.45 where the author says: 'Whatever fragments of the Old or New Testaments of the lives of the saints, of the sayings of the Jewish Fathers or of ordinary folklore happened to be in the prophet's memory were regarded by him as suitable matter for the Koran.'

105. *Ibid.*, pp.102–3. *Paternoster* – 'Our Father', is the Lord's Prayer which the Gospels say was taught by Jesus Christ. See *Matthew* 6: 9–13; *Luke* 11: 2–4.

106. Margoliouth, 'On the Origin and Import of the Names Muslim and Hanif', *op. cit.* p.492.

107. *Ibid.*

108. Charles Lyall, 'The Words "Hanīf" and "Muslim" ', *op. cit.*, pp.771–2.

109. *Ibid.*

110. *Ibid.*, p.777.

111. *Ibid.*

112. *Ibid.*, p.784. See also pp.779–84.

113. *ERE*, p.875.

114. Frank Hugh Foster, 'Is Islam a Christian Heresy', esp. pp.128–30; and Margoliouth's criticism in his article bearing the same title (see note 26 of this chapter).

115. See note 27.

116. Margoliouth, *Mohammed*, p.61.

117. *Ibid.*, p.107.

118. *Ibid.*, p.131.

119. *Ibid.*, p.135.

120. F.H. Foster, 'Is Islam a Christian Heresy', esp. pp.128–32.

121. Margoliouth, *Mohammed*, esp. pp.35–40.

122. Robertson, *A Short History of Christianity*, Part II.

123. See *Sūrah al-Anʿām* 6: 31, 48; *Sūrah Ibrāhīm* 14: 4–6. Also: Abūl Ḥasan ʿAlī Nadwī, *Prophethood in Islam*, *passim*; Roston Pike, *Encyclopaedia of Religion and Religions* (1951), p.308; *Encyclopaedia Judaica*, Vol. 13, pp.1150–81, on 'Prophets and Prophecies'.

124. See *Sūrah al-Baqarah* 2: 285; and vv. 136, 253 of the same *sūrah*; *Sūrah al-Nisā'* 4: 150–2. In fact, in the last passage, those who pick and choose are described as unbelievers.

125. This raises the issue of *Taḥrīf* (Manipulation, Perversion) in Islamic critique. See *Sūrah al-Baqarah* 2: 42, 75, 146; *Sūrah Āl ʿImrān* 3: 71; *Sūrah āl-Nisā'* 4: 46; *Sūrah al-Mā'idah* 5: 14–15. See also Abdel Majid Charfi, 'Christianity in the Qur'ān Commentary of Ṭabarī', *Islamo Christiana*, Vol. 6 (1980), pp.105–48, and M.H. Ananikian, '*Tahrif* or the Alteration of the Bible According to the Muslems', *MW*, Vol. 14 (1924), pp.61–84.

126. Margoliouth, *Mohammed*, p.149.

127. *Ibid.*, pp.150–1.

128. *Ibid.*, p.149.

129. *Ibid.*, p.387.

130. *Ibid.*, p.388.

131. *Ibid.*, p.413.

132. See *Sūrah al-Baqarah* 2: 43 and vv. 110, 177 and 277; *Sūrah al-Nisā'* 4: 162; *Sūrah al-Mā'idah* 5: 58. For further reading on *zakāh,* see G. de Zayas Farishta, *The Law and Philosophy of Zakat,* Vol. 1, edited A.Z. Abbasī (1960); As-Sayyid Ṣābiq: *Fiqh-us-Sunnah,* Vol. 3 (1986), esp. Part 1 on *az-zakāh.*

133. Margoliouth, *Mohammed,* p.272.

134. *Ibid.*

135. *Ibid.*, pp.389–90.

136. *Ibid.*, p.393.

137. *Ibid.*, pp.393–4.

138. *ERE,* p.873.

139. *CMI,* Vol. 51, p.244. As we have already intimated, we are cognizant of the Church atmosphere and the expectations of those at St. Aldate's Church, Oxford, where the sermon was given. Nevertheless, we expected a more sobre reflection from a scholar of Margoliouth's calibre. See p.56 for discussion on Margoliouth's sources.

140. *Islam and the West,* esp. pp.167–9, 265, 269–70, 292, 298, 306, 311, 351–3 and 381–4.

141. Margoliouth, *Mohammed,* p.66. This sounds very much like an anti-Arab sneer from the Jews which is unproven and unprovable. Margoliouth, however, believes in it first perhaps because of his Jewish background and second and more importantly, because it fits his purpose.

142. *Ibid.*, p.176.

143. *Ibid.*, pp.176–7.

144. *Ibid.*

145. *Ibid.*, p.183. See also notes 89 and 90 above.

146. *Ibid.*, p.184.

147. *Ibid.*, pp.340–1.

148. *Ibid.*

149. *Ibid.*, p.343.

150. *Ibid.*, p.351.

151. *Ibid.*, pp.351–2.

152. *Ibid.*, p.369.

153. See his article on Muḥammad in the *ERE.*

154. Margoliouth, *Mohammed,* pp.371–2. This incident is indicative of the Prophet's sincerity and the fact that he was not a man of pleasure and the flesh as he is being depicted to be. For further reading on the postponement of the wedding feast, see Guillaume's translation of Ibn Isḥāq's *Sīrat Rasūl Allāh,* p.531; Fārūqī's translation of Haykal's *The Life of Muhammad,* pp.384–5; and Martin Lings' *Muhammad – His Life Based on the Earliest Sources* (1983), Ch. 72, esp. pp.281–2.

155. *Islam and the West,* Ch. 3.

156. Margoliouth, *Mohammed,* p.127.

157. See *Matthew* 21: 12–13; *Mark* 11: 15–17; *Luke* 19: 45–6.

158. Abūl Ḥasan ʿAlī Nadwī, *Muhammad Rasulallah,* p.412. See also Saiyīd Sulaiman Nadwi: *Muhammad – The Ideal Prophet,* translated by Mohiuddin Ahmad (1981), esp. Ch. 4.

159. *Sūrah al-Anʿām* 6: 68. Abu'l Kalām Āzād explains: 'When people who have no urge to seek out truth and who try to twist it to serve their purposes indulge in spurious argumentation, it would be well for the truth loving to keep aloof of them; for, truth does not emerge through wilful controversy over it.' See his *The Tarjumān al-Qur'ān,* edited and translated by Syed Abdul Latīf, Vol. 2 (1967), p.353. Sayyid Abu'l Āʿlā Mawdūdī also explicates that the main duty of the believers is to present the truth to the unbelievers but, if they reject it, they '. . . should not waste their time and energy by entering into useless polemical disputes, discussions and argumentations with disbelievers'. See his *The Meaning of the Qur'ān,* Vol. 3 (Lahore: Islamic Publications, 1972), p.119, note 45. In fact the Qur'ān makes this a principle, that arguments must always serve a useful purpose and not be for the mere sake of it or to cause strife in society. See *Sūrahs* 16: 125; 29: 46.

160. Margoliouth, *Mohammed,* p.276.

161. *Ibid.*, p.278.

162. *Ibid.*, p.279.

163. *Ibid.*, p.278.

164. *Ibid.*, p.281.

165. *Ibid.*, pp.282–3.

166. *Ibid.*, pp.286–7.

167. *Ibid.*

168. *Ta'ākhin* or *Mu'ākhāt* refers to the institution of Brotherhood which the Prophet instituted after the *Hijrah* between the *Anṣār* (literally, the Helpers, from the inhabitants of Madīnah) and the *Muhājirūn* (literally, the Migrants who migrated from Makkah to Madinah). The *Anṣār* not only welcomed the newcomers as their brothers-in-faith, but readily shared their wealth and property with the *Muhājirūn*. This institution of brotherhood, in many ways, is unparalleled in human history.

169. Margoliouth, *Mohammed*, p.288.

170. *Ibid.*

171. *Ibid.*, p.338.

172. *Ibid.*, p.362.

173. *Ibid.*, p.363. See Shiblī Nuʿmānī's explanation in *Sīrat an-Nabī*, p.156 ff.

174. Margoliouth, *Mohammed*, p.363.

175. *CMI*, Vol. 5 (1900), p.245.

176. *ERE*, p.873.

177. *Ibid.*, p.878.

178. See *Sūrah al-Baqarah* 2: 256; *Sūrah Āl Imrān* 3: 20, 104, 110; *Sūrah al-Tawbah* 9: 6; *Sūrah Yūnus* 10: 99; *Sūrah al-Naḥl* 16: 125; *Sūrah al-Ḥajj* 22: 68–70; *Sūrah al-Shūrā* 42: 13–15; *Sūrah al-Muzzammil* 73: 10–11; *Sūrah al-Ghāshiyah* 88: 20–6. See also T.W. Arnold, *The Preaching of Islam* (1896), esp. Chs. 1, 2 and *passim*.

179. M. Cherāgh ʿAlī, *A Critical Examination of the Popular Jihād* (1885), esp. pp.55–91. See also Ḥasan Moinuddin, *The Charter of the Islamic Conference and Legal Framework of Economic Co-operation Among its Member States* (1987), esp. Ch. 2 on 'Islam and International Law'.

180. See p.65 ff. above.

181. Margoliouth, *Mohammed*, p.97.

182. *Ibid.*, p.98.

183. *Ibid.*, p.114.

184. *Ibid.*, p.376.

185. *Ibid.*, p.407.

186. *Ibid.*

187. *Ibid.*, pp.227–8.

188. Muhammad Hamidullah, *The First Written Constitution in the World* (1981); Afzal Iqbal, *Diplomacy in Islam* (1965); Abdulrahmān Abdulkādir Kurdī, *The Islamic State: A Study Based on the Islamic Holy Constitution* (1984), esp. the Appendix entitled 'The Declaration of Medina', pp.131–7.

189. Margoliouth, *Mohammed*, pp.226–7.

190. *Ibid.*, p.228.

191. *Ibid.*, p.231. See also the Bible, *Proverbs* 19: 17; the Qur'ān, *Sūrah al-Baqarah* 2: 245; *Sūrah al-Ḥadīd* 57: 11, 18; *Sūrah al-Taghābun* 64: 17; *Sūrah al-Muzzammil* 73: 20.

192. Margoliouth, *Mohammed*, p.232.

193. *Ibid.*, p.233.

194. *Ibid.*, p.238.

195. *Ibid.*, p.249. Muslims believe that the Qur'ān makes it clear that the changing of the *qiblah* was not according to Muḥammad's personal whim but a directive from God. See *Sūrah al-Baqarah* 2: 142–5, 149–50. One scholar comments on this: 'The Qur'an has dealt with this problem beautifully, saying that the ceremonial and ritualistic aspects of religion, if at all necessary, have secondary importance; they are not the essentials of faith. Directions of space have little meaning intrinsically in spiritual communion with a Being whose Light, according to the Qur'ān is "neither Eastern nor Western" (24: 35).' ('Abdul Ḥakīm Khalīfah, *The Prophet and His Message* (1972), p.110.)

196. *Mohammed*, p.249.

197. *Ibid.*, pp.247–51.

198. *Ibid.*, p.310.

199. *Ibid.*, p.314.

200. *Ibid.*, pp.314–15.

201. *Ibid.*, pp.312–25 and *passim.*

202. *Ibid.*, p.323.

203. *Ibid.*, pp.333–4.

204. *Ibid.*, p.325.

205. *Ibid.*, p.336.

206. *Ibid.*

207. *Ibid.*, p.355.

208. See p.99 ff. for a discussion on the Ḥudaibiyyah Treaty.

209. Margoliouth, *Mohammed*, p.367.

210. *Ibid.*, p.369.

211. *Ibid.*, p.364.

212. *Ibid.*, p.431.

213. *Ibid.*, p.434.

214. *Ibid.*, p.435.

215. For further reading on the delegation's visit, see: Guillaume's translation of Ibn Isḥāq's *Sīrat Rasūl Allāh*, pp.270–7; Nuʿmānī's, *Sīrat an-Nabī*, p.369; and Fārūqī's translation of Haykal's *The Life of Muhammad*, pp.195–6, 478.

216. 'Is Islām a Christian Heresy?', *passim.*

217. *Ibid.*, p.244.

218. *Ibid.*

219. *Ibid.*, p.345.

220. For further reading on the Ḥudaibiyyah Treaty, see Shiblī Nuʿmānī, *Sīrat an-Nabī*, pp.390–400; Guillaume's translation of Ibn Isḥāq's, *Sīrat Rasūl Allāh*, pp.499–507; Fārūqī's translation of Haykal's *The Life of Muhammad*, pp.340–59; Abūl Ḥasan ʿAlī Nadwī, *Muhammad Rasulallah*, pp.261–72.

221. Margoliouth, *Mohammed*, p.345.

222. *Ibid.*, p.348.

223. *Ibid.*, p.349.

224. See above, p.99.

225. See *Sūrah al-Fatḥ* 48: 1 and *passim.*

226. Cited by Muḥammad M. Pickthall, in his translation of the Qur'ān, *The Glorious Qur'an* (Makkah: Muslim World League, 1977), p.557. He remarks that Ibn Khaldūn's statement agrees with that of Ibn Hishām on the subject.

227. Fārūqī's translation of Haykal's *The Life of Muhammad*, p.355. See also p.356. Shiblī Nuʿmānī reiterates the same view: 'The Treaty of Hudaybiyah has been a victory by Allah; it was not a victory of bodies but of hearts. Islam wanted peace for its propagation and this was secured through the treaty.' (*Sīrat an-Nabī*, Vol. 2, p.409.)

228. Margoliouth, *Mohammed*, p.364.

229. T.W. Arnold, *The Preaching of Islam*, esp. Ch. 1 on the missionary nature of Islam. See also: *Sūrah al-Baqarah* 2: 143; *Sūrah Āl ʿImrān* 3: 104, 110, 187; *Sūrah al-Aʿnām* 6: 48; *Sūrah Ibrāhīm* 14: 4–6; *Sūrah al-Naḥl* 16: 125; *Sūrah al-Aḥzāb* 33: 45–7. These passages make the duty of the Prophet and indeed his followers clear. They have to spread the Word of God so that mankind will do what is right and forbid what is wrong (*al-Baqarah* 2: 104, 110).

230. Margoliouth, *Mohammed;* see the page facing p.364 for the 'original text' and p.365 for the translation.

231. See pp.365–7.

232. *Ibid.*

233. *Ibid.*, p.368.

234. See S. Ahmed Qureshi, *Letters of the Holy Prophet* (1983), *passim*; Guillaume's translation of Ibn Isḥāq's *Sīrat Rasūl Allāh*, pp.653–9; Fārūqī's translation of Haykal's *The Life of Muhammad*, pp.374–9; Abūl Ḥasan ʿAlī Nadwī, *Muhammad Rasulallah*, Ch. 15; Shiblī Nuʿmānī, *Sīrat an-Nabī*, pp.401–9; Afzal Iqbāl, *Diplomacy in Early Islam, passim.*

235. See note 227 above.

236. See the suggested references in note 234 above, esp. the works of Ahmed Qureshi, Afzal Iqbāl and Abūl Ḥasan ʿAlī Nadwī.

237. Margoliouth, *Mohammed*, pp.70–1.

238. *Ibid.*, p.236.

239. *Ibid.*

240. *Ibid.*

241. *Ibid.*, p.397.

242. *Ibid.*

243. *Ibid.*, pp.440–1.

244. *Ibid.*, p.443.

245. *Ibid.*, p.453.

246. *Ibid.*, pp.14, 61, 234–5, 321 and 342.

247. *Ibid.*, p.450.

248. *Ibid.*, p.456.

249. *Ibid.*

250. *Ibid.*, p.458.

251. *Ibid.*, pp.458–61.

252. *Ibid.*, p.462.

253. *ERE*, p.876.

254. H.A.R. Gibb, *Mohammedanism* (1949), p.23; (emphasis ours).

255. Margoliouth, *Mohammed*, p.90.

256. *Ibid.*, p.91.

257. The '*Lawḥ Maḥfūẓ*'. See *Sūrah al-Burūj* 85: 22.

258. See *Sūrah Yūsuf* 12: 2; *Sūrah al-Fuṣṣilat* 41: 44; *Sūrah al-Shūrā* 42: 7.

259. Margoliouth, *Mohammed*, p.91.

260. For further reading on the subject of Revelation in Islam, see Guillaume's translation of Ibn Isḥāq's *Sīrat Rasūl Allāh*, esp. Part 3 on 'Muhammad's Call and Preaching in Meccah'; Muhammad Rashīd Riḍā, *The Revelation to Muhammad*, translated from the Arabic by Abdus-Samad Sharafuddīn, Part 1, 2nd Revised Edition (1960), esp. Ch. 1 on 'Divine Message and Messengers', and *passim*; Abūl Ḥasan 'Alī Nadwī, *Islamic Concept*

of Prophethood (1979), *passim*; Fazlur Rahman, *Islam*, 2nd. Edition (1979), esp. Ch. 1 on 'Muhammad and the Revelation'.

261. See *Sūrah al-Baqarah* 2: 23–4; *Sūrah Yūnus* 10: 38.

262. Cited in Margoliouth, *Mohammed*, p.134.

263. *Ibid.*, p.156.

264. Christian Snouck Hurgronje, *Mohammedanism: Lectures on Its Origin, Its Religious and Political Growth, and Its Present State* (1916), p.18.

265. (New York, Painsville, 1834), p.12.

266. See his *The City of the Saints Across the Rocky Mountains to California* (1861); reprint by F.M. Brodie (New York: Knopf, 1963).

267. A.H. Green, 'The Muhammad-Joseph Smith Comparison: Subjective Metaphore, or a Sociology of Prophethood', in Spencer J. Palmer, *Mormons and Muslims – Spiritual Foundations and Modern Manifestations*, Conference Papers (1985), p.67.

268. See p.56 ff. above.

269. Thomas Carlyle, *On Heroes, Hero Worship and the Heroic in History* (London, 1891).

270. Margoliouth, *Mohammed*, p.218.

271. *Ibid.*, p.245 (emphasis ours). ʿAmr ibn al-Haḍramī is reputed to be the first person to die at the hands of the Muslims. It was at Nakhlah, when a group led by ʿAbdullah ibn Jahsh and sent by the Prophet to investigate the movement of the Quraysh caravan and report back, confronted ʿAmr and he was killed. The Prophet was displeased at this because he pointed out that he did not send them to fight, especially since it was the month of Rajab, in which traditionally, fighting was banned. In fact, Shiblī Nuʿmānī claims that this incident was the real cause of the battle of Badr (see *Sīrat an-Nabī*, pp.317–20). For further reading on this subject, see Fārūqī's translation of Haykal's *The Life of Muhammad*, pp.208–11; Guillaume's translation of Ibn Isḥāq's *Sīrat Rasūl Allāh*, pp.286–9.

272. See Margoliouth, *ibid.*, pp.258–66.

273. '*Mohammed: The Rise of Islam* by D.S. Margoliouth' (Book Review), *CMI*, Vol. 57 (July 1906), pp.545–6.

274. 'Professor Margoliouth's "Life of Mohammed" ', *MW*, Vol. 2, No. 3 (July 1912), p.311.

275. *Islam and the West*, p.49.

276. Shiblī Nuʿmānī, *Sīrat an-Nabī*, Vol. 1, p.95.

277. *Ibid.*, p.180. See also the footnote in which he criticizes Margoliouth's allegation that Muḥammad and Khadījah used to worship the idol al-ʿUzza before going to bed. On his other claim that the couple sacrificed a brown sheep dedicated to al-ʿUzza, Shiblī Nuʿmānī points out that Kalbī, on whose authority the statement is given, is a notorious liar.

278. Margoliouth, *Mohammed*, p.158. See also the footnote.

279. Shiblī Nuʿmānī, *Sīrat an-Nabī*, p.221, note 3.

280. Sh. Inayatullah, 'Personalia', *IC*, Vol. 12, No. 4 (October 1938), p.535.

281. See p.106 ff. above.

282. See p.49 above

PART II

CHAPTER FOUR

Survey of Twentieth-Century Literature

Introduction

The appearance of Margoliouth's book *Mohammed and the Rise of Islam*, published in 1905, opened the floodgates within the English scene for a plethora of writing on Muḥammad and his ministry. Without making any claim to exhaustiveness, we make a survey of that literature which appeared in Europe between 1910 and the 1980s.

Our interest lies mainly in English works published in Europe and especially in Britain. Included in these are those translated from other European languages into English and which are deemed to have made an impact on the intellectual landscape. However, more attention will be paid to those English works which we believe have occupied centre stage in studies on Muḥammad.

This survey will enable us to set a proper context for William Montgomery Watt whose works this chapter, in the main, sets out to analyze.

The First Half of the Twentieth Century

Leones Caetani's monumental ten-volume work first began to appear in the same year as Margoliouth's principal book on

Muḥammad.[1] Rodinson writes that after Caetani's '. . . massive study on the life of the prophet (and also on the subsequent period) . . . the researcher could rightly feel a sense of discouragement'.[2] Any discouragement felt here being in the sense that everything that needed to be said had already been said. Rodinson goes further to say that Caetani's work '. . . marks both the culmination and the end of a period of scholarly investigation'.[3] Perhaps, Margoliouth might have generated that kind of feeling as well among admirers who could not fathom his intellectual capability.

However, the context of the twentieth century, especially in light of political developments, made Islam an important theme in the West. People were literally looking for both the origin and the 'originator' of this 'phenomenon' called Islam.[4]

Rodinson mentions an interesting poll conducted in France by a Book Club asking its members to choose personalities whose biographies they would like to see published ranking them in order of preference. Muḥammad topped the list by a wide margin.[5]

Nineteenth-century historical posture and critical approaches to scholarship fostered the kind of works on Muḥammad in particular, and Islam in general, in the twentieth century. Nevertheless, as Rodinson points out, a lot of tares are mixed up with the wheat but these are to be excused when one takes into account the general euphoria generated by early scholars. Some of the material could rightly be described as hypercritical and excessive. Rodinson cautions that: 'The accounts found in our Muslim sources of events which occurred at the beginning of Islam do require special methodological study, for the process of oral transmission constitutes a problem whose implications have not yet been fully explored.'[6] Not long after Caetani, Th. Menzel's *The Life and Religion of Mohammed, the Prophet of Arabia* was published.[7]

The Rev. Canon Edward Sell followed with his *The Life of Mohammad*.[8] Having previously written extensively on Islam, he concentrates on the 'political factor' in the Prophet's life because he felt it to be an area neglected by previous scholars. Among his sources he counts Muir and Margoliouth. He agrees with Muir that the kind of Christianity the Prophet became acquainted with was of the depraved kind, hence Muḥammad's image of Christianity as reflected in the Qur'ān. Sell also mentions that when the angel Jibrīl appeared to Muḥammad in the Cave of Ḥirā', the Prophet's family was with him; this Sell views as 'historical fact'. He further follows writers like Muir, MacDonald and Margoliouth in believing the theory about epileptic fits.

He portrays Muḥammad as the culprit of a whole episode of confrontations with non-Muslims and directs his sympathy towards the Jews in their confrontations with Muḥammad. He writes of the Banū Qurayẓah issue that Muḥammad's actions:

> . . . cannot be justified by comparison with other men. They belong to a different category; they are according to Muslim theology, the result of a divine impulse within him, the deeds of a sinless and therefore perfect man. They form the highest ideal and the most perfect conception of life which Islam can present. All apologies based on the fact that other leaders, religious or secular have done similar deeds are altogether beside the question.[9]

One wonders what Sell's analysis of the fall of Jericho would be when that depicted the typical use of Divine power to destroy a whole city.[10]

In his conclusion, and as can be expected of a man of that vocation, Sell categorically states that Muḥammad could not be a Prophet. He writes:

> The impartial student of history will come to the conclusion on a careful review of Muhammad's life and work, that, although he was a very successful Arab chief, and did much to maintain and spread a belief in one God, he has entirely failed to establish his position as a divinely commissioned prophet, or to show that he was sent with 'the guidance and the religion of truth that he might exalt

> it above every religion', and make it set aside all that had gone before. We cannot, therefore, admit that Muhammad was sent from God . . .[11]

One important factor to consider here is Sell's total reliance on Muir and Margoliouth as his authorities.

We might also draw attention to the work of G.M. Draycott, first published in 1915.[12] Anees and Athar describe this book as, 'A biographical study of the prophet with an extremely harsh tone.'[13]

In the first three decades after Margoliouth, Father Henri Lammens' *Islam – Beliefs and Institutions* appeared in 1929.[14] Even though this work contains only one chapter on Muḥammad, its dominant theme of the Prophet and the institutions of religion justifies its mention. In fact, Lammens, a Belgian Jesuit priest, wrote extensively on Islam, especially on the Prophet and his family. Rodinson sees him as a scholar who '. . . dominated European studies on Muhammad during the first third of the century'.[15] Despite his fine Arabic scholarship, Lammens had his own biases and as a Francophile denounced Muslim resistance to French imperialism. As Rodinson again indicates, Lammens '. . . was filled with a holy contempt for Islam, for its "delusive glory" and its works, for its "dissembling" and "lascivious" Prophet, for the Arabs of the desert who in his judgement were cowards and swaggerers, plunderers and destroyers'.[16] In his effort to discredit the Prophet and Islam, he went a little too far in employing methodologies which could hardly withstand academic scrutiny. The only accounts acceptable to him were those that reflected unfavourably on Muḥammad and his family. His excessive prejudice, his violation of the texts rather too often, and his errors have justly called forth severe judgements.[17] In fact, the attacks were such that some Christian writers expressed disquiet about the impact of his methodology. Rodinson mentions an instance in which Ignaz Goldziher expressed such concern in a private discourse with Louis Massignon. Goldziher is reported to have said: 'What would remain of the Gospels if he applied to them the same methods he applies to the Qur'an?'[18]

Some people, however, see one benefit from such unrestrained use of extreme criticism. For Rodinson, such approaches '. . . have forced us to be much more highly demanding of our sources. With the traditional edifice of history definitely brought down, one could now proceed to the reconstruction'.[19]

In 1926, Richard Bell published his *The Origins of Islam in its Christian Environment.*[20] Bell follows the reductionist approach trying to prove that Islam is a borrowed, rather perverted form of Christianity. He wrote extensively on Muḥammad, focusing on his revelation which he dismisses as not genuine.

Rodinson's optimism for reconstruction has been very slow indeed. However, in 1930, the emergence of the German expanded edition of Frantz P.W. Buhl's original Danish work broke the lull.[21] Though the work itself remains in German, parts have appeared as articles in the *Encyclopaedia of Islam* and the *Shorter Encyclopaedia of Islam*. Buhl's work:

> . . . contains a considerable mass of information taken from all the available sources, studied and analyzed critically in the light of the discussions of European Islamists, of whom he had an almost exhaustive knowledge. With the robust sense of a good researcher, he rejected both the hypercriticism of certain Arabists and the blind confidence of Muslims in their sources.[22]

Rodinson continues that, 'Within the area of its concern, the work has not been excelled and remains an indispensable tool.'[23]

Another work which needs mention here is Emile Dermenghem's *La Vie de Mahomet* which was translated into English and published in 1930.[24] Two years later, Theodora Barton's *Talks on Mohammed and His Followers* joined the list.[25] In the same year, one of the most experienced European writers on Islam, Arent Jan Wensinck, published *The Muslim Creed – Its Genesis and Historical Development*[26] with the basic premise that Islamic doctrines were influenced by Greek philosophy in their formative periods. Though the book is not primarily a biographical piece, his arguments display a lot of his understanding of the Prophet. Arguing that the Prophet was not concerned with creedal matters, Wensinck writes: 'We may call him a Prophet, a Politician, or both; but he was certainly no religious philosopher. Moreover, the change in his career brought about by the *hidjra* and its consequences, produced a change in his general attitude.'[27]

His sympathy for the Jews shows when he suggests that Muḥammad's failure to win their crucial recognition was a huge blow to him, making him plan to be rid of them.[28] Wensinck has also contributed a large number of articles to the *Shorter Encyclopaedia of Islam* covering various aspects of the Prophet's life and those of his family and Companions.

In the same period a German Jew using a Muslim pseudonym, Mohammad Essed Bey, wrote his *Mahomet* which was later translated from the French original into English under the title *Mohammed A Biography*.[29] This work can only be described as deficient in any scholarly methodology and, therefore, of little worth.[30]

Possibly the real limelight in the field was taken by Tor Andrae whose *Muḥammad, hans liv och hans tro* was published in Swedish.[31] This is an examination of Muḥammad from the perspective of the psychology of religion. In his Preface to the English edition, Menzeil writes: 'The study of Mohammed's life and work is advancing so rapidly that no apology is needed for publishing this excellent study. We have reached a stage where it is possible to approach his personality with a measure of understanding and balance impossible of attainment a few decades ago.'[32] In the Introduction, Andrae himself points out that some past amateurish writings looked at religions as entities without any real force behind them. In this way, the prophetic initiative of the main personality was played down and even, in some extreme cases, the very historicity of the Prophet doubted. He argues further that, 'The development of Islam – at least, as compared with the other religions – is open to the clear light of history . . .'[33] and therefore lends itself, most amenably, to any investigation.

Though he agrees with other Western writers that Muḥammad 'borrowed' from other than existing religious sects, he questions the extent to which this theory of lack of originality is sometimes carried. He states that '. . . it is cheap wisdom to think that this disposes of the question of Mohammed's originality'.[34] He emphasizes that all the 'borrowing' notwithstanding, Islam has a uniqueness which defies understanding from others. He explains that much of the causes for Western neglect of Muslim piety can be traced to ignorance or vestiges of the already debunked theories from the confrontation era of the Middle Ages. He says:

> The cause lies deeper, and may perhaps be expressed by the proverb: 'Relatives understand each other least of all'. A Christian sees much in Islam which reminds him of his own religion, but he sees it in an extremely distorted form. He finds ideas and statements of his own religion, but which, nevertheless, turn off into strangely different paths.[35]

Andrae, thus justifies the writing of this book, saying that there is a need for people to know more about Islam, and especially about the Prophet, because what they are used to is biased.

Some works of this period focused on the search for the origins of Islam. Many, of course, as Andrae points out, found the answer in Judaeo-Christian traditions. Indeed, he traces much of what the Prophet preached from Mani and other Gnostic sects of those days. He presumes that Muḥammad learned from these sects that Christịanity was just one of many groups around which had been graced with Divine guidance. Again, the Prophet, he argues, learnt that every people had had their own prophet. This, to Andrae, was the secret of the Prophet's vocation. He asserts that, 'To imagine that the revelation came first – and Mohammed's conception of his call was only an interpretation which had already occurred – does away with any possibility of explaining the matter psychologically.'[36]

Rodinson, on reflection on the subject, agrees with the argument that 'Islam was not born in a sealed container in an environment sterilized against the germs of other ideologies as contemporary Muslim authors and certain others frequently imagine.'[37] However, he also advises that the idea should be applied judiciously and not be allowed to run into excessiveness. Because, as he reasons, this theory contains the inherent danger of denying the fundamental originality of every tradition, including Islam. He further argues that there is this '. . . evident fact that a study of influence cannot fully explain the origin of a new ideological phenomenon or its own particular dynamism. One must never under any circumstances or in any area shun a structural analysis which takes into account the functional necessity of the new ideology'.[38]

In Andrae's concluding chapter on 'Mohammed's Personality' he points out that, 'The concepts of the period of Enlightenment permitted a more just estimate of Mohammed's personality.'[39] Despite this, the book carries some very medieval images of the Prophet. He mentions Muḥammad's 'craftiness and trickery', his slyness, and his moral weakness which made him give ' . . . free rein to his sensual impulses'.[40]

Samuel M. Zwemer, in his comments on the book, cites some such views which are critical of Muḥammad.[41] To Marmaduke Pickthall, Tor Andrae has '. . . two voices in his work, one suave and judicial, the other harsh and fanatical'.[42] He gives examples of such 'two-voice' methodology when he writes: 'He rules out the idea of deliberate imposture, yet on many pages he seems to write of the Qur'an as the work of the man Muhammad and even charges him with such manipulation of it as might as well be described as deliberate imposture.'[43]

Pickthall again refers to a statement from page 55 of the book which says: 'It is said that he was known by the epithet Al-Amin, "the reliable", *and even if this designation does not seem to express the most apparent trait of Mohammed's character*, it does show that he had an unusual power of inspiring confidence.'[44]

The reviewer cites several other examples with the result that the stated objectives of the book lose their significance and probably it becomes just another of those typical in the field of Orientalism. That is why, we can perhaps assume, Pickthall ends his review with the statement: 'The translator in his preface expresses with, perhaps, unconscious sarcasm a hope that the book will appeal, among others, to "adherents of Islam".'[45]

Following Tor Andrae, came Richard Bell's two-volume work *The Qur'ān – Translated with a Critical Rearrangement of the Sūrahs.*[46] As the title suggests, Bell sets out to rearrange the *sūrahs* of the Qur'ān, according to him, chronologically. As the author says in his Preface to the first volume: 'The main objective has been to understand the deliverances of Muhammad afresh, as far as possible in their historical setting, and therefore to get behind the traditional interpretation.'[47] Bell is of the opinion that because of their attachment to dogmatic beliefs Muslim commentators are sometimes not able to get to the bottom of things. His work is, therefore, meant to clear up some of the 'difficulties' as he sees them. He does however admit that he very often relies on his own presuppositions to resolve some seemingly knotty issues.[48] He even supplies words which are not there in the English,[49] and believes that the Qur'ān is a document produced by Muḥammad himself.

Bell's other major work, also on the Qur'ān, was published in 1953 and was supposed to be a companion volume to his translation of the Qur'ān.[50] In this latter work, he emphasizes that the central place the Qur'ān occupies in the general thought and life of a large section of the world's population makes it imperative that it be studied. This work is, therefore, not meant for specialists but rather for the general public. On Muḥammad, Bell believes that, 'All intimate questions regarding the prophet's personality, his inspiration, claim and purposes, can be answered only on the basis of study of the Qur'ān.'[51] This reasoning flows from his earlier opinion that Muḥammad was the author of the Qur'ān and, therefore, Bell views it as a sort of autobiography.[52]

William Montgomery Watt revised and enlarged this work in 1970 as part of the Islamic Survey Series.[53] Watt was one of Bell's students but he nevertheless sets out to examine his teacher's work critically. As he points out in the Foreword: 'The sincerest tribute to a scholar is to take his views seriously and criticize him frankly.'[54] He disagrees with Bell's notion that the Qur'ān was Muḥammad's own handiwork. He stresses:

> Courtesy and an eirenic outlook certainly now demand that we should not speak of the Qur'ān as the product of Muhammad's conscious mind; but I hold that the same demand is also made by sound scholarship. I have therefore altered or eliminated all expressions which implied that Muhammad was the author of the Qur'an, including those which spoke of his 'sources' or of the 'influences' on him.[55]

In a critical analysis of the book, S. Vahiduddin further points out that Bell's appreciation of the Qur'ān is typical of Western Orientalists' 'arid criticism'.[56] Looking at the prejudiced way in which some of these critical methodologies are applied when it comes to the Qur'ān or the Prophet, Vahiduddin states with regret that:

> Generally, the European scholars, who have undertaken a critical scrutiny of the Qur'an, seem to believe in God and in the possibility of divine communication but seem to deny it in the particular case of the prophet of Islam . . . They then try to understand the Qur'an by a psychological analysis of the prophet's life, by the historical situation and social environment in which he grew. Mr Bell, like others before and after him, is of this way of thinking.[57]

He seriously questions the methodology of finding Muḥammad outside himself and cites a statement purported to have been made by Hegel, that, 'The sun of the spirit is always new, . . .' continuing that ' . . . it is to be observed that every work of a genius, whether in religion or art or thought, is unique in its own way and cannot be understood by anything outside itself'.[58] Vahiduddin further advises that by judging the Prophet through our own lenses, we need also to ponder over the question whether the criteria we are using would stand up to all the rigours of testing as required in modern critical scholarship. If not, we would be reading ourselves into the Prophet.

In the decade which followed, worthy of mention is the doctoral thesis of J.C. Wilson submitted to the University of Edinburgh.[59] Perhaps the significance of this thesis lies in the fact that it was written in Edinburgh, the place where both Muir and Watt were professors and at a time when Richard Bell was also at that university.

In 1949, Gibb's *Mohammedanism* was published.[60] One of Gibb's essential objectives was to improve upon Margoliouth's work published under the same title in 1911. In essence, he argued that after 35 years, the time was ripe for a relook at the subject. He explains thus: 'Between one generation and the next, the bases of judgement necessarily suffer change. They are modified firstly in the material or scientific sense, by the discovery of new facts and the increase of understanding which results from the broadening and deepening of research.'[61] He also talks of what he calls '. . . the spiritual and imaginative sense',[62] pointing out that factual knowledge alone is not enough.

Gibb identifies two camps in the writings on Islam. The first group consists of Muslims, and basically produces apologetic literature in answer to Islam's critics. The second group, mainly comprised of Christian clergy, seek to project Islam and indeed Muḥammad as inferior. He explains that there is some element of prejudgement in both groups. In his work, he indicates an effort to steer clear of both groups.

He then writes that he tackles the subject with the fundamental thesis that '. . . Islam is an autonomous expression of religious thought and experience, which must be viewed in and through its own principles and standards . . .'[63] Together with this, he stresses: '. . . upon the ideals which it strives to realise than upon the failings of our common humanity'.[64]

Though only Chapters Two and Three might strictly be called relevant to our present work, these stated objectives are quite significant in the development of works on Muḥammad and Islam in the West.

Gibb looks at the confrontations the Prophet had with his enemies and defends him thus: 'It would . . . be a serious mistake to imagine that Mohammed's interest and attention during these years were given up solely to politics and war. On the contrary, the centre of all his preoccupations was the training, educating and disciplining of his community.'[65] He ends his discussion on Muḥammad with the following appreciative statement:

> For us, it goes without saying that the hold which Muhammad gained over the wills and affections of his companions was due to the influence of his personality. Without that they would have paid little heed to the claims of the prophet. It was because of his moral qualities, not because of his religious teaching, that the men of Medina invoked his assistance.[66]

William A. Polk's article on Gibb gives a glimpse of his capabilities. He describes Gibb's tenure at both Oxford and Harvard, his expertise in Oriental languages, history and culture and the holistic approach he used in his works. He then writes in the conclusion: '. . . Gibb must be reckoned as the last and perhaps the greatest of the true Orientalists, a man who rode nearly to the end of its most productive course that great wave of intellectual inquiry.'[67]

The Second Half of the Twentieth Century

The 1950s witnessed a new wave of biographies. The French work by Regis Blachère, though not yet rendered into English, deserves to be mentioned simply because of its reputation.[68]

According to Watt,[69] Blachère based his theory on the notion that the Qur'ān is the only reliable source for the biography of Muḥammad. Rodinson's comments on the book read as follows:

> It is clear, precise, and well thought out. Taking a mediating position between an uncritical view of the source and a hypercritical stance, and thoroughly steeped in the literature on the subject, Blachère underscores very clearly the serious problem presented by the sources viewed from a critical perspective. He regards the Qur'an as the only fully reliable source and utilizes biographical tradition with great caution.[70]

Geo Widengren published his *The Ascension of the Apostle and the Heavenly Book* in 1950,[71] followed in 1955 with *Muhammad the Apostle of God and His Ascension.* The latter is the second part of the former. The author states in his Preface to the 1955 publication that some Arabic material he was waiting for could not be obtained and that this resulted in some inconsistencies in the work. He further admits his lack of expertise in Arabic literature. He follows Tor Andrae's theory of Muḥammad, appropriating many of his ideas on revelation from Mani.[72]

In his deduction of Shī'ism and Sunnī Islam, Widengren concludes that just as it was in ancient Mesopotamia and other ancient kingdoms, the Prophet's ascent was necessary if he were to be invested with the desired authority. He explains:

> Thus within Islam two types of religion equally well known from the history of Christianity stand out clearly against each other: the institutional type, asserting the Revelation is brought once [and] for all in its definite form by a Divine Saviour, or by a prophet who is not to appear again until possibly at the end of time, and the other, the charismatic type, claiming that inspiration is carried on by means of visions from God, through the incarnation of God, or God's Light or Spirit, or of the Heavenly Apostle in new earthly representatives who together form a long

> chain of successive 'descents' of the same Divine Being, the Heavenly Apostle.[73]

Rodinson remarks: 'Widengren attempts to situate Muhammad in the framework of a typology of the Celestical messenger.'[74]

In 1953 and 1956 respectively, Watt published his definitive works on Muḥammad, *Muhammad at Mecca* and *Muhammad at Medina*. These were later abridged into a single volume, *Muhammad – Prophet and Statesman*, published in 1961. These works have had a considerable impact on English medium students of Islam. Again, since they form the main basis for this chapter, we will return to them later.

Alfred Guillaume's *The Life of Muhammad – Translation of Ibn Isḥāq's Sīrat Rasūl Allāh*[75] which appeared in 1955 deserves particular mention. In his Introduction, Guillaume concedes that, 'My predecessors in translating the Sira have made many mistakes and I cannot hope to have escaped all the pitfalls.'[76] The work itself is based on Ibn Hishām's recension, and has been heavily reviewed by both Muslim and non-Muslim scholars alike, some of whom deserve mention here.

One significant thing that Guillaume does in his book is to point out general Muslim scholarly opinion on the reputation of Ibn Isḥāq as a historian. This perception has largely been unfavourable. However, the general view of Western scholars is that Ibn Isḥāq's reputation is not impugned as such. Guillaume himself argues that since much of the criticism directed against Ibn Isḥāq relates to his work on *Sunan*, his biographical writings should not be affected.[77]

In his review of the book,[78] James Robson lauds Guillaume for the invaluable service he has performed for *Sīrah* scholarship by rendering Ibn Isḥāq's work into English. On Ibn Isḥāq himself, Robson says:

> While we may speak highly of him, his detractors vary in their opinion, some regarding him as an authority on biographical details but not on legal matters, others refusing

> to have anything to do with him. We are here interested in him as a biographer, and there is every reason to believe that he tried to be as accurate as possible.[79]

Robson then says of the translation itself that it is '. . . very good and very readable. . . . One is grateful for this accurate and attractive translation . . .'[80]

R.B. Serjeant, in his review,[81] describes the work as an outstanding piece, and a fitting memorial to Guillaume's position as Professor of Arabic at the University of London. After suggesting a number of changes in the rendering of certain Arabic expressions, Serjeant concludes rather appreciatively: 'The achievement of its author in presenting Muhammad to the English-speaking world with a sweet clarity unknown before, will be immediately recognized by scholars and writers as outstanding.'[82] Rodinson's estimation of the book is that despite the criticisms, which he considers minor, '. . . it is on the whole deserving of confidence'.[83]

A.L. Tibawi, on the other hand, writes a rather lengthy and near-dismissive critique of Guillaume's translation. He starts by saying that '. . . Professor Guillaume is not merely offering a translation of the received text of the biography of Muhammad, as recorded by Ibn Hishām from al-Bakkā'i, from Ibn Isḥāq. His work is a translation of his own reconstruction of Ibn Isḥāq.'[84]

He goes on to argue that the German rendering of Ibn Hishām by Weil (1864) and the earlier one by Wüstenfeld (1858–60) were much better and did not merit the criticisms meted out by Guillaume. He adds: 'The reviewer (and the reader) who is in a hurry need have no qualms: the translator has an established reputation; the book is well produced and has the imprimatur of a famous publishing house. But if he has time for close examination, comparison, and check, he will find that this translation raises more problems than it solves.'[85]

Tibawi questions the propriety in Guillaume's methods of reconstruction, omission, conjecture, abbreviation and addition, citing a number of cases. These, he argues, have greatly affected the quality of the translation and has possibly resulted in the '. . . dismemberment of Ibn Hishām and the adulteration of Ibn Isḥāq'.[86] He goes on to catalogue a number of minor mistakes in the translation of certain Arabic expressions but explains that the cumulative effect of the same gives grounds for serious concern.[87]

He expresses dissatisfaction with, what he believes to be, the lack of detailed estimation of Ibn Isḥāq as a historian. Furthermore, he argues that, 'Any detailed study of the Sīra – and one cannot translate it scientifically without such a study – should yield new information or throw fresh light upon early Muslim historiography.'[88]

None of these is obviously found in the work. Tibawi accuses Guillaume of not making a clear distinction between the usage of 'Allah' in pre-Islamic belief and its Islamic meaning. Citing examples from the translation, he rightly indicates that this could lead to a serious misconception.[89] He ends the critique with this rather harsh judgement: 'The specialist would no doubt make his own assessment; but to the general reader, and in particular the student of comparative religion, a word of warning is absolutely essential. As it stands, Professor Guillaume's translation cannot be accepted as a reliable reproduction of the received Arabic text of the Sīra.'[90]

Guillaume, in the previous year (1954), published his other work entitled *Islam*[91] which was supposed to present the essence of the teachings of the Prophet to the Western reader. In this book, the second, third and fifth chapters, respectively dubbed 'Muḥammad', 'The Qur'ān' and 'Apostolic Tradition', are of some significance to this general survey. In his opening statements on the chapter on Muḥammad, Guillaume declares:

> In writing of a man who is loved and venerated by millions of the world's citizens today, one would wish to be purely objective so far as the greatest monument to Muhammad's memory – the Qur'an – is concerned, that is not difficult;

> but his biography is much more difficult to deal with. To translate without comments the statements of his biographers without historical criticism would be misleading; on the other hand, to generalize as some Western scholars have done would be rash.[92]

This sets the tone for appreciating the enormity of the strain the Western non-Muslim scholar has to undergo in handling Islamic material. Perhaps this is also true of all scholars who deal with religious material of faiths they do not profess.

Though Guillaume repudiates some of the old theories about Muḥammad, such as the one of epilepsy, he sticks to the traditional Orientalist argument that he fell under the heavy influence of the religious environment of the day. He asserts that since not much is known of Muḥammad's life between the period of his marriage and that of his call, he might have learned some of his beliefs from Jews and Christians.[93]

Hasan Karmi reviews this book and points out some controversial issues that Guillaume raises.[94] He takes issue with the author on his interpretation of some *Ḥajj* rituals as heathen practices and also his comments on confrontations with the Jews as not expected '. . . from one who comes with a message from the Compassionate and Merciful'.[95] The general perception of the reviewer, therefore, is that Guillaume has misrepresented much of the material concerning the Prophet, the Qur'ān and Islam in general.

In the same decade, Kenneth Cragg wrote his *The Call of the Minaret*.[96] Even though it has only a chapter which directly relates to the field currently under discussion, its general tone makes it worthy of mention. Cragg's focus was mainly on Christian-Muslim Relations, and this major work focuses on the *adhān*, seeking to unearth '. . . the clue to Islam, and from that clue to learn the form and dimension of Christian relation to what it tells . . .'[97]

The 1986 edition contains additional material to take care of some contemporary changes in religious history since the

1950s, when the original work was published. Despite his stated efforts to present Islam as it could be gleaned from the *adhān*, the author seems to have been caught in the same web as earlier Western Christian writers. He has a particularly emotive sympathy for the Jews and portrays Muḥammad as perhaps a callous man who dispossesses the weak to enrich his followers. A typical example is his comment on the Banū Qurayẓah, where he writes: 'There followed the massacre of the Banu Qurayzah which marks the darkest depth of Muslim policy, a depth which palliatives suggested by some modern Muslim historians fail to measure.'[98]

Muhammad Hamidullah also reviewed the original edition *in extenso.*[99] He is of the opinion that despite the charming methodology, Cragg's book '. . . gives a new look to Christian polemics against Islam, and presents a sugar-coated pill'.[100] He accuses Cragg of displaying an underlying thesis of the superiority of Christianity over Islam. He therefore invites Muslims to read the book '. . . if they wish to be up to date regarding the contemporary methods of Christian Missions'.[101]

Cragg has written quite vigorously on Islam and his other major work relevant to this study is *Muhammad and the Christian – A Question of Response.*[102] This work is supposed to be a reaction to a consistent Muslim call for Christian appreciation, and indeed acceptance of Muḥammad, ostensibly reciprocating Muslim acceptance of Jesus. It is therefore meant to educate the Christian as to how to respond to such Muslim desire. As he himself says in the Preface: 'It is the aim of this study to offer at least one Christian's view of a resolution of the problem, a resolution which, no more than tentative, remains loyal to Christian criteria while outlining a positive response to Muhammad.'[103] The author picks upon one central issue which, he argues, keeps the intransigence between Muslims and Christians alive. It has to do with the question of prophethood. He points out that, to Christians, it was something of an affront for Muḥammad to claim to supersede the finality of the person of Jesus which he believed and trusted in so much.

Hermansen, in his review of the book, has this to say:

> . . . the Muslim reader may be disturbed by Cragg's recurrent hints that it would be preferable for Muslims to have a more Christ-like appreciation of Muhammad (p.79). Cragg's work has in the past been criticised by Islamicists and Historians of Religion for 'Christianizing' Islam by making comparisons which misrepresent the insider's view. This trend is not absent in the present work, . . .[104]

A typical example is when Cragg looks at some Muslim salutations on the Prophet and suggests that there is an intrinsic meaning of the 'sonship' of Muḥammad to God. He likens it to the New Testament declaration: 'This is my Son, My Beloved, hear him.'[105]

The 1960s saw another 'fruitful' decade of writings on Islam in general and on Muḥammad in particular. In 1960, Norman Daniel's voluminous *Islam and the West – The Making of an Image* was published.[106] This work, revised in 1993, is a compendium and critique of attempts by mainly Christian writers to shape public opinion on Muḥammad through some derisory writings. The author passed away not long before the revised edition went to press. In the blurb on the jacket of the new edition we read the following commendations. F.J. Ziadeh says: 'No scholar of Islam can afford to miss it.' Sir Hamilton Gibb describes it as a 'Masterly analysis', and J. Kritzeck sees it as an '. . . excellent book . . . now the indispensable work on the subject'. He further says, it is 'Wonderfully learned, beautifully written.'

Daniel presents a myriad of medieval invectives against Muḥammad and points out that a 'communal opinion' has been built in the Western non-Muslim consciousness about the Prophet which is difficult to excise.[107] He does, however, suggest that contemporary Orientalists have somehow moved away from the ignorance and prejudice of their medieval predecessors.

Anees and Athar, in their partly annotated bibliographical

work call this '. . . an unsuccessful attempt to absolve the modern Orientalists of their prejudice against Islam'.[108]

M.M. Ahsan, in his review of the work points out that Daniel's opinion is true only '. . . in the sense that the naked malice of the attack on Islam, characteristic of the academic and pseudo-academic writings of the medieval period, has somehow worn away. But to claim that hostility to Islam has ceased is an over-simplification or perhaps misrepresentation of the fact'.[109]

In 1961, P.S.R. Payne's *The Holy Sword – The Story of Islam from Muhammad to the Present*[110] appeared. The title of the book perhaps offers a clue to the author's hidden agenda. Michael Edwarde's *The Life of Muhammad, Apostle of Allah* followed in 1964.[111] This is described by Anees and Athar as, 'Based on selections from Ibn Isḥāq's Sīrat Rasūl Allāh.'[112]

1967 saw the re-issued edition of C.C. Torrey's *The Jewish Foundation of Islam* originally published in 1933.[113] The work is a compilation of five lectures delivered as part of The Hilda Stich Stroock Lecture Series. It mainly uses a reductionist methodology where the origin of 'Muḥammad's ideas' are traced to Judaism. The objective was primarily to refute the then ongoing general opinion that Islam was founded on Christian principles, a theory that Julius Wellhausen, Tor Andrae, Karl Ahrens and others tried to propagate. Torrey, like Bell and others, sees Muḥammad as the author of the Qur'ān. To reinforce this assumption, he has to forcefully deny the fact that Muḥammad was not formally educated. The reasoning being that if he was not formally educated, how could anyone attribute authorship of the Qur'ān to him? So he needs to be educated to fit the thesis. He writes in the 1933 edition that, 'The Orthodox Muslim dogma that Muhammad was an unschooled man is utterly untenable, though even the most recent treatises continue to give it some credence.'[114] He continues that Muḥammad '. . . was at all times sincere, never doubting that the self-hypnotism which he had learned to produce, and which he continued to practise at critical times, brought him a divine revelation'.[115]

In a well-written Introduction to the 1967 edition, Franz Rosenthal describes the academic arrogance often associated with Torrey. He criticizes Torrey for making assertions which are difficult to sustain in a scholarly manner. For example, he writes: 'It is unmistakable that an approach concerned primarily with attempts to demonstrate dependence on earlier stages of the historical process is no longer able to command the loyalty of historians and is considered by many rather elementary or even primitive.'[116] He ends the piece thus: 'Torrey's work contains a good deal that is debatable or even wrong. It may no longer be within the mainstream of Islamic Research, and many of today's Islamists may be unresponsive to its approach and its technique.'[117]

E.R. Pike's *Mohammed – Prophet and the Religion of Islam*, originally published in New York in 1962, was re-issued in London in 1968.[118] Finally, the work of Francesco Gabrieli, originally in Italian, and which appeared in 1968, also needs to be mentioned as an attempt at a balanced historical account of Muḥammad and the spread of Islam.[119]

During the 1970s, the major works perhaps begin with John Bagot Glubb's *The Life and Times of Muhammad*[120] which carries a detailed discussion on the *sunnah*.

The French work of Maxime Rodinson, translated into English by Anne Carter, appeared in 1971.[121] An academically well-written book by a Jewish-Marxist author, it seeks to present a sociological analysis of the life of the Prophet. His subsequent writings have always elicited scholarly interest and attention.

In this major book on the Prophet, Rodinson states that he took up certain issues which he felt had not been considered sufficiently enough. He writes that his objective was:

> . . . to show the relationship between the eschatological visions of the early preachings of Muhammad and the international political situation of that period. Taking the sociological correlations of his preachings as established (notably by Watt), . . . to show how a personal, psychological evolution shaped Muhammad into an

> instrument capable of formulating and communicating an ideology that correspond[ed] to the needs of the time and the milieu.[122]

Rodinson's work carries evidence of his Marxist leanings. He yearns for an interpretation of Muḥammad and Islam through a '. . . historiography freed from the chains of theology'.[123] Though he is cautious about the psychoanalytic explanation of the personality of Muḥammad as advocated by scholars like the Frenchman Regis Blachère, the Finn Harri Holman and the Swede Tor Andrae, Rodinson recommends that scholars '. . . should go beyond the purely religious sphere and give a total explanation to this exceptional personality'.[124] His comments on the development of *aḥādīth* put so much emphasis on the role played by political interests, individual curiosity and piety that the reader senses his rejection of the whole package. He asserts that though scholars tried to sift the myriad of reports, '. . . they made no claims to any degree of certainty. Instead, they were content to repeat contradictory traditions on the same subject, one after the other, quoting their sources for each. It was up to the reader to decide which one he liked to believe'.[125]

His analysis of the battles the Prophet and his people were involved in and other minor confrontations in Madīnah betrays where Rodinson's sympathy lies. The Jews are portrayed as innocent people who happened to be at the wrong place at the wrong time, and in each case their fate had already been decided before the incident which finally brought either their expulsion or execution.[126]

The 1980s onwards saw an increase in the writings on Islam but mainly in the area of Inter-Faith relations and other fields of Islam.

On the Prophet, perhaps mention should be made of the work edited and translated by Merlin L. Swartz.[127] The most significant paper here is the lengthy 'A Critical Survey of Modern Studies on Muhammad' by Rodinson of which we have made extensive use.

Michael Cook's *Muhammad* was published in 1983.[128] It is important to point out that it is this same Cook, who together with Patricia Crone wrote *Hagarism: The Making of the Islamic World* (in 1977).[129] This latter work which follows a reductionist methodology, does not see any originality in Islam and indeed in Muḥammad. In fact, Anees and Athar describe it as, 'Relying on documents of questionable authority coupled with gross aberrations of style, . . . It is a mockery of scholarship that set[s] out to show that the Muslim concepts of revelation and prophethood were born in the Judaic cradle.'[130]

M.D. Valimamed in his review of this joint publication also seriously questions the authors' central argument and the methodology they applied. He writes:

> On points of historical methodology, one wonders how the authors are justified in using circumstantially tenuous tracts, putting them together and inferring from these documents conclusions to back a passionate thesis which is clearly untenable? In all seriousness, how can one use the following to substantiate that the tradition of prophethood in Islam is actually a botched stem from the Judaic Messianic glory: a tenuously dated and located anti-Jewish tract, the 'Doctrine of Iacobi', an eschatological document written by a rabbi probably in the eighth century; the propensity of Jews to announce the coming of the Messiah as a man dressed in Arab garbs (apparently a tradition that was found socially more acceptable amongst the Jews at the time); and an Armenian opus which is chronologically questionable?[131]

With all this, one would naturally not expect Michael Cook to veer too far away from this central philosophy in *Hagarism* in this subsequent biographical work on Muḥammad.

H.T. Norris, also reviewing the book, criticizes Cook for forcing certain conclusions, especially about the origins of Islam. However, he ends by saying that the book '. . . provides a fresh gust of air through the windows of a library of musty books on the subject. Many such books are little more than sanctimonious apologia. This life of Muhammad can hardly be counted amongst their number'.[132]

Cook offers a questionable analysis of the Prophet's life. His interpretations of the Prophet's marriages, the status of women in Islam, the so-called 'Satanic Verses' and the encounters with the Quraysh and others are seriously flawed. He gives the impression that Muslim scholars are not to be trusted and, therefore, he offers them no room at all in the book.

Anees and Athar see the book as a '. . . biased, hostile writing about the Sira and Islam'.[133]

A.W. Boase, in his review of the book describes it in rather scathing words. He writes: '. . . Michael Cook exhibits great hostility and prejudice for the man Muhammad (peace and blessings be upon him) and the doctrines of Islam . . . This is surely a very biased, atheist-tinted vision of Islam.'[134]

It is within this morass of intellectual (and sometimes otherwise) perspectives of the Prophet that William Montgomery Watt falls, and given this scenario, we might well be able to appreciate the works of Watt and other contemporary writers that much better.

We therefore discuss Watt's works with the conviction that no scholar falls into a vacuum. His place in a particular historical, environmental, intellectual and any other context is bound to be of significant interest to the student who undertakes to study him and critique his views.

The Choice of Watt

From the foregoing rather cursory survey of twentieth-century literature on Muḥammad, it is obvious that many authors treated the subject not as an area of substantial interest but as an ancillary issue. Even in cases where they have specifically written biographical material, either their previous or subsequent works indicate a general interest in Islam and the life of Muḥammad as part of this wider interest.

Among twentieth-century British scholars of Islam, William Montgomery Watt stands out as the most prolific writer on Muḥammad.

Despite the general condemnation of the works of Western non-Muslim scholars by Muslims, especially in the field of *Sīrah* scholarship, Watt has received some fairly appreciative comments. Of the Western Orientalist school, he is perhaps the most respected.

In the Foreword to Watt's book *Islam and Christianity Today*, Shaikh Ahmed Zaki Yamani alludes to Watt's eminence among British, and generally, English-speaking scholars on Islam. Shaikh Yamani says:

> Professor Watt has done much in the effort to free the Western mentality of the shackles of prejudice and hatred that originated in the hostilities of medieval times and that have for so long blinded the Western world to the merit of trying to understand Islam. In spite of the phenomenal difficulties inherent in attempting to reconcile positions that are generally regarded as irreconcilable he has achieved a high level of open-mindedness.[135]

He continues that Watt shows '. . . aspirations to the highest degrees of objectivity . . .',[136] which become evident in some of his statements.

Again, in his review of the same book, 'Alī Qulī al-Qarā'ī the editor of *Al-Tawhid* describes Watt as '. . . one of the leading living Orientalists, who has written and compiled a large number of books on various aspects of Islam, Muslim history and Islamic thought'.[137] He also points out that Watt has a sympathetic regard and respect for Islam.[138] He sees Islam as the ground for Watt's expertise and Watt as having a more balanced attitude to Islam than most of his contemporaries.

Antonie Wessels also says of Watt: 'In our days, of course,

there are very profound and respectable accounts of Muhammad's life (by "Westerners") like the two volumed one by W.M. Watt, *Muhammad at Mecca* and *Muhammad at Medina*, which have been translated into Arabic.'[139]

'Imāduddīn Khalīl in his critical study of Watt's thought, speaks of him favourably. He states: 'Unlike the authors of his era he is the first who rendered it necessary to maintain the respect and impartiality while writing about the unseen foundations in the background of the facts and events of the prophet's life.'[140] He then offers evidence of Watt's impartiality. He cites Watt's statement in the Introduction to his *Muhammad at Mecca* in which Watt states that he has tried to be as respectful and impartial as possible. Khalīl continues, giving assurances to his Muslim readers that:

> I have endeavoured, while remaining faithful to the standards of Western historical scholarship, to say nothing that would entail rejection of any of the fundamental doctrines of Islam. There need be no unbridgeable gulf between Western scholarship and Islamic faith; if some of the conclusions of Western scholars have been unacceptable to Muslims, it may be that the scholars have not always been faithful to their own principles of scholarship and that, even from the purely historical point of view, their conclusion requires to be revised.[141]

Khurshid Ahmad, in his *Islam and the West* puts Watt among those who, in this age, have endeavoured to change the attitude of Western scholarship on Islam. He sees Watt as being somewhat dispassionate and sympathetic.[142]

A.L. Tibawi, reviewing Watt's *Muhammad – Prophet and Statesman* censures many a Western scholar for their often hypercritical stance usually using standards which could end up giving the wrong impressions about Islam and especially the Prophet. However, he sees in Watt's contributions '. . . an honest attempt to redress the balance'.[143] He further says of

Watt: 'His command of the facts and his imaginative reconstruction of events is admirable, . . .'[144]

Watt's place in contemporary English-speaking Orientalists' scholarship on the *sīrah* is further boosted by Syed Ali Raza Naqvi, who describes him as, 'One of the most prominent modern biographers of the holy prophet, . . .'[145] Considering that this statement, together with others which see Watt as rebutting the harsh criticisms of his fellow Western writers, was made in a paper read at the National Seerat Conference held at Islamabad, it demonstrates the regard in which Watt is held among some Muslim scholars.[146]

Khurram Murad also places Watt among the top scholars in the field. He says: 'Watt is a sort of doyen of that "new" school of orientalist thought to have been kind enough to lend a sympathetic ear and pen to Islam. He is also aware of the serious difficulties he faces as an heir of a "deep-seated prejudice" from which, he frankly admits, "we are not yet wholly freed" . . .'[147]

In another review of *What is Islam?*, A.S. Bazmee Ansari despite his critical remarks, admires Watt's openness, and honesty in pointing out the problems a non-Muslim Western scholar faces in the field of Islamic Studies.[148]

Watt's discerning scholarship is also referred to by Muhammad Benaboud, in his review of the *festschrift, Islam: Past Influence and Present Challenge.*[149] Benaboud describes Watt as someone who has '. . . contributed so positively to the field of Orientalism . . .'[150] In a rather lengthy but very appreciative comment, he says that:

> W.M. Watt stands out as a scholar by the high intellectual calibre of his numerous books . . . his attitude towards the Easterners he studies and those he contacts is different from that of many of his colleagues. Given his background, training and general orientation, his (*sic*) is an Orientalist by definition. Yet he has been able to overcome the cultural arrogance that has for so long been widespread among

> Western Orientalists and to which Easterners are so sensitive. The Easterners are not offended by his criticism which is sometimes quite sharp in substance, but never in form because he is equally critical of the West. This explains his credibility. Furthermore, it is difficult to detect any sense of evil motivation behind his criticism, because he usually criticises to improve and construct.[151]

Benaboud sees Watt as a scholar who accepts criticism with forebearance, and asserts that, 'As an orientalist, he respects the Islamic Culture and is in turn respected by Muslim scholars.'[152]

Also in the book in question, Josef Van Ess in his tribute, explains Watt's capabilities and his methodology. He points out that Watt shows:

> . . . the ability to understand a culture on the level it deserves, by comparing its ideals with our ideals and its deficiencies with ours, without confusing both things in a hasty, even worse, polemical way . . . Through his books, the Europeans – and Christians – have learnt that there are values and modes of life equivalent to theirs, similar in origin and intention, though dissimilar in their individual realization, and the Muslims have felt understood without being unduly flattered.[153]

Valerie J. Hoffman-Ladd states that Watt is a '. . . well-known Edinburgh scholar of Arabic and Islamic Studies who, in a long and distinguished career, has contributed many original works that have become part of the core literature in Western scholarship on Islam'.[154]

Andrew Rippin adds to the long list of appreciative comments on Watt in his review of one of Watt's latest publications, *Early Islam – Collected Articles*. He affirms:

> There can be no doubt about William Montgomery Watt's contribution to our field of study. Many of us remember

> very well the role Watt's writings played in our postgraduate years and it would be churlish not to acknowledge the debt which we owe to this scholar. His works will continue to be significant, will continue to be studied, and, indeed, continue to be refuted where necessary.[155]

Maxime Rodinson also praises Watt's scholarship. Commenting on Watt's book *Muhammad at Mecca*, Rodinson states:

> The clear and direct way in which he formulates his conclusions on the various events of the prophet's life, the confident fashion in which he employs his conclusions, has appeared to some to indicate an exaggerated confidence in the reliability of these latter. But above all, he is the first one in a very long time to pose the problem of the success of Muhammad's preaching by going beyond the history of religions' viewpoint to which Orientalists, since the trenchant response of Snouck Hurgronje to the simplistic theses of Grimme regarding the purely 'socialist' character of this preaching, have clung.[156]

The foregoing shows Watt's prominence, the respect in which he is held by contemporary English-speaking Western scholars of Islam, and that his work evokes special interest.

Notes

1. *Annali dell' Islam* (1905–26).

2. M. Rodinson, 'A Critical Survey of Modern Studies on Muhammad', in Merlin L. Swartz (trans.), *Studies on Islam* (1981), p.23.

3. Rodinson, 'A Critical Survey', p.23.

4. *Ibid.*, p.23.

5. *Ibid.*, p.24.

6. *Ibid.*

7. London: Sands & Company, 1912.

8. London: The Christian Literature Society for India, 1913.

9. *Ibid.*, pp.173–4.

10. See *Joshua* 5: 13 – 6: 27.

11. Sell, *The Life*, pp.231–2.

12. *Mahomet – The Founder of Islam* (1915).

13. Munawar Ahmad Anees and Alia Athar, *Guide to Sira and Hadith Literature in Western Languages* (1986), Item No. 315, p.40.

14. Translated from the French by E. Denison Ross (1929).

15. Rodinson, 'A Critical Survey', p.26.

16. *Ibid.*, p.26.

17. *Ibid.*

18. *Ibid.*, p.62, note 16.

19. *Ibid.*, p.27.

20. London, 1926.

21. *Das Leben Muhammeds*, translated from the Danish original by H.H. Schaeder (1930).

22. Rodinson, 'A Critical Survey', p.27.

23. *Ibid.*

24. It was published under the English title *The Life of Mahomet.*

25. London: Edinburgh House Press, 1932.

26. New York: Macmillan Company, 1932.

27. *Ibid.*, p.17.

28. *Ibid.*, p.18. See also his *Muhammad and the Jews of Madina* with an Excursus *Muhammad's Constitution of Madina* by Julius Wellhausen. Translated and edited by Wolfgang Behn (1975).

29. French original in Paris in 1934, the English translation in 1936.

30. Rodinson, 'A Critical Survey', p.62, note 19.

31. The original was published in Stockholm in 1930. The English edition, *Mohammed – The Man and His Faith*, was translated by Theophil Menzeil and published by Allen & Unwin, London in 1936.

32. *Ibid.*, Preface, p.5.

33. *Ibid.*, p.10.

34. *Ibid.*, p.11.

35. *Ibid.*, p.12.

36. *Ibid.*, p.149. See also Ch. 4 on 'Muhammad's Doctrine of Revelation'.

37. Rodinson, 'A Critical Survey', p.25.

38. *Ibid.*

39. Tor Andrae, *Mohammed*, p.243.

40. *Ibid.*, p.265. See also pp.256–69.

41. See his 'Tor Andrae's Mohammed', *MW*, Vol. 26, No. 3 (July 1936), pp.217–21.

42. Book Review of *Mohammed: The Man and His Faith*, in *Islamic Culture*, Vol. 11, No. 1 (January 1937), p.150.

43. *Ibid.*, see pp.59–65 of Tor Andrae's text.

44. *Ibid.* The italics belong to the reviewer – Pickthall.

45. *Ibid.*, p.154.

46. Edinburgh: T. & T. Clark, 2 vols. (1937–39).

47. *Ibid.*, p.v.

48. *Ibid.*

49. *Ibid.*, pp.vii–viii.

50. *Introduction to the Qur'ān* (1953).

51. *Ibid.*

52. See his *The Qur'ān*, p.vi; and his articles: 'The Development of Mohammed's Personality', *MW*, Vol. 4, No. 4 (October 1914), pp.353–64; and 'Muhammad's Visions', *MW*, Vol. 24, No. 2 (April 1934), pp.145–54; see also F.H. Foster, 'An Autobiography of Mohammed', *MW*, Vol. 26, No. 2 (April 1936), pp.130–52.

53. Bell's *Introduction to the Qur'ān* (1970), (reprinted 1990). Islamic Surveys – 8.

54. *Ibid.*, p.v.

55. *Ibid.*, p.vi.

56. 'Richard Bell's Study of the Qur'an: A Critical Analysis', *IC*, Vol. 30, No. 3 (July 1956), pp.263–72; see p.263.

57. *Ibid.*, p.264.

58. *Ibid.*, p.272.

59. *Muhammad's Prophetic Office as Portrayed in the Qur'ān*, Ph.D. Thesis, Edinburgh University, 1949.

60. H.A.R. Gibb, *Mohammedanism – An Historical Survey* (1949).

61. *Ibid.*, Preface, p.v.

62. *Ibid.*

63. *Ibid.*, p.vii.

64. *Ibid.*

65. *Ibid.*, p.30.

66. *Ibid.*, pp.33–4.

67. 'Islam and the West – Sir Hamilton Gibb Between Orientalism and History', *IJMES*, 6 (1975), pp.131–9; see p.139.

68. Regis Blachère, *Le Probleme de Mahomet, Essai de biographie Critique du fondateur de l'Islam* (1952).

69. W.M. Watt, Bell's *Introduction to the Qur'ān;* see p.177.

70. Rodinson, 'A Critical Survey', p.46. Bell used the same argument in his *Introduction to the Qur'ān*; see note 50 above. See also the articles in note 52.

71. Uppsala, Sweden A–B, Lundequistska Bokhandeln, 1950.

72. Tor Andrae, *Mohammed*, Ch. 4.

73. *Muhammad, The Apostle of God and His Ascension*, pp.215–16.

74. Rodinson, 'A Critical Survey', p.54.

75. Oxford: Oxford University Press, 1955.

76. *Ibid.*, p.xli.

77. *Ibid.*, p.xxxiv.

78. *MW*, Vol. 46, No. 3 (July 1956), pp.272–3.

79. *Ibid.*, p.272.

80. *Ibid.*, p.273.

81. *Bulletin of the School of Oriental and African Studies*, 21, Pt. 1 (1958), pp.1–14.

82. *Ibid.*, p.14.

83. Rodinson, 'A Critical Survey', p.45.

84. 'Ibn Isḥāq's Sīra, A Critique of Guillaume's Translation (The Life of Muhammad)', *IQ*, Vol. 3, No. 3 (October 1956), (pp.196–214), p.197.

85. *Ibid.*, p.198.

86. *Ibid.*, p.199.

87. *Ibid.*, pp.200–6 for the examples which Tibawi enumerates.

88. *Ibid.*, p.207.

89. *Ibid.*, pp.211–12. See Guillaume's translation, pp.49, 51 and 68 for examples.

90. Tibawi, 'A Critique of Guillaume's Translation', p.214.

91. Harmondsworth, Middlesex: Penguin Books, 1954.

92. *Ibid.*, p.20.

93. *Ibid.*, p.30.

94. *IQ*, Vol. 2, No. 1 (April 1955), pp.61–5.

95. Guillaume, *Islam*, p.48. See also Hasan Karmi's Review, p.62 ff.

96. Published originally in New York by Oxford University Press, 1956. Several editions of this book were issued and this is indicative of the interest it caused. For example: Reprinted in 1964 as a Galaxy Book by Oxford University Press; Second Revised Edition published by Orbis Books, 1985; and William Collins & Sons published another edition in 1986.

97. *Ibid.*, p.viii.

98. *Ibid.*, p.87 (1956 original). The statement survives in the 1986 edition.

99. *IQ*, Vol. 3, No. 4 (January 1957), pp.245–9.

100. *Ibid.*, p.245.

101. *Ibid.*, p.249.

102. London: Darton, Longman & Todd, 1984. His other works include: *The Event of the Qur'ān* (London: Allen & Unwin, 1971); *The Mind of the Qur'ān* (London: Allen & Unwin, 1973); *The Wisdom of the Sūfīs* (London: Sheldon, 1974); *This Year in Jerusalem* (London: Darton, Longman & Todd, 1982); *Readings in the Qur'ān* (London: Collins, 1988); and *Troubled by Truth – Life Studies in Interfaith Concern* (Edinburgh, Durham etc.: The Pentland Press, 1992).

103. *Muhammad and the Christian*, p.ix.

104. M.K. Hermansen, 'Kenneth Cragg, *Muhammad and the Christian*' (Maryknoll, NY: Orbis Books, 1984), *AJISS*, Vol. 2, No. 1 (July 1985), p.131.

105. *Muhammad and the Christian*, p.65. See *Matthew* 17: 5; also 3: 17 and *Mark* 9: 7.

106. Edinburgh: Edinburgh University Press, 1960.

107. *Ibid.*, see Ch. 9 entitled 'The Establishment of Communal Opinion'.

108. Anees and Athar, *Guide to Sira*, Item No. 1574, p.179.

109. *MWBR*, Vol. 1, No. 3 (Spring 1981), p.53.

110. London: Robert Hall, 1961.

111. London: The Folio Society, 1964.

112. Anees and Athar, *Guide to Sira*, Item No. 923, p.104.

113. New York: KTAV Publishing House, 1967. The 1993 original was also from New York published by the Jewish Institute of Religion Press.

114. *Ibid.*, Preface, p.v.

115. *Ibid.*

116. *Ibid.*, p.xv.

117. *Ibid.*, p.xxii.

118. London: Weidenfeld & Nicolson, 1968. Originally published as *Mohammed – Founder of the Religion of Islam* (New York: Roy Publishers, 1962).

119. *Muhammad and the Conquests of Islam*, translated from the Italian by Virginia Luling and Rosamund Linelli (London: Weidenfeld & Nicolson, 1968), esp. Chs. 1–5.

120. London: Hodder & Stoughton, 1970.

121. *Mohammed* (1971).

122. Rodinson, 'A Critical Survey', in: Swartz, *Studies on Islam*, p.50.

123. *Ibid.*, p.51. How this methodology could still leave 'Muḥammad the Prophet' intact is something that might puzzle the student of theology and even history.

124. *Ibid.*, p.53.

125. *Mohammed*, p.43.

126. *Ibid.*, see Ch. 5, characteristically entitled 'The Prophet in Arms'.

127. *Studies on Islam.*

128. Oxford: Oxford University Press.

129. Cambridge: Cambridge University Press, 1977. We point this out because of the disparaging reviews this joint publication received.

130. Anees and Athar, *Guide to Sira*, Item No. 1655.

131. *MWBR*, Vol. 1, No. 2 (Winter 1981), pp.7–8.

132. *BSOAS*, Vol. 48, Pt. 1 (1985), p.131.

133. Anees and Athar, *Guide to Sira*, Item No. 305, p.39.

134. *MWBR*, Vol. 4, No. 3 (1984), pp.6–7.

135. *Islam and Christianity Today* (1983), p.ix.

136. *Ibid.*

137. *Al-Tawhid*, Vol. 11, No. 3, p.136, footnote.

138. *Ibid.*

139. 'Modern Biographies of the Life of the Prophet Muḥammad in Arabic', *IC*, Vol. 49, No. 2 (April 1975), (pp.99–105), p.99.

140. See his five-part article entitled 'Maqālāt Sīrat Nabawī Awr Mustashriqīn Montgomery Watt Kā Afkār Kā Tanqīdī Jā'izah' (Urdu), in *Sīrat Nabawī Awr Mustashriqīn* (August 1987), p.90.

141. p.x.

142. Lahore: Islamic Publications, 1979, 4th. Edition; see p.18.

143. Review in *IQ*, Vol. 6, Nos. 3/4 (July/October 1961), (pp.127–8), p.127.

144. *Ibid.*

145. 'Prophet Muhammad's Image in Western Enlightened Scholarship' (A paper read at the National Seerat Conference held in Islamabad, 19–20 January 1981), *IS*, Vol. 20, No. 2 (Summer 1981), (pp.137–51), p.147.

146. *Ibid.*, p.148.

147. Review of Watt's *What is Islam?*, *MWBR*, Vol. 1, No. 3 (Spring 1981), (pp.3–9), p.5.

148. *HI*, Vol. 4, No. 3 (Autumn 1981), pp.91–7.

149. Alford T. Welch and Pierre Cachia (eds.), (Edinburgh: Edinburgh University Press, 1979).

150. *IQ*, Vol. 26, No. 1 (First Quarter 1982), (pp.56–7), p.56.

151. *Ibid.*

152. *Ibid.*, p.57.

153. Welch and Cachia (eds.), *Islam – Past Influence*, p.xiii.

154. Review of Watt's *Islamic Fundamentalism and Modernity*, *IJMES*, Vol. 23, No. 3 (August 1991), (pp.414–17), p.414.

155. Review in *BSOAS*, Vol. 55, Pt. 1 (1992) (pp.195–6), p.196.

156. 'A Critical Survey of Modern Studies on Muhammad', in Swartz, (trans. and ed.), *Studies on Islam*, p.46.

CHAPTER FIVE

W. Montgomery Watt

Watt's Intellectual Biography

Since there is no detailed biographical publication on Watt, much of his personal background material is derived from a private interview with Watt at his home in Dalkeith, Midlothian, Scotland in June 1990; further information is taken from a questionnaire sent him in May 1994. Perhaps the only published information on Watt appears in the 1993 edition of *Who's Who.*[1]

William Montgomery Watt was born on 14 March 1909 in Ceres, Fife, Scotland. He was the only child of Andrew and Jean Watt. His father, a Presbyterian minister, passed away when Watt was only a year old. His mother, whose maiden name was MacDonald, is described by Watt in our interview as a truly religious person. He does not say to which Christian denomination she belonged but from Andrew Watt's position as a Presbyterian minister one could conclude that she too was a Presbyterian. Watt had his secondary education at George Watson's College, Edinburgh and then went on to Edinburgh University. He continued his education at Balliol College, Oxford and later at the University of Jena in Germany. He holds the degrees of MA, Ph.D (Edinburgh), and MA, B.Litt (Oxon.). His academic career began at Edinburgh University, where he was an assistant lecturer in Moral Philosophy from 1934 to 1938.

Watt was ordained as a minister in the Anglican Communion in 1940 and was curate at St. Mary Boltons, London (1939–41) and at Old St. Paul's, Edinburgh (1941–43). To an item in our questionnaire as to his ambitions as a youth, Watt answered that he wanted to be a scientist and then later a philosopher. However, he ended up as a clergyman and an academic. When asked how he became interested in Islamic Studies, his answer was tempered with modesty. He said: 'On my mother's death, to enable me to pay for a housekeeper, I asked a Muslim friend to come as a paying guest and we had long religious discussions over meals. Then I heard that the Anglican bishop in Jerusalem wanted to work at the intellectual approach to Islam and I accepted a post under him.'[2] When we later enquired how his interest in Inter-Faith relations developed, he explained that it grew out of his work in Jerusalem.

It is important to note that, though Watt's interest in Islamic Studies at the intellectual level increased during his time in Jerusalem, the starting point was the encounter with his Muslim friend. This is significant, because many scholars who deal with Islam without this personal, positive encounter with those who profess the faith are likely to have a very different view of and attitude to Islam.

Watt's time as academic specialist to the Bishop of Jerusalem spanned about three years (1943–46). He then returned to his Alma Mater, Edinburgh University, where he lectured in Ancient Philosophy (1946–47) and later became lecturer and then senior lecturer and Reader in Arabic (1947–64). He became Professor of Arabic and Islamic Studies in 1964 and for a further fifteen years Watt dedicated his life to a serious study of Islam especially in the areas of *Sīrah*, history and theology.

Watt was also a visiting Professor: of Islamic Studies in the University of Toronto (1963); College de France, Paris (1970); of Religious Studies, University of Toronto (1978); and of Arab Studies, Georgetown University (1978–79). He was chairman of the Association of British Orientalists (1964–65). In addition to his academic degrees, he holds an honorary degree (Hon. DD.) from the University of Aberdeen (1966) and was also awarded the Levi Della Vida Medal, in Los Angeles in 1981.

Watt is by nature reserved and introspective, even elusive, as we found during our interview in June 1990.

Watt's publications are too numerous to mention. Stretching over more than half a century they are indicative of an able scholar on almost every aspect of Christianity and Islam, though he has written more on the latter than the former. He began writing in 1937 and at the time of this study, 1994, continues to do so. However, we concern ourselves mainly with some of his most important writings and those which fall within the ambit of this study.

Before this, we make a general appraisal of the character of his writings. With Watt's interest in Islamic Studies being partly attributed to his early personal contact with a Muslim friend, from the very beginning, Inter-Faith encounter has been at the root of his thinking.

In our interview, Watt expressed concern regarding the rise of fundamentalism in all religions but also a belief that Inter-Faith relations would improve. When asked for his advice to those engaged in Inter-Faith relations, he emphasized an appreciation of the strengths of the positive assertions of the other side. This concern reverberates throughout most of Watt's writings on Islam. His dialogical consciousness, however, can be seen to have grown tremendously in his later publications.

However, as Josef Van Ess points out, Watt has been an Anglican clergyman throughout his life and so sometimes his writings could be described as didactic or possibly 'propagandistic'.[3] He was able to achieve this simultaneously with his academic vocation as an Islamist. Van Ess explains that:

> From the very beginning, he saw his task as an Islamist in the dialogue; it was his destiny that he came to live in an ecumenical age. The dialogue was twofold: with his own society which, in happy ignorance, always tended to take

> its own values for granted, and with the Muslims who did just the same. This is why he tried to distil the fundamental notions of Muslim civilization out of a recalcitrant mass of material; he wanted to make clear the alternatives which Islam, growing out of the same roots as Christianity, is able to offer. It is only with the awareness of these alternatives that a meaningful and unprejudiced dialogue can be started.[4]

This then accounts for why Watt's writings are so different from his contemporaries and predecessors in the English West on Islam in general and on the *Sīrah* in particular.

Watt's first book, published in 1937, was entitled *Can Christians Be Pacifists?*[5] His Islamic material started with an article, 'Freewill and Predestination in Early Islam',[6] which was part of his Ph.D thesis submitted to Edinburgh University in 1944. The thesis itself was published as a book in 1948 under the same title. As Van Ess writes:

> . . . his thesis demonstrated an unusual gift for textual interpretation, combined with a certain lucidity of arrangement which made the argumentation immediately clear to the reader. Yet there was more than sound method and persuasive style. There was also a feeling for the individuality of historical situations and ideological decisions which was not so common among philologists. Theology was not treated as an impersonal fight of ideas or, even worse, as a catalogue of notions and values, but as an expression of the way specific persons or groups reacted to the demands of their time.[7]

Theology, in the hands of Watt, became more realistic and meaningful. In the Introduction to the book under discussion, Watt states his aim as trying to explain '. . . the great underlying principles and influences in men's hearts and minds, and the manner in which these are derived from the original intense realization of God'.[8] He goes on to point out that, 'In order to achieve this aim it is necessary to rid ourselves, as far as may be, of the preconceptions and prejudices of Western thought of the 19th and 20th centuries.'[9]

Watt's realization of the encumbrances which weighed heavily on the minds of many a Western scholar of Islam is admirable. This also contributed to his attempts at objective scholarship which many scholars have alluded to, as explained in the early part of this section of the work.

Watt accepts that biased or subjective and opinionated material abound in the non-Muslim world, therefore a scholar should be willing to do a lot of unlearning to escape censure. He demands a fresh and open mind as an indispensable tool in dealing with Islam. Despite this, he states: 'Since complete impartiality is impossible, the best I can do is to make explicit the position I myself hold.'[10]

Watt's plain-spoken and forthright manner is found in his works where his stance on a particular subject is laid out. A man of dialogue, Watt seeks positive elements in both Islam and Christianity. In an article, for example, he concludes: 'I would therefore contend that the difference between Western Christianity and Islam (which undoubtedly exists) is not so much a difference between the religions in their pure state as between the cultures and civilizations in which they are embedded.'[11] Few would disagree with this sentiment because Muslims have often argued that the original message of Jesus Christ was of Divine origin and it is because of this that the Qur'ān emphasizes that belief in the original word revealed to the prophets will ensure salvation.[12]

After a series of articles and book reviews in the late forties and the early fifties, Watt's next major work, published in 1953, was *The Faith and Practice of al-Ghazali*.[13] This is a collection of some of the works of al-Ghazālī which the author translates into English. The book is part of a series, the objective of which was to '. . . place the chief ethical and religious masterpieces of the world, both Christian and non-Christian, within easy reach of the intelligent reader who is not necessarily an expert – the ex-serviceman who is interested in the East, the undergraduate, the adult student, the intelligent public generally.'[14]

The series, initiated by some scholars from Oxford, was a result of the feeling brought about by the two world wars. People felt they needed to know each other better and what better way was there than to share the moral and spiritual ideals of both sides.

Watt's appreciation of al-Ghazālī is evident from his Introduction. He points out that a 'deep study of al-Ghazali may suggest to Muslims steps to be taken if they are to deal successfully with the contemporary situation. Christians, too, now that the world is in a cultural melting-pot, must be prepared to learn from Islam, and are unlikely to find a more sympathetic guide than al-Ghazali.'[15] This further demonstrates Watt's original passion for Inter-Faith relations.

In 1953, Watt's first book on the *Sīrah, Muhammad at Mecca*[16] appeared. This was followed by *Muhammad at Medina*[17] and the two books were summarized into one volume five years later under the title *Muhammad – Prophet and Statesman.*[18] Our discussion on Watt's works centres around these three books. The two earlier works, which provide a fairly detailed account of Muḥammad's life, and the ideas set out therein, received much acclaim.

These books, which have been reprinted several times, have been translated into many languages including Arabic, French, Japanese, Spanish and Turkish.[19]

In a recently-released work, F.E. Peters compares his own effort to those of Watt and submits that his pales into insignificance in the face of the latter's. He writes that '. . . undoubtedly, Montgomery Watt's two-volume life of Muhammad written at the mid-century has become the standard for students and scholars alike. Works of such magnitude and conviction usually signal a pause, the reshaping of a new *communis opinio*, and such seems to have occurred here: no one has since attempted a like enterprise in English.'[20]

He says that while Watt's works '. . . closed one large door, they opened many others',[21] his belief being that if Watt's efforts are judged to have initiated a methodological shift in the area of the life of Muḥammad in British scholarship, and literally shut the door in the face of the old attitude, they also kindled new interests. These works asked new questions and raised issues which question known accepted sentiments and hence opened other doors for productive research.

Returning to the subject of Watt's intellectual biography, in 1952 Watt's article 'The Condemnation of the Jews of Banū Qurayzah', expressed a marked sympathy for the Jews.[22] He argues, on the basis of Caetani's understanding of the event, that traditional Islamic accounts of the incident strive to save Muḥammad from culpability. He points out that the fact that Saʿd b. Muʿādh is made to pronounce the judgement is beside the point because, 'The sentence . . . was in any case dictated and inspired by the Prophet, who certainly made him understand what was the decision required of him. The responsibility for the slaughter falls entirely on the Prophet.'[23] He is of the opinion that the idea that the Jews themselves picked Saʿd as the judge is a later interpolation to make the traditional version more appealing. Watt's assertion is patently contrary to the account provided by authentic sources.

Watt's concern for Christian-Muslim dialogue started quite early and is apparent in some of his earlier writings. For example, in 1953, in an article he expresses concern about the Christian usage of the Arabic word 'Allah' instead of 'God' when communicating with Muslims.[24] He argues strenuously that whatever the motives for this widespread usage, it is inappropriate and he questions whether by doing this Christian missionaries and scholars are not engaged in a '. . . dangerous subjectivism that is tantamount to a denial of the essential realism of Christianity?'[25] He asserts that Muslims have an imperfect conception of God because God did not reveal Himself to them but only to Christians. Hence, he continues, the use of 'Allah' instead of 'God' would emasculate the Christian faith, which gives a fuller understanding of the Being Muslims themselves claim they also worship. He refers to the Qur'ān, which talks of the same Being that Christians and

Jews worship, and points out that even though the Muslim '. . . conception of God was faulty . . . their intention to serve Him cannot be doubted.'[26] He reasons that a sound theological communication can only take place when the basis of the discussion is 'God' and not 'Allah', because that conveys a more comprehensive understanding and it is only from here that issues like God's attributes, and revelation could be looked at. Though the deduction in this article might be difficult to follow, it must be appreciated that this was Watt's formative period in becoming an established scholar in the field.

In a review of Watt's book on al-Ghazālī,[27] Muhammad Hamidullah,[28] though he lauds Watt for his efforts in translating the work, points out certain areas where he claims Watt has offered an incorrect rendering of al-Ghazālī's original. When Watt remarks that despite al-Ghazālī's acceptable opinions, sometimes '. . . dark forces of superstition are prominent in the background . . .,[29] Hamidullah retorts: 'Perhaps this remark shows the background also the translator's approach to Islam.'[30]

Watt's next published material was his paper on Thomas Carlyle read at the Carlyle Society, Edinburgh on 24 October 1953.[31] This paper, an appreciation of the Scotsman's famous lecture in 1840, asserts that Carlyle's statements represent the first attempt in European literature to strongly affirm the sincerity of Muḥammad.

Watt questions how Carlyle came onto the scene so suddenly, despite centuries of invectives against the Prophet. He looks at the ideas current before and in Carlyle's time, pointing out that the medieval geopolitical picture was too frightening for Western Christendom. He concludes: '. . . on every frontier of Christendom where there was inhabited land, Islam was dominant. Is it surprising that Islam came to be thought of as the great enemy?'[32] As far as influences on Carlyle are concerned, he finds Goethe the dominant force.[33]

Carlyle, he argues, '. . . was the first writer in either East or West to attempt to fathom the inner experience of the founder of Islam'.[34]

He adds that while most earlier researchers were interested in the historical record of Muḥammad, 'Carlyle alone was interested in the man, the human person, grappling with the problems of human life and destiny that are common to all men.'[35]

Watt sees Carlyle's portrayal of Muḥammad as the true picture and his effort as '. . . an important step forward in the process of reversing the medieval world-picture of Islam as the great enemy, and rehabilitating its founder, Muhammad'.[36]

In 1953, a conference in Liege and Spa in Belgium on 'Unity and Variety in Muslim Civilization', resulted in a book under the same title published in Chicago in 1955 edited by Von Grunebaum.

An article by Watt, in 1956, reflects the conference proceedings.[37] He looks at the issue of whether Islam is monolithic, a unity or a multiplicity and explains that the answer, depending upon one's influences, is not easy to find. He refers to a theory of Karl Marx in which it is asserted that people's opinions are influenced by their position in the social structure, and points out that '. . . for example, in the case of Islamic Studies, . . . racial, national and cultural allegiances'[38] are factors. Therefore, he argues, '. . . whereas Marx thought that he and the proletariat were exempt from the distorting effect of material factors, nobody is immune from the "taint of ideology" '.[39] Watt explains that this view does not necessarily question the scholarly aptitude of those concerned and the merit of their researches. It merely states the position that at the end of the day, selection of material, interpretation of data and the evaluation of their acceptability or importance would have been due to the particular orientations of a particular scholar.

The claim is very true regarding the issues discussed at the conference, Watt says. He gives as an example the differences between the perceptions of Islam in Africa by the French and British colonists. While the French feared a *Pax-Islamica* which would destroy the Union Française, the British, he insists, were more perceptive and saw Islam in its local context and not as part of a world-wide movement.[40]

He is, however, of the view that a greater unity of the Muslim world would bring better prospects for peace both within the Muslim world and the world in general than is normally thought. It is in this context that he advocates a greater study of sociology and its application to Islam and religion in general. He believes this would reduce the tension between Western-educated Muslims and their 'traditional' religionists.[41]

The Reality of God[42] is one of Watt's few works on Christian theology. It is primarily an attempt to help Christians, and of course, all men of faith to resolve the tensions which have arisen because of the clash of religious beliefs and scientific humanism. Watt writes with a philosophical methodology tempered by his Christian faith.

Again, it is indicative of Watt's concern for a multi-faith approach to issues. Here, though he writes basically as a Christian, he intimates that Muslims and Jews might be confronting the same enigma of scientific humanism in contemporary times. He writes: 'It may therefore be that, though writing chiefly for my fellow Christians, I shall say something of value for members of other religions.'[43] Watt states his position clearly, allowing the reader to follow him through the work, as he does with practically all he writes. He states:

> What I am attempting . . . in this book is to contribute to the relieving of this tension in our lives by stating the Christian conception of God in terms and thought forms which we use in the world of scientific humanism.
>
> . . . I am restating what is already known and believed, but not revising it. I am translating it from the language of the New Testament and Christian Theology into that of scientific humanism or, more vaguely, modern thought; but a translation can never supplant the original. As befits a translator, I have no intention of saying anything at variance with the ecumenical creeds of Christendom, which I fully accept.[44]

Watt further shares his positive attitude to Inter-Faith relations in his review of Constance Padwick's *Muslim Devotions – A Study of Prayer Manuals in Common Use.*[45] He emphasizes that today's inter-religious contacts demand a shift in our attitude when studying faiths other than our own. He points out that we must change from the aloof, detached academic methods to a more pragmatic recognition that, 'We and the members of the religions we study are in the same crowd, jostling one another at every turn; to continue to think in terms of an I/it relationship is no longer adequate.'[46] He sees the book's merit as hinging on the fact that it is a representation of a real and ordinary Muslim's inner attitudes to his faith. Though he agrees that the work is entirely reflective of the Muslim attitude, he finds an extraordinary resemblance to the concerns of ordinary Christians, and says: 'This makes one think.'[47]

He concludes the review with a statement which shows his deep respect for other people's faith. He writes: '. . . in this materialistic and atheistic world it is important that many more Christians should realize that, despite the recalcitrance of their genuine dogmatic differences from Islam, there is a spiritual blood-relationship between themselves and the Muslims.' He then asks: 'Are not both spiritually, sometimes also physically, the seed of Abraham?'[48]

Norman Daniel's epoch-making *Islam and the West: The Making of an Image*, published in 1960, was also reviewed by Watt.[49] He sees the book in the light of today's psychological theory, of the positive effect of bringing early experiences back into one's consciousness. He explains that Daniel's book takes one back to the 'war psychosis' era of Christian attitudes to Islam, and points out that this is the best way to shake off the neurosis that seems to survive in the present. He describes the work as scholarly and a bold attempt, which '. . . is a pioneer work in a field likely to be much cultivated in the coming decades, namely, the historical and psychological roots of communal images and attitudes'.[50] He concludes that the book would have a Carthatic effect on the Western mind.

Watt's *Islamic Philosophy and Theology*, published in 1962,[51] was the first in the 'Islamic Surveys' series, a series '. . . designed to give the educated reader something more than can be found in the usual popular books. Each work undertakes to survey a special part of the field, and to show the present stage of scholarship here'.[52]

Watt was the first General Editor of the series and the first contributor. He introduces the book by discussing his sources, explaining the problems that a scholar who deals with Arabic philosophical manuscripts faces. He points out that these might lead to a serious misrepresentation of facts and so render the whole effort fruitless.

He specifically mentions the myriad of interpretations open to a naïve researcher handling manuscripts without diacritical marks. He advises that astuteness in following the story is crucial in order not to be misled and leave oneself open to censure.

Watt accepts that this work might be criticized along the same lines. He spends considerable time on his various sources, both primary and secondary, giving the reader an insight into the quality of the main book.

The paperback edition, published in 1985, has instructive comments on both the front and back covers. On the back cover, one reads:

> The product of a lifetime of study by one of the leading Islamists of our time, Watt's book represents an important contribution to the study of Islamic thought. It is clearly the best introduction to the subject presently available in English and will prove to be a valuable asset to both scholars and general readers interested in the history of Islamic thought. Highly recommended for graduate, undergraduate and public libraries.

In 1964, Watt published a paper on the nature of the Muslim community and the requirements for entering into that fold.[53] His main thesis is that Islam is a communalistic religion which allows little room for individualistic attitudes. Looking at Islamic institutions like *zakāh* and *ṣalāh*, Watt reasons that these essential characteristics of a believer or follower of Muḥammad show a deep sense of communal feeling. Referring to the Khawārij argument on the *kabā'ir* (major) sins, he argues that the main reason why such a person faces excommunication is because of the effect of his sins on the community as a whole, endangering their status as people of paradise (*ahl al-jannah*).[54] His conclusion is that '. . . there is more communalistic thinking in Islam than is usually realized'.[55]

Companion to the Qur'an Based on Arberry's Translation[56] was Watt's next major publication. Meant to be a handbook of explanation, albeit sketchy, of the Qur'ānic text to the uninitiated English reader, as Watt himself says in the Introduction: 'The aim of the present *Companion* is to provide the English reader with the chief background material needed to facilitate the understanding and appreciation of the Qur'an in translation.'[57] Watt, emphasizing the richness of the Arabic language, in a way also acknowledges the inadequacy of the English tongue and hence the immense difficulties faced by a translator of the Qur'ān.[58]

Probably, the most problematic part of appreciating the Qur'ān is that of interpretation. Watt refers to this but makes a comment which might be somewhat objectionable to Muslims. With regard to particular references as explained in the science of *Asbāb al-Nuzūl,* he accuses Muslim scholars of making dubious conjectures in their explanations.

Looking at the interpretation he puts on the last verse of *Sūrah al-Fātiḥah,* one can understand his anxiety with regard to some of the classical expositions. He writes that traditionally, the verse refers to '. . . Jews and Christians respectively . . . but this is not possible if the Sura is early Meccan, while the phrases would suit the pagan Arabs'.[59] In general, however, Watt steers clear of controversy, often making casual reference to what Muslims themselves believe.

That Watt's interest in the Qur'ān developed further is evident from his analysis of the Qur'ānic critique on Christian doctrines in an article published in 1967.[60] The main objective of the paper is to examine the Qur'ānic criticisms of Christianity and to find out whether these were directed against mainstream Christianity or some heretical groups. Referring to Waraqah and Negus and their apparent friendliness or sympathy for Muḥammad, Watt claims that Qur'ānic ideas were revised, so that critiques which were earlier known to be directed at Jews were now applied to Christians. He insists that the Qur'ānic understanding of the Christian doctrine of Trinity is at best described as 'Tritheism', which Christians vigorously deny.[61]

Even in the specific Qur'ānic reference to the Christian doctrine of the sonship of Jesus, in *Sūrah al-Tawbah* (9: 30), Watt maintains that '. . . this was not intended as an attack on the Orthodox Christian conception of the sonship of Christ, but on something else'.[62]

On the Qur'ānic claim that Jesus was not killed on the Cross but it was made to appear like it to the people (*Sūrah al-Nisā'* 4: 157–8), Watt interprets it in a unique way. He writes: 'Once again, the primary denial is of something heretical, namely, the Jewish contention that the crucifixion had been a victory for them, and this same denial would of course be most vigorously affirmed by Christian Orthodoxy.'[63] His conclusion is that rather than attacking primary Christian Orthodoxy, the Qur'ān is championing its cause in the face of heresy and Jewish invectives.

In another article which appeared the same year, he expresses some ideas on Inter-Faith relations which were of specific concern to him.[64] He says that the term 'dialogue' presupposes a group of academics who reflect on pure intellectual issues, and he does not see much benefit from that exercise. He advocates instead what he terms 'Inter-religion', which reflects a living dialogue rather than a mere intellectual reflection. He points out the opportunities afforded by new scientific and technological developments and argues that this should give us more faith in inter-religion than ordinary dialogue.[65]

He further elaborates on the idea that Christian thoughts

should be presented to Muslims and people of other religions through secular scientific arguments. He writes: '. . . we are called to seek involvement in contemporary secular thought as a response not merely to the internal concerns and tensions of Occidental culture (in which Western Christendom is comprised) but also to the great new fact of our century, namely, our condition of "inter-religion" '.[66]

1968 saw the publication of Watts' work on a sociological and psychological outlook on religious truth.[67] Here again, Watt begins with a layout of his objectives and methodology, explaining his presumptions underpinning the study. His multi-faith interests are again evident. He states: 'I have attempted to defend religion in general and not Christianity specifically, since I think that in the present world situation the great religions whether they realize it or not, are allies against opposing forces.'[68] Discussing the problems and presuppositions, he touches on prejudice going back to the period when opinions about Islam were shaped by the '. . . "War propaganda" of medieval times'.[69] He criticizes Western scholars who perceive Divine Truth as found only in Christianity.

In his last chapter, Watt discusses approaches to religious harmony, especially among the Abrahamic faiths. He brings back his argument of Inter-religion, stressing that there is global contact of all religious communities. In the ensuing reasoning, however, he expresses apprehension that even though the inevitable existential contacts are positive signs, these in themselves might generate a struggle for supremacy. He therefore proposes a four-point maxim which would enhance harmony. He states clearly that the maxims do not preclude missionary work but reject abuse in the form of proselytization.

The definition of proselytization is offered as '. . . seeking to get people to attach themselves to your community, chiefly because you want to glorify the community and not out of genuine concern for the welfare of the people themselves'.[70]

He further explains that his approach denounces the 'superiority complex' attitude, where others are seen as clinging to an inferior system and therefore need to abandon it. The method he proposes means, he says, that, 'Any genuine mission in future must more and more be a mutual personal relationship in which we are ready to receive as well as to give. It is a case of letting the other person see in us the "fruits" of our religion, while learning to appreciate in him the "fruits" of his.'[71]

Watt in his Conclusion insists that world peace, and indeed unity, can only be attained with religion as the basis. All other forms of foundations be they economic, political or cultural are skirting the real problem, he argues.

Watt's next book, *Islamic Political Thought*, came hard on the heels of his work on the socio-psychological study of truth in religions.[72] It reiterates the religious foundations of political consciousness in Islam and its development based on the politico-religious formation structured by the Prophet and his successors. The comments on the book's jacket are instructive: 'Any fruitful understanding of the polities of Islam must be based on knowledge of these religious attitudes and comprehension of the historical processes by which they continue to influence both the body politic and the wider life of society.'

The book, sixth in the 'Islamic Surveys' series, was meant as an addition to ordinary material on Islam. In the Introduction, Watt argues for the need for a close affinity between religion and politics. He elucidates:

> When politics becomes serious and it is a question [of] men being ready to die for the cause they support, there has to be some deep driving force in their lives. Usually this force can only be supplied by a religion, or by an ideology that is acquiring some of the functions of religion (such as making man aware of the powers on which his life is dependant).[73]

Yet again, Watt makes his position clear, emphasizing that his primary concern is the political process in the history of Islam with allusions to religious underpinnings. However, he states that the book '. . . will attempt to preserve the neutrality proper to the Social Scientist; that is to say, it will neither affirm nor deny the metaphysical truth of the religious ideas, but will consider them as ideas influencing the life of society'.[74]

A.L. Tibawi, in his review of the book, though he has misgivings about certain aspects of the book's style, says of Watt: 'His writing is clear, logical and sparkles with inventive comments.'[75]

1968 was perhaps one of the richest periods in Watt's academic life. A third book, *What is Islam?*,[76] was published as part of the 'Arab Background' series under the general editorship of Nicolas A. Ziadeh then of the American University of Beirut. In his Preface to this work, Ziadeh explains that the series was meant to educate the English-speaking populace on the role of Islam as the guiding principle of the Arab world, a subject he argues, the world could no longer do without. He points out that it was the intensity of Islam which fired the Arabs to contribute so much to world civilization and enabled a hitherto rather obscure nation to become a world power.

In the Introduction, Watt looks at Thomas Carlyle's public lecture in May 1840 in Edinburgh in which, perhaps for the first time, a Westerner pronounced Muḥammad as sincere with an open and earnest soul. Still, Watt argues, Carlyle had one basic hurdle to overcome, a hurdle which has plagued and will possibly continue to plague European scholarly circles: '. . . deep-seated prejudice which goes back to the "war propaganda" of medieval times'.[77]

The enormous spiritual and military threat posed by Islam was instantly seen as the greatest enemy to Christendom. Therefore:

> In deadly fear Christendom had to bolster confidence by placing the enemy in the most unfavourable light possible, consistent with some genuine basis in fact. The image created in the twelfth and thirteenth centuries continued to dominate European thinking about Islam, and even in

> the second half of the twentieth century has some vestigial influence.[78]

Watt examines the definition of religion in the West as compared to the Islamic concept of *dīn*, explaining that to the average Western Christian, religion might not go beyond the basic needs of an individual in his day to day life. Certainly, it would have nothing to do with commerce, or economics or whatever one might see as general hygiene and etiquette.

To a Muslim, however, *dīn* (religion) encompasses all these and more. This, Watt points out, makes it difficult for the ordinary Western Christian to appreciate the reasoning of the average Muslim. Watt's book claims to seek to bridge the gap between the two; to create a sociological understanding of religion which has some affinity with the Durkhiemian notion, which affirms the importance of the deep-seated social function of religion.

In the opening chapter, Watt focuses on the nature of Muḥammad's vision, seeing it as a new irruption with its own distinctiveness yet, at the same time following the general trend of scriptural history. He virtually dismisses the theory of the Qur'ān's literary and historical dependence on existing ideas and the milieu of the then Arabia and the world. He emphasizes that '. . . studies of sources and origins satisfy our intellectual curiosity and show us something of the mechanisms which play a subordinate part in literary creativity, but the essential creative work of genius eludes such studies'.[79]

Watt advises against acceptance of the idea, fixed in many scholars' consciousness, that Islam is merely a garbled form of previously established monotheistic systems of thought be it Christianity or Judaism. He invites people to note the 'particularity of the Islamic vision', citing Tor Andrae who went so far as to say that Muḥammad's image of God did not indicate any influence from Judaism or Christianity.[80]

Watt's argument continues that, whatever the natural effect of the contemporary environment on Muḥammad, '. . . this would not prevent the distinctive Qur'anic teaching from being a fresh irruption, any more than Jesus' appreciation of contemporary Jewish religion reduced his originality'.[81]

Though Watt leaves room for acceptance of the Qur'ān as embodying a large measure of truth, he writes: 'At the same time we cannot fully accept the standard Islamic view that the Qur'an is wholly true and the criterion of all other truth; for in the strictly historical field, we cannot hold that the Qur'an overrides the usual canons of historical evidence.'[82]

In the concluding chapter, Watt looks at Islamic values in the contemporary world. He examines the Muslim perception of Muḥammad as the archetype, the paradigmatic embodiment *par excellence* and in some ways seems to question the historicity of many of the traditions. He acknowledges, nevertheless, that: 'So much moral abuse has been hurled at Muhammad in Europe over many centuries that it is difficult if not impossible, for any Occidental to think of him as a moral exemplar.'[83]

He is of the view, not entirely different from the general Western perception of the traditions of Islam, that a large proportion of the accounts about Muḥammad's life consist of the projections of Muslims. He argues that since '. . . projection is a justifiable epistemological procedure in theological matters . . .', these 'idealistic expectations' by Muslims of Muḥammad are not entirely devoid of historical authenticity. He offers an analogy of a novelist whose imaginary creations might have the capacity of conveying truth because they are embodied in some reality.

In a statement which Muslim readers might have some difficulty in accepting, he says that, 'Some Muslims must have put these stories into circulation, and, if challenged, would have presumably have said, "This is the way one would have expected Muhammad to have acted".'[84]

In his concluding paragraph, Watt looks back at his analysis of the question raised by the very title *What is Islam?*, and reassures himself that he has done justice to it by appealing to both Muslims and non-Muslims to acknowledge his efforts. He writes: 'It is my hope that this book will enable Occidentals to understand better this living and powerful community which is both their partner and their rival, and also that it will show Muslims how a sympathetic Occidental sees them and thus bring them to appreciate another facet of their own identity.'[85]

One of the most significant issues that Watt raises is the methodological problem, as to how an Occidental or anyone who is not a Muslim can study Islam adequately. Does he have to be 'kind' or 'sympathetic' or satisfy other criteria outside those in strict academic scholarship? We will resume discussion of this point in the concluding part of this book.

Khurram Murad's review of the book acknowledges Watt's expertise but comes to the conclusion that the book is '. . . to say the least, disappointing. Islam could perhaps have done without such help in making it comprehensible to the West'.[86]

To A.S. Bazmee Ansari, 'Strictly speaking the book . . . does not describe Islam as a religious system but only attempts to give a philosophical and sociological and to some extent historical explanation of what, according to the author, may be called religion.'[87] Despite his critical review, Ansari shares the thoughts and concern of Watt about the destructive effects that colonialism has had on Muslim polity and expresses the hope that the original and undiluted Islamic vision will direct contemporary Muslims to build the Islamic society envisioned while drawing on those Occidental values which are compatible.[88]

In 1970, Watt's revised edition of Bell's work on the Qur'ān, *Bell's Introduction to the Qur'ān* was published.[89] Despite, and curiously enough, due to a profound respect for Bell, his teacher, Watt expresses his opinions frankly which, again, is indicative of his academic integrity.[90] He questions Bell's view that the Qur'ān is the work of Muḥammad and explains that, 'With the greatly increased contacts between Muslims and Christians during the last quarter of a century, it has become imperative for a Christian scholar not to offend Muslim readers gratuitously, but as far as possible present his arguments in a form acceptable to them.'[91]

Watt explains the paramount place of the Qur'ān in Muslim piety and everyday life, emphasizing that such a book, which moulds the life and thoughts of a large segment of the world's population, obviously merits attention. He advises against the attitude of nineteenth-century Occidental scholarship which pontificated about Islam and other religions. He recommends a reverential approach to the Qur'ān in particular even though one might not share its reasoning. This is the foundation for Watt's critique of Bell's work.

In the second chapter of this work, entitled 'Muhammad's Prophetic Experience', Watt reminds us of the early Christian scholars' criticism of Muḥammad's vocation. He writes: 'In Medieval Europe there was elaborated the conception of Muhammad as a false prophet, who merely pretended to receive messages from God; and this and other falsifications of Medieval war propaganda are only slowly being expunged from the mind of Europe and of Christendom.'[92] He catalogues a series of scholars and their basic ideas – some of them attempting to present a more balanced view of Muḥammad and Islam while others merely continue wallowing in the medieval derision.

While mentioning Thomas Carlyle, P.W. Buhl, Richard Bell and Tor Andrae as examples of those who try to rescue Muḥammad, he lists Gustav Weil, Aloys Sprenger, William Muir, David S. Margoliouth and Theodor Nöldeke as typical of those with surviving vestiges of 'war-propaganda views' in their works.[93] He criticizes such approaches, especially those of the latter group, as depending too much on certain traditions which might not have any certainty instead of the Qur'ān the veracity of which could be relied upon. He states:

> It is incredible that a person subject to epilepsy or hysteria or even ungovernable fits of emotion, could have been the active leader of military expeditions, or the cool far-seeing guide of a city-state and a growing religious community; but all this we know Muhammad to have been. In such questions the principle of the historian should be to depend

> mainly on the Qur'ān and to accept tradition only in so far as it is in harmony with the result of Qur'ānic study.[94]

Watt here is in consonance with *ḥadīth* scholarship itself, where an underlying principle is that if a *ḥadīth* contradicts an express Qur'ānic principle then that statement is basically rejected as unauthentic.[95]

Watt advocates repudiation of the medieval opinionated conceptions and acceptance of Muḥammad '. . . as a man who sincerely and in good faith proclaimed messages which he believed came to him from God'.[96]

In 1972, Watt turned his attention to Islam and Europe with *The Influence of Islam on Medieval Europe*, the ninth in the 'Islamic Surveys' series.[97] The book was a result of Watt's visiting professorship at the College de France in 1970.

In the opening chapter, Watt decries the lack of European scholarly writings on the influence of Islam on Europe and its subsequent contribution to the flowering of European civilization. The main objective of the book is therefore to offer '. . . a comprehensive view of this influence . . .'[98]

He points out that as far as Islamic cultural indebtedness is concerned, '. . . we Europeans have a blind spot. We sometimes belittle the extent and importance of Islamic influence in our heritage, and sometimes overlook it altogether'.[99]

Watt also looks at commerce and technology, Arab advances in science and philosophy and how these have influenced Europe. He again reminds us of the '. . . way in which a distorted image of Islam has dominated thinking in Europe from the twelfth century almost until the present day'.[100]

J.D. Latham in a review of the book[101] offers a glimpse of Watt's place in the circle of those who struggle for some form of objective study of Islam and indeed of any other faith they do not profess themselves. Latham writes: 'The most refreshing feature of this book is that the author – a committed Christian – approaches his subject as free from prejudice, whether conscious or subconscious, against Islam as it is possible to be.'[102] He commends Watt for making a serious attempt to study Islam from a new perspective.[103]

Watt has carved out an enviable place in the area of *Sīrah* in English scholarship. This is attested to by the invitation extended to him to deliver a paper at the First International Congress on Seerat, held in Islamabad under the auspices of the Ministry of Religious Affairs, Pakistan and the Hamdard National Foundation, in March 1976.[104]

Watt, introducing his paper, looks at the basic issue of common concern for both Christians and Muslims, which he identifies as *kufr* (atheism) or materialism hence the pressing need for dialogue. He explains that one fundamental requirement for a proper atmosphere for dialogue is to be prepared to listen and learn from each other. He mentions Massignon and Arberry among others who bravely took up the serious study of Islam and were thereby enriched.[105]

He goes on to discuss the twelfth- and thirteenth-century Christian defensive study of Islam and the resultant distortion. He then points out the process of change which started in the seventeenth century, mentioning the names of Leibniz, Goethe and Carlyle who, in their various approaches had a positive appreciation of Islam. He asserts that '. . . hostility was due to [the] personal attitudes of the writers and not to scientific historical methods. On the contrary, it will be maintained, these methods are essentially neutral to Islam, Christianity and other religions.'[106]

In his Conclusion, Watt expresses the hope that Muslims will take scientific historical study of the *Sīrah* seriously. He points out that even though there will be hostility, only this method will enable the persevering researcher to reach the required goal – that of the truth. This would contribute enormously to an understanding of Islam among those who do not share the faith.

In 1983, in 'A Muslim Account of Christian Doctrine',[107] Watt looks at al-Shahrastānī's *Kitāb al-Milal wa'l-Nihal*. He finds al-Shahrastānī's study of the three main Christian sects generally

'. . . objective and, so far as it went, reliable'.[108] In his translation of the study, Watt gives elaborate footnoted comments, appreciating the presentation on the Christian Trinitarian and Christological doctrine.

Also in 1983, Watt's *Islam and Christianity Today – A Contribution to Dialogue*[109] appeared, in which Watt looks at the whole subject of scholars studying 'other' religions and seeks avenues for positive dialogue. Watt sees this book as a culmination of his own 'inner dialogue', since he considers the study of a religion other than one's own a dialogue in itself.[110]

He sets out the concern of the work as '. . . the doctrinal aspects of the meeting of the two religions, and hardly anything has been said about ethical or other aspects. Ethical aspects, in particular, are so complex that they would require a book to themselves'.[111] He examines the traditional approaches and attitudes of both Christians and Muslims to each other and comes to an interesting and quite objective conclusion. He writes:

> The 'distorted image', however, has continued to influence the Western understanding of Islam into the present century, despite the efforts of scholars for two hundred years or more to correct the flagrant distortions. Just as their efforts appeared to be successful certain events linked with the present revival of Islam are causing not a few Westerners to turn back to the 'distorted image'.[112]

This therefore makes dialogue, which he considers despite all its inherent scepticism and possible dangers as mutual witnessing, to be imperative. He counts himself among those who advocate destruction of the 'defences' erected over the ages due to the old thinking and asks for a 'quantum leap' to be made on both sides.

In his Conclusion, he insists that every believer in God owes it as a duty to his Creator, to himself and to his community to strive for a better understanding of people of other faiths. He does not share the fear that dialogue would lead to an amalgamation of faiths, pointing out that rather it involves a '. . . mutual recognition where the various world religions accept one another as fellow-climbers of the cloud-covered mountain on whose summit in the mists God dwells unseen'.[113]

In an extensive review article, ʿAlī Qulī al-Qarā'ī looks at the book critically.[114] Acknowledging what he sees as a positive posture towards Islam, and in fact all religions, he detects a dual effort in Watt's writing. He finds that Watt's 'inner dialogue' is prompted by the need to defend his own faith against the continuous growth of scientism, and by defending Christianity, he would be defending aspects of Islamic beliefs as well.

Al-Qarā'ī also finds in Watt a pragmatic approach which defends religious pluralism and the axiology of religious faith in general.[115] He cites Watt's argument that religion over the course of history has offered man a quality of life that is largely satisfactory[116] but questions the assertion. He questions the criteria Watt employs to judge the quality of life as satisfactory and whether that on its own ensures salvation.[117]

He takes issue with Watt's contention that the two most contentious issues between Islam and Christianity, the prophethood of Muḥammad and the incarnation of Jesus, are not that divergent when closely examined.[118]

To al-Qarā'ī, Watt's attempt to explain the complication through symbolic language could be seen as a demand that Muslims should accept the divinity of Jesus in exchange for Christians accepting the authenticity of Muḥammad's prophethood.[119] He accuses Watt of naïvety, in his interpretation of religious doctrines and of deep infatuation '. . . with the desire to defend the Christian doctrines by diluting Islamic disapproval of them'.[120]

The central issue in this reaction derives from Watt's insistence that Jesus' crucifixion is beyond doubt a historical fact and is as irrefutable as saying that '. . . Muhammad proclaimed the religion of Islam in Mecca about the year 610 . . .'[121]

Al-Qarā'ī dismisses the views of secular historians as mere

conjecture based on an empirical world-view. To him, Watt follows other Orientalists in using such conjecture and sophistry in their analysis of Islam.[122]

Watt's book is also reviewed at length by Zāhid Azīz, who describes Watt as a most distinguished Western scholar of Islam.[123] He, however, expresses surprise that despite his extensive knowledge, Watt completely omits the Islamic view of Inter-Faith dialogue. Like al-Qarā'ī, Azīz is of the view that '. . . Watt's concept of "dialogue" appears to be not much more than Muslims being asked to alter the interpretation of those Qur'anic verses which militate against Christian beliefs'.[124]

He also attacks Watt's suggestion that Muslims should reinterpret the Qur'ānic verses on the alleged corruption of the Biblical text to mean either 'limited' or 'temporary' corruption and Christians should change some of their medieval views about Islam. Azīz points out that such a suggestion '. . . is clearly a retrograde step so far as modern research and knowledge are concerned'.[125]

Watt, in his discussions on the charge of scriptural corruption levelled against Christians by Muslims, sees this as part of the Muslim efforts to promote the self-image of Islam by emphasizing its self-sufficiency. He then refers to a story in which the *Khalīfah* ʿUmar ibn al-Khaṭṭāb was said to have ordered the burning down of the Alexandrian library after the city fell to the Muslim army. ʿUmar was supposed to have said, rather cynically, that if the books in the library did not contradict the teachings of the Qur'ān then they were an unnecessary duplication and therefore should be destroyed. Again, if they contradicted the Qur'ānic teachings then they should be destroyed since they constituted a danger to truth.

Watt expresses scepticism about the story but the mere fact that he recounts it has immense implications. He says: 'This story is probably not factually true, but it expresses exactly a belief still common among Muslims, namely, that all the religious and moral guidance required by the human race, from now to the end of time is to be found in the Qur'an (coupled with the example of Muhammad).'[126] He then attempts to assign reason to this perceived notion among Muslims which, he thinks, '. . . may go back to the feeling of the nomadic Arab that he was superior to all peasants and city-dwellers and had nothing to learn from them'.[127]

Azīz, in his review, takes the issue of 'Umar's story very seriously and accuses Watt of presenting '. . . a totally false story fabricated centuries ago to discredit Islam, . . . and proceeds to draw a conclusion from it about Muslim beliefs . . .'[128] He expresses displeasure with this kind of academic scholarship in which weight is attached to a false story and deductions then made. He believes that the fact that Watt himself expresses some scepticism should have been enough for him to omit the story altogether.

Azīz further detects a lacuna, which he considers as significant taking into consideration the purported objective of the book. He points out that the book '. . . completely omits to give the history of the contact between the two faiths over the last hundred years or so, . . .'[129] He is of the opinion that the lack of this important historical dimension, in which vigorous missionary activities feature considerably, seriously undermines the value of the book.

In 1984, an article by Watt entitled 'Muḥammad as the Founder of Islam' appeared in *Studia Missionalia*.[130] The article opens with a discussion on the human element of the Prophet as a linkage between God and man. Watt points out that in the drama of revelation '. . . there is a wide field for human co-operation with the divine initiative'.[131] He holds that the same is true in the case of Muḥammad.

In his attempt to justify the use of the concept 'founding' of religion, Watt says that since Muḥammad was instrumental in the establishment and management of the Muslim *Ummah* especially in the post-*Hijrah* period in Madīnah, then the epithet 'founder of Islam' is justified.[132]

Touching on the pre-Islamic milieu, Watt asserts that apart from a sprinkling of monotheistic ideas from a handful of Jews and Christians, '. . . the average Arab of Mecca, or indeed of Medina, seems to have had only slight and imperfect knowledge of the Jewish and Christian religions'.[133] He pictures Muḥammad as being in a dire search for a new monotheism which would have relevance for the problems of the Makkan society. In this search, Muḥammad's views of God are presented as being very fluid and within the context of the contemporary Jewish and to a lesser extent Christian views.

Referring to the Qur'ānic narrative on Muḥammad's sighting of the angel Jibrīl, Watt asserts that Muḥammad thought he had seen God, '. . . though later, when he learnt the Jewish view that God cannot be seen, he thought of this being as an angel'.[134]

Touching on the dating of the revelations in terms of the *Sūrahs*, Watt acknowledges the enormity of the problem since, to him, the Muslim science of *Asbāb al-Nuzūl* does not offer much help in this. He points out that the 'unofficial' acceptance of these views in the *Asbāb al-Nuzūl* by Muslims has prompted Western scholarly circles to devise their own critical criteria to arrive at a solution. This question of assigning dates for Qur'ānic passages has been further complicated by the fact that many similarities exist among them. Watt offers advice as to one's attitude in this exercise. He writes: 'In all this process sound scholarship requires that we hold Muhammad to have believed sincerely that to God and not himself were due not only the original revelations but also the repetition of revelations with modifications and his putting together of revelations into suras.'[135]

The issue of the 'satanic verses' is mentioned, pointing out how the so-called repudiation of the alleged verses affect the Prophet's image and also that of his followers. Watt then acknowledges how this story is subjected to serious discussion by Muslims and its renunciation. He, however, adds: '. . . it is difficult to understand how any Muslim could have invented or accepted it, if it had no basis in fact'.[136]

With regard to the 'Aqabah pacts which resulted in the

Hijrah to Madīnah, Watt reasons that Muḥammad envisaged the opportunities for raids on Makkan caravans that Madīnah offered and that is why he accepted the invitation to move.[137] Hence, the whole motive for the *Hijrah* is seriously questioned. The argument is developed to interpret even the motive for the spread of Islam in general. Watt claims that, 'The expeditions of the following century, however, which caused Muhammad's federation to expand into an empire stretching from Spain and Morocco to Delhi and Samarqand, were really only glorified razzias, whose aim was not to make converts but to gain booty.'[138]

The article then looks at Muḥammad's attitude towards the Jews and Christians, which Watt characterizes as a transformation from amity to hostility. He suggests that Muḥammad's attitude worsened as more and more statements came through the revelation criticizing certain Christian doctrines. In this he again affirms, as he does in his *Islam and Christianity – A Contribution to Dialogue*,[139] that there is no semblance of what the Qur'ān criticizes as Orthodox Christian doctrine but there were probably some heretical beliefs in existence in Makkah and Madīnah in Muḥammad's time.[140]

He attributes the change in the direction of prayer (*qiblah*) and the institution of the annual fast during the month of Ramaḍān to a shift in Muḥammad's attitude towards the Jews, in particular, and what he believes were worsening relations between Muḥammad and people of other faiths. He discusses briefly the confrontations with the three main Jewish tribes in Madīnah and considers the way the issues were handled as cruel.[141] However, he points out that the 'cruelty' has to be seen within the proper historical period where '. . . there was much violence . . .',[142] and therefore asks that '. . . the modern historian, remembering the distortions of the medieval image, will tend to give Muhammad the benefit of the doubt'.[143]

Watt calls for a complete rejection of the medieval charges of impostor and liar levelled against Muḥammad, explaining that contemporary, sound scholarship does not accept such frivolous charges. Muḥammad's proven sincerity, he further insists, leaves no room to doubt that Muḥammad was able to discern revelation from his own unconscious activities.

In conclusion, Watt reiterates the underlying assumptions regarding the status of Muḥammad. He writes:

> This study has been based on the belief that Muhammad was a genuine prophet in the sense that God used him to communicate truth about himself to human beings; but this assertion has to be qualified by holding also that prophets can make mistakes of a sort, as the Old Testament prophets Haggai and Zechariah did when they thought that Prince Zerubbabel was the Messiah.[144]

Noting that Muḥammad was used by God to found a religion, Watt holds that '. . . perhaps a part of his role in these purposes is to challenge Christians to more profound reflection on some of their basic beliefs'.[145]

In 1985, another article by Watt, 'The Expedition of al-Hudaibiyya Reconsidered',[146] appeared in response to an article by Farrukh B. 'Alī, who asserts that the whole issue of Ḥudaibiyyah '. . . constitutes a strange chapter in the history of Islam and the life of the prophet Muhammad. The accepted version of these events and the terms of the treaty raise many questions and create many difficulties'.[147]

'Alī questions the episode as understood in traditional literature, finding it incompatible with the status of Muḥammad as a prophet with divine patronage. He also finds the Ḥudaibiyyah episode too humiliating to be true. By implication, the accepted version is just not rational enough. He insists that the terms of the treaty '. . . bear no logical relationship to the general situation prevailing in Arabia at the time, nor to the particular situation existing at Hudaybiya on that occasion. It appears unlikely that he could have agreed to such a treaty'.[148]

Watt expresses his strong disagreement with the underlying rationale for 'Alī's paper, maintaining that, 'In the actions of the Prophet there was nothing dishonourable or cowardly and no neglect of principles.'[149] He explains that the episode rather offers a further exposition on the immense skills of the Prophet as a master tactician. He points out that though a cursory look at the issue might present a picture of victory for the Makkans, a perceptive analysis shows a desperate Makkan attempt to boost their self-confidence. On the other hand, the composure of the Prophet and his people was indicative of immense self-confidence that victory was inevitable and the desperate attempts by the Makkans to stop them were signs to that effect.[150]

ʿAlī asserts that the accepted version has been based on the *Ḥadīth* of Miswar b. Makramah and Marwān b. al-Ḥakam, some details of which are not found in the main text of the *Ḥadīth* when compared with the version in Ibn Isḥāq, al-Ṭabarī and al-Wāqidī. He is of the opinion that the details of the *ḥadīth* are ahistorical. He lays the blame at the door of the *quṣṣās* (story-tellers) who used to embellish certain historical events.[151]

Watt points out that ʿAlī's reasoning is faulty because he '. . . fails to recognize that these developed a sharp distinction between the disciplines of Hadith and Sira, and between the methods employed'.[152] He explains that there were other means of obtaining details of expeditions, especially the accounts of the people themselves, which might have nothing to do with the *Ḥadīth*. These accounts were widespread enough in many cases to merit the status of *tawātur*.[153] He hence affirms his position: '. . . the standard account of the expedition of al-Hudaybiyya and what followed is not dependent on any Hadith but is part of the "widely transmitted" (mutawatir) and generally accepted chronological framework'.[154]

Watt's interest in things Islamic is further evidenced by his immense positive regard for al-Ghazālī. Having previously written on this great scholar Watt, in 1986, published another article entitled 'A Great Muslim Mystic'.[155] Perhaps Watt is sharing in the general Western scholars' fascination for al-Ghazālī but it seems that he also has a deep respect for Islamic spirituality which al-Ghazālī symbolizes for him.

This article is mentioned merely to show Watt's interest in, and respect for Islam and it is not discussed here since its subject matter does not fall directly within the concern of the present work.

Our attention now shifts to the series entitled *The History of al-Ṭabarī* to which Watt contributed. Watt teamed up with M.V. McDonald, working on the annotation and translation of Volumes VI and VII in the series.[156] The translation offers only a glimpse of Watt's thought; perhaps a better insight can be obtained from the Translator's Foreword to both volumes which were written by Watt, since the ideas here are presumably entirely his.[157]

In the seventh volume, which incidentally appeared earlier (1987) than the sixth (1988), Watt begins the Foreword with a note that the period under discussion '. . . was a time of critical importance both for Islam as a religion and for the political community in which it was embodied'.[158] He touches on the Constitution of Madīnah and what he assumes was an apparent lack of political authority in Muḥammad.

He asserts that the selection of Friday as a special day for the Muslims was made by Muḥammad on the principle of expedience. He says that Friday was a market day in Madīnah and the day that the Jews prepared for the Sabbath and, since it was already part of the customary practice, Muḥammad accepted it as such.[159]

On the Prophet's marriages, Watt claims that all of them '. . . and those he arranged for his daughters were made for political reasons'.[160]

On 'Ā'ishah and her personal qualities as traditionally expounded in Muslim literature, Watt is of the opinion that the extolment had a political undertone and was directed against the Shī'ites who were immoderate in their praise for Fāṭimah.[161] This seems to suggest that perhaps 'Ā'ishah did not merit those qualities usually attributed to her but these were meant to serve a political purpose.

Watt looks at the early expeditions undertaken by Muḥammad

and his Companions and expresses surprise at al-Ṭabarī's version as compared to those of al-Wāqidī and Ibn Isḥāq. With respect to dating he has more confidence in al-Wāqidī because, for Watt, he makes things clearer than al-Ṭabarī.[162]

Watt, commenting on the battle of Badr looks for reasons for the spectacular Muslim victory. After mentioning the military tactic of the Muslims in occupying the main wells in the area, he says: 'It is likely, too, that the Ansar, because they gained a livelihood by cultivating date-palm and cereal crops, were in better condition physically than the Meccans, whose lives as merchants were probably much more sedentary.'[163] However, Watt also recognizes that their belief in a supernatural backing and their expectation of being rewarded with Paradise heightened their morale.[164]

Watt draws attention to the relationship with the Jews, pointing out that, 'One of the limitations of al-Tabari's method of writing history is to be seen in the fact that he more or less attaches less importance to the Jewish question.'[165] Watt explains that even though it could be argued that Muḥammad and his followers had a marked interest in the wealth of the Jews, the primary grounds for the expulsion of the Jews from Madīnah was that they became a real danger to the very basis of the new religio-political entity.[166] At least, in this particular instance, Watt shifts from his usual reasoning where economic considerations were central to any decision taken by the Prophet.[167]

In his concluding remarks, Watt looks at al-Ṭabarī's sources, making reference to omissions from his main source – the *Sīrah* of Ibn Isḥāq as seen in the recension of Ibn Hishām and additions from al-Wāqidī's accounts.

The sixth volume, published in 1988, focuses on the Makkan situation. Again, Watt analyzes the sources that were at al-Ṭabarī's disposal. He further notes that Ibn Isḥāq remains the dominant influence.[168] In addition, al-Ṭabarī is noted as a scholar who balances the accounts he picks from Ibn Isḥāq either through Ibn Hishām or elsewhere with other versions.

This often has to do with issues relating to *Shīʿah* concerns.[169]

Reflecting on the reliability of such early Islamic material, Watt mentions the attempts by Wansbrough and his pupils Patricia Crone and Michael Cook to pour scorn on them. They claim that the materials cited in primary scholarship is ahistorical since it either developed more than a century and a half after the 'alleged' events or related to some other ideology entirely.[170]

Watt, however, insists that there is enough proof that the early Islamic sources could be relied upon to reconstruct early Islamic history. He points out that, 'Neither book has been favourably received by scholars in general, since both are based on many unjustified assumptions, and there seems little point in offering a detailed criticism of them.'[171]

The historicity of such material is taken further in an elaborate discussion centring on the works of eminent Islamists such as Goldziher, Schacht, Lammens, Becker and Blachère who all questioned the reliability of the earlier Islamic scholars.[172] Watt, noting that much of the discussion in these works centres on the *ḥadīth*, claims that, 'A saying which is of dogmatic or juristic interest is usually irrelevant to the historian.'[173] Though the statement appears a bit extravagant, by careful wording, and inserting the adverb 'usually', Watt leaves little room for criticism. After all, any survey of the historical development of Islamic Religious Thought would have to be interested in dogmatic and juristic matters as historical events.

Watt concludes that '. . . the critique of Hadith by Goldziher, Schacht, and others does not necessarily apply to the materials used in the Sirah'.[174] He maintains that from the relative ages of some of the early writers, it is possible to at least assume that writings of considerable historical significance existed in the early days of Islam. He gives ʿUrwah b. al-Zubayr and al-Zuhrī as examples of people who were old enough to have seen history in the making or at least heard from people who were eyewitnesses or active participants in events.[175]

Referring to Schacht's theory of 'family *isnāds*', which were thought to be merely attempts by certain families to glorify themselves through spurious *aḥādīth*, Watt takes the view that there is a real danger of unlimited application of this theory replacing genuine historical issues. He points out that some of the details are so minor that a family would not find it worthwhile to invent them. However, he advises against dismissing everything out of hand, arguing, 'Each, however, should be considered on its merits and examined for inherent improbabilities and the presence of distorting motives.'[176]

Genealogy with its strong base in the Arab psyche, poetry, and eventually the Qur'ān itself have all been considered by scholars as offering glimpses of history. To some, like Blachère, the Qur'ān is the only reliable source of material to reformulate the biography of Muḥammad.[177] Watt cautions against using the Qur'ān as a historical textbook, pointing out the crucial difficulty of chronology.[178] He explains that genealogies offer a rough guideline to history and poetry and also '. . . give some insight into people's feelings and attitudes, including the attitudes of a tribe or clan towards its rivals. Even when poems are not by the authors to whom they are ascribed, the information they give about attitudes may still be accurate'.[179] He emphasizes that the critical challenge to modern scholarship is how to harmonize the plethora of sources to arrive at an objective history of Islam and in this enterprise it is not logical to reject anything without a sober analysis.

S. Salmān Nadvī reviews the two volumes under discussion and commends them highly.[180] He picks up on one significant point, concerning the change of the *qiblah* from Jerusalem to Makkah which, Watt claims, reflected the worsening relations between the Prophet and the Jews. He writes that because Watt is suggesting that the change was the Prophet's own decision, this reflects Watt's perception of the Qur'ān. He insists that:

> If one studies the Qur'anic verses (2: 125, 142–50) together with the reports in al-Bukhari, it is clear that the original

> Qiblah (the Ka'bah) was changed temporarily to Jerusalem by Divine Command (2: 143) and then God restored the original Qiblah in Madinah (2: 144). . . . As soon as the Divine Command for the change of Qiblah came to the Prophet, it was changed in a single day during prayers (salah) in a mosque which is known to this day as the Mosque with two Qiblahs (Masjid al-Qiblatayn).[181]

Despite his largely appreciative stance, Nadvī sees many conjectures in the analysis of some of the issues in the annotation and even in the translation itself.[182]

In our interview with Watt in 1990, one of his fundamental concerns about contemporary Islam was what he felt to be the rise of Islamic fundamentalism. In fact, in his book *Islamic Fundamentalism and Modernity*, published in 1988,[183] Watt claims to demystify a subject which is often misunderstood and has therefore caused a lot of Islamophobia especially in the West.

Watt's objective is two-fold. He sets out to offer a discerning exposition of Islam to the West and also to study what he considers to be a harmful Muslim introspective self-image which does not allow them to understand the West in modern times and, according to him, pushes Muslims to the periphery of world affairs.

Without a Preface or Introduction, Watt plunges into his analysis, looking at the traditional self-image of Muslims. He gives the thesis of the book, and says:

> . . . the thinking of the fundamentalist Islamic intellectuals and of the great masses of ordinary Muslims is still dominated by the standard traditional Islamic world-view and the corresponding self-image of Islam. This is a fact of great importance at the present time when the influence of Islam is increasing throughout the world, since it means that how contemporary problems are seen by many Muslims may be different from how they look to Western observers and statesmen.[184]

Touching on the title of the book, Watt admits the inappropriateness of the journalistic parlance, 'fundamentalism', but prefers to stick to it because it offers him the interpretation of 'literalism' which suits his critique.

Discussing the sub-section entitled 'The Unchanging Static World', Watt seems to run into a minefield. He sees Islam as a religion tied to the philosophy of 'unchangingness'. He states: 'It is very difficult for the Westerner to appreciate the outlook of those in whose thinking there is no place for development, progress or social advancement and improvement.' He then adds: 'It was in my studies of the Islamic sects that I first became aware of the complete absence of the idea of development.'[185]

Watt continues with what might be perceived as a diatribe on Islam: that the Muslim argument, that since there is no fundamental change in human nature and the principles of the *Sharīʿah* are eternal, means that Islam does not accept any social reform. He even links this theory to the pre-Islamic 'primitive' Arab desert nomad life which was not amenable to change hence, he argues, the development of the *Sunnah* of the progenitors traditionally translated as 'the beaten path'.

Referring to the Islamic concept of the finality of prophethood, Watt postulates that verse 33: 40 which pertains to this has been misinterpreted by Muslims. He speculates: 'To the first hearers this probably meant that Muhammad was the seal which confirmed the truth of previous prophets, but it is now universally interpreted by Muslims to mean that Muhammad is the last of the prophets, after whom there will be no other.'[186]

The book has a sub-section, entitled 'The Idealization of Muhammad and Early Islam', where Watt suggests that frantic efforts by Muslims to portray Muḥammad as the archetype make them propound 'theories' about him and reject events with historical evidence which do not promote such thinking. He gives examples, such as Muslims 'covering' Muḥammad's 'pagan past', and rejecting the 'satanic verses' even though the available sources allude to these.

Watt makes a quick comparison of the Christian slogan 'Back

to the Bible' and the Muslim demand for 'Back to the Qur'ān and *Sunnah*', condemning the Muslim idea while lauding the Christian conception. He argues that:

> . . . the idea of going back to the Qur'an and the example of Muhammad means the idealization of a period of little more than twenty years in a region of the world where life was still somewhat primitive and barbaric. Nearly all Westerners whether God-fearing or not, are horrified that Muslims of today can contemplate the amputation of a hand as a punishment for theft or stoning as a punishment for adultery, even if only in a few precisely defined cases.[187]

In the epilogue, he exhorts Muslims not to exist in '. . . the fortress of their medieval world-view', but to fully participate and share in '. . . the whole intellectual and cultural life of the human race'.[188]

He recommends that Muslims should broaden and reframe the *Sharīʿah* because, he assumes, it is out of touch with modernity. This is because, he reasons, 'Human beings in a mature civilization cannot accept such practices of the distant past as an ideal to be followed.'[189]

This book has been reviewed by many scholars. V.J. Hoffman-Ladd sees Watt's exposition in the book as '. . . remarkably clear, insightful, and provocative . . .',[190] and Watt as playing the role of a 'Big Brother' who offers 'helpful intellectual advice' to Muslims to '. . . join believers in the West in facing modernity without bankrupting themselves spiritually'.[191] In general, this review is very appreciative of the book's message.

A. Qamaruddin offers a rather different view.[192] He questions the whole motivation behind the thesis of the book: 'What the author does not tell us is to what degree contemporary or even relatively late expressions of fundamentalism are motivated by sectarian, economic, sociological and political factors, and to what extent they are, in spite of an orthodox legalism, essentially of modern Western inspiration.'[193]

Watt's definition of 'development' or 'social reform' is denounced by Qamaruddin, who points out that '. . . the author's idea of development is clearly characterized by temporal evolution, . . .'[194]

He is indignant about what he believes is the apparent posture by Watt, that the future of Islam, and Muslims for that matter, lies in the extent to which they ape others especially the West and the Christian way of doing things.[195] He concludes:

> The ameliorative content of the book, in so far as modernity is concerned, is obvious and perhaps symptomatic of the approach. The error of this approach has been in its assuming that the questions posed by it were the only questions, whereas in reality they are based on premises which are not consonant with the realities they attempt to gauge.[196]

J.S. Nielsen, in his review of the same work, pays tribute to Watt's authority in the field, acknowledging that the book offers some helpful ideas.[197] However, in his overall assessment, he writes:

> There is a rough edge to the evaluations and judgements spread right through the book. It lacks the subtlety and flexibility of analysis which characterises the author's earlier works. This leads towards generalizations which sometimes tend to be simplistic. The reader with little previous knowledge in the field is likely to find stereotypes of Islam reinforced here.[198]

Nielsen takes issue with the central thread in Watt's argument, that Islamic self-image moulded in the seventh century has become unshakeably static. He argues that the emphasis put on this completely denies the tremendous metamorphosis that has taken place in Islam over the centuries, and that is a very unfair and even untenable academic position to take. To completely ignore the profound elasticity in Islamic thought is unfortunate. He also expresses dissatisfaction with the general tone of the book, dealing as it does with 'ideals', and points out the obvious absence of looking at realities in the Islamic world. He concludes that, 'The "Islamic revolution" or resurgence has, as some scholars are recognizing, represented an enfranchisement of the broader "masses" of the Muslim world. Islam is, in such circumstances, not static. It is, on the contrary, at the beginning of a period of a *Kulturkampf* of immense proportion.'[199]

Also published in 1988 was Watt's study *Muhammad's Mecca – History in the Qur'an.*[200] The book looks for '. . . as much historical material as possible for the Meccan period of Muhammad's career from the Holy Qur'an'.[201] It also continues the discussion begun in the earlier *Muhammad at Mecca* (1953).

Watt points out that many twentieth-century scholars have concluded that the Holy Qur'ān is the only credible source on the life of Muḥammad. This, he says, has come about because of the harsh criticisms against *ḥadīth* literature, rejecting them as unreliable material for Muḥammad's biography. Though Watt himself does not seem to subscribe totally to this theory, he is of the view that much *ḥadīth* literature does not have any relevance for the historian. He argues that the *aḥādīth* are mainly useful for legal experts and theologians and not historians as such.

Watt makes a bold statement regarding the prophethood of Muḥammad:

> Personally, I am convinced that Muhammad was sincere in believing that what came to him as revelation (Wahy) was not the product of conscious thought on his part. I consider that Muhammad was truly a prophet, and think that we Christians should admit this on the basis of the Christian principle that 'by their fruits you will know them', since through the centuries Islam has produced many upright and saintly people. If he is a prophet, too, then in

> accordance with the Christian doctrine that the Holy Spirit spoke by the prophets, the Qur'an may be accepted as of divine origin. In saying this, however, I do not exclude the possibility that God makes his revelations through a person's unconscious mind; and indeed something of this sort seems to be required if we are to explain adequately all the phenomena.[202]

He stresses the 'Arabic' origin of the Qur'ān, and cites the statement in *Sūrah* 12: 2 explaining that this does not merely imply that the language of revelation was Arabic but its first addressees were Arabs, whose perception of things had to be adequately addressed. The stakes are raised further by dwelling on the hypothesis that Muḥammad's journey to prophethood and his whole life were shaped by the environment. It is this which makes him suggest that the Qur'ān contains mistaken ideas about Christian and Jewish beliefs and also that its cosmology is primitive.[203]

Looking at chronology in the Qur'ān, Watt refers to some Western studies on this subject and their attempts at rearranging the Qur'ān in a 'proper' order. Here, he mentions Muir, Grimme, Nöldeke, Bell and Blachère. He sees Nöldeke's study as the most successful, while he admits that Blachère's is the most modern and hence he relies on it.

He rejects the rendering of the term '*ummī*' as 'illiterate' and interprets it as 'gentile' or 'unscriptured', arguing that the general level of literacy in Makkah was high. Coupled with Muḥammad's business transactions on behalf of Khadījah, he argues further, he must have been literate enough to at least keep commercial records. He states: 'Thus the *ummī* prophet is the non-Jewish, or Gentile prophet, whom Muslims held to be foretold in the Bible, and who was sent by God to his own non-Jewish or heathen people, as well as to the Jews and perhaps Christians.'[204] He emphasizes, however, that Muḥammad's literacy does not mean he had a direct insight into the Bible.

Watt also explains his criterion for sanctioning Muḥammad's

prophethood. He writes: 'In any case the experienced "manner" of revelation is not a guarantee of genuineness, since Muhammad at first thought the "satanic verses" were genuine. It is the "fruits" which are the ultimate criterion of genuineness.'[205]

Sami Angawi, in his review of the book in the *Journal of Islamic Studies*,[206] points out some assertions in the book which will '. . . not only fail to satisfy scholarly criteria but would also be unacceptable to Muslims for whom the Qur'an is a divine book protected by Allah from any alteration'.[207]

In his general assessment of the book, Angawi is of the opinion that it has a particular tint which Muslims would find highly objectionable. He points out some examples: 'Qur'anic cosmology, for instance, is referred to as being not only "mistaken" (1) but also "primitive" (6). Similarly certain Qur'anic statements about Judaism and Christianity are said to be not just "mistaken" (2, 37, 45) but "palpably false" (44) . . .'[208] He accuses Watt of having a shallow understanding of the Qur'ānic concepts he deals with. He also points out that even though Watt makes passing reference to the universal message of the Qur'ān, there is an implicit denial of this in the tone of the book. He thus concludes that:

> The book is highly speculative and thus at best inconclusive in its claims . . . . A certain amount of speculation is of course necessary in this sort of attempt at historical reconstruction; but if the author had recognized a little more universality in the phenomena being discussed, he might at least have understood them rather better from his own experience instead of being limited to such unconvincing conclusions.[209]

In 1989, an article by Watt entitled 'Islam and Peace' appeared in *Studia Missionalia*.[210] Watt asserts at the beginning of the article, that though Islam is presented by Muslims as the religion of peace their approach to peace is different from that of Christians. He argues that the reason is because Islam began as a political movement while Christians were apolitical until some three centuries after the death of Christ.

He continues that the *'pax Islamica'* Muḥammad established was deeply steeped in the old Arabian pastime of raiding others and when many tribes around Madīnah accepted Islam, a new outlet had to be sought for their 'excessive energy' to satisfy their war-like passion. He speculates that lands in Syria and Iraq, and probably beyond, came under the purview of Islam through such an arrangement.[211] He refers to the deduction of law from Qur'ānic principles and also from the mass of Traditions from the Prophet and his four Rightly-Guided caliphs, saying that Muslims believe that through these all mankind's problems can be solved. He then writes: 'This simple-minded and unrealistic assertion is almost certain to lead to disillusionment among the Muslim masses when it is realized that the problems are not being solved.'[212]

Touching on a talk said to have been given by an *Imām* of the Ahmadiyyah Community concerning Islamic ethics of war, Watt comments that there do not seem to be any *Sunnī* jurists who would look at the issue of peace in a realistic way and differentiate the period of Muḥammad from our present times. He continues: 'We still wait for Muslim traditionalists to convince non-Muslims that Islam as they conceive it has an important contribution to make to world peace.'[213] This seems to be a veiled indictment of Islam as a religion of hostility instead of peace. However, he notes attempts by what he calls liberal and better-educated Muslims, represented here by the late Fazlur Rahman and Mohammad Arkoun, to change the traditionalist image of Islam which he considers not conducive to the modern world.[214]

Another significant work is *Early Islam – Collected Articles* published in 1990.[215] This is an anthology of articles by Watt that appeared in eminent journals during the period 1943 to 1983. They are put into two groups, the first group covering 'Muhammad and the Qur'ān' and the second centring on 'Early Islamic Thought'.

We have already covered in our discussion some of the articles in the first group. As Watt himself states in the Introduction, the articles focus on his main disciplines of research.

The items are not arranged chronologically, but significantly Watt begins with his article on the Banū Qurayẓah issue. This, in most of Watt's works, is a favourite theme and one wonders whether, by putting it first, Watt is giving credence to the assertion that his selection of themes is often biased against Muslims.

However, Watt, the careful historian that he is, points out a methodological dictum in research which is very significant. In the article on 'The Reliability of Ibn Isḥāq's Sources', he writes: '. . . it is worth reminding ourselves of a general principle of all historical research, namely, that the ostensible sources for any series of events are always to be accepted unless some grounds can be shown for their rejection or partial rejection'.[216]

Andrew Rippin, in his review of this book appreciates the tone and general arrangement of the articles.[217] However, he refers to the above statement and argues that Watt seems to hold a view not very different from the outlook of the eighth- and ninth-century Muslim historians, which basically means '. . . retelling "what really happened", filtered of course, through our own contemporary sense of "what makes sense" '.[218] Rippin believes that this perspective is not good enough in view of the enormity of the mission facing the researcher. However, he values the articles as a '. . . fitting reminder of the contribution he has made'.[219]

1991 saw the publication of one of Watt's most recent books, *Muslim-Christian Encounters: Perceptions and Misconceptions.*[220]

Peter B. Clarke of King's College, London in his estimation of the book remarks that Watt shows an exceptional expertise in dealing with a rather complex subject.[221] The work itself is said to be the culmination of half a century of Watt's involvement in the field of academic study of Islam and Christianity.

The book begins with an assessment of the kind of Christianity that Islam met in Arabia. This is another passionate theme for Watt, with the underlying argument being that Islam encountered a garbled form of Christianity which no 'true' Christian could recognize. He then reasons that that is exactly why the Qur'ānic critique of Christian doctrine is, as he finds it, so strange.[222] He recycles his arguments on the lack of historical consciousness among the Makkans, explaining that it accounts for the nature of the Qur'ānic 'caricature' of Christianity.[223]

Watt looks at Muslim encounters with Greek philosophy, with Christians and others when Islam was in its period of ascendancy, and with medieval Europe. He also discusses encounters in the present period, ending with a reflection on future prospects. In the concluding chapter, Watt devotes a section to the question of religious exclusivity, pointing out that '. . . exclusivist views cannot be held within the emerging world culture, because social science is part of the Western intellectual outlook, and social-scientific observation of religions shows that they are all doing more or less the same things, with similar aims and with a measure of success'.[224]

It is on this basis that he employs the 'Sermon on the Mount' criterion of evaluating a religion, a religious personality or religious teachings. However, he notes that since religion is dynamic despite the fact that scripture might not undergo change, the yardstick of 'fruits' is an unstable one since the 'fruits' might differ from year to year. He calls on Muslims '. . . to abandon their exclusivism . . . reinterpret their conception of the finality of Islam and of Muhammad being the last prophet'. He continues: 'In respect of Muslim-Christian relations it is essential that Muslims accept the historicity of the Bible and reject the doctrine of its corruption. That doctrine contradicts known facts, such as the existence of manuscripts dating from long before the time of Muhammad.'[225]

Watt refers to the enormous amount of critical scientific scholarship which has been brought to bear on the Christian scriptures over the years, and pleads that these writings have inspired Jews and Christians since the earliest times, and hence, by implication could not be false. Therefore, he says finally: 'What Muslims and other non-Christians are asked to accept in this world where religions mix is this core of historical fact about the teaching and achievement of Jesus as a human being, but without the theological interpretations.'[226]

In his review of the book, Jorgen S. Nielsen,[227] commends Watt's earlier scholarly works on Islam and Christian-Muslim relations and welcomes the work at what he sees as a critical moment in the history of such relations especially in the light of the Gulf crisis. Nielsen points out that the title of the book should be understood as both positive and negative encounters between Christians and the Muslim world as such and not the narrow confines of Islam and Christianity.

In Watt's effort to reflect on and search for solutions to the problems of Inter-Faith relations, he falls back on his theological roots, asking both Christians and Muslims to take a hard look at their scriptures and the interpretations and theologies built around them which often seem to reinforce the attitude of exclusivity. Nielsen asks a question which a non-theologian would feel is at the heart of the issue. He writes:

> . . . from outside the field of theology however, I feel that one must ask the theologians why it should not be possible to live together in reasonable harmony even if one differs in one's theological views. Equally, though, the question must be asked of the social scientist why theological doctrines so easily become the ammunition for material interests.[228]

Mary Hossain's review is rather less complimentary.[229] While she agrees that the book contains valuable information on many issues, she is at pains to point out that '. . . there are also many examples of dubious arguments presented as proven facts without reference to the work of Muslim scholars'.[230] She identifies the second chapter as particularly problematic, where the expressions Watt uses suggest that the revelation of the

Qur'ān was almost wholly contingent upon the environment that it came from.

She then takes issue with Watt regarding assertions in the book that the Qur'ān presents a wrong perception of Christianity and that there are many inaccuracies with respect to certain historical personalities.[231] She notes with concern the criterion that Watt uses to judge the validity of a religious faith – 'the fruits' – which in itself is overtly Christian. She then writes: 'Suitable for those religions whose doctrines are expressed in symbolic terms, this would dilute unnecessarily the straightforward and unambiguous message of the Qur'an. It is the first step towards a free-for-all in which language can mean whatever one wants it to mean and religious truth disappears . . .'[232]

In her concluding appraisal she observes:

> This is a stimulating and interesting, but irritating book. Watt has covered an enormous amount of ground and, in his suggestions for the future, has posed questions which must be answered. His book, however, although full of scholarly information, useful brief critical surveys, and much that is positive, also contains, as well as the dogmatic statements already mentioned, unconvincing speculation, notably on Muslim motives behind the strong reaction to the satanic verses (42, 122) and the Islamic resurgence (124), and strange comparisons between, for example, the suffering of Jesus and the hypothetical suffering of non-fundamentalist Muslims trying to establish a different kind of Islam (37).[233]

In 1991, Watt's article 'Women in Early Islam' in *Studia Missionalia*,[234] was an attempt as a non-anthropologist, as he says, to give a summary of his findings on the subject as reflected in his earlier study in 1956.[235]

Watt asserts that the Qur'ānic amelioration of the existent social system was to change from the matrilineal to the patrilineal system, which was indicative of the economic situation at the time which promoted individualism. He acknowledges the advances that Islam brought to the women in that environment. He quotes from his earlier work *Muhammad at Medina*: 'Both by European Christian standards and by those of Islam, many of the old practices were immoral, and Muhammad's reorganization was therefore a moral advance.'[236]

In 1992, also in *Studia Missionalia*, on the theme 'Religious Sects and Movements – Christianity and Other Religions', Watt contributed an article on 'Islamic Fundamentalism'.[237] Trying to identify the reasons for fundamentalism, he notes that it is essentially a form of response to a highly sophisticated world where advancement in science and technology has led to a stranglehold on cultures. People, he argues, are facing an identity crisis and fear the loss of their culture which would be tantamount to losing their very souls.[238]

Though he identifies fundamentalism in Protestant Christianity, he suggests that this fear of the extensive domination of science and technology is more pervasive in Islam. He again asserts that developments in the modern world, with its concomitant effect of loss of authority among traditional Islamic scholars, led to the latter offering '. . . the intellectual form to Islamic fundamentalism . . .'[239] in anticipation of retention of their authority. He refers to Qur'ānic claims on finality of prophethood and revelation as seen in the person of Muḥammad and the Qur'ān respectively, and reasons that the original meaning of these verses might have been something other than the contemporary Muslim understanding. This position then, of course, dismisses the role of *ḥadīth* in exegesis.

Watt then asserts that the cultivation of this self-image of Islam led Muslims to perceive '. . . the non-Islamic world not as a field for making conversions as Christian missionaries might have done, but as a sphere to be dominated by force'.[240] This method of using a Christian yardstick to measure Islamic principles and comparison of the ideals of the one religion with the realities of the other is not a very helpful principle in scholarship. Here again, Watt seems to be reinforcing the old perception of Islam and its obsession with forcing people to the faith.

Many of the arguments in this article are also to be found in Watt's 1988 publication, *Islamic Fundamentalism and Modernity*.[241] Watt looks at the Western perception of Islam and the response from Muslims which has generally been critical. However, he explains that criticism of Western scholars has come about because '. . . some of the objective facts found by orientalists in Islamic sources are contrary to features of the traditionalist self-image of Islam'.[242] However, he admits that the 'Orientalists' have had a very selective attitude to Islamic studies. He notes: 'The orientalists at most thought of themselves as correcting faulty views held by Muslims. What should certainly be admitted, however, is that for the most part they showed little interest in the positive religious values of Islam.'[243]

Watt looks at the Muslims' criticism levelled against Christian missionaries of collaborating with colonialists to destroy Islam, and he rejects the arguments as exaggeration. He claims that Christian missionaries did not make many inroads into Muslim communities and therefore there was a change of emphasis to the provision of humanitarian assistance. He mentions schools and hospitals in particular.

Again, he refers to the Christian initiatives in Inter-Faith dialogue and seems to suggest that this proves the Christians' sincerity in the promotion of mutual understanding and co-operation. He then writes: 'It should also be admitted, however, that some minor Christian bodies have a hostile attitude towards Islam and produce books criticizing it, though such books have little academic value. Thus, though the accusation of missionaries by the fundamentalists is not wholly mistaken it is very wide of the mark (*sic*).'[244] This statement is not entirely in accordance with the popular perception of the missionary enterprise and the position of Christendom *vis-à-vis* the Muslim world. Until recently, the official position of the Catholic Church, for example, was very different from what Watt suggests.[245]

Watt concludes by admitting that what he calls Islamic fundamentalism is not representative of Islam as a whole. Acknowledging that both Muslims and Christians have a responsibility to oppose secularism and consumerism in the contemporary world, he advocates that every effort be made towards Inter-Faith dialogue and real co-operation in matters of mutual practical significance.

In 1993, Watt again contributed an article, 'Islamic Attitudes to Other Religions', in the *Studia Missionalia* volume dedicated to 'Theology of Religions – Christianity and Other Religions'.[246] He writes that the Muslims' attitude towards people of other faiths were basically conditioned by the Prophet's environment. This could be read as against the universalistic nature of the Qur'ānic message and the fact that the revelations, indeed any revelations, cut across time and space.

Watt then makes a statement similar to an earlier one he made in his *Muhammad's Mecca – History in the Qur'an*, on the status of Muḥammad.[247] He writes: 'Personally I hold that we must accept Muhammad as a prophet who was similar to the Old Testament prophets.'[248] He then clarifies his position by saying:

> The traditional Muslim view, however, is that the revelations in the Qur'an are the actual words of God, and therefore inerrant. This view the Christian cannot admit, since there is in the Qur'an a denial of the death of Jesus on the Cross. What I would say, however, is that, while the central doctrines of the Qur'an are from God, its teaching is expressed in terms, not merely of the Arabic language, but of the views about the world and human life held by the people of Mecca, including some of their misconceptions.[249]

By suggesting that Muḥammad was a Hebrew prophet, Watt leaves room for the ideas of the Arab world to 'slip' into the Qur'ān. He reiterates that these ideas were not concocted by

Muḥammad though '. . . but came to him in some other way'.[250]

Noting that Muḥammad and his people had some semblance of Christian and Jewish influence Watt, however, claims that even though many Biblical prophets and personalities are mentioned in the Qur'ān, '. . . the Qur'anic picture of them is completely different, especially in the earlier passages'.[251] He mentions specific examples like Noah, Abraham, Moses and Jesus, providing extensive references to the Qur'ān to support his contention. He continues: 'While there are thus numerous references to Biblical matters in the Qur'an, it must be insisted that its presentation of the Jewish religion is seriously inadequate and indeed misleading.'[252]

Watt is of the view that the way the Qur'ān presents events in a 'haphazard' or 'disconnected' way, is in line with pre-Islamic thought which did not pay much attention to continuity.[253] He claims that in the early period of Islamic scholarship when the doctrines of Islam were agreed upon, every effort was made to outlaw the study of other cultures and especially other religions. Muslims, according to this assertion, were living in intellectual isolation and this fostered an unhealthy attitude towards others.

He mentions as an exception the twelfth-century Ash'arite theologian al-Shahrastānī, whose study of sects offers an extensive insight into Christianity.[254]

In his concluding remarks, Watt maintains that, 'If the attitude of Islam to other religions is to be summed up in a word, it is that, as far as possible, they were to be ignored . . . At the moment the safest conclusion would be that the objective study of other religions by Muslims is still in its infancy.'[255]

Watt's work *Islamic Creeds – A Selection*[256] published in 1994 is a collection of classical credal works by Muslim theologians. The interest here lies in the introductory chapters before the creeds themselves. These deal with the historical background of Islamic theology, a discussion on basic articles of belief, a note on literature and some technical terms which appear in the translated texts. After noting the structural differences in

Christianity and Islam, Watt seeks to identify the reason for such differences. He suggests that Christians needed the elaborate structural arrangement of bishops and others to look after a community that often found itself as a minority. In the case of Islam, however, he asserts that the political nature of the faith enables it to find some form of self-sufficiency or autonomy and even though '. . . in some of the conquered lands they were for a time in a minority, they were still politically supreme. Because the Muslim community had a political structure, no need was felt to have some further structure to deal with purely religious matters.'[257]

He acknowledges that in spite of the lack of such an authoritative body in Islam, even in theological issues Muslims displayed a '. . . considerable skill in reaching a common mind or consensus . . . in these fields, and this justified al-Shafiʿi's inclusion of consensus among the roots of law'.[258]

The discussions on some articles of faith, the short sections dealing with the *shahādah*, the Qur'ān, the Prophethood of Muḥammad and so forth are largely non-commital. They state the Muslims' basic beliefs without any overlay of Watt's own interpretation as in his earlier works. It would appear that since the creeds are merely being translated, Watt did not feel there was any need for elaborate, critical remarks.

The foregoing survey of Watt's thought, essentially on Islam, gives a fairly accurate picture of his outlook on Islam in general and on the Prophet Muḥammad in particular. Following is a specific appreciation of his two books, *Muhammad at Mecca* (1953) and *Muhammad at Medina* (1956).[259]

MUHAMMAD AT MECCA

Structure of the Book

This book was published in 1953; a short introduction on the back cover sets out, basically, the status of the book in the context of academic study of Islam in general and Muḥammad in particular, and states that the book was written to satisfy an apparent appetite in academia for '. . . a fresh life of the Holy Prophet set in a fuller historical context'.

The reader is also informed that Watt takes special note of traditional sources and uses the Qur'ān as a key source, and examines Muḥammad afresh looking at the economic and socio-political factors which were operative during the period. However, Watt does not give these constituents as the only ones which offer a fuller explanation of the issues of Muḥammad's era. He does not think that pure academic paradigm *per se* is enough to study Muḥammad comprehensively.

From this information, one is given the impression that Watt breaks fresh ground and sets himself apart from the mass of material that has been produced over the ages on the subject. Indeed, in the Preface to the work, Watt mentions, among other things, that his teacher, Richard Bell, deserves a mention since he consulted him on a number of issues. He also points out that Bell had some misgivings about the thesis of the book.

The fact that Watt mentions differences of opinion with Bell is significant. It is indicative of his preparedness to try to break free from the dominant paradigm in the interpretation of Muḥammad at this time. In fact, in his revision of Bell's work, *Introduction to the Qur'an*, Watt remarks critically on the assumptions in the book and points out the need for a new perspective befitting the present age.[260]

The book[261] is in six main parts each with well-defined sub-divisions. Watt sets out his objectives and ground plan for the work in the Introduction.

Part One looks at the Prophet's Arabian background, probing the socio-political, economic, religious and intellectual context.

Part Two focuses on Muḥammad's early life up to the prophetic call and discusses his ancestral history, birth and infancy, marriage, and the call to mission. Then, in a sub-section, Watt discusses Muḥammad's prophetic consciousness, followed by a short chronology of events in the Makkan era.

Part Three examines the Prophet's message, analyzing the

Qur'ān regarding its dating, and the essence of the earliest revealed passages, setting them in the context of early seventh-century Makkah. This part concludes with a section entitled 'Further Reflections', which is divided into two sub-sections, taking up the issues of the effect of the economic situation in Makkah on the Message of Islam and the theory on the originality of the Qur'ān.

Part Four, entitled 'The First Muslims', investigates conversions and accounts of converts, ending with the general impact of Muḥammad's message on the society.

Part Five focuses on the issue of opposition. It investigates the so-called 'Satanic Verses', the first migration to Abyssinia, the methods of opposition and presents what Watt deems to be Qur'ānic evidence to show that what happened could not be termed persecution in the strictest sense.[262] This analysis follows Watt's dominant method of relying on the Qur'ān as a primary source of historical material. The prominent opposition leaders and their motives are discussed at the end of this part.

Part Six, bearing the title 'Expanding Horizons', looks at Muḥammad's attempt to widen the spectrum of his mission by venturing outside Makkah. It studies the difficult personal problems the Prophet faced following the demise of both his wife and uncle within the first decade of his call. The abortive preaching mission to Ṭā'if is discussed, together with the advances he made towards inviting the Bedouins to accept his message. A section is devoted to the ʿAqabah discussions culminating in the main *Hijrah.* This, and indeed the main part of the book, ends with a short, two-page assessment of the Makkan era of the Prophet's work.

The book closes with an 'Eight-Point Addendum', which runs through a discussion of the Ahabish theory, the question of Judaeo-Christian influences, the Ḥanīfs, a survey of prominent Makkan Muslims and unbelievers, to a short analysis of traditions from ʿUrwah b. az-Zubayr with regard to the Makkan period. The addendum ends with the first *Hijrah* to Abyssinia and looks at those who were supposed to have returned to join the Muslim forces at the various battles which ensued. Finally, Watt attempts to account for what he perceives as a short-fall in the numbers of those who migrated and those who returned.

Sources

One characteristic, which could probably be described as Watt's *marque de fabrique*, is his concern for the sources he makes use of. In almost every work, the reader is given a foretaste of what to expect. Watt lays bare the sources of his material, usually analyzing them to set the tone for the discussion. Whether one agrees with his interpretation of the sources or not, he affords the reader the opportunity for a follow up. He almost always makes his standpoint clear, so that the reader, if he happens to take issue, might be able to find a foundation for that critique.

In this particular work, Watt follows his usual pattern. In the introductory pages, he sets out a handsome bibliography, giving the classical works he uses and explaining the symbols that one might encounter, especially in the footnotes. He divides the Introduction into two sections. The first section deals with his standpoint while the second concerns the sources used.

He points out that his target readership could fall into three groups – historians, Muslims and Christians. He again states that he has endeavoured to be as dispassionate as possible with respect to references to Qur'ānic verses. He writes: '. . . for example, in order to avoid deciding whether the Qur'an is or is not the Word of God, I have refrained from using the expressions "God says" and "Muhammad says" when referring to the Qur'an, and have simply said "the Qur'an says".'[263] He then continues: 'I do however, regard the adoption of a materialistic outlook as implicit in historical impartiality, but write as a professing monotheist.'[264]

Watt argues against a purely academic outlook on

Muḥammad, which he thinks is not adequate to understand such a figure, and demands a theological appreciation as well. He maintains that despite the fact that he considers he has respected the demands of Western academic historical scholarship, nothing is expressed in the book which could suggest vilification of any cardinal article of faith in Islam. He does not see any problems in applying the principles of Western academic lore in the study of Islam. He argues:

> There need be no unbridgeable gulf between Western scholarship and Islamic faith. If some of the conclusions of Western scholars have been unacceptable to Muslims, it may be that the scholars have not always been faithful to their own principles of scholarship and that, even from the purely historical point of view, their conclusion requires to be revised.[265]

Watt then goes further, asking Muslims to reconstruct or modify their doctrines without, as he puts it, '. . . any change in essentials'.[266] He reasons that students of Islam in the twentieth century have been craving for a new look at Muḥammad not necessarily because of the availability of new material. It is primarily '. . . because in the last half-century or so historians' interests and attitudes have altered, and in particular because they have become more conscious of the material factors underlying history'.[267] He explains that this suggests that many more questions are now being raised in the context of the socio-political and economic milieu in which Islam found itself.

Watt asserts that the present work does not merely analyze material more carefully than others on the market but perhaps, more importantly, it '. . . attempts to answer many questions that have hardly been raised in the past'.[268]

Watt states that his primary source is the Qur'ān and the classical material from the third and fourth centuries after *Hijrah.* He focuses on the *Sīrah* of Ibn Hishām, the *Annals* of al-Ṭabarī, the *Maghāzī* of al-Wāqidī and the *Ṭabaqāt* of Ibn Saʿd. Material is also derived from Bukhārī, Aḥmad ibn Ḥanbal, Ibn al-Athīr and Ibn Ḥajar. He praises Ibn Isḥāq, for whose work he relies on Ibn Hishām, pointing out that he organized his materials carefully.[269] He also praises Ibn Hishām, for both his faithful recension of Ibn Isḥāq and his own valuable additions.

He refers to a statement by P.W. Buhl which gives valuable advice on dealing with historical data, especially in periods of great rivalry within the organization or group under survey. It says: '. . . in dealing with the traditional material one must always be on one's guard, where a definite party-interest may be supposed, not to be led astray by its sometimes innocent-looking appearance'.[270]

Watt, however, urges that the possibility or even probability of such a bent being brought to bear on a historical narrative should not, in itself, deprive us of the opportunity to make a sound judgement. One could, he points out, '. . . make allowance for the distortion and . . . present the data in an unbiased form; . . .'[271]

He further explains that this theory, called 'tendential shaping' of events, and due to party interests, occurs especially when people try to assign reasons for a particular event. Often, he says, the main actor would assign a meritorious motive for the act while his opponents would attribute to it the exact opposite. The student should therefore keep this in mind while interpreting data, especially in periods when history was not distinct, and he suggests, as an example, Islam's pre-*Hijrah* times.[272] He advises a self-reconstruction of motives in cases where reasonable doubt seems to exist.

Watt then gives his own procedure for dealing with such issues in the book under discussion. He writes:

> In dealing then, with the background of Muhammad's career and his Meccan period I have proceeded on the view that the traditional accounts are in general to be accepted, are to be received with care and as far as possible corrected where 'tendential shaping' is suspected, and are

> only to be rejected outright where there is internal contradiction.[273]

For example, he considers the genealogical structure in Ibn Saʿd as fascinating and probably unbelievable to the average Western mind. However, he reasons, the fascination in itself should not make the material implausible because, he asks: 'Who would have taken the trouble to invent all this intricate network, and for what reason?'[274]

In his consideration of the Qur'ān as primary source-material, Watt notes the difficulties of '. . . determining the chronological order of the various parts and the uncertainty of many of the results', and the fact that '. . . the Qur'an is partial and fragmentary'.[275] He is of the view that, due to these difficulties, there is a need to look at the socio-political and economic environment in which Islam was cradled in order to have a balanced picture.

He has a rather interesting methodology concerning traditional reports in the Makkan and the Madīnan periods. In the former period, he accepts the material, basing himself solely on the *Matn* (the text of the tradition) neglecting the *Isnād* (the chain of narrators); in the latter period, he accepts the *Matn* through an analysis of the *Isnād*. The rationale for applying this inconsistent methodology is unfortunately not very clear from the discussion.

In the following discussion we examine the themes Watt selects as significant in his assessment of Muḥammad in Makkah, note any lacunae and attempt to discover why he selects particular themes and avoids others which, we think, are also important.

Selected Themes

In this section, Watt's dominant themes are considered. This approach, apart from the fact that it is consistent with other parts of the study, enables us to understand Watt's favourite issues and, hopefully, makes it possible for us to discern whether he merely follows other late nineteenth- and early twentieth-century scholars, especially those we are studying, or is able to break the mould and set out a fresh outlook on Muḥammad. If the latter is the case, then Watt will have really lived up to his promise to provide his readers with a fresh insight into the subject.[276]

The Background

Watt states the aim of this discussion, the subject of Chapter One, as, to bring into focus '. . . those features of the background which are most important for a proper understanding of . . .' the life and work of Muḥammad.[277] Taking up the economic issue, he argues that though Gibb has maintained that the desert environment *per se* was irrelevant in the shaping of Islam, '. . . nonetheless in the total phenomenon of Islam the desert has a role of first importance'.[278]

The position of the two dominant cities in early Islamic history, Makkah and Madīnah, with the constant interchange between them and the Bedouin tribes, provides an opportunity to look at desert economics *vis-à-vis* Islam.

Watt discusses the climatic differences in various parts of the Ḥijāz and the Nejd, resulting in the need for migration of shepherds and their flocks. The crucial importance of the camel and the date is also pointed out. Owing to the nature of the land, the constant – usually rough – interaction of the nomads and the settlers in the lush green belts is unavoidable hence the question of raiding and general brigandry.

Watt's analysis brings into sharp focus the harsh realities of the differences between Makkah on the one hand and areas in Ṭā'if and Madīnah on the other. These concern agricultural viability. He emphasizes that in Makkah agriculture was almost non-existent while in the other areas (Ṭā'if and Madīnah) the land was suitable for agriculture and the settlers engaged in extensive farming.

He underlines Makkah's status as a nerve-centre for commerce and its favourable geographical position. He also stresses the city's prominence as a financial centre of the day, with many eminent residents being '. . . financiers and skilful in the manipulation of credit, shrewd in their speculations, and interested in any potentialities of lucrative investment from Aden to Gaza or Damascus'.[279]

The Qur'ān, therefore, he reasons, '. . . appeared not in an atmosphere of the desert, but in that of high finance'.[280]

He raises the question of whether the birth of Islam and its later expansion into other parts of the world, especially Persia, Syria, and North Africa, had anything to do with economic upheavals in the Ḥijāz. However, he discounts any plausible economic explanation for this, arguing that despite the many conquests, the Ḥijāz settlers almost always returned to their native land, suggesting the place was still 'peaceful' and attractive.[281]

The second issue Watt looks at under environmental factors is the political climate in Makkah at the time. Despite the suspicions that many Western scholars have about accounts of Arabic sources with respect to the political arrangements and tribal bickering in Arabia at the advent of Islam, Watt takes a positive stance and accepts these accounts as largely dependable. He admits that while extreme hostile relations between the ʿAbbāsids and the Umayyads, for example, might have had some telling effects on later historical narratives, he does not believe that these caused much damage to the overall spectrum of the history of the period.

He examines the 'extreme antiquity' of Makkah, mentioning various clans who held sway in the political structure of ancient Arabia. He relies on al-Masʿūdī, Ibn Hishām, Ibn Isḥāq and al-Ṭabarī in his analysis of the thorny relations among the clans with the resultant effect of strengthening some while weakening others.

He points out that L. Caetani's opinion that the *Ḥilf al-Fuḍūl* was a general alliance to fight injustice and oppression does not seem to be supported by the available material.[282]

Watt interprets what he thinks were the various groupings and political alliances at play before the advent of Muḥammad,[283] and assigns reasons for his understanding. In terms of the wielding of authority in Makkah, he sees the rather low-key consultative council of chiefs and elders (*The Mala'*), who technically had no executive powers, as the one having that power. He points out that '. . . the boycott of the clans of Hashim and al-Muttalib is an example of how economic and social pressure could be brought to bear'.[284]

He also refers to the smaller office-holders in the intricate arrangement in Makkah. Notable among these were the office of the *Siqāyah*, responsible for water supplies, especially for the benefit of pilgrims; the *Rifādah*, in charge of arrangements for pilgrims; and the *Liwā'*, the office in charge of keeping the banners and flags during battle. All these offices, however obscure their influence, had a significant behind-the-scenes impact on the political arrangements in Makkah.

Watt goes on to identify two main factors as responsible for a person's influence and status in the Makkan society, namely, '. . . his clan and his personal qualifications'.[285]

He compares the Makkan institution of *Mala'* with the Athenian arrangement of *ekklesia* and pronounces the former as a '. . . much wiser and more responsible body . . .' because '. . . its decisions were more often made on the solid merit of men and their policies and not on specious rhetoric that could make the worse appear the better cause'.[286] However, he notes a significant difference between the two bodies, pointing out that in the Athenian philosophy, honesty and uprightness were the main principles for honourability while in the Makkan situation, the more pressing elements were practical skills and efficient leadership qualities.[287]

In the next discussion, focusing on the status of the Quraysh as compared to the other tribes, Watt argues that though there could be some justification for the claim that the Qurayshī authority was derived from superior military strength, the suggestion by Lammens that this was achieved because of the employment of black slaves is not convincing. He is of the opinion rather, that the Qurayshī eminence did not derive from '. . . their military prowess as individuals. The secret of their prestige was the military strength they could bring to bear on an opponent. This was not their own military strength, but that of a whole confederacy. This confederacy they had built up on the basis of their mercantile enterprises'.[288] He attributes the success of the Quraysh rather to their political wisdom and skilful display of statesmanship which, in Makkan society, as he argues in his comparison of Athenian *ekklesia* and Arab *Mala'*, were crucial in determining one's honour.

Watt's attention then shifts to the foreign policy of Makkah. He notes that the city was sandwiched between the two major powers of the then known world, the Byzantine and Persian empires, and also to some extent the Abyssinians.

Makkah was important because it offered an alternative trade route to the Byzantines since the Persians, taking advantage of their geographical location, were creating serious problems for them in their trade with the outside world especially China, India and Ceylon. In peace-time the Persians exacted huge tariffs on trading and, of course, in war-time trading activities were seriously affected. Makkah was the most appropriate route remaining.

Therefore, he notes, the Byzantines, in the early and mid-sixth century, had an arrangement with the Abyssinians which, indirectly, meant they had an influence on South Arabia, a position which, of course, changed during the Persian conquest in the latter part of that century. In this struggle between the superpowers, Makkah was relatively unaffected and made significant gains. This culminated in an attempt by Arabia to destroy the *Kaʿbah* in order to re-focus attention on the shrine at Ṣanʿā' in Yemen in the south. In his understanding of the traditional accounts, Watt says that the '. . . expedition came to nothing as the Abyssinian army was destroyed, apparently by plague'.[289]

Watt refrains from explaining his understanding of events in the Year of the Elephant in the face of traditional accounts often based on Qur'ānic references.[290] He does, however, provide a view of his honesty and pragmatism. In the analysis dealing with very intricate issues, he admits that he might not be absolutely right. He acknowledges: 'Owing to the scantiness of our materials there is much in this account of Meccan policies that is conjectural.'[291]

However, he insists that '. . . even if many of the details are incorrect, the general picture is, I believe, sound. Muhammad grew to maturity in a world in which high finance and international politics were inextricably mixed up'.[292] Watt's preparedness to admit that one's interpretation does not in itself constitute the 'real' or 'only' basis for scholarly understanding of events is indicative of his probity as a seasoned academic.

The third issue in the background discussion has to do with social and moral factors. Watt notes the importance of the tribe in the conditions existing in Arabia in Muḥammad's time. However, he then reminds us that the tribal units themselves were not absolute and could break up into sub-units or even disappear, and in the case of Makkah, animosities were rife. Therefore the need for strong bonds amongst tribal members or those of a particular unit. The language that was best understood was based on force and, within the circumstances, was found to be the most expedient to keep law and order. The principle of *lex talionis* might be repugnant in our age but, in that scenario, there was perhaps no better alternative.[293] Despite the pervasive consciousness of tribal solidarity, there was an underlying, carefully woven unity in which these apparently diverse groups were welded together by the force of '. . . a common language (though with variations in dialect), a common poetical tradition, some common conventions and ideas, and a common descent'.[294]

Watt argues, with some justification, that the strong tribal solidarity among the Arabs, especially those in Makkah, was responsible for the relative ease with which Muḥammad was able to preach in Makkah in the first place. Despite the problems he encountered later, he says, it was because of Muḥammad's tribal unit, the Banū Hāshim, and his being a Qurayshī that his enemies found it too risky to attack him personally for fear of retribution. Nevertheless, he reminds us, tribal solidarity was not absolute. The Arabs loved and cherished their individual freedom. In fact, as Philip Hitti puts it, 'The Arabian in general and the Bedouin in particular, is a born democrat. He meets his sheikh on an equal footing.'[295] Watt stresses that:

> The members of the tribe were not automatons, but human beings prone to selfishness – or what Lammens calls '*individualisme*'; it would only be natural if sometimes they put private interests above those of the tribe . . . While tribal solidarity continued to govern the actions of the best people, yet a certain individualism began to make its appearance in their thinking . . .[296]

Watt again assigns the circumstances of a mercantile society to the individualistic tendencies amongst some Makkans. He refers to business alliances which sometimes did not respect tribal or clan boundaries and mentions also that Abū Lahab, for example, took a different stance with regard to Muḥammad as against other members of the Banū Hāshim due to palpable economic reasons. He then asserts that these economic exigencies of the time had what he calls a 'correlation' with the genesis of Islam. However, he quickly tries to make a distinction between this assertion and '. . . the absolute dependence of religion and ideology on economic factors as maintained by the Marxist'.[297]

The discourse moves on to moral ideals and refers to the Arab moral ideal as based on *murūwah* or manliness, Goldziher's favourite terminology. It is this which R.A. Nicholson is said to have explained as '. . . bravery in battle, patience in misfortune, persistence in revenge, protection of the weak, defiance of the strong'.[298]

Basic moral values as understood by the Arabs are discussed.

Principles such as generosity and hospitality bordering on profligacy, loyalty and fidelity and general heroism are mentioned.[299] Perhaps it is from this basic rationale that succession by primogeniture was markedly absent. Watt says this was the case '. . . for obvious reasons; if the eldest son of a chief was inexperienced when his father died (as would frequently happen), the tribe could not jeopardize its very existence by having such a man as leader. The chief must be a man of wisdom and sound judgement, and so was usually the most respected male in the family.'[300]

On the religious and intellectual setting, the discussion is based on three assumptions: that the existent religion had become decadent and archaic, there was in vogue what could be described as 'tribal humanism'; and that shadows of monotheism were visible on the horizon.

On the first point, Watt refers to the works of T. Nöldeke, J. Wellhausen and H. Lammens, each of them touching on ancient Arabia and its religious vestiges. They describe the 'pagan' beliefs prevalent before the advent of Muḥammad.

Watt, however, makes it clear that since the material in this area is scrappy and perhaps more importantly for his theory, derived from Islamic sources, '. . . there is ample scope for conjecture'.[301] Perhaps it is primarily this conjectural attitude which prevents him from venturing into a deeper discussion on religion.

'Tribal humanism', which Watt sees as the other considered alternative and calls the '. . . effective religion of the Arabs',[302] was also waning in its impact as was the worship of cosmic objects, trees, stones and other aspects of nature. He describes 'tribal humanism' as the religion one detects from the poets for whom '. . . the realization of human excellence in action is an end in itself, and at the same time usually contributes to the survival of the tribe, which is the other great end of life. This is humanism in the sense that it is primarily in human values, in virtuous or manly conduct, that it finds significance.'[303]

Again, he is at pains to differentiate this type from

contemporary humanist philosophy. The cardinal difference here, he points out, is that the focus in Arab belief is the tribe while in modern humanism individualism becomes the centre of orientation. The deliberation touches on the concept of fate in the Arab society where the perception was not a total but a limited fatalism.

As Watt had argued earlier in his Ph.D thesis, which was later published as *Freewill and Predestination in Early Islam*,[304] he reiterates that this limited fatalism was, among other things, carried over into Islam. At the advent of Muḥammad, this perception of the immortality of the tribe had tapered off almost into oblivion. Individualism held sway but, as he indicates, the shift of axis did not create a new 'religion' since, even though tribal humanism itself did have a form of religious belief behind it, the Arabs did not have a clear concept of individual immortality. He argues that this made a transfer of the idea impossible.

Watt begins the discussion on the last part of this section with a criticism of the *communis opinio* in Western scholarship regarding the Judaeo-Christian roots of Islam. He notes that despite the discussion of this theory *ad nauseam*, it is basically flawed because it intrinsically denies the authentic independent theological roots of Islamic tenets. He writes:

> Even from the standpoint of the best Western scholarship the Western studies on the Qur'an have often been unfortunate. They have made a fetish of literary dependence and have forgotten that literary dependence is never more than one side of the picture; there is also the Creative work of the poet, or dramatist, or novelist; and the fact of literary dependence never proves the absence of creative originality.[305]

Comparing the religious domain to this, he points out that too much stress on a religious personality's dependence on the environmental influences *per se* would seriously diminish the opportunity of appreciating '. . . the originality and the uniqueness of the Divine revelation'[306] at play. Yet, he goes on to assert that though Muslims generally hold the Qur'ān to be the divinely-revealed word of God, internal evidence suggests the influence of Judaeo-Christian ideas.

He notes the existence in pre-Islamic religious culture and diction of *al-ilāh* which, he claims, was transposed into Allah by Muḥammad. However, he does not think that *al-ilāh* in the Makkan consciousness had any monotheistic originality in itself. The later monotheistic interpretation, he asserts, was supplied by Judaeo-Christian influences. The issue is so important to him that he devotes an addenda to it, entitling it 'Arabian Monotheism and Judaeo-Christian Influences'.[307]

In this article in the Excursus, Watt argues strenuously that the assumption that '. . . there was no monotheism among the Arabs to whom Muḥammad preached . . . is unsound'.[308] He refers to the works of Nicholson, Margoliouth, Torrey and Jeffery to support his position.[309] His thesis is encapsulated in the statement:

> Thus sound scholarship as well as the theological impartiality of the historian suggests that the chief question to be asked in this field is the extent of Jewish and Christian (and perhaps other) influences upon the Mecca of AD 600, not upon Muhammad himself, or rather upon the Qur'an; and to this question the answer can be neither simple nor absolutely certain.[310]

Watt does not totally discount the possibility of some influence because he thinks that some rumours about and from Jews and Christians and other peoples could certainly have reached Muḥammad and he could have made use of the information. Granted that this reasoning is correct, Watt still depends solely on this to assess the originality of the doctrines of Islam. He revives his original line of thinking thus: 'There is no great difficulty in claiming that the precise form, the point and ulterior significance of the stories came to Muhammad by revelation and not from the communications of his alleged informant.'[311]

Though he argues that Muḥammad and the early Muslims wanted to learn more about the earlier prophets from the Jews and Christians, he maintains that '. . . before this interest in the prophets arose, the essential message of the Qur'an had been proclaimed . . .'[312]

It is also reasonable to assume that the intense superpower politics between the Byzantines and the Persians could have resulted in contacts which went beyond mere military or trade encounters. In both empires and that of the Byzantine surrogates the Abyssinians, Christianity was strong and therefore the influence from this direction on the Arabs cannot be altogether ignored.[313]

As for the types of Christianity or Judaism the Arabs were influenced by, Watt is content to sum up his ideas by stating that those Christian and Jewish denominations '. . . must have had many strange ideas'.[314]

Watt's analysis is significant because it is a general departure from the rather dominant arguments which seek to establish that Muḥammad did not have original ideas of his own.[315]

Muḥammad's Early Life

Every biography of Muḥammad has been concerned with his early life and the discussion often delves into his descent, often with varied objectives. Watt, for example, identifies what he feels is a significant question regarding Muḥammad's pedigree. He writes: 'The chief question to be considered in the life of Muhammad is whether his ancestors were as important in the politics of Mecca as the sources suggest, or whether (as some Western scholars have thought) their importance has been exaggerated.'[316] Whichever way one looks at it, someone with a hidden agenda would be able to reach a conclusion which might not necessarily be in accordance with sound scholarship.

Watt seems to have a theory at the back of his mind when he suggests that the extant material seems to have given prominence to the generation of Hāshim over and against that of ʿAbd Shams, since scholars were under the considerable influence of ʿAbbāsid political intrigue. However, he does not give much weight to the leverage which was applied. He notes that '. . . there are no grounds for supposing serious falsification or large-scale invention'.[317]

The crucial issue in this argument is not merely the level of influence but essentially how this could have a negative effect on the whole historical spectrum of Muḥammad's life. In conclusion, Watt is of the opinion that though Muḥammad's family was once prominent in Makkan society, in Muḥammad's own time that prominence had certainly declined.[318]

Touching on his birth, Watt seems to express some doubt about Muḥammad being born posthumously, saying this was a presumption.[319]

He states some basic facts about Muḥammad's childhood and adds a footnote that as far as the secular historian is concerned these are the only relevant facts though, even with these, some doubts have been raised. He then refers to a large mass of material, theological in character, and of significance only to the believer. Watt writes: 'It is almost certain that they are not true in the realistic sense of the secular historian, for they purport to describe facts to which we might reasonably have expected some reference at later periods of Muhammad's life; but there is no such reference.'[320] He then cites a lengthy passage from Ibn Isḥāq, detailing some of the narratives from Halīmah, Āminah herself and other events which border on the miraculous and which explain why the secular historian might find it ahistorical.[321]

He then looks at Muḥammad's marriage to Khadījah and immediately expresses doubt about her age at the time of the marriage and that it '. . . has perhaps been exaggerated'.[322] His argument is simply that granted that the seven children Khadījah had were born at yearly intervals, the last would have been born when she was about forty-eight years old. He expresses disquiet about this and argues that though, 'This is by no means impossible, . . . one would have thought it sufficiently unusual to merit comment; it is even the sort of thing that might well have been treated as miraculous. Yet no single word of comment occurs in the pages of Ibn Hisham, Ibn Saʿd, or al-Tabari.'[323] Again, he doubts whether Khadījah was quite the woman of substance that the traditional accounts portray her as being.

In his search for material on Muḥammad's early married life during prophethood, Watt says he draws a blank and therefore he has to deduce from passages of the Qur'ān and he draws on *Sūrah al-Ḍuḥā* where references are made to Muḥammad's past.[324]

The Call to Prophethood

Watt discusses the account of Muḥammad's call to prophethood in the work of al-Zuhrī and examines what he considers to be some inconsistencies in the various reports. He casts doubt on the interpretation given to Muḥammad's early visions which involved the angel Jibrīl and asserts that Muḥammad might have thought that he saw God Himself. Acknowledging that this does not agree with the Muslim understanding of the nature of God, he reasons that the position is reinforced by the fact that Jibrīl does not appear in the verses revealed in Makkah until the Madīnan period. He points out that, 'The formal interpretation of the vision, however, is not so important from the standpoint of the life of Muhammad as the significance of it for his religious development.'[325]

Referring to the practice of retreat – *Taḥannuth* – in the Cave of Ḥirā', Watt is sceptical of the standard account that the first encounter with the angel Jibrīl happened here, saying that '. . . the comparative dates of the different features of Muhammad's call are uncertain'.[326]

On the visit to Waraqah by Muḥammad and Khadījah, Watt

does not find it expedient to doubt it. He reasons that the incident shows how desperate Muḥammad was to boost his confidence after the initial experience in the cave and therefore it could not have been fabricated.[327]

Probably precisely because of this, Watt goes on to suggest that the expression in the first revelation in *Sūrah al-ʿAlaq* concerning the 'teaching of the pen', might have reminded Muḥammad of his indebtedness to Waraqah. He therefore concludes that '. . . Muhammad had frequent communication with Waraqah at an earlier date, and learnt much of a general character. Later Islamic concepts may have been largely moulded by Waraqah's ideas, e.g., of the relation of Muhammad's revelation to previous revelations'.[328] He is of course, aware that this is a mere assumption since there is no evidence that Muḥammad met Waraqah before the incident connected with the first encounter in the Cave of Ḥirā'. The assumption itself is interesting considering that Waraqah might have died some three or four years after the incident.[329]

Discussing the Western appreciation of the form of Muḥammad's prophetic consciousness, Watt reiterates his view that the picture has generally been unfavourable. He points out that 'Western writers have mostly been prone to believe the worst of Muhammad, and, where an objectionable interpretation of an act seemed plausible, have tended to accept it as fact.'[330]

He insists that plausibility in itself is not a strong criterion on which to judge a particular case and it is important that solid, sound evidence should be presented as the basis for assessing the Prophet. He writes: 'Thus, not merely must we credit Muhammad with essential honesty and integrity of purpose, if we are to understand him at all; if we are to correct the errors we have inherited from the past, we must in every particular case hold firmly to the belief in his sincerity until the opposite is conclusively proved; . . .'[331] He goes on to argue that one cannot sustain the view that Muḥammad interposed his own views into the revealed text. Yet, he believes the Prophet '. . . may have tried to induce emending revelations where he felt that a passage required emendation – it is part of orthodox Muslim theory that some revelations were abrogated by others'.[332]

Watt attempts to look at the nature of the Qur'ān in relation to Muḥammad's own psyche. He mentions the opinions of Muslim orthodoxy, secular scholarship and a third stance generally shared by some Christian scholars of Islam.

The first opinion is of the divinity of the Qur'ān (its divine origin), the second discounts the Divine origin and focuses on Muḥammad's personality as the source of the Qur'ān. The third opinion allows room for divine involvement but sees Muḥammad's personality as being an influential factor in the 'formation' of the Qur'ān.

Watt claims that as a historian he does not lean towards any of these theories and endeavours to be dispassionate.[333] With this, he launches an investigation into the nature of the revelation which Muḥammad received and, relying on A. Poulain's *The Graces of Interior Prayer*, identifies two main forms of religious experience as it occurred to Muḥammad – 'Locutions' and 'Visions'. He explains that in 'locution' the messages are '. . . received directly without the assistance of the ear; they can be said to be received by the imaginative sense; . . .', while in visions, there is '. . . a simple communication of thought without words, and consequently without any definite language'.[334]

Looking at the opinions of al-Suyūṭī and others, Watt finds that these two forms could be identified with the experience of Muḥammad. He is of the opinion that the traditional accounts as to the various forms through which the revelation came to Muḥammad are largely acceptable. Therefore, he points out that, 'To assert that Muhammad's visions and locutions are hallucinations as has sometimes been done, is to make theological judgements without being fully aware of what one is doing, and thereby to show a woeful ignorance of the science and sanity of writers like Poulain and the discipline of mystical theology which they represent.'[335]

He explains further that the main point is not the question of authenticity of the revelations but the fact that the revealed word and Muḥammad's own thoughts could be distinguished. Watt then touches on the pathology theory where Muḥammad was thought to be epileptic. He repudiates the theory on the basic grounds that none of the medical symptoms associated with this condition were present in Muḥammad. Further, he argues, even if it were the case '. . . the argument would be completely unsound and based on mere ignorance and prejudice; such physical concomitants neither validate or invalidate religious experience'.[336]

Muḥammad's Basic Teachings and the Contemporary Situation

This theme occupies the third chapter of the book. Starting with the question as to the original teaching presented by Muḥammad, Watt says that though the Muslim accounts can be relied upon, there are problems which cannot be solved from the available material because of what he claims are inconsistencies and contradictions. Hence, to the Western scholar many issues remain unsolved, unless of course some reconstruction is resorted to. Most of the problems have to do with the chronology of the revealed passages. Nöldeke and Bell attempted to reorganize the Qur'ānic material to suit the Western quest for chronology. Watt tries to introduce a paradigm which he thinks could help solve the problem. His principle is basically that he identifies all passages which reflect opposition to be late Makkan, since, as he argues, '. . . before opposition could arise some message which tended to arouse opposition must have been proclaimed'.[337]

He indicates that as far as the early passages are concerned they must have concentrated on subjects like 'God's goodness and Power'; 'The return to God for Judgement'; 'Man's response – gratitude and worship, generosity and purification'; and

'Muḥammad's own vocation'. In these, he specifies verses which, he thinks, fit his paradigm.[338]

Again, Watt discusses the social, moral, religious and intellectual significance of Muḥammad's message in the then environment, underlining the kind of transformation it sought to initiate.[339]

The rest of the chapter is devoted to general comments which centre on two main parts – economic conditions and viability of religion, and the originality of the Qur'ān.

Watt revisits the economic argument, stating that Makkah's economic environment during Muḥammad's time is very significant for obtaining a fuller understanding of Muḥammad. He argues that the economic conditions created an individualistic philosophy and the society was in need of a balance to sustain it and that moral and religious balance came in the form of Islam. He is of the opinion that the manifest needs of the society were primarily religious and therefore, in a way, the society was ripe for Islam.[340]

As for the originality of the Qur'ānic message, Watt writes: 'The secularist would have to say that it was by chance and for secondary reasons that Muhammad stumbled across ideas that held the key to the solution of the fundamental problems of his day; and that is not plausible. Neither empirical grouping nor hard and acute thinking adequately account for the Qur'anic *kerygma*.'[341] He endeavours to steer a middle course between this secularist position and the Muslim belief that the Qur'ān was divine intervention in the world with Makkah a mere cradle. He emphasizes that his position does not discount the fact that the Qur'ān had a particular significance for the Makkan milieu. He refers to certain relevant issues which could only be understood by the Makkans.[342]

He illustrates it with an example of the Qur'ānic critique of usury and asks rather rhetorically why the issue of usury was not mentioned in the Makkan passages since Makkah, with its elaborate financial system should have been the starting point. However, he answers himself by noting that the situation in

Makkah was such that the message of usury could not have been effectively conveyed and hence it was more sensible for the issue to be raised in the Madīnan period.[343]

Watt then attempts to look at the relation of the Qur'ān to the Judaeo-Christian teachings in existence at the time. Trying to create an analogy between this and the 'sources', he obviously recognizes the inherent danger and abandons the exercise. Curiously, he then says: 'This latter conception, however, is contrary to the beliefs of Orthodox Muslims, and therefore to be avoided.'[344]

This is a remarkable statement because all along the impression one gathers is that Watt sticks to historical scholarship without necessarily agreeing with what Muslims believe. This apparent contradictory rationale will be taken up in the Conclusion and an attempt made to point out which of the two is dominant in his analysis.

Watt goes on to argue that many fundamental ideas expressed in the Qur'ān were already public knowledge in Makkah and it was therefore necessary to 'Arabize' these old 'Judaeo-Christian ideas' to make them more relevant to the Arabs since only an Arab could have made these 'ideas' relevant to his tribesmen.[345]

The reasoning appears to be not very different from the Muslim scholarly position – where it is emphasized that the essential message of the Qur'ān is dissimilar to what has already been revealed to others. After all, the Qur'ān recognizes itself as a 'Reminder' and a 'Confirmation' of the earlier message.[346]

Watt observes that the 'originality' of the Qur'ān *vis-à-vis* these 'ideas', '. . . consists in that it gave them greater precision and detail, presented them more forcefully, and, by its varying emphasis, made a more or less coherent synthesis of them; above all, it gave them a focus in the person of Muhammad and his special vocation as a messenger of God'.[347]

A problem is identified here, that, in the case of what Watt calls 'illustrative material, like the stories of the prophets', wide discrepancies between the Judaeo-Christian views and the Qur'ānic views are detected. Often, the argument has been that the Qur'ānic views agree more with what the Jews and Christians would call non-canonical or apocryphal works. The conclusion has therefore almost always been that Muḥammad merely heard these heretical stories from the society and uncritically 'adopted' them into 'his Qur'ān'.[348]

'The Satanic Verses'[349]

The 'Satanic Verses' is one of Watt's favourite themes and in Chapter Four he spends ten pages on it. Looking at it from the context of the beginning of opposition, he divides the discussion into three sections. In the first section he considers a letter cited in al-Ṭabarī written by ʿUrwah b. az-Zubayr, the second looks at 'The Satanic Verses, the facts' and the last focuses on what he calls motives and explanations for the Satanic Verses.

ʿUrwah's letter refers to the beginning of preaching, the eruption of opposition, the involvement of certain prominent personalities in Ṭā'if and the eventual migration of part of the nascent community of Abyssinia. Watt's analysis of the satanic verses is thus based partly on this letter. Regarding the 'facts', of the satanic verses, he claims that, 'The most notable mention of idols in the Meccan part of the Qur'an is in Surat al-Najm (53), and thereby hangs a tale.'[350] He recounts and comments on the versions of the tale in al-Ṭabarī. His conclusions rest on two main issues. He suggests that the story could certainly be true because there is no reason to assume that it was invented by Muḥammad's enemies and, also, that since the tales say that the actual expressions were abrogated it means the incident actually occurred. He writes:

> Firstly, at one time Muhammad must have publicly recited the satanic verses as part of the Qur'an; it is unthinkable that the story could have been invented later by Muslims or foisted upon them by non-Muslims. Secondly, at some later time Muhammad announced that these verses were

> not really part of the Qur'an and should be replaced by others of a vastly different import. The earliest versions do not specify how long afterwards this happened; the probability is that it was weeks or even months.[351]

In his attempt to look for motives and explanations, Watt is of the opinion that Muslim scholars, without the sophistication of their Western contemporaries made the mistake of assuming that the concept of monotheism was fully clear to the Prophet from the beginning. Hence, he goes on to assert, rather condescendingly, that the satanic verses cannot be explained effectively. Claiming a better insight into Muḥammad's prophethood, Watt then says: 'The truth rather is that his monotheism was originally, like that of his more enlightened contemporaries, somewhat vague, and in particular was not so strict that the recognition of inferior divine beings was felt to be incompatible with it.'[352] For Watt, the message of the 'satanic verses' is indicative of '. . . views which Muhammad had always held'.[353]

He goes on, assigning some rationale for the 'satanic verses' and what Muḥammad might have thought to gain out of making such a statement. He assumes that the Prophet was probably trying to seek a closer alliance with the Qurayshī elites and thought this concession would do the trick. Or, he again asserts, the Prophet wanted to reach out to the wider community and felt that by mentioning these popular deities in such important places his own self-image would be heightened. Watt even attributes material gains to Muḥammad's 'recognition' of these deities. He insists that: 'The promulgation of the satanic verses is doubtless to be linked up with this bargain.'[354]

In the whole discussion one discerns Watt's argument that Muḥammad's views on the Oneness of God was a gradual development and at various points in time he felt pressured to offer some acknowledgement to idolatry, which he did with the satanic verses episode. However, the argument further suggests, when he realized that the compromise would deal a fatal blow to his whole ideology, he recanted his statement and brought in more forceful anti-idolatry statements.[355]

OPPOSITION AND PERSECUTION

Looking at the reasons why some of the early Muslims emigrated to Abyssinia, Watt finds the argument of persecution unconvincing. He reasons that the Prophet's main opponents came from the Makhzūm and the ʿAbd Shams and, if at all, pressure on converts would come from members of these clans.

Discussing the people who left for Abyssinia as stated by Ibn Isḥāq, Watt notes the reference to the fact that some belonged to groups other than the Makhzūm and the ʿAbd Shams who were high finance people. To him, therefore, it does not make sense that others who possibly did not face persecution chose to emigrate.[356] He then asks: 'If the Muslims went to Abyssinia merely to avoid persecution, why did some of them remain there until A.H. 7, when they could safely have rejoined Muhammad in Medina?'[357]

He asserts that there is possibly a more important reason but this is avoided. A second assumed reason, ostensibly made by Western scholars, is stated but immediately discounted as not being viable. It is suggested that Muḥammad sent these people to Abyssinia to avoid a possible relapse into idolatry. Watt, rejecting this view, points out that there are no grounds to believe that Muḥammad could have promised them a safer Makkah at a later date.[358] Another assumed reason is that they went there for trade; but this also, Watt says, is not acceptable because Muḥammad was more preoccupied with religious reform than mere trade.

His analysis now shifts to the reasons for the military help from the Abyssinians. Was it to make Abyssinia a Muslim base from which later to invade Makkah or to form an alliance with Abyssinia to destroy the Makkan monopolistic hold on trade? Referring to the Makkans sent to seek their repatriation, Watt notes that there might have been economic and political objectives, 'But the precise nature of the mission and its result must remain a matter for conjecture.'[359]

Watt discovers a motive which he finds irresistible, to do with alleged dissent within early Islam. He claims that ʿUthmān b. Mazʿūn, whom Ibn Hishām identifies as the leader of the first group that went to Abyssinia, led a dissenting group within the Muslims. He mentions Khālid b. Saʿīd from the ʿAbd Shams who was of a similar inclination. This Khālid also emigrated. These people, and others mentioned were allegedly opposed to the prominent position of Abū Bakr. Watt, therefore, assumes that the emigration was due to this factionalism in early Islam. He writes, for example:

> It is in accordance with Muhammad's character that he should quickly have become aware of the incipient schism and taken steps to heal it by suggesting the journey to Abyssinia in furtherance of some plan to promote the interest of Islam, of whose precise nature we remain unaware since in its ostensible aim it met with little success.[360]

As far as the details of the persecution are concerned, Watt plays down the severity and considers them as exaggerated. Resting on the theory that tribal security in Makkah was very strong and nobody who belonged to a tribe could have been freely attacked or molested, he concludes that, 'The persecution of the Muslims was thus mostly of a mild nature.'[361]

He discusses the boycott of the Banū Hāshim, and is of the view that the boycott could not have been strictly enforced as traditional accounts say because there were inter-marriages amongst the members of the clans involved. Watt reduces the most severe persecutions to mere verbal criticisms of the Qur'ānic message and also of Muḥammad's prophethood. He acknowledges that there were schemes and plots against the Prophet and the Muslims but insists that there was '. . . hardly

. . . anything that really merits the name of persecution'.[362]

Despite the fact that he does not approve of reliance on the Qur'ān for historical facts, in this particular discussion Watt dwells on Qur'ānic references following the methodology of Caetani.[363]

His conclusion is thus a reiteration of the position he has taken all along, that there is evidence in the Qur'ān of some verbal harassment and arguments but these in themselves do not fit the picture normally portrayed. He maintains: 'The criticisms may have included false assertions, the plots may have led potentially to disaster, but there is no evidence for any severe persecution or anything that could be called oppression.'[364]

MUHAMMAD AT MEDINA

Structure of the Book

This book, published in 1956, was a sequel to the 1953 volume which concentrated on the Makkan phase of the Prophet's biography.

In the Preface, Watt acknowledges that in spite of his efforts, the extensiveness of the available material has meant picking and choosing or emphasizing certain parts and downgrading other aspects. However, he is confident that it is the best he could produce and, if he were to add more to it, it is '. . . as likely to mar as to better the impression . . .' he has endeavoured to present.[365]

He identifies two gaps which he believes are crucial to a more adequate treatment of the subject at hand. In his view, '. . . the normal type of European or American Orientalist is incapable of fulfilling' these gaps.[366] He names the first as a map that would adequately reflect the period. He continues: 'The other serious gap is that the study of life in pre-Islamic Arabia has not kept pace with the development of social anthropology.'[367] He explains that it takes a skilled social anthropologist to deal with the Arabic source material, to be able to make a sound study of the early history of Islam, since the non-anthropologist is bound to pass over some vital issues.

The book has ten chapters and a twelve-point addendum. In Chapter One, Waṭt seems to suggest that the primary blame for the confrontations between the Muslims and the Quraysh in Madīnah should be laid at the door of the Prophet. The chapter examines the situation during the early period of Muḥammad's settlement in Madīnah, the earliest expeditions, the initial skirmish which became the *casus belli* of the battle of Badr, the battle itself and its aftermath.

Chapter Two focuses on the Qurayshī attempt to avenge the disaster at Badr. It then looks at the battle of Uḥud and the siege of Madīnah.

Chapter Three discusses the circumstances in which the Makkans were becoming more amenable to the Prophet's message. It touches on the expeditions after the episode of Khandaq, the Ḥudaibiyyah incident and its aftermath and the general reaction of the Makkans to the apparent successes of the Prophet, ending with the battle of Ḥunayn and attempts to consolidate the victory.

Chapter Four, 'The Unifying of the Arabs', considers the tribal system in Arabia and Muḥammad's policies which were meant to be the cementing force.

In Chapter Five, 'The Internal Politics of Medīnah', Watt investigates the social and political organization in Muḥammad's time. It also incorporates sections on Muḥammad's supporters and the internal opposition that he had to grapple with.

Chapter Six is devoted entirely to the Jewish question, looking at the social standing of the Jews in general before and after the *Hijrah*. The discussion also takes in what Watt terms the intellectual and physical attacks on the Jews. This chapter has a Conclusion in which Watt wraps up the discussion.

Chapter Seven, 'The Character of the Islamic State', deals with the Constitution of Madīnah, Muḥammad's status within the arrangement, the nature of the *Ummah* and the financial affairs of the new community.

Chapter Eight focuses on the elaborate social reform inaugurated by Muḥammad, security of life and property, marriage and family, and inheritance.

Chapter Nine examines the new religious establishment, covering Islamic religious institutions, Islam and Arab paganism and ending with a discussion on Islam and Christianity.

Chapter Ten concentrates on Muḥammad's greatness. It looks at his appearance and mien, his supposed moral bankruptcy and ends with the foundations of his greatness.

The addendum, which Watt terms 'excursus', contains further comments on the sources, a list of expeditions with dates, a list of slaves and freedmen among the *Muhājirūn*, and comments on the letters the Prophet sent to eminent personalities in the then known world. It continues with a discussion on 'those whose hearts are to be reconciled', the translation of some twenty-one letters and treaties, a list of administrators, *zakāh* and *ṣadaqah*, and marriage and family in pre-Islamic times. It ends with a look at some technical vocabularies in selected verses of the Qur'ān dealing with marriage and comments on Muḥammad's marriages.

As usual, Watt provides a guide to his sources, preceding the first chapter with notes on bibliographic details. The book also has a handsome set of indexes.

Selected Themes

Confrontations

The first two chapters basically focus on the early encounters between the Muslims of Madīnah and their Qurayshī adversaries. The title of Chapter One, 'The Provocation of the Quraysh', is suggestive; Watt seems to make the Quraysh the 'innocent victims' of the episode. The tone of the discussion implies that it was the Muslims who provoked a rather 'peaceful'

Quraysh and this led to the confrontations experienced over a long period.

The title can be read in two ways: either in an objective genitive sense which would mean it was the Prophet who provoked the Quraysh, or a subjective genitive sense which would mean the provocation was by the Quraysh. However, we read it in the first sense because internal evidence in the discussion does not make the second sense plausible.

Starting with the situation at the *Hijrah*, Watt notes the intolerable conditions in Makkah and the demands on the people to accept Muḥammad as a prophet and a political arbiter in Madīnah.[368] Looking at the earliest expeditions, Watt refers to some seventy-four incidents mentioned by al-Wāqidī, seven of which are noted to have occurred in the first eighteen months after the *Hijrah*. He then writes: 'They are of slight importance, in that nothing seemed to happen, but they are excellent illustrations of Muhammad's attitude towards the Meccans shortly after his departure from the city.'[369] Despite the acknowledgement that nothing of substance occurred, Watt calls on his readers to take a point into consideration. He says: 'The chief point to note is that the Muslims took the offensive.'[370]

The discussion goes on to explain the relative geographical positions of Makkah and Madīnah, explaining that the expeditionary force was to accost only the detachment accompanying the caravan. The rationale for these *ghazawāt*, Watt remarks, '. . . was doubtless to catch the opponents at a disadvantage – by ambushing them, for instance'.[371]

Referring to some of the initial attempts and the numbers involved, Watt reiterates that: 'In all this we may see a deliberate intention on Muhammad's part to provoke the Meccans.'[372]

Trying to discover the motive for Muḥammad's 'provocation' of the Makkans, Watt speculates whether it was for the conquest of Makkah or control of the trade routes which passed close to Madīnah. In each case he does not find a valid point. He argues that the Prophet did not seem to be that strong militarily to risk such an adventure.

Regarding the 'incentives' which made the Prophet's followers heed his 'call' to fight, Watt notes that the Qur'ānic references carry the strongest incentive where promises of reward in the Hereafter reinforced the people's resolve. He then ends this section of the discussion, saying: 'Clearly the Muslims regarded their political and military activities as taking place within a religious setting.'[373]

The discourse continues with the Nakhlah incident, in which ʿAmr b. al-Haḍramī was killed. Watt emphasizes the clandestine nature of the expedition, explaining that this was for security reasons in the light of the elaborate Qurayshī intelligence operations. As to the ethic of the operation, Watt's own assessment can be gleaned from the statement regarding what those who took part might have felt. He asserts that they were more concerned with '. . . the obvious danger of the enterprise and not any scruples about possibly dishonourable aspects of what they were asked to do'.[374] To him, of essence were the Prophet's instructions for the expedition to 'ambush' the Makkan caravan. Therefore, he rejects the interpretation of the objective of the expedition to be to keep track of the caravan. He writes: 'The further clause (in some versions) about bringing back a report to Muhammad is clearly a later addition intended to give the word *taraṣṣadū* the meaning "keep a watch" instead of "lay an ambush"; in this way all responsibility for blood shedding would be removed from Muhammad.'[375]

Watt speculates that Muḥammad might have assumed that the caravan would have only token protection, but he is not able to find an answer to why Muḥammad would order an attack during the sacred month of Rajab.

Again, to reinforce his arguments regarding apportionment of blame, Watt refuses to take into consideration the reasoning that those who attacked the caravan were probably unaware that they were still in the inviolable month. He is of the opinion that this argument '. . . looks like an attempt to whitewash what is known to be black'.[376]

The speculation continues that even if Muḥammad meant

to violate the hallowed month he did not do so primarily because he intended to be unethical. However, Watt continues to assume, the Prophet might have violated the hallowed month because it was in accordance with his mission which rejected heathen practices. Since the concept of a sacred month dates from the pagan past, violation of it would not tarnish his image as a prophet. However, there is a problem in this reasoning. It is that Watt cannot find any explanation for the fact that the Prophet was not very pleased with the outcome of the Nakhlah incident and was not keen to take the *khums* from the booty. To wriggle out of this, Watt suggests an idea. He says: 'The easiest solution is to hold that after the event he discovered that there was a far greater feeling on the question of violation than he had anticipated.'[377]

A revelation then came to settle matters, by comparing 'violation of the sacred month' to 'turning people away from God' and the latter was pronounced a more heinous sin.[378] The section under this concludes with the insistence that, 'It is tolerably certain that Muhammad himself had few scruples about 'fighting in the sacred months . . .'[379]

Turning to the major confrontations, Watt looks at the battle of Badr and at the very beginning of the section makes a suggestive statement. He says that, 'The booty from Nakhlah gave a fillip to the policy of raiding Meccan caravans . . .'[380] This is to say that the 'provocation' of the Makkans continued and this then led to the real battle at Badr. He even makes the Makkans, despite the unproportionately large force sent to 'protect' Abū Sufyān's caravan, appear only to have intimidated the Muslims rather than anything else. Nevertheless, he acknowledges the emotions whipped up by Abū Jahl to avenge ʿAmr b. al-Haḍramī and possibly eliminate Muḥammad.

After describing the general outcome of the battle, the treatment of prisoners and Muḥammad's general policy on prisoners of war, Watt turns to the factors leading to the defeat of the Quraysh. He notes two main issues: disunity and over-confidence.[381] On the Muslim side, he notes: 'Their belief in a future life probably gave them greater courage in battle, and Muhammad's confidence inspired them with confidence. His generalship also won for them a tactical advantage. These seem to be the main reasons for the Muslim victory.'[382] He questions some details of the traditional accounts concerning those killed, suggesting they were exaggerations and even claims that with the Makkans, '. . . at least many of those killed, were considerably older than the majority of the Emigrants, and were probably suffering from thirst'.[383]

This assumption discounts all arguments for Divine intervention. At this point, Watt is strictly a historian applying 'scientific criteria' in assessing the material and therefore miracles would not make much sense here. In fact, he makes a passing remark to this effect in his discussion of the impact of the battle, saying: 'Very naturally they regarded it as miraculous, the work of God, as the Qur'an asserted (8: 17) . . .'[384]

As far as the aftermath was concerned, while the result of the battle boosted the resolve of the Muslims, the Makkans interpreted it that Muḥammad had thrown down a challenge which needed to be taken up, hence the subsequent clashes.

The first major clash after Badr was the battle of Uḥud, in which Watt takes considerable interest. Relating the story of preparation for the battle itself, he does not accept the part about ʿAbdullāh ibn Ubayy who withdrew his supporters from the Muslim army. Watt interprets his action to be an attempt to '. . . defend the main settlement against a possible enemy attack'.[385] He continues arguing on ʿAbdullāh ibn Ubayy's behalf that, 'In sources not friendly to him his motives could easily be blackened, especially when, after the battle, he made no secret of his joy at the discomfiture of his rival Muhammad.'[386]

Curiously, Watt does not notice a contradiction here. If he accepts that ʿAbdullāh ibn Ubayy openly expressed joy at the turn of events, then one would have thought that there was no attempt by his enemies to slander him but that was what actually happened. His activities were judged as treachery and treated as such.

Regarding the details of the battle itself, Watt continues this theory that most of the initial Muslim successes were exaggerated while activities attributed to the Quraysh, either as individuals or as a group, were peddled by their enemies though they were not true.[387]

On the outcome of the Uḥud encounter, Watt attempts a reconstruction of the traditional accounts. He writes: 'Western scholars have sometimes thought that the sources try to hide the full extent of the disaster at Uhud. Scrutiny suggests, however, that the opposite is rather the case, and that the Muslims themselves paint Uhud in gloomier colours than it merits.'[388] Again, he attributes this to political considerations with the *Anṣār* making the most of the accusations against the Quraysh and the Umayyads. Further, he mentions the 'spiritual chaos' into which the Muslims were thrown as a result of the outcome of the battle and also the damage it did to Muḥammad's prophetic authority. He ends the discussion with a comparative account of Badr and Uḥud. He notes:

> If Uhud was not an out-and-out defeat for the Muslims, still less was it a Meccan victory. The Meccan strategic aim was the destruction of the Muslim community and nothing less, and they had fallen far short of this. For many of the Meccans the conscious motive was revenge for the blood shed at Badr; and, if we take the lower figure of about fifty four Meccan dead at Badr, then the Muslims killed at Badr and Uhud together are slightly more than the Meccans killed in the two battles (though with the higher figure of seventy Meccans killed at Badr the total Muslim dead are slightly fewer).[389]

Turning to the Makkan attempts to solicit the support of the tribes in a grand coalition against Muḥammad, Watt mentions two techniques that Muḥammad used to avert that. The first, he says, was pre-emptive strikes to break up any threatening activities and the second was assassinations. He details situations in which, in his judgement, the Prophet was personally responsible for the 'elimination' of certain active opponents.[390]

The chapter ends with the siege of Madīnah. After giving the general details of this desperate attempt by the Quraysh to complete unfinished business, Watt again looks for reasons for the unsuccessful outcome of the siege on the part of the Makkans. He writes that, 'Exceptionally cold weather and a storm of wind gave the *coup de grace* to the morale of the besiegers.'[391] He attributes the Muslims' apparent success to efficient organization and the superior military strategy of the Prophet aided by what he believes was an efficient intelligence network.

In addition, Watt remarks that the Muslims were united and brimming with confidence while the Makkan camp was divided and the various groups did not seem to have confidence in each other. Again, he charges the Makkans with lack of proper planning and foresight, especially since by the time they arrived at the battlegrounds the fields had been harvested and they could not find fodder for their horses.[392]

In view of the elaborate but unsuccessful attempts to annihilate Muḥammad, Watt is of the view that, 'It would be strange if some of the Meccans – a practical people – had not begun to wonder whether it would not be best to accept Muhammad and his religion.'[393]

Ḥudaibiyyah and its Aftermath

For Watt, this theme opens up a wider perspective of Muḥammad's character and long-term objectives. The Ḥudaibiyyah incident made it clear that the Prophet had a more expansive intention than most scholars assume. Therefore, Ḥudaibiyyah is of special interest because it is a fertile field '. . . to understand the underlying aims of Muhammad's overt actions'.[394]

Watt maintains, through this argument, that the intention to cast the net of Islam beyond the immediate environs of Madīnah and Makkah was a later development. He continues: 'On the other hand, the suggestion of some Muslim sources, though not the earliest, that he conceived of Islam as a universal religion and summoned the Byzantine and Persian emperors and other lesser potentates to accept, is almost certainly false.'[395] He acknowledges that Islam, from the beginning had the potential to be a universal religion and this potential was actualized in the expansion period. However, he does not offer any tangible reasons for the rejection of the invitations Muḥammad was known to have sent to various emperors and other rulers, other than that there are alleged inconsistencies in the reports about the messengers. He remarks that '. . . It is barely credible that a wise statesman like Muhammad should have made this precise appeal at this precise stage in his career . . .'[396]

One notes a slight change in Watt's perception of Muḥammad at this stage of his career. Perhaps for the first time, Watt uses the epithet 'statesman' rather than 'prophet'. Within just two pages one senses a marked change.[397] He speculates that the best one could settle for on this issue is that Muḥammad might have sent a political message because, to him, it is incredible that the Roman emperor or the Negus could have been invited to Islam. Unfortunately he does not say why this could not be done apart from the fact that they were very powerful. Curiously, he surmizes that granted that the emissaries were actually sent, '. . . It is not impossible that the contents of the letters have been somewhat altered in the course of transmission. This may be either because the details were not known to the messenger (who is the presumptive source of information), or because later developments made the message seem trivial and unworthy of a great prophet'.[398]

The discussion refers to Muḥammad's interest in the tribes along the northern route to Syria and, looking for the factors which led to this interest, Watt discounts religion as one of them. He sees Muḥammad as primarily being interested in strengthening the Madīnan economy. Further, he alleges that as more and more tribes came to accept Islam, and with the legal prohibition of in-raiding amongst Muslims, Muḥammad had '. . . to find an alternative outlet for their energies'.[399]

He continues with an uncharacteristically harsh vocabulary: 'The peace of Islam, as administered by the *iron hand of Muhammad*, would bring prosperity for the Arabs, but only if the means of subsistence was correspondingly increased.'[400] For him, the expansion of Islam was not for religious reasons but for political and economic objectives. The expedition to Ḥudaibiyyah is thus portrayed as a fitting conclusion to the efforts to achieve these goals.

Recounting the details of the premonition which led to the trip to Ḥudaibiyyah, some of which he discounts as later embellishments, Watt claims that when the objective of pilgrimage was not achieved, Muḥammad '. . . was naturally puzzled when what he regarded as a Divine promise was not fulfilled'.[401]

Watt notes that though the Prophet intended to perform the pilgrimage, he was more interested in the political rather than the religious implications. These, he notes, are that the pilgrimage would have buttressed his argument that Islam was not an alien religion and hence was not a danger to the Makkan establishment. Again, he points out that the performance of the pilgrimage would have demonstrated to the Makkans that Muḥammad was friendly towards them.

Watt, unlike many of his predecessors pays considerable attention to the Ḥudaibiyyah incident, discussing the factors leading to the journey, the course of events, the text of the treaty and its implications for both the Quraysh and Muḥammad. He sees the treaty as a face-saving exercise for the Quraysh while it offered Muḥammad more than he could possibly have obtained on the battlefield. However, he states that the Prophet's followers were not happy with the outcome and therefore he needed to forestall a potential crisis. He then writes: 'It is against this background that the Pledge of Good Pleasure (bayʿat al-riḍwān) must be considered.'[402]

The Khaybar expedition, Watt says, came about as a result of this incident, to reward those who took part in the *baiʿat al-riḍwān*. He claims that: '. . . Muhammad had evolved the scheme of attacking the rich Jewish settlement of Khaybar, but allowing only those who took the pledge at Ḥudaybiyah to participate'.[403]

In his concluding assessment of the Ḥudaibiyyah treaty, despite what he has already said, Watt states that: 'The treaty of al-Hudaybiyah was only satisfactory for the Muslims in so far as one believed in Islam and its attractive power.'[404] He suggests that if Muḥammad had not handled the Muslim community as deftly as he did, the Ḥudaibiyyah agreement would not have been that profitable.

Looking at the conversions which came about as a result of the treaty, Watt points out that material factors were certainly instrumental but he also advocates that Muḥammad's deep conviction that he was bearing a Divine message meant for the whole of mankind and that Islam had both religious and political significance has to be acknowledged.

For the post-Ḥudaibiyyah period, Watt catalogues a number of expeditions which, he suggests, were carried out because of the enormous boost Muḥammad received at Ḥudaibiyyah.

The Fall of Makkah

In discussing the Ḥudaibiyyah topic, the significance of Makkah in Islam is emphasized. Hence, under this theme, Watt intimates that, all along, Muḥammad had been eyeing Makkah but merely as a means to an end – ostensibly more expansive policies. It is further argued that the Muslims had an almost nostalgic attachment to Makkah, it being the preparatory ground for Islam, and so wanted unimpeded access to the city. In addition, Watt asserts that Muḥammad was convinced that, 'Could Mecca be brought under his sway, his prestige and power would be greatly increased; without Mecca his position was comparatively weak.'[405] He adds that the Prophet was also thinking of the vast military and administrative resources that Makkah could bring to the Islamic state. Makkah therefore had to be taken.

In all this, the religious objective is played down and prominence given to political and economic ends. As we have already noted, this is like a thread that runs through the whole of the Madīnan era of Watt's biography. It is therefore suggested that political and economic motives made Muḥammad assemble a force large enough to intimidate the Makkans, cowering them into submission.

Noting that Makkah fell with virtually no bloodshed, Watt looks for reasons for Muhammad's magnanimity to the residents including his avowed enemies. Again, he assigns material considerations for the Prophet's gesture. He says: 'Muhammad's policy of forbidding all pillage meant that some of his poorer followers were now in want, and from some of the rich men of Mecca whom he had treated so magnanimously Muhammad requested loans.'[406] He further notes that those leaders who offered large sums of money were not forced to accept Islam, implying that they 'bought' their independence with the loans. Watt ends the section with the reasons for Muḥammad's successes and counts two main elements. He identifies '. . . the attractiveness of Islam and its relevance as a religious and social system to the religious and social needs of the Arabs'.[407] He also argues that the success owed much to '. . . Muhammad's own tact, diplomacy, and administrative skill . . .'.[408]

Unification of the Tribes

This theme, in Chapter Four, takes up the most space as compared to other chapters. One could argue that this is indicative of the significance Watt attaches to the subject.

The discussion takes the form of an overview of the Prophet's policy towards the tribes around the peninsula and the tone of the argument implies that Muḥammad was more interested in personal aggrandizement than spreading the message of his mission. Yet again, the theory which downgrades purely religious motives for Muḥammad's activities is at play.

Referring to the traditional view that most of the tribes in Arabia accepted Islam, Watt doubts the accuracy of this and interprets the various *wafds* (delegations) that the Prophet received as being for political alliances rather than acceptance of the Prophet's religious mission. From this platform he argues that strictly speaking the *Riddah* wars were not about apostasy but concerned political disloyalty. He asserts that, 'The supposed "deputations" of all the tribes and their conversion are largely pious inventions to magnify the achievement of Muhammad (and perhaps to minimize that of Abū Bakr).'[409]

Watt then enters into an elaborate discussion of the various tribes and their alliances with Madīnah, dividing them into geographical groups possibly to make for easier analysis and for maximum impact in his argument. He looks at the tribes to the west of Makkah and Madīnah, those to the east, the northern tribes and those in the south and the rest of Arabia.

Often in the discussion one reads of Muḥammad encouraging some tribesmen who had joined him to attack others to force them into the alliance, while others were more or less coerced into Islam through economic blackmail.[410] Watt does not attach much weight to material which does not seem to support this line of argument. For example, concerning some of the documents used in the classical sources, he writes: 'Some of the passages which have been thought to indicate that Muhammad made agreements without demanding acceptance of Islam are inconclusive.'[411] However, he makes a distinction, between agreements made with 'pagans' and those made with Christians. With the latter, room was left for them to be members of the *Pax Islamica* subject only to the payment of the *jizyah*.

Concluding the chapter, Watt examines the success of the Prophet's policy. He points out that though the Arabs had some ideas about unification of the tribes in the peninsula, it was

Muḥammad who actually gave real form to such ideas.[412] He reiterates his argument that Muḥammad initially thought he was sent merely to his own people and Islam's universalistic image developed later. Again, he reasons, the alliances the Prophet built initially in Madīnah were based on secular foundations. He states: 'The whole of Muhammad's work may be regarded as the building on religious foundations of a political, social and economic system; and his tribal policy was merely an aspect of this.'[413]

He rationalizes his argument by pointing out that Makkah had no religious demands made on it before it capitulated and even at the time of the Prophet's demise there were a number of tribes who had only political alliances with Madīnah. The argument continues, asserting that the Prophet did not want the whole of Arabia to become Muslim otherwise, especially since there would be no place left to raid, there would be too many people making demands on the dwindling resources of Madīnah.[414]

Despite all this, Watt acknowledges that people did not accept Islam merely on material or emotional grounds as asserted in some Western writings. He points out that 'Islam provided an economic, social, and political system, the *Pax Islamica.* Of this system religion was an integral part; it may be called the ideological aspect of the system. The peace and security given by the system were "the security of God and of His Messenger".'[415] He adds that Islam gave the people a standard of living they were probably not used to and the Prophet's attitude towards his followers was one of respect and courtesy. As far as the religious aspect is concerned, Watt explains that a seed was always in people's hearts awaiting the 'fertile season' to sprout and the advent of Muḥammad inaugurated that long-awaited 'season'. He likens this to the political sphere where, he says, '. . . there is the familiar phenomenon of "the rush to get on the bandwagon" '.[416]

In these sections concluding the discussions on the theme, one sees Watt the historian exhibiting his theological sense and allowing religious sentiments to be part of the underlying factors which made people join Islam. He indicates that though Western scholarship saw the phenomenal increase in Muslim membership in the ninth and tenth years of the *Hijrah* as being for political reasons, one cannot doubt the intrinsic religious explanations since, '. . . in the integral reality of the events the religious and political factors were inseparable'.[417]

He advises that it would be an error to consider 'religion' in the European understanding while looking at a situation of this nature instead of looking at it from the point of view of the Arab. When it is viewed in the sense of the latter, then, 'The Riddah was a movement away from the religious, social, economic and political system of Islam, and so was anti-Islamic.'[418]

As for the unification of Arabia, Watt points out that though it was not achieved in its entirety, Muḥammad '. . . had done more than sceptical European scholars have allowed. Moreover, his personal influence doubtless gave him power and authority beyond that conferred by formal agreements, . . .'.[419]

In his final deliberation, Watt argues that there were 'great upheavals' during the age, especially with respect to superpower conflicts between Persia and Byzantium and many people needed some spiritual support. He then states that, 'The "false prophets" tried to meet this need, but had little success.'[420] He adds that the Christians were in dire need of this spiritual solace since their links with the Byzantine empire had been severed. Hence, he continues, Islam with its alluring successes might have offered a great appeal and, 'Only a deeply rooted Christianity could withstand such fascination.'[421]

The implications of these statements are for the reader to infer.

The Jewish Question

In the preceding chapters of the book, Watt makes cursory reference to Muḥammad's relationship with the Jewish tribes, who in fact, are mentioned more than any other tribe in the whole book.

Mention is made of the expulsion of the Banū Qaynuqā and the assassination of Kaʿb b. al-Ashraf for which the Prophet is held responsible. In the latter incident, Watt writes that Kaʿb's head was '. . . carried off and flung at Muhammad's feet', adding that it became '. . . clear that Muhammad was not a man to be trifled with. For those who accepted him as leader there were material advantages; for those who opposed him there were serious disadvantages'.[422]

Again, the Banū al-Naḍhīr and the Banū Qurayẓah and the charges against them are briefly mentioned. It is however in Chapter Six that the discussion of the Jewish question is the central point. The chapter is divided into sections dealing with the Jews of Yathrib, the situation of the Jews at the time of the *Hijrah* and the alleged attempts by Muḥammad to make overtures to them and to impress upon them the affinity that Islam had with the teachings of Moses.

Perhaps the main force of the argument has to do with what Watt describes as intellectual and physical attacks on the Jews. He poses questions about the origins of the Jewish tribes, noting that they were largely at odds with one another in their Yathrib settlement.

Speculating on the pre-*Hijrah* situation, Watt suggests that there might have been attempts to win over the Jews but these were spurned except that they were prepared to enter into a political arrangement with Muḥammad. The *Hijrah*, therefore, the assumption continues, was seen by Muḥammad as a good opportunity to achieve success where initial efforts had failed.[423]

As the situation unfolds, he points out that: '. . . the great majority of the Jews not merely did not accept Muhammad, but became increasingly hostile. . . . Very soon after the Hijrah it must have become clear that few Jews were likely to accept the Gentile prophet'.[424]

Moving on to the Prophet's attempts to 'get closer' to the Jews, Watt asserts that Muḥammad increasingly '. . . tried to model Islam on the older religion'.[425] He mentions that Waraqah's statement that Muḥammad had encountered the same *nāmūs* as experienced by Moses must have left the Prophet thinking and hence, in Madīnah, he taught his followers to observe the Jewish Sabbath. Watt again claims that '. . . the Friday worship, which became a distinctive feature of Islam, was somehow connected with Judaism'.[426]

Further, he refers to the *qiblah*, which was initially Jerusalem, as further evidence supporting his reasoning. He is sceptical of the existence of a *qiblah* in pre-*Hijrah* times. However, he acknowledges that even if Muḥammad asked his people to face Jerusalem in prayer this does not necessarily indicate Jewish influence because, apparently the Christians also had a similar practice.[427] This apparent contradiction is solved by remarking that the 'Jerusalem *qiblah*' idea was taken by Muḥammad from his Madīnan followers.

In addition, Watt argues, is the incontrovertible issue of the Fast of 'Āshūrā' which was established to coincide with the Jewish Day of Atonement. Even the midday prayer (*Ṣalāt al-Ẓuhr*) is considered as another case in point since, it is said, it was introduced in the Madīnan period.[428] Watt goes on, relying on Buhl, Caetani, Wensinck and Becker, to suggest that '. . . in building the mosque at Madina Muhammad had in mind the Jewish synagogue; . . .'.[429]

To the seemingly unending catalogue of so-called Jewish practices followed by Muḥammad is added the Qur'ānic permission to eat the same food as the People of the Book and to marry their pious women.[430] The main motive behind all these 'overtures', Watt maintains, was for Muḥammad to endear himself to the Jews and also to seek some authentication for his religious status if he was recognized as preaching virtually Jewish ideas.

Watt then focuses on Muḥammad's alleged sudden change of attitude towards the Jews. The change in *qiblah* and the institution of the Ramaḍān fast are mentioned, with the latter being speculated as being of Christian influence because of its observance of Lent.[431] Citing Bell however, Watt develops another theory, that the fast of Ramaḍān was instituted to commemorate the battle of Badr since it was similar to God's deliverance of the Jews from Pharaoh's pursuing army.[432] Concluding this section of the chapter, Watt writes: 'These marks of "the break with the Jews" are in fact indications of a completely new orientation both politically and religiously. The Medinan state now began a series of attacks on the Jews in the physical sphere, and at the same time the Qur'an carried on polemics against their religion in the intellectual sphere.'[433] Thus, the ground is prepared for a discourse on the alleged intellectual and physical aggression against the Jews.

The contention starts with the reasoning that in the pre-*Hijrah* period, the Arabs and Muḥammad, and his people for that matter, had no idea as to the linkage of Abraham and his son Ishmael with the *Kaʿbah*. It was only in Madīnah, after learning about Abrahamic stories from the Jews, that Muḥammad introduced a connection between Islam and Abraham. The argument is based on the premise that the Qur'ān does not refer to this connection in the Makkan texts. Abraham therefore became an important personality and an instrument to be used in a critique of both Jews and Christians.[434] Hence the whole spectrum of Qur'ānic critical references to Jewish behaviour in terms of their devotion to God, their original scripture and to the Prophet is interpreted as later developments which arose because of Muḥammad's apparent frustration in failing to get the Jews to accept him despite all his elaborate overtures. The Qur'ān is therefore pictured as resorting to polemics against the Jews. Watt advises that this point has to be taken into consideration since it forms the basis of '. . . the actual hostilities between Muhammad and the Jews'.[435]

The discussion then leads on to the physical confrontations between the Jews and the Muslims. The events leading to the expulsion of the Banū Qaynuqāʿ from Madīnah are revisited and the picture presented suggests ṭhat the actual event was trivial but, 'Muhammad regarded the matter as a *casus belli*, and collected a force to besiege the clan'.[436]

Perhaps, the case of the expulsion of the Banū al-Naḍīr is presented in an even more interesting style. It starts with the murder of Kaʿb b. al-Ashraf of the al-Naḍīr who, Watt says, was murdered at the active encouragement and to the delight of the Prophet. As for the *causa proxima* of the banishment, after relating the story Watt writes that the decision taken '. . . seems to be out of proportion to the offence, or rather to the apparently flimsy grounds for supposing that treachery was mediated'.[437]

In an attempt to find the rationale behind what he maintains to be a harsh verdict, he returns to the *causa remota* which is the assassination of Kaʿb b. al-Ashraf, arguing that with that incident at the back of his mind, Muḥammad always feared an attack from the al-Naḍīr. It is then noted that, 'The expulsion of an-Nadir from Medina was not the end of their dealings with Muhammad. From Khaybar some of them continued to intrigue assiduously against Medina, and played a considerable part in the formation of the great confederacy to besiege Medina in April 627.'[438]

If there is any incident in Muḥammad's biography that causes revulsion among Western scholars, it is the case of the Banū Qurayẓah. Watt is no exception in this. In relating the narrative concerning the matter, the Banū Qurayẓah are portrayed as having behaved neutrally in so far as the Khandaq episode is concerned even though it is admitted that they had some discussions with the Quraysh and could have attacked the Muslims if they really trusted the Quraysh. Hence it is stated that: 'Muhammad attacked Qurayzah, to show that the rising Islamic State was not prepared to tolerate such "sitting on the fence".'[439]

Muḥammad himself is said to have selected Saʿd b. Muʿādh as judge and Saʿd to have pronounced the verdict with his advanced age and devotion to Islam in mind. He is said to have put Islam ahead of his tribal affiliations for fear of upsetting Muḥammad and being seen as sliding back into his pre-Islamic situation.

Watt rejects the usual Western reasoning that it was Muḥammad's definite strategy to rid Madīnah completely of Jews, referring to the Madīnan constitution, where references are made to the Jews, as evidence. Whilst it is true, he admits, that the main Jewish tribes had been expelled, other smaller units of Jews remained.

The expedition to the Jewish settlement of Khaybar on Muḥammad's return from Ḥudaibiyyah is mentioned. The main motive, Watt says, was '. . . for him to have booty to distribute to his followers whose expectations had recently been disappointed'.[440] The result was that 'Khaybar was . . . reduced to a position of subservience and rendered innocuous'.[441]

In his concluding remarks on the theme, Watt speculates what would have happened if the Jews had not opposed Muḥammad but accepted him. He conjectures that among other things Islam would have become '. . . a sect of Jewry'. He immediately adds: 'How different the face of the world would be now, had that happened!'[442]

He is of the opinion that despite the validity of the Jewish refusal to acknowledge Muḥammad due to their traditional exclusive claims, their hostile and derisive attitude towards Muḥammad was unnecessary. As for Muḥammad, it is argued that the Jews' behaviour was a real danger to everything he stood for and therefore he could not overlook them.

Again, Watt continues to argue, Muḥammad had the Jews' wealth in mind in his confrontations with them but that alone does not fully explain the rationale behind the history of the hostile relationship. He puts a finger on what he considers to be the key point. He says: '. . . the fundamental reason for the quarrel was theological on both sides. The Jews believed that God had chosen them specially, Muhammad realized that his prophethood was the only possible basis of Arab Unity. As so often in the history of the Middle East, theology and politics are intermingled'.[443]

THE CONSTITUTION OF MADĪNAH

To this subject, often left untouched or treated either superficially or in a slipshod manner, Watt pays particular attention, discussing it in the context of his outlook on the larger question of 'The character of the Islamic state'. He reproduces the text as found in Ibn Isḥāq's work but follows Wensinck's paragraphing of it.[444]

Discussing its authenticity and dating, Watt asserts that it is not clear if the document had the prominence as is often allotted it. However, he finds some evidence which indicates that it could not have been forged. He comments that, 'No later falsifier, writing under the Umayyads or ʿAbbasids, would have included non-Muslims in the Ummah, would have retained the articles against Quraysh, and would have given Muhammad so insignificant a place.'[445]

From its style, language and other details, the document is attributed to the Madīnan period though its precise dating is uncertain. Watt refers to differences amongst Western writers such as Wellhausen, Grimme and Caetani as to whether it is a pre- or post-Badr document.[446]

Watt's passion for fine detail is displayed here in his scrutiny of the document – in trying to put a precise date on it and understand what he considers to be crucial lacunae especially regarding the absence of the three main Jewish clans mentioned.[447] In the end, he is of the view that the so-called Constitution of Madīnah was probably not one whole document but a series of enactments issued at different periods and put together later. He finds no solid proof though, and is perhaps content with saying, finally, that '. . . there is much that is bound to remain conjectural and obscure'.[448]

As far as he could glean from the document regarding the position of Muḥammad, Watt notes that the Prophet remained as a sort of *primus inter pares* without any specific authoritarian powers. Even where actions were carried out on 'his behalf', the argument says, it is always not clear if Muḥammad was openly behind it. His powers, in a way, were 'limited'. Watt gives the Banū Qurayẓah issue as a typical example, where Muḥammad had to 'use' someone to achieve an objective. The point discussed here gives force to the arguments regarding Muḥammad's political dexterity.[449]

Muḥammad's Personality

The last important theme in the work is an assessment of the Prophet's personality and in this Watt stands undeniably poles apart from his predecessors. In the first section, the discussion is devoted to the Prophet's physical characteristics and some personal traits regarding his emotions, management of time and general behaviour in public.

Watt refers to the traditional accounts and remarks that despite the possibility of attempts to paint an ideal man, '. . . the probability is that the general picture is sound'.[450] Muḥammad's affection for children, his '. . . courage, resoluteness, impartiality, firmness inclining to severity but tempered by generosity',[451] are all noted.

Turning to a more thorny matter, Watt discusses Muḥammad's 'alleged moral failures'. He points out that, 'Of all the world's great men, none has been so much maligned as Muhammad.'[452]

He refers to the medieval pictures of the Prophet, due primarily to the then geo-political situation of the world, where Islam, and Muḥammad for that matter, were seen as a threat. Watt writes: '. . . medieval war-propaganda, free from the restraints of factuality, was building up a conception of "the great enemy" '.[453]

Referring to the various derisory images of Muḥammad, he then mentions the attempts of Peter the Venerable to offer a reliable picture of Islam and Muḥammad. Nevertheless, he admits, 'Since then much has been achieved, especially during the last two centuries or so, but many of the old prejudices linger on.'[454]

He advocates a more objective appraisal of Muḥammad, arguing that as a reaction to the biased theses, there have been attempts by some scholars to offer a romantic Muḥammad as an alternative. He rejects both the disparaging and romantic methodologies and claims to give an objective view, basing his discussion on three areas: Muḥammad's alleged insincerity, sensuality and treachery.[455]

On the question of insincerity or imposture, Watt agrees with Carlyle's famous rebuttal and states that the whole theory is preposterous and does not in any way explain the real character of Muḥammad. He is, however, quick to clarify his acceptance of Muḥammad's sincerity. He states emphatically that it should not be misunderstood as an acknowledgement of the Qur'ān as an authentic revelation from God. He maintains that '. . . a man may without contradiction hold that Muhammad truly believed that he was receiving revelations from God but that he was mistaken in this belief'.[456]

He continues this reasoning rather interestingly thus: '. . . the alleged fact that the revelations fitted in with Muhammad's desires and pandered to his selfish pleasure would not prove him insincere; it would merely show him to be capable of self-deception'.[457]

Further, he argues that the allegations made against Muḥammad by some Western scholars such as Bell and others, that he sometimes modified Qur'ānic statements, do not imply he was insincere. He even refers to the science of abrogation in Qur'ānic scholarship as proof that the so-called 'changes' were sincerely believed by Muḥammad to have come from God.

On the issue of moral debauchery and duplicity, Watt is of the view that there could be problems in justifying the cases of the Prophet's marriage to Zaynab and what he calls 'breaking the treaty of al-Hudaibiyyah', but even here, he argues, '. . . there is ample room for dispute about circumstances and motives'.[458]

He cautions against applying the standards of one age to judge the acts of another. He notes that even if all those acts attributed to Muḥammad were true, very often by the standards of that age and environment one could not categorize them as immoral or treacherous. Perhaps on behalf of Muḥammad, Watt argues that the primary objective was formation of the society based on what he believed was revelation from God and, therefore, '. . . the religious aspect was probably more important than the purely moral one'.[459]

Further, he states, '. . . the common European and Christian criticism that Muhammad was a sensualist or, in the blunter language of the seventeenth century, an "old lecher", fades away when examined in the light of the standards of Muhammad's time'.[460]

The Prophet's marriage to Zaynab bint Jahsh is taken up as an example of the topics of criticism. Watt gives the details as he understands it from the sources and largely rejects the charge of incestuous relationship or sensuality levelled against the Prophet. He explains that in the first place the Qur'ān sanctioned the marriage but again, and probably for him more importantly, it was not blind lust which led to the Prophet marrying Zaynab, rather it was for political ends.[461] He points out that: 'In his day and generation Muhammad was a social reformer, indeed a reformer even in the sphere of morals. He created a new system of social security and a new family improvement on what went before.'[462]

Watt maintains that there is no real evidence suggesting a decline in Muḥammad's character in the later years of his mission. He remarks that in contemporary times, Muslims see Muḥammad as a model for mankind and call people to acknowledge this but there have been no sober reflections on this call. He asks, in this context, 'Are any principles to be learnt from the life and teaching of Muhammad that will contribute to the one morality of the future?'[463] He continues that non-Muslims in general have not yet given any firm response to this but he insists, perhaps correctly, that the response would definitely depend upon the way Muslims themselves live Islam or present Muḥammad to the non-Muslim world.

He is, however, sceptical of Muslims being able to meet this demand. He asserts bluntly: 'A combination of sound scholarship and deep moral insight is essential, and this combination is rare. I will not conceal my personal view that Muslims are unlikely to be successful in their attempt to influence world opinion, at least in the sphere of morals.'[464] However, intriguingly, he accepts that Islam as a 'religion' has something to remind other monotheistic faiths of.

In the concluding section of the book, Watt attempts to examine the reasons for Muḥammad's greatness, noting various incidents which he thinks contributed to this. He mentions a favourable period in history and an environment where despite a general social malaise, coupled with troubled conditions among the then empires, and what he calls an increasing consciousness among nomadic tribes to raid and plunder others, the people were content to lead a normal settled life. He acknowledges that without Muḥammad's unique personal traits Islam would not have attained the heights it did. He identifies three of Muḥammad's characteristics which were crucial contributory factors for his huge success. These are Muḥammad's gift as a seer, his being a wise statesman and a shrewd and skilful administrator.[465] He finally observes that without these traits in addition to '. . . his trust in God and firm belief that God had sent him, a notable chapter in the history of mankind would have remained unwritten'.[466]

In 1961, Watt's two-volume biographical work on Muḥammad was published as one volume, entitled *Muhammad – Prophet and Statesman*.[467] Watt makes it clear in the 'Note on the Sources' that:

> The present work is essentially an abridgement of my books *Muhammad at Mecca* and *Muhammad at Medina* (Oxford, 1953, 1956). The chief difference is that in the present volume the chronological order has been more strictly adhered to. Here and there this may have produced a slight change of emphasis, *but there is no fundamental change in the views presented.*[468]

This is very true; and as for the slight emphasis in certain places that Watt mentions, one specific example has to do with the Jewish question, which now takes up forty-nine pages of a book of two hundred and forty-five pages.[469]

The next chapter of the present work, the Conclusion, recapitulates essential issues and focuses on some of the central arguments of the three key scholars we have examined – Muir, Margoliouth and Watt. It also raises issues of sound Western academic scholarship, the scientific study of religion and their application in the study of Islam. The question of how one academically deals with a faith one does not share is posited and an attempt made to analyze it.

Notes

1. *Who's Who – An Annual Biographical Dictionary* (London: A. & C. Black, 1993); see p.1974.

2. Questionnaire, May 1994.

3. 'Tribute to William Montgomery Watt', in Welch and Cachia (eds.), *Islam – Past Influence*, p.ix.

4. *Ibid.*, p.xiii.

5. London: Student Christian Movement Press. A more comprehensive list of Watt's writings up to 1979 can be seen in the Appendix to Welch and Cachia (eds.), *Islam – Past Influence.*

6. *MW* ,Vol. 36, No. 2 (April 1946), pp.124–52.

7. *Islam – Past Influence*, p.ix.

8. *Freewill and Predestination*, p.1.

9. *Ibid.*

10. *Ibid.*, pp.1–2.

11. *Freewill and Predestination*, p.152.

12. *Sūrah al-Baqarah* 2: 62; *Sūrah al-Mā'idah* 5: 68–9.

13. Eighth in the series entitled 'Ethical and Religious Classics of East and West' (London: George Allen & Unwin, 1953).

14. *Ibid.*, p.5, General Introduction.

15. *Ibid.*, p.15.

16. Oxford: Clarendon Press, 1953.

17. Oxford: Clarendon Press, 1956.

18. Oxford: Clarendon Press, 1961.

19. See *Islam – Past Influence*, p.x.

20. *Muhammad and the Origins of Islam* (1994), Preface, p.xi.

21. *Ibid.*

22. *MW*, Vol. 42 (1952), pp.160–71.

23. *Ibid.*, p.160; cf. L. Caetani, *Annali dell' Islam*, Vol. 1 (Milano: Ulrich Hoepli, 1905–26), p.632.

24. 'The Use of the Word "Allah" in English', *MW*, Vol. 43, No. 3 (July 1953), pp.245–7.

25. *Ibid.*, p.245.

26. *Ibid.*, p.246.

27. *The Faith and Practice of al-Ghazali* (London: Allen & Unwin, 1953).

28. *IQ*, Vol. 1, No. 1 (April 1954), pp.62–4.

29. Watt, *The Faith and Practice*, p.14.

30. Hamidullah. See his review of the book, p.64.

31. 'Carlyle on Muhammad', *HJ*, Vol. 52 (October 1954–July 1955), pp.247–54.

32. *Ibid.*, p.248.

33. *Ibid.*, p.252.

34. *Ibid.*, p.253.

35. *Ibid.*

36. *Ibid.*, p.254.

37. 'Thoughts on Islamic Unity', *IQ*, Vol. 3, No. 3 (October 1956), pp.188–95.

38. *Ibid.*, p.189.

39. *Ibid.*

40. *Ibid.*, p.191.

41. *Ibid.*, pp.194–5.

42. London: SPCK, 1957.

43. *Ibid.*, p.2.

44. *Ibid.*

45. London: SPCK, 1936. See Watt's review in *HJ*, 59 (October 1960–July 1961), pp.385–6.

46. *Ibid.*, Watt's review, pp.385–6.

47. *Ibid.*, p.386.

48. *Ibid.*

49. *HJ*, 59 (October 1960–July 1961), pp.209–12.

50. *Ibid.*, p.212.

51. Edinburgh: Edinburgh University Press, 1962.

52. *Ibid.*, p.v.

53. 'Conditions of Membership of the Islamic Community', *SI*, Vol. 21 (1964), pp.5–12.

54. *Ibid.*, pp.6–7.

55. *Ibid.*, p.12.

56. London: George Allen & Unwin, 1967.

57. *Ibid.*, p.10.

58. T.B. Irving has delineated this problem in an article entitled 'Terms and Concepts – Problems in Translating the Qur'ān', in K. Aḥmad and Z.I. Anṣārī (eds.), *Islamic Perspectives – Studies in Honour of Mawlānā Sayyid Abul Aʿlā Mawdūdī* (Leicester: The Islamic Foundation, 1979), pp.121–34.

59. Watt, *Companion*, p.14.

60. 'The Christianity Criticized in the Qur'an', *MW*, Vol. 57, No. 3 (July 1967), pp.197–201.

61. *Ibid.*, p.198.

62. *Ibid.*

63. *Ibid.*, p.200.

64. 'Thoughts on Muslim-Christian Dialogue', *MW*, Vol. 57, No. 1 (January 1967), pp.19–23.

65. *Ibid.*, p.19.

66. *Ibid.*, p.23.

67. *Truth in Religions – A Sociological and Psychological Approach* (1968).

68. *Ibid.*, p.vii.

69. *Ibid.*, p.1.

70. *Ibid.*, p.173.

71. *Ibid.*

72. Edinburgh: Edinburgh University Press, 1968.

73. *Ibid.*, p.ix.

74. *Ibid.*, p.x.

75. Review in *IQ*, Vol. 14, No. 1 (January–March 1970), (pp.53–4), p.53.

76. London and Harrow: Longmans, Green & Co., 1968 and Beirut: Librarie du Liban, 1968.

77. *Ibid.*, p.1.

78. *Ibid.*, p.2.

79. *Ibid.*, p.12.

80. Tor Andrae, *Mohammed – The Man and His Faith* (1936), p.86.

81. Watt, *Islam*, p.17.

82. *Ibid.*, p.21.

83. *Ibid.*, p.228.

84. *Ibid.*, p.229.

85. *Ibid.*, p.234.

86. *MWBR*, Vol. 1, No. 3 (Spring 1981), (pp.3–6), p.5.

87. Review in *HI*, Vol. 4, No. 3 (Autumn 1981), (pp.91–7), p.91. Bazmee Ansari uses almost the same wording in his appreciation of Watt as a scholar, in his opening paragraph, as Khurram Murad on p.5 of his (the latter's) review.

88. Watt, *Islam*, pp.168–9, 233 and Bazmee Ansari's review, pp.96–7.

89. Edinburgh: Edinburgh University Press (paperback edition, 1977; reprinted 1990). We have mentioned this work in the section on twentieth-century literature; see p. 140, esp. note 55.

90. Watt says that: 'The sincerest tribute to such a scholar is to take his views seriously and criticise them frankly'. See p.v of the book.

91. Watt, *Bell's Introduction*, p.vi. This, further, brings to the fore the methodological conundrum as to how a scholar studies a faith he does not share.

92. *Ibid.*, p.17.

93. *Ibid.*, pp.17–18.

94. *Ibid.*

95. See M.M. Azami, *Studies in Ḥadīth Methodology and Literature* (1977) and *On Schacht's Origins of Muhammadan Jurisprudence* (1993); M.H. Kamali, *Principles of Islamic Jurisprudence*, revised ed. (1991); M.Z. Siddīqī, *Hadith Literature – Its Origin, Development and Special Features* (1961); G.H.A. Juynboll, *The Authenticity of the Tradition Literature* (1969) and *Muslim Tradition – Studies in Chronology, Provenance and Authorship of Early Hadith* (1983); S.M. Yusuf, *An Essay on the Sunnah – Its Importance, Transmission, Development and Revision* (1977).

96. Watt, *Bell's Introduction*, p.18. See also his discussion on 'The Qur'an and Occidental Scholarship', in Ch. 11, pp.173–86, where he again raises the problem of methodology.

97. Edinburgh: Edinburgh University Press, 1972. Reprinted in 1982, 1987 and 1994.

98. *Ibid.*, p.1.

99. *Ibid.*, p.2.

100. *Ibid.*, p.72.

101. *IQ*, Vol. 17, No. 3 (July–December 1973), pp.191–2.

102. *Ibid.*, p.191.

103. *Ibid.*

104. 'Secular Historians and the Study of Muhammad', *HI*, Vol. 1, No. 3 (1978), pp.51–3. See also the full text of the paper published as: 'Western Historical Scholarship and the Prophet of Islam', in *Message of the Prophet*, a selection of articles presented at the First International Congress on Seerat, Islamabad, 1976, pp.68–75.

105. See the full text, 'Western Historical Scholarship', pp.68–9.

106. *Ibid.*, p.72.

107. *HI*, Vol. 6, No. 2 (Summer 1983), pp.57–68. Cf. his 'The Christianity Criticized in the Quran', *MW*, Vol. 57, No. 3 (July 1967), pp.197–201.

108. *Ibid.*, p.57.

109. London: Routledge & Kegan Paul, 1983. See initial mention of this work in the section on 'The Choice of Watt' above.

110. *Ibid.*, Preface, p.xiii.

111. *Ibid.*

112. *Ibid.*, p.4.

113. *Ibid.*, p.146.

114. *Al-Tawhid*, Vol. 11, No. 3 (April–June 1985; Rajab–Ramaḍān 1405), pp.136–76.

115. *Ibid.*, p.137.

116. Watt, *Islam and Christianity*, see pp.21–2.

117. Al-Qarā'ī's review, p.137.

118. See Watt, *Islam and Christianity*, pp.23–31.

119. Al-Qarā'ī's review, p.138.

120. *Ibid.*, p.171.

121. Watt, *Islam and Christianity*, p.144.

122. Al-Qarā'ī's review, p.176, note 11.

123. *The Islamic Guardian*, Vol. 5, No. 2 (April–June 1984), pp.18–28.

124. *Ibid.*, p.19.

125. *Ibid.*, p.21. Cf. Watt, *Islam and Christianity*, p.3.

126. Watt, *Islam and Christianity*, p.3.

127. *Ibid.*

128. Azīz's review of Watt's *Islam and Christianity*, p.21.

129. *Ibid.*, p.24.

130. Vol. 33, pp.227–49.

131. *Ibid.*, p.227.

132. *Ibid.*, pp.227–8.

133. *Ibid.*, p.230.

134. *Ibid.*, p.231.

135. *Ibid.*, p.232.

136. *Ibid.*, p.234.

137. *Ibid.*, p.238.

138. *Ibid.*, p.242.

139. See above.

140. 'Muhammad as the Founder', pp.242–3.

141. *Ibid.*, p.243.

142. *Ibid.*, p.248.

143. *Ibid.*, p.249.

144. *Ibid.*

145. *Ibid.*

146. *HI*, Vol. 8, No. 1 (Spring 1985), pp.3–6. Cf. Farrukh Ali's article entitled 'Al-Ḥudaybiya: An Alternative Version', *MW*, Vol. 71, No. 1 (1981), pp.47–62.

147. 'Al-Ḥudaybiya: An Alternative Version', p.47.

148. *Ibid.*, p.48.

149. 'Al-Hudaybiya Reconsidered', p.3.

150. *Ibid.*, pp.3–4.

151. 'Al-Ḥudaybiya: An Alternative Version', pp.48–52.

152. 'Al-Hudaybiya Reconsidered', p.4.

153. *Ibid.*, p.5.

154. *Ibid.*

155. *Studia Missionalia*, Vol. 35 (1986), pp.161–78.

156. *The History of al-Ṭābarī (Ta'rīkh al-rusul wa'l Mulūk) Vol. VII, The Foundation of the Community* (Albany: State University of New York Press, 1987), and *The History of al-Ṭabarī (Ta'rīkh al-rusul wa'l Mulūk), Vol. VI, Muhammad at Mecca* (Albany: State University of New York Press, 1988).

157. In fact, he himself points out that the main translation was done by M.V. McDonald while he wrote the Introduction and the annotation. See *ibid.*, Vol. VII, p.xxxviii.

158. *Ibid.*, p.xv.

159. *Ibid.*, p.xvi.

160. *Ibid.*, p.xviii.

161. *Ibid.*

162. *Ibid.*, see pp.xxi–iv.

163. *Ibid.*, p.xxvi.

164. *Ibid.*

165. *Ibid.*, p.xxvii.

166. *Ibid.*, p.xxviii.

167. See above his arguments for Muḥammad's acceptance to migrate to Madīnah and also the rationale for the battle of Badr.

168. See Vol. 6, pp.xii–xvii.

169. *Ibid.*

170. See J. Wansbrough, *Qur'anic Studies, Sources and Methods of Scriptural Interpretation* (1977); P. Crone and M. Cook, *Hagarism – The Making of the Islamic World* (1977).

171. *The History of al-Ṭabarī*, Vol. VI, p.xvii.

172. *Ibid.*, pp.xvii–xxi. See also Watt's other paper entitled 'The Material's Used by Ibn Isḥāq', in B. Lewis and P.M. Holt (eds.), *Historians of the Middle East* (1962), pp.23–34; I. Goldziher, *Muhammedanische Studien Vol. II*, English edition by S.M. Stern, *Muslim Studies* (London, 1971); J. Schacht, *The Origins of Muhammadan Jurisprudence* (1950); C.H. Becker, *Islamstudien* (1924) (also in *Der Islam*, 4 (1913), pp.263 ff.); R. Blachère, *La Probleme de Mahomet* (1952).

173. *The History of al-Ṭabarī*, Vol. VI, p.xviii.

174. *Ibid.*, p.xix.

175. *Ibid.*, pp.xx–i.

176. *Ibid.*, p.xxiii.

177. See his *La Probleme de Mahomet.*

178. *The History of al-Ṭabarī*, Vol. VI, pp.xxiv–v. See his *The Meccan Prophet in the Qur'an* (1987).

179. *The History of al-Tabari*, Vol. VI, p.xxxv.

180. *Journal of Islamic Studies*, Vol. 3, No. 1 (January 1992), pp.114–16.

181. *Ibid.*, p.116.

182. See *ibid.*

183. London and New York: Routledge.

184. *Ibid.*, p.1.

185. *Ibid.*, p.3.

186. *Ibid.*, p.7.

187. *Ibid.*, p.19.

188. *Ibid.*, p.141.

189. *Ibid.*, p.142.

190. Review in *IJMES*, Vol. 23, No. 3 (August 1991), pp.414\17, quotation on p.417.

191. *Ibid.*, p.416.

192. *IQ*, Vol. 35, No. 2 (2nd Quarter, 1991), pp.140–5. Also published in *Islamica* (Journal of the Islamic Society of the London School of Economics), Vol. 1, No. 2 (March 1993), pp.26–7.

193. Review in *IQ*, *ibid.*, p.142.

194. *Ibid.*, p.143.

195. *Ibid.*, pp.143–4.

196. *Ibid.*, p.145.

197. *New Community*, Vol. 15, No. 4 (July 1989), pp.639–40.

198. *Ibid.*, p.640.

199. *Ibid.*

200. Edinburgh: Edinburgh University Press, 1988.

201. *Ibid.*, p.vii.

202. *Ibid.*, p.1.

203. *Ibid.*, pp.2–3, 5–6, 36–8. See our own review of the book in *ICMR*, Vol. 1, No. 2 (December 1990), pp.286–9.

204. *Muhammad's Mecca*, p.53.

205. *Ibid.*, p.68.

206. Vol. 3, No. 2 (July 1992), pp.240–3.

207. *Ibid.*, p.242.

208. *Ibid.*

209. *Ibid.*, pp.242–3.

210. Vol. 39, pp.167–78. This particular volume of *Studia Missionalia* is on the theme 'Peace and Religions'.

211. *Ibid.*, pp.168–9.

212. *Ibid.*, p.171.

213. *Ibid.*, p.173.

214. See pp.175–6.

215. Edinburgh: Edinburgh University Press.

216. *Ibid.*, pp.13–14.

217. *BSOAS*, Vol. 55, Part 1 (1992), pp.195–6.

218. *Ibid.*, p.196.

219. *Ibid.*

220. London: Routledge.

221. *Ibid.* See the comments on the back cover.

222. *Ibid.*, Chs. 1, 2 and 3, *passim.*

223. See his other work, *Muhammad's Mecca – History in the Qur'ān, passim.*

224. *Muslim-Christian Encounters*, p.138.

225. *Ibid.*, p.149.

226. *Ibid.*, p.150.

227. *New Community*, Vol. 18, No. 2 (January 1992), pp.342–3.

228. *Ibid.*

229. *JIS*, Vol. 3, No. 2 (July 1992), pp.257–8.

230. *Ibid.*, p.257.

231. *Ibid.* Such reasoning can also be found in his *Muhammad's Mecca.*

232. Mary Hossain's review, p.258.

233. *Ibid.* The numbers in parenthesis refer to page numbers from the book itself.

234. Vol. 40, pp.161–73.

235. *Muhammad at Medina.*

236. 'Women in Early Islam', p.163.

237. Vol. 41, pp.241–52.

238. *Ibid.*, pp.241–2.

239. *Ibid.*, p.243.

240. *Ibid.*, p.246.

241. London and New York: Routledge.

242. *Islamic Fundamentalism*, p.248.

243. *Ibid.*

244. *Ibid.*, pp.249–50.

245. It was the second Vatican Council which brought about this quantum leap in the perception of the Catholic Church as far as Islam is concerned.

246. Vol. 42, pp.245–55.

247. See p.1 of this work.

248. 'Islamic Attitudes', p.245.

249. *Ibid.*

250. *Ibid.*, p.246.

251. *Ibid.*

252. *Ibid.*, p.250.

253. *Ibid.* See also p.245.

254. *Ibid.*, pp.252–3.

255. *Ibid.*, pp.254–5.

256. Edinburgh: Edinburgh University Press, 1994.

257. *Ibid.*, p.3.

258. *Ibid.*, p.4.

259. Later summarized into one volume: *Muhammad – Prophet and Statesman* (1961).

260. See above, p. 140, note 54.

261. *Mecca.*

262. *Ibid.*, p.123.

263. *Ibid.*, p.x.

264. *Ibid.*

265. *Ibid.*

266. *Ibid.*

267. *Ibid.*, p.xi.

268. *Ibid.*

269. For further insight into Watt's regard for Ibn Isḥāq, see his article 'The Materials Used by Ibn Ishaq', in B. Lewis and P.M. Holt (eds.), *The Historians of the Middle East* (1962), pp.23–34.

270. Watt, *Mecca,* p.xiii. (See F. Buhl, *Das Leben Muhammeds*, German translation by H.H. Schaeder (1930).

271. Watt, *Mecca*, p.xiii.

272. *Ibid.*, p.xiv.

273. *Ibid.*

274. *Ibid.* In modern scholarship, however, this ignores the social-anthropological view of genealogy.

275. *Ibid.*, p.xv.

276. See the jacket of the book.

277. *Mecca*, p.1.

278. *Ibid.* See H.A.R. Gibb, *Mohammedanism – A Historical Survey* (1969), p.1.

279. *Mecca*, p.3.

280. *Ibid.*

281. The economic background of the Hijāz and its concomitant effects on early Islam has been examined in other works by Watt. See his 'Economic and Social Aspects of the Origin of Islam', *IQ*, Vol. 1, No. 2 (July 1954), pp.90–103 and the 'Ideal Factors in the Origin of Islam', *IQ*, Vol. 2, No. 3 (October 1955), pp.160–74. See also Patricia Crone, *Meccan Trade and The Rise of Islam* (1987), Robert Simon, *Meccan Trade and Islam – Problems of Origin and Structure*, trans. by Feodora Sos (1989) and F.E. Peters, *Muhammad and the Origins of Islam* (1994), see esp. Ch. 3, 'The Arabian Oikoumene'.

282. Watt, *Mecca*, p.6. Cf. L. Caetani, *Annali dell' Islam*, Vol. 1 (1905), pp.164–6.

283. *Mecca*, pp.6–8.

284. *Ibid.*, p.8.

285. *Ibid.*, p.9. It is worth noting that wealth was also an important element in the estimation of a person's status.

286. *Ibid.*

287. *Ibid.*, pp.9–10.

288. *Ibid.*, p.10. It is to support his interpretation of events that he presents an addendum entitled 'The Ahabish', focusing on this 'Black-slave mercenaries' theory of Lammens. See Excursus A, *ibid.*, pp.154–7.

289. *Ibid.*, p.14.

290. *Sūrah al-Fīl* 105: 1–5.

291. *Mecca*, p.16.

292. *Ibid.*

293. *Ibid.*, p.17. It is perhaps significant to note that *lex talionis* and feuding in traditional societies are considered by social anthropologists as significant factors for social and political stability and security.

294. *Ibid.*, p.18.

295. *The Arabs – A Short History* (London: Macmillan, 1968), p.15. The statement might be described as a romantic exaggeration but it gives a further glimpse of the traditional Arab society.

296. *Mecca*, pp.18–19.

297. *Ibid.*, p.19.

298. *Ibid.*, p.20. R.A. Nicholson, *A Literary History of the Arabs* (1953), pp.82–5, 178–9.

299. *Mecca*, pp.20–2.

300. *Ibid.*, p.22.

301. *Ibid.*, p.23.

302. *Ibid.*, p.24.

303. *Ibid.*

304. Published in London in 1949. See p.25 and *passim.*

305. *Mecca*, pp.25–6.

306. *Ibid.* Cf. T. Andrae, *Mohammed – The Man and His Faith* (1936), esp. pp.10–12 and Ch. 4.

307. *Mecca*, see Excursus B, pp.158–64.

308. *Ibid.*, p.158.

309. D.S. Margoliouth, 'The Origins of Arabic Poetry', *JRAS*, Vol. 57 (1925), pp.417–49, esp. p.434 ff.; R.A. Nicholson, *A Literary History* (1953), p.139 ff.; C.C. Torrey, *The Jewish Foundation of Islam* (1967), esp. pp.33, 48, 50–4, 71, 76; A. Jeffery, *The Foreign Vocabulary of the Qur'an* (1938), esp. p.10.

310. *Mecca*, pp.158–9.

311. *Ibid.*, p.160.

312. *Ibid.*

313. See Rodinson, 'A Critical Survey of Modern Studies on Muhammad', p.25.

314. *Mecca*, p.27. See his article 'The Christianity Criticised in the Qur'an', *MW*, Vol. 57, No. 3 (July 1967), pp.197–201.

315. See R. Bell, *The Origins of Islam in its Christian Environment* (1926), *passim*; A. Guillaume, *Islam* (1954), esp. p.30; C.C. Torrey, *The Jewish Foundation of Islam* (1967), *passim*; F. Rosenthal, 'The Influence of the Biblical Tradition on Muslim Historiography', in B. Lewis and P.M. Holt (eds.), *The Historians*

of the Middle East, pp.35–45; and A.N. Papathanassiou, 'Christian Missions in Pre-Islamic South Arabia', *Theologica*, Vol. 65 (1994), Issue 'A', pp.133–40.

316. *Mecca*, p.30.

317. *Ibid.*

318. *Ibid.*, pp.32–3.

319. *Ibid.*, p.33.

320. *Ibid.*, pp.33–4.

321. *Ibid.*, pp.34–8.

322. *Ibid.*, p.38.

323. *Ibid.*

324. *Sūrah al-Ḍuḥā* 93: 6–8.

325. *Mecca*, p.43.

326. *Ibid.*, p.44.

327. *Ibid.*, p.51.

328. *Ibid.*, pp.51–2.

329. *Ibid.*, p.51.

330. *Ibid.*, p.52.

331. *Ibid.*

332. *Ibid.*, p.53.

333. *Ibid.*

334. *Ibid.*, p.54.

335. *Ibid.*, p.57.

336. *Ibid.* With respect to this, see the interesting study of J.C. Archer, *Mystical Elements in Mohammed* (New Haven: Yale University Press, 1924). See especially the summary (p.87) where Archer thinks that Muḥammad practised 'self-hypnotism' to induce the events which he experienced. Yet, he also states that this '. . . did not in the least affect their character as the means of God's revelation to his chosen prophet'.

337. *Mecca,* p.61.

338. *Ibid.,* pp.62–72.

339. *Ibid.,* pp.72–9.

340. *Ibid.,* p.80.

341. *Ibid.,* pp.80–1.

342. *Ibid.,* p.81.

343. *Ibid.* The traditional argument that the message of the Qur'ān was graded to allow for human capability to bear and absorb it could be stated here.

344. *Ibid.,* p.83.

345. *Ibid.*

346. See the Holy Qur'ān, e.g.: 2: 87; 7: 63; 11: 17; 12: 104; 18: 101; 20: 3, 99, 124; 25: 29; 36: 11, 69; 43: 44; 65: 10; 72: 17.

347. *Mecca,* pp.83–4.

348. *Ibid.,* p.84.

349. For further reading on this subject see: M.M. Ahsan, 'The Qur'ān and the Orientalists. A Note on the Authenticity of the So-Called Satanic Verses', *IQ,* Vol. 24, No. 3/4 (1980), pp.89–95; M.M. Ahsan and A.R. Kidwai (eds.), *Sacrilege Versus Civility: Muslim Perspectives on The Satanic Verses Affair* (1991); S.A.A. Mawdudi, *Tafhīm al-Qur'ān,* Vol. III (1972), pp.238\45; M.H. Haykal, *The Life of Muhammad,* trans. from the 8th ed. by Ismail R. al-Fārūqī (1976); Sayyid Qutb, *Fī Ẓilāl al-Qur'ān,* Vol. IV (1974), pp.2431–3.

350. *Mecca,* p.101. The expression 'hangs a tale' seems to suggest that Watt takes a particular view of the issue. One wonders why Watt thinks the expressions in *Sūrah al-Najm* are of particular significance.

351. *Ibid.,* p.103.

352. *Ibid.,* p.104.

353. *Ibid.*

354. *Ibid.,* p.105.

355. *Ibid.,* pp.104–9.

356. *Ibid.*, p.113.

357. *Ibid.*

358. *Ibid.*, p.114.

359. *Ibid.*, p.115.

360. *Ibid.*, p.117.

361. *Ibid.*, p.119.

362. *Ibid.*, p.123.

363. *Ibid.*, pp.123–33.

364. *Ibid.*, p.133.

365. *Medina*, p.v.

366. *Ibid.*

367. *Ibid.*, pp.v–vi.

368. *Ibid.*, p.3. This is an interesting comment because Watt has maintained that Muḥammad and his followers did not suffer any severe hardship which could pass for persecution. One wonders why the situation had become that intolerable and making it impossible to live in Makkah. See *Mecca*, esp. pp.117–36.

369. *Medina*, p.2.

370. *Ibid.*

371. *Ibid.*

372. *Ibid.*, p.4.

373. *Ibid.*, p.5.

374. *Ibid.*, p.6.

375. *Ibid.*, p.7.

376. *Ibid.*

377. *Ibid.*, p.8.

378. *Sūrah al-Baqarah* 2: 217.

379. *Medina*, p.9.

380. *Ibid.*, p.10.

381. *Ibid.*, p.13.

382. *Ibid.*

383. *Ibid.*

384. *Ibid.*, p.15.

385. *Ibid.*, p.22.

386. *Ibid.*

387. *Ibid.*, pp.24–5.

388. *Ibid.*, p.27.

389. *Ibid.*, pp.27–8. If his version of counting is accepted, how can it be argued that the Muslims were out to create a gloomier picture than what was actually the case?

390. *Ibid.*, pp.29–35.

391. *Ibid.*, p.37.

392. *Ibid.*, pp.37–8.

393. *Ibid.*, p.39.

394. *Ibid.*, p.40.

395. *Ibid.*, p.41.

396. *Ibid.*

397. *Ibid.*, pp.40–1.

398. *Ibid.*, p.41.

399. *Ibid.*, p.45.

400. *Ibid.* The emphasis is ours.

401. *Ibid.*, p.47.

402. *Ibid.*, p.50.

403. *Ibid.*, p.51.

404. *Ibid.*

405. *Ibid.*, p.65.

406. *Ibid.*, p.67.

407. *Ibid.*, p.69.

408. *Ibid.*

409. *Ibid.*, p.80. It is curious why this comparison of Muḥammad's achievements as against those of Abū Bakr has arisen so suddenly.

410. *Ibid.*, see esp. pp.113–24.

411. *Ibid.*, pp.125–6.

412. *Ibid.*, p.143.

413. *Ibid.*, p.144.

414. *Ibid.*, esp. pp.145–6.

415. *Ibid.*, p.146.

416. *Ibid.*, p.147.

417. *Ibid.*

418. *Ibid.*, p.148.

419. *Ibid.*, p.149.

420. *Ibid.*

421. *Ibid.*, p.150.

422. *Ibid.*, p.19. See also pp.8, 15, 18.

423. *Ibid.*, pp.195–6.

424. *Ibid.*, pp.197–8.

425. *Ibid.*, p.198.

426. *Ibid.*

427. *Ibid.*, p.199. He cites Tor Andrae's *Ursprung des Islams* and Buhl's work as authorities for this opinion.

428. *Medina*, p.199.

429. *Ibid.*

430. *Ibid.*, pp.199–200. See *Sūrah al-Mā'idah* 5: 5.

431. *Ibid.*, p.203.

432. *Ibid.* Cf. Bell, *The Origins of Islam in its Christian Environment* (1926), p.124 ff.

433. *Medina*, p.204.

434. *Ibid.*, pp.204–6.

435. *Ibid.*, p.208.

436. *Ibid.*, p.209.

437. *Ibid.*, p.211.

438. *Ibid.*, p.212.

439. *Ibid.*, p.214.

440. *Ibid.*, p.218. See above for the discussion on the theme of Ḥudaibiyyah.

441. *Ibid.*

442. *Ibid.*, p.219.

443. *Ibid.*, p.220.

444. *Ibid.*, see pp.221–5.

445. *Ibid.*, p.225.

446. *Ibid.*, pp.225–6.

447. *Ibid.*, pp.226–8.

448. *Ibid.*, p.228.

449. *Ibid.*, see pp.228–38.

450. *Ibid.*, p.322.

451. *Ibid.*, p.323.

452. *Ibid.*, p.324.

453. *Ibid.*

454. *Ibid.*

455. *Ibid.* Since we have dealt with some of these charges in the discussion on the medieval views (see Ch. 1), we do not intend to repeat them here. We restrict ourselves mainly to Watt's opinions on these issues.

456. *Ibid.*, p.325.

457. *Ibid.*

458. *Ibid.*, p.327.

459. *Ibid.*, p.328.

460. *Ibid.*, p.329.

461. See his arguments in *ibid.*, pp.329–32.

462. *Ibid.*, p.332.

463. *Ibid.*, p.333.

464. *Ibid.*, p.334.

465. *Ibid.*, pp.334–5.

466. *Ibid.*, p.335.

467. Oxford: Clarendon Press. This volume has seen many reprints through the various branches of the Oxford University Press throughout the world.

468. *Ibid.*, p.242. The emphasis is ours.

469. *Ibid.*, see pp.127–75.

CHAPTER SIX

Conclusion

General Comments

Throughout the foregoing discourse, one of our main objectives has been an analysis of how the medieval portrayal of the life and ministry of the Prophet Muḥammad has survived in later times, especially in the period of enlightened scholarship.

As far as the main medieval attitudes are concerned, we have attempted to explain these in Chapter One, delineating some of the motives behind them.

In our concluding discussion we do not intend to repeat those comments except perhaps to reinforce them with other arguments and opinions.

On this theme, some of the most interesting arguments are found in the works of Norman Daniel and Edward Said.[1] However, being aware of the controversy surrounding Said's later works, especially after publication of his *Orientalism*, we deem it appropriate to refer to some later opinions which might be perceived as providing useful correctives and a more systematic overview than those of Daniel and Said. In fact, in Daniel's 1993 revised edition of his work which, sadly, he did not live to see published, a few additions are made to the last chapter on 'The Survival of Medieval Concepts', a theme of much interest to this work and to which we therefore refer.[2]

In the same vein, the 1995 reprint of Said's work has a new Afterword which makes a significant impact on the original ideas.[3] While we are aware that the project has entered the controversial Orientalist debate, our primary objective is not to join the fray but merely to analyze the works of the three British authors who have had a significant influence on students of Islam.

Again, part of our investigation has crossed into the territory of Inter-Faith relations and we shall be making some comments on this. After all, our three scholars were either ordained Church ministers or had a close association with the Church. In fact, generally, a significant number of the Western writers in this field can be categorized as such. On the face of it, this might not be regarded as relevant since Western enlightened scholarship is supposed to create a forum for dispassionate, scientific investigation or analysis. However, when a theologian seeks to become a historian or at least portray himself as one, the distinctive line between theology and history often becomes blurred. We believe that in the case of our three scholars, this has sadly been the case.

Hal Koch, in his work on Constantine, writes that: 'The task of the historian is to let history itself speak; to describe, as honestly as possible, what did happen; and to bring the past and our times into contact.'[4] However, Koch was 'found guilty' of writing a theologian's construction of history.[5] G. Zuntz in his review article on Koch's work observes that the theologian in the scholar has tipped the balance in his favour and this has damaged '. . . the correctness of his historical vision'.[6] Possibly, a similar observation could be made of the three scholars we have investigated. Zuntz, in his final remarks on the book writes:

> He who merely collects historical data is in danger of missing the significance of each and all of them; while he who strives to understand them as strands in a meaningful web may lose his hold upon the infinity of concrete details which in their combination make up that whole which he strives to grasp. This antinomy to be overcome calls for a combination of historical mastery and philosophical penetration . . . .[7]

Our study has sought to point out instances where historical data have either been misinterpreted or scholars have allowed their theological stance to lead them to an interpretation or over-simplification, even bordering on falsity. We now make our concluding observations on the subject, beginning with the medieval setting where the Orientalist debate is an issue.

The Medieval Setting and the Orientalist Debate

Edward Said

Maxime Rodinson, in his thoughts on the future of researches in Islam, advises students not to be too dogmatic about the phenomenon called Orientalism. He goes as far as to point out that, 'There is, . . . no such thing as Orientalism, Sinology, Iranology, and so forth. Rather, there are scientific disciplines defined both by the object of their study and by the direction the study takes, such as sociology, demography, political economy, linguistics, anthropology, ethnology or the various branches of general history.'[8] Of course he is not denying the existence of a particular field of study labelled 'Orientalism' as such but is merely stating that this method of study is supposed to be scientific.

In a follow-up comment, he says that Orientalism as a concept was born out of a particular pragmatic necessity which faced Europe. He continues: 'This situation was reinforced by European dominance over the other societies, and the result was a greatly distorted vision of things.'[9] One suspects that his comments have to do with the work of Edward Said which he criticizes severely.

After commending Said for attacking the self-satisfaction of many Western scholars, Rodinson opines that the book carries a militant philosophy and a particular tone which is indicative of Said's nationalistic views.[10] Hassan Gai Eaton considers Said's *Orientalism* to be a 'counter-attack' against Western Orientalists.[11]

To Muhammad Benaboud, the work is the '. . . most scholarly study of the phenomenon up to date, which has placed the problem in a new light'.[12] He then goes on to laud the book as a serious study which has achieved tremendous success both in the East and the West.

Said's work has instigated enormous debate and this is referred to by Fred Halliday in a paper given at the Annual British Society for Middle Eastern Studies Lecture in March 1993.[13] Halliday notes that Said comprehensively criticizes the dominant writings of Westerners on the Middle East and that this has influenced many works which have sought to label such Western studies as '. . . Eurocentric, imperialist, racist, essentialist, and so forth'.[14] In his view, Said's work carries a 'Foucauldain perspective', where the main motivation behind Orientalist' works is seen to be the desire for power over others.[15]

A serious analysis of 'Orientalism' and the efforts of Orientalist studies is presented, always cautioning that the term is open to abuse. For example, he writes that, 'Orientalism in Said's usage acquires an almost metaphysical power to pervade very different epochs and genres of expression; in so doing it loses analytic or explanatory purchase.'[16] Criticizing Said for being too one-sided in his analysis, Halliday argues that '. . . when it comes to hypostasis, stereotyping, the projection of timeless and antagonistic myths, this is in no sense a prerogative of the dominator, but also of the dominated; . . .'[17] While accepting that what Halliday says might be true, these projections of the enemy are art forms which perhaps, it could be argued, the dominator excels in.

Donald P. Little, in his article 'Three Arab Critiques of Orientalism', examines the works of A.L. Tibawi, Anouar Abdel-Malek and Edward Said.[18] Criticizing Tibawi for what he sees as his closure of the door of study of Islam in the face of non-Muslims, Little does not see much difference in Abdel-Malek except that the latter has Marxist inclinations. Hence, colonialism, to Abdel-Malek has always gone hand in hand with Orientalism.[19] One wonders what happened to Orientalism in the post-colonial period. Perhaps the argument can be likened to the usual arguments about Christian missionary activities which were seen as being carried out in the shadow of the colonialists. Of course, in this case, and possibly in the case of Orientalism as well, colonialism built a foundation on which it could thrive.

Little continues his analysis, considering all Orientalists to be the same and therefore lumps them together. He understands Said's argument to be that all Orientalists '. . . share the same beliefs and assumptions which invariably distort their vision'.[20] Again, he considers that Said and Abdel-Malek hold a similar view, that Orientalism is merely an imperialist tool. Said is accused of not reading wide enough to realize that a large amount of material does not fit his pattern of critique.[21]

However, Said has obviously realized the controversy his work has generated. He writes in the Afterword to the 1995 re-issue: 'In both America and England (where a separate UK edition appeared in 1979) the book attracted a great deal of attention, some of it (as was to be expected) very hostile, some of it uncomprehending, but most of it positive and enthusiastic.'[22]

The hostility towards the book was, perhaps, responsible for the enormous publicity it achieved. The book has now been translated into many languages including Arabic, French, German, Italian, Japanese, Polish, Portuguese, Serbo-Croat, Spanish and Swedish.

Said maintains that the book is not anti-Western as is sometimes argued by its critics, and that it should not be misunderstood as projecting a philosophy where the entire Western world is seen as an enemy of Islam. He is at pains to refute the accusations of him being a '. . . supporter of Islamism or Muslim fundamentalism'.[23]

Calling the critiques mostly 'caricatural permutations' of the work, he insists that the book explicitly states that the concepts 'Orient' and 'Occident', '. . . are an odd combination of the empirical and imaginative'.[24] He explains that the hostility to the book was essentially defence of a particular position. He says further, that: 'Part of the resistance and hostility to books like *Orientalism* . . . stems from the fact that they seem to undermine the naive belief in the certain positivity and unchanging historicity of a culture, a self, a national identity. Orientalism can only be read as a defense of Islam by suppressing half of my argument . . .'[25]

Said's critique of that perhaps amorphous phenomenon needs to be understood as a reaction to a particular mode of thinking, which sees a '. . . dynamic, and complex human reality from an uncritically essentialist standpoint; . . .',[26] a reasoning this work seeks to share. Instead of it being seen as anti-West or even anti-non-Muslim, it needs to be viewed as an endeavour to redress the situation which has become endemic, the consequences of which do not serve any good cause. It is a critique of a system of thought which invariably creates negative reactions to sincere scholars.

It is not anti-West or anti- a particular scholar, be it Muir, Margoliouth or Watt, to suggest that a particular line of reasoning or a model used to assess the Prophet of Islam needs rethinking or may even be entirely wrong. After all, if we are to be faithful to contemporary enlightened scholarship then critiques, even frequent ones, have to be encouraged.

Norman Daniel

Many of our arguments in Chapter One were built on Norman Daniel's *Islam and the West – The Making of an Image*, which we also briefly commented upon in the discussion under the survey of twentieth-century literature.[27] We are returning to it because of its revised edition published in 1993. This new edition has the advantage of an expanded Introduction and also a concluding chapter. Though the material could be criticized as not being structured particularly well, it still offers a large body of information in the field which we would be foolish to ignore.

In the Introduction, Daniel reiterates the position that there are still differences between Christianity and Islam, '. . . so that Christians have always tended to make the same criticisms; and even when, in relatively modern times, some authors have self-consciously tried to emancipate themselves from Christian attitudes, they have not generally been as successful as they thought'.[28] The results of our investigation with respect to the three British scholars under study, show this to be the case. There are glimpses of efforts where detachment seems to have triumphed but, more often than not, the inherited attitudes seem to be creeping back. What Daniel calls 'war psychosis' can almost always be discerned in the writings of the present age where the scientific method has claimed victory.

From the beginning, John of Damascus was known to have been the source of a formula for new converts to Christianity, heavily laden with pejorative statements against Islam.[29] Such ideas became sharper as the years went by and the feared dominance of Islam seemed to become a reality. It was with this in mind that caustic polemics, and of course its toned-down and sophisticated modern versions, were developed. The works of Alvarus and Elogius are cases in point to which both Daniel and Southern refer.[30]

Daniel points out the significance of avoiding the popular opinion of the uninformed masses. In our case, perhaps the remark is valid as well. After all, it is the opinions of the specialists in the field which shape the *communis opinio*. The works of Muir, Margoliouth and especially those of Watt, have been largely responsible for the general views about Muḥammad in the English-speaking West and even in institutions in Muslim communities where English is the main or only medium of instruction.

In his analysis of the survival of medieval ideas, Daniel points out that in the medieval era, even though a considerable amount of knowledge about 'authentic' Islam was available, particular choices were made to serve what was thought to be a crucial end. Consequently, 'A communal mode of thought developed. Establishing great internal coherence, it represented the doctrinal unity of Christendom in its political opposition to Islamic society, a clear social function that correlated military and intellectual aggression.'[31]

Daniel looks at the medieval canon and summarizes the main concepts regarding Muḥammad, the Qur'ān and Islam in general, comparing some values in Islam to those in Christianity. These ideas, which were developed mainly during the twelfth to early fourteenth centuries, were carried over into later times.[32] Curiously, Daniel points out, these distorted images of Muḥammad in particular and of Islam in general were so zealously passed on that even later generations, 'If they did look at them, . . . did so through the eyes of their predecessors; . . .'[33]

Even in the post-enlightenment period, with the secular and humanist perspectives of the Prophet, the difference in attitude has not been that great. Though Carlyle shook the British academic world with his lecture on Muḥammad, even here his sincerity regarding what he is prepared to allow Muḥammad, is open to question. Carlyle, despite his alleged openness and even accusations of pandering to the wishes of Muslims, remained rather sceptical or at best ambiguous about the revelation the Prophet received.[34]

Discussing the gradual development of the academic approach to the study of Islam, Daniel comments that in the medieval era a particular situation fostered the development of those distorted ideas. He continues: 'As these reasons ceased to exist, a scientific attitude, that is an attitude of pure science, interested in the thing itself was free to develop. There is still reciprocal distrust between the cultures to which the key is "secularism".'[35]

Whether the scientific attitude has been applied, as it was supposed to be in nineteenth- and twentieth-century literature, is debatable. As for Daniel's prescription of secularism as the panacea for the rivalry, this has to be received with some disquiet. The issue of secularism *vis-à-vis* Islam is expertly discussed by Syed Muhammad al-Naquib al-Attas, who argues that by its very character and definition secularism cannot understand religion and therefore it is bound to take a sceptical attitude to things religious, which would then not solve problems but perhaps raise new ones.[36]

The reason why Daniel seems to have lost interest in the scientific paradigm is apparent in his comment which follows his prescription of secularism. He declares:

> Although I personally believe in the 'scientific' historical ideal of objectivity, I think it certain that it has been infiltrated by subjective ideas of cultural, political and social prejudice. The condemnation by Edward Said in his *Orientalism* of the assumed superiority and cultural intolerance of the Orientalist tradition in the West was not only justifiable but overdue.[37]

To Daniel, contemporary academics and Orientalist scholars of Islam for that matter, often sound patronizing and display evidence of double standards in their 'scientific' discourse. Such scholars have not been able to break free from the medieval legacy of hatred and bias. In the works of Muir, Margoliouth and Watt on Muḥammad one detects evidence of this albeit in different shades and strengths.

Referring to some contemporary material, the work of Patricia Crone and Michael Cook[38] comes in for particular criticism, for being almost maverick and making a mockery of scholarship by rejecting almost all Muslim sources. Daniel explains that '. . . this is just what Medieval writers did when they hung on to poor evidence that contradicted the Muslim witness'.[39] He describes their comments on the Qur'ān as reminiscent of twelfth- to fourteenth-century scholarship.

Such critique could well apply to certain aspects of the works of the three authors this work investigates, the evidence of which can be gleaned from the foregoing chapters and some points we intend to raise now.

In the last section, Daniel devotes some pages to Christian-

Muslim relations in our time, accusing British Christians of perhaps being the most guilty in the retention of some medieval attitudes. Pointing out the inability of Western Christian opinion to adequately transform itself in accordance with the changing conditions in the era of colonialism, he adds that some Christians even saw the triumph of technology and colonialism as proof of the supremacy of Christianity. He mentions Montgomery Watt as sounding like one who views the superiority of Western technology in that light.[40] Daniel also reminds us of a medieval attitude in William Muir. He writes: 'A collection of papers by Sir William Muir, founder of Islamic Studies at Edinburgh, which was published in 1897 under the general title *The Mohammedan Controversy*, includes the remark, soon to be outdated, "Mohammedanism is perhaps the only undisguised and formidable antagonist of Christianity".'[41] He then comments that the statement lacked the foresight of other, perhaps, real adversaries of the Church. He also comments that the attitudes of missionaries like W.H.T. Gairdner, Karl Krumm and Vincent of Beauvais were not dissimilar to that of their medieval colleagues.[42]

For Daniel, efforts for a new understanding of Islam in this century began to yield fruit with the publication in 1949 of the work of a Muslim convert to Christianity, who sought to find out what lessons Christians could learn from Muslim spirituality.[43] Others who have made advances in the field include Kenneth Cragg, Jacques Jomier, and Louis Gardet. Gardet is given a special place for being more detached than others.[44] Daniel observes that in reality, 'There has been a considerable advance in such study, not only of Islam itself, but also of the history of relations between the two religions, not only as communities, but as faiths, and here the explicitly Christian contribution has its own insights.'[45]

Montgomery Watt's contribution in the field is commended and his two-volume work on Muḥammad gets a special mention. However, Daniel points out that these works did not do much to radically transform the existing opinions about Muḥammad in the Christian psyche. But, he adds, Watt's works '. . . change the emphasis, so that the reader, through the historico-anthropological approach, is drawn into and allowed to some extent to share the Muslim awareness of the Prophet'.[46] This opinion about Watt is well placed. Often his reader is taken on a journey to explore what one might call 'authentic' Muslim beliefs sometimes without any critical comments. And on occasions he declines to make any remark on a topic because it might go against orthodox belief.[47]

Daniel advocates a strengthening of Inter-Faith dialogue, explaining that there is much that both Muslims and Christians could work for together. He is, however, cautious about what he calls extremists, whose philosophy is that all the ills of the Muslim world can be attributed to the 'Christian West'. He stresses that the West is no longer Christian, an argument he admits that finds little sympathy amongst the larger Muslim populace. The main characteristic of Western society, he insists, is secularism not Christianity. He sees some truth in the Muslim perception though. In a world where many of the scholars who deal with Islam are either ordained ministers or have close links with the Church, and where daily global issues seem to typify Christian ideals, how can people disabuse their minds of this perception that the West is Christian?

In his closing remarks, Daniel calls for new scholarship to see Islam from the Muslim point of view. The empathy, he stresses is necessary otherwise estrangement, distrust and survival of caricatural opinions will persist. He explains that the argument does not mean a full acceptance of Muḥammad and hence embracing Islam but that, for methodological reasons, Christians need to replace their jaundiced views with Muslim perceptions to enable them to obtain a better discernment of Islam and especially of Muḥammad.

We align ourselves with these sentiments because this work endeavours to contribute to this call, so that the methodological requirements of the scientific study of religion are adhered to as much as possible.

William Muir

Albert Hourani hails Muir's works as yet to be superseded, though he admits that Muir's perspective of Islam is typically traditional Christian.[48]

To Norman Daniel, Muir is not very different from his contemporaries or others in the field, who have '. . . maintained an attitude that is not fundamentally sympathetic to Muhammad or to Islam'.[49]

Clinton Bennet argues that '. . . Muir, who combined the scholar, the colonial administrator with support for missions, influenced Missions in India towards a less conciliatory view of Islam'.[50]

Muir's general attitude towards Muslims can only be described as confrontational. His works on Islam, and on Muḥammad in particular, are written in this spirit. In fact, he was known to be a keen supporter of the CMS missionary in India, Karl Pfander who was constantly associated with polemical discourses against Muslims.

Clinton Bennet again points out this fact, and even observes that Muir's work *The Mohammedan Controversy*, '. . . is much more than a description of Pfander's debates'.[51]

Against a background of such comments, it is difficult to agree with Lyall, who describes the book as being 'systematic', excellent, and offers 'sobriety of judgement'.[52]

Muir's subjectivity is displayed when pointing out the kind of yardstick he intends to employ in evaluating Muḥammad. In the preliminary discussions forming the Introduction, he calls the Christian yardstick a '. . . purer morality . . .',[53] and it is this that he uses in his analysis. In fact, he states that he is going to apply the '. . . canon of Christian criticism, that any tradition whose origin is not strictly contemporary with the facts related is worthless exactly in proportion to the particularity of detail'.[54]

Syed Ahmad Khan rightly rejects this position, pointing out that any conclusions arrived at from this methodology can only be false.[55]

Muir confidently tells us that he is dealing with original source material. In fact this information is incorporated within the title itself, but this one great asset of the book is perhaps the root of its weaknesses. With access to the original sources, Muir owed the academic world (not only the Western or Christian world), a duty to be honest, sincere, fair and consistent. Without doubt, one can conclude that his understanding of the sources and the interpretations he puts on them have had a marked negative effect on his scholarship.

However, we do not intend to reject everything that has been said, for in the face of bias and prejudice any small amount of fairness still has to be acknowledged. This is why we appreciate his exhaustive analysis of the sources, noting some of the inevitable problems which existed with the traditional accounts. We ourselves have pointed out that Muslim scholarship does not gloss over this and the whole elaborate science of *Ḥadīth* criticism is evidence of that.[56]

Because of the intricacy of the traditions, Muir falls back on the theory that unfavourable comments about Muḥammad could be true but favourable ones, especially from Muḥammad's followers, need to be treated with care.[57] His blanket application of this theory, which achieved currency even in Watt's later works is an abuse of methodology.

Muir seems to have missed the opportunity of seeing Islam in the Muslim perspective, a principle advocated by scientific scholarship. Instead, he uses a methodology which exhibits a continuation of the medieval attitudes.

Looking at the various themes he selects and the tone of the discourse, our hypothesis that change in methodology *per se* does not necessarily imply change in attitude, seems justified. By repeating medieval Christian arguments and exhibiting similar attitudes, Muir has made objectivity elusive. His emphasis on wars, Muḥammad's sexuality and so-called fabrication of revelation leaves much to be desired. Very important themes, such as the treaty Muḥammad signed with the tribes of Madīnah (usually called the Madīnan Charter or the Madīnan Constitution), the Prophet's honesty, his commitment to strict monotheism, his compassion, the treaty of Ḥudaibiyyah and others are either not mentioned at all or treated very casually.

The argument is reinforced if one looks at his other work which was supposed to be an abridgement of the main volume on the biography. This is meant to contain all the essentials of the main work.[58]

Muir's Christian background weighs heavily on him and one senses this in the way he deals with revelation and inspiration in Islam.[59] His understanding of religious experience is not very different from that of his co-religionists and contemporaries Rev. Canon Sell and Rev. W.H. Temple Gairdner. Sell, for example, states that inspiration in Islam is '. . . quite illogical and entirely contrary to the inspiration in the Bible'.[60]

In the Christian concept, expertly explained by Gairdner and Sell, and which would no doubt have been accepted by Muir as valid, Jesus Christ becomes the *ne plus ultra* (the highest point, fulfilment) of revelation. The Muslim concept of revelation, during which the medium becomes seized-up completely, does not make much sense in Christianity.

In the Christian understanding, the Prophet maintains his composure and his senses while being inspired and, therefore, he is fully responsible for whatever he utters and his words cannot be said to be those of the Divine. One seems to hear Muir echoing Gairdner that, 'It is impossible for us to accept any revelation subsequent to Christ. The Word was made flesh – what need of further words? God, after that He spake to the fathers in the Prophets hath at last spoken to us in a *Son* – how then go back to any prophet? No, it is impossible.'[61] Muir therefore seems heavily constrained in his assessment in spite of his scholarly capabilities and sees almost everything about Muḥammad as having human meaning.

But that is not the point. The issue is not whether to accept Muḥammad as a true prophet or not. Of significance here is proper application of sound scholarship, so that the object being analyzed is recognizable in the light of the original sources that Muir himself claims he had access to.

The book's concentration on the theory that Islam is a garbled form of earlier monotheistic faiths, the pathological theory, that the messages the Prophet received were from his subconscious mind and not the Divine, and the Satanic Verses, all point to an attitude which can be traced to the medieval period.[62]

Muir's comments on Muḥammad's *Isrā'* and *Mi rāj* experience is indicative of his utter derision.[63] Here, as we have pointed out in the main discussion, Muir is inconsistent in his outlook on similar experiences, such as the doctrine of transfiguration of Jesus and even the bodily ascension of Elijah which, as a Christian, he should have had no qualms about.

Again, mention must be made of Muir's use of the miracle criterion to assess Muḥammad. Daniel has elaborated on this in his work and it seems Muir is rehearsing medieval opinions again.[64] Further, Muir, with his Christian yardstick then censures Muḥammad's sexual behaviour, accusing him of violating a Christian canon.[65]

Having dealt with some of these issues in the text itself, it would serve little purpose to repeat them here. Again, in our concluding remarks at the end of the chapter, we reiterate that Muir was not able to divorce himself from the communal opinion dating from the medieval period. Therefore, even though in some instances, he is positively appreciative of Muḥammad as the available sources suggest, his work lacks the merit of consistent, sound academic scholarship.

David Samuel Margoliouth

Having been analytical in our discussion on Margoliouth, there is no point in recounting those remarks. We would, however, like to reiterate some significant points.

If Muir, writing to encourage the missionary propaganda of

Karl Pfander in India, failed to live up to his promises of objectivity, one would not expect Margoliouth to fall into the same category. As a British colonial officer, having to pursue the 'unofficial official' British policy, something which Clinton Bennet reminds us of, Muir was in a rather different situation compared to Margoliouth.[66] Also, in terms of academic standing, Muir and Margoliouth are perhaps worlds apart and therefore one might, understandably, excuse Muir some of his lapses.[67] It should also be noted that Margoliouth's work appeared almost half a century after Muir and therefore a more judicious use of fair and sound academic principles would be expected.

A *cause célèbre* in the field among his contemporaries, Margoliouth's attitude should be markedly better than that of Muir.[68] In fact, his expertise in Arabic language is readily accepted but, significantly, he is also portrayed as rather conceited, always insisting that his view is right.[69]

Granted this observation, one might be sceptical about Margoliouth's preparedness to be fair and just with the material he deals with. The argument basically is that expertise in a language in itself does not necessarily guarantee objectivity when the expert is working on material in that language. Therefore, though Margoliouth might be aware of all the extant classical material on the Prophet's biography and could delve into its intricacies, at the end of the day his interpretation cannot be guaranteed as objective. After all, in the Prophet's time there were perhaps greater experts in the Arabic language, and yet because of particular motives they scorned Muḥammad. In the medieval age, even those scholars who could be described as well acquainted with Arabic chose to interpret Muḥammad the way they did.

One can discern in Margoliouth's *Mohammed* that his expertise has not guaranteed fairness. It is pertinent to point out here, as we have done in the case of Muir, that we are not demanding that his expertise should have led him to accept Muḥammad and become a Muslim. Our argument is that his expertise should have led to a fairer assessment of the Prophet.

In his discussion on the sources, Margoliouth's demand that scholars should go to the original biographical sources for a better appreciation of Muḥammad is, no doubt, commendable. So is his detailed discussion of the scholarship in existence at the time.[70] In fact, he makes a bold statement, that the existing '. . . works are ordinarily designed to show the superiority or inferiority of Mohammed's religion to some other system; an endeavour from which it is hoped that this book will be found to be absolutely free'.[71]

However, in the next few pages, in his discussion of pre-Islamic Arabian history, he accuses Islam of adding to the already volatile arena by introducing religious zealotry.[72] This opinion goes against history in the sense that Islam came rather to ameliorate the situation and not to increase the insecurity. In fact, the issue of the *Hijrah* to Madīnah is primarily linked with the question of security and peace. This has nothing to do with belief; it is a matter of history and Margoliouth, on this particular score has not been fair to his material.

His choice of themes, his interest in the pathological theory and his view that this was evident in Muḥammad's state when receiving revelation, confirm that Margoliouth's objectivity is questionable. He is therefore not very different from many of the scholars he criticizes as being unscholarly.[73]

One would have expected Margoliouth to show more perspicacity on this subject. He lays himself open to the charge of falsehood by commenting that a particular Qur'ānic order, which he sees as coming from Muḥammad himself, had to be retracted. As we have already remarked, this view does not have any truth in it.[74] He even claims that Muḥammad's Companions used to collect and drink the water he had used for ablution. Later, he claims, Muḥammad '. . . took to bottling up the precious liquid and sending it, after the style of saints, to new adherents'.[75] Margoliouth does not question the authenticity of this story in the light of the personality of the Prophet. This approach is not very helpful in sound scholarship.

Margoliouth's understanding of the Qur'ān is questionable

and sometimes the vocabulary he applies to it is not academic.[76] His denial of the existence of metaphysical issues in the Qur'ān is not justified. Though one might not believe in the Hindu Scriptures, for example, scholarly rectitude requires that one acknowledges the enormous metaphysical concerns they carry.

Margoliouth's charge of imposture against Muḥammad again reminds one of the medieval thoughts. Though he rejects some of the outdated stories peddled during the age of 'war propaganda', he does not try unduly to ensure fairness.[77]

The doubts he casts upon Muḥammad's visit to Waraqah ibn Naufal is strange, and even more so his reason for doubting it. His reasoning that, because Waraqah does not appear in the later narratives the story could have been concocted by Muslims to support the authenticity of Muḥammad, has no support from the general material available. We have already dealt with this and pointed out that the premise of the reasoning is faulty.[78]

Margoliouth's imputation of idolatrous practices against Muḥammad looks very much like medieval polemic. Norman Daniel recounts a series of these charges which were manufactured in those emotive periods.[79] Rosalind Hill, in her paper 'Crusading Warfare: A Camp-Follower's View 1097–1120', notes how the prosecutors of the Crusades relied on these fanciful stories in order to boost the morale of the Christian soldiers who interpreted the wars as theologically necessary since they were fighting against idol worshippers.[80] Relying greatly on the *Patrologia Latina* and the *Gesta Francorum*, Hill points out that, 'The belief in Moslem Polytheism certainly outlasted the Crusade and survived in the Latin states.'[81] This is very true and one can argue that vestiges are seen in Margoliouth's work.

Another theme around which Margoliouth uses a high level of speculative theory is the infamous 'Satanic Verses' issue. As we have argued, it is not merely the story itself but the skilful way he attempts to find a basis for it. Margoliouth with his expertise should at least have questioned the accounts.

Margoliouth does not divorce himself from old arguments

that, since Muḥammad's prophethood cannot be genuine, and he was an impostor, then those ideas which sound acceptable must have been borrowed from existing faiths. And, that without Judaism and Christianity, or at least their ideas in various forms in Arabia there would have been no Prophet. This reasoning has, of course, like many others continued beyond Margoliouth. In the whole analysis, conjecture is the main ingredient of his work. However, he strongly rejects any idea that Islam is a Christian heresy.[82] There is a contradiction here. If, for argument's sake, Muḥammad relied on the Bible or on Christian and Jewish teachers to establish his religion and if his central ideas are wrong as far as the main Christian teachings are concerned, then why the objection that it is a wrong form of Christianity?

As for Muḥammad's morals, Margoliouth's assessment cannot be distinguished from that of the medieval Church fathers whose philosophy was to show the enemy in the worst possible light. Even Margoliouth's language is sometimes unbecoming of such a respected academic.[83]

Even in Muḥammad's behaviour at the fall of Makkah, for which Margoliouth himself praises the Prophet's magnanimity, he finds an ulterior motive. He asserts that Muḥammad was so merciful only because he was looking beyond Makkah.[84]

Comments on the Prophet's sexuality begin on a sympathetic note but soon run into severe censure, reminiscent of the days of ignorance mixed with animosity. Muḥammad is pictured by Margoliouth as a bad-tempered and violent man, again digging deep into the archives of the subculture built over the ages. Despite his claims that this work is going to break fresh ground, this characterization does not support that. In the work edited by Samir and Nielsen this question is expertly dealt with.[85]

If Muir is criticized for omitting the Madīnan Charter, Margoliouth should be given credit for finding it significant enough to discuss. Acknowledging that it was an important document meant primarily for the security of Madīnah and its environs is commendable. However, even here, the implications of the charter as far as Muḥammad's personality is concerned are clearly absent. Any analysis of the Prophet's biography ought to take cognizance of what issues like the Madīnan Charter tell us about the Prophet and his mission.

The Jewish question receives exhaustive attention and, though one mostly detects Jewish sympathy, occasionally we come across statements which can be described as anti-Semitic. Margoliouth's Jewish background could be the reason for this. Though he often identifies with the Jews, coming from a family of converts to Christianity this other side also shows. While charging Muḥammad with violence against the Jews, he also accuses the Jews of being stupid enough not to break off relations with Muḥammad especially when faced with the change in *qiblah*.[86]

When discussing Muḥammad's relationship with the Christians, Margoliouth becomes emotional and this makes him act even less like an academic.[87]

The Ḥudaibiyyah treaty also receives much attention and Margoliouth perhaps gives it more space than many of his contemporaries. However, he avoids comments on what it means as far as Muḥammad's personality is concerned.

His observation regarding the letters the Prophet sent to various eminent personalities of the day as embodying a programme of world conquest, is unfortunate. Even here, the Jewish issue crops up when Margoliouth alleges that Heraclius was much like Muḥammad because the Prophet had massacred Jews. Considerations like these cloud any fairness.

When Margoliouth looks at the general character of Muḥammad, he makes some fair comments. The greedy, violent, power-hungry, bad-tempered, robber-chief suddenly becomes affectionate, abstemious and honest. However, this does not seem to match the bulk of the discussion.

Margoliouth, having reflected on Muḥammad's teachings as having something to do with Christianity, has to put him somewhere; hence the proto-Mormon argument. As we have already pointed out, Margoliouth, with his academic stature should have known the spuriousness of the theory.[88] This is very similar to the medieval argument of the Anti-Christ which both Muḥammad and the Pope were supposed to be.[89]

In our concluding remarks to the chapter we reiterate our supposition that medieval ideas continued to survive and that a change in methodology *per se* does not necessarily lead to a change in attitude. Margoliouth's work does not disprove these assertions.

William Montgomery Watt

In both Muir and Margoliouth we detected serious lapses in interpretation of data on the Prophet's biography. However, one has to take into account the period in which both produced their works. Margoliouth's constant reference to Muir suggests that the latter's was the main serious academic study of the age. It thus shows the paucity of sound material.

In Watt's case, the situation is very different. Writing almost half a century after Margoliouth and almost a century after Muir, Watt falls into a very different category. In Watt's time and certainly that of his students, the Christian biographical approach to the Prophet shifted significantly from confrontation to dialogue. This is borne out by the enormous amount of twentieth-century literature we surveyed as a prelude to our discussion of Watt. Such a survey for the periods of Muir and Margoliouth would be extremely difficult, which is indicative of the dearth of English material. Therefore, since our interest lies mainly with English sources we thought it prudent to avoid that.

The tremendous change in the level of discussion and the rapid growth in material in the early part of the century and after can be attributed to several reasons. These might include the situation in Egypt in the twenties and thirties with the rise of figures such as Muḥammad Husayn Haykal and Ṭāha Husayn. Also, the 1920s Indian scene and the Khilāfat Movement along with all their manifestations cannot be left out. Further, the collapse of the *Khilāfah*, the triumph of secularism in Turkey, together with the Middle Eastern situation played a significant part in putting Islam and Muslims on the Western agenda. The growing profile of Islam dictated an interest in Islam and Muḥammad.

Watt was writing during a period of great development in the field and therefore we are justified in spending much more time on him than the others. Again, as we have indicated in our rationale for choosing him, Watt's impact on English-speaking students of Islam, and the Prophet's biography for that matter, is more pervasive than any of his predecessors or contemporaries.[90] But, if Watt was fortunate enough to be born in this period of tremendous advance in scholarship, then primarily because of that, our level of critique has to be more stringent as compared to the others. Watt's books have been seriously reviewed by various scholars and we refer to some of these here.

Alfred Guillaume reviews Watt's *Muhammad at Mecca* and calls it a useful project. He notes Watt's concern with the economic theory as the basis of the episode in Makkah. He writes: 'Dr. Watt's observations on the stresses and strains of social and economic solidarity brought about by financial alliances bring to the fore a factor of considerable importance, though it is possible to exaggerate it.'[91] He is, however, critical of Watt's theory of the level of individualism and what Watt calls 'tribal humanism' in pre-Islamic Arab society. He points out that Watt's suggestion that without belief in immortality, it would have been impossible for the society to pass on from 'tribal humanism' to individual humanism, '. . . seems to me to go beyond the evidence'.[92]

Watt's attempt to be fair to Muḥammad concerns his view about his sincerity and here Guillaume censures him for failing as a historian. This has to do with Watt's insistence that there is no plausible evidence to suggest that the Qur'ān is Muḥammad's own composition.[93] For Guillaume, the historian's proper position is that the Qur'ān is indeed Muḥammad's own composition. On this, Watt's position is a distinct improvement in scholarship and a significant shift away from the medieval position which Guillaume seems to hold on to. Guillaume's final statement is, however, complimentary. He writes: 'Whether one agrees with Dr. Watt or not, it is beyond doubt that he has written a stimulating and informative book which will provoke both thought and further research. The excurses which must have given the author much labour, are of great value.'[94]

This same volume is reviewed by W. Arafat.[95] Arafat, noting Watt's claims to neutrality on theological issues, reviews the book as a work of history. Welcoming the economic analysis of pre-Islamic Makkah, he, however, cautions that Watt has theorized too much on this without marshalling enough evidence. On Watt's theory of individualism and tribal humanism, on which Guillaume also comments, Arafat feels that there is a danger of forcing the argument. He points out that '. . . individualism seems deep rooted in the Arab, and it is a fact that individualism and tribal solidarity existed side by side'.[96] He accuses Watt of relying on too many theories and hypotheses which are not conclusively proved.

Watt thinks that the reports of persecution of the Muslims in Makkah are exaggerated.[97] On this, Arafat says that it is not fair to suppose that the Muslims emigrated due to 'base motives' and not because of persecution. He reasons that although perhaps the level of persecution was not the same as that endured by the Christians in Rome, that does not reduce the severity of it within the Makkan context.[98]

Again, reacting to Watt's acceptance of pre-Islamic poetry of the *Sīrah*, Arafat calls this a dangerous position to take. He elaborates thus: 'The poem attributed to Abu Talib, which Dr. Watt is inclined to accept is mostly doubted by I.H. himself and rejected by his authorities.'[99] Could it be that Watt misread the text or forced his own conclusions on it? If the account is doubted by the same authority Watt cites, Ibn Hishām, why Watt, with his knowledge, accepts it is not clear.

As further evidence of Watt's different level of scholarship and the scope of his work, Arafat in the end says of the book:

'There are many points in this book for praise and comment. The excurses and some of the discussions are extremely valuable. Even if one finds much to disagree with, it is a great merit of the book that it should stimulate interest or provide further research.'[100]

A.L. Tibawi reviews Watt's third volume on the biography and notes that Watt has tried to change the face of negative scholarship against Islam.[101] He is, however, of the opinion that Watt is often too speculative, sometimes to the point of incredulity.[102] Tibawi points to instances of contradiction, specific examples being to do with Muḥammad's prophethood and his sincerity. While Watt acknowledges these, he argues about the roots of Muḥammad's teachings being Biblical and speculates that Muḥammad attempted to make his religion Jewish. Tibawi then writes: 'The lavish, if cautious use of "perhaps", "may", and "if", followed only too often by far-reaching conclusions, is a disturbing feature of this scholarly work.' He continues: 'There is a great deal of intelligent guess-work which sounds reasonable and may be acceptable, but apart from a solid core of factual survey, this work contains too much speculative deduction. Not the least significant of these deductions is the so-called Judaeo-Christian "origins".'[103]

Tibawi points out that since Watt should have been aware that the theory of Judaeo-Christian 'origins' of Islam is alien to Muslims, as a dispassionate historian he should have stated the Muslim position on this matter.

This raises the question of method in historical inquiry. If the historian is to 'let the text speak for itself' or merely 'let history speak for itself' as Koch has suggested,[104] then Watt, in this case, has not allowed history to speak.

In discussing the Madīnan period of the Prophet's life, Watt often makes the Prophet look like someone who had the conquest of the whole of Arabia and beyond as his primary aim.[105] Tibawi, however, notes an inconsistency in that Watt at the same time rejects the letters Muḥammad sent to various rulers and eminent people of the then known world as spurious.[106] If

Muḥammad's life ambition was to bring the whole world under his power, then this is one of the most natural courses of action he could have taken.

In our own analysis of Watt's material, we found it necessary to put him in perspective by presenting a general survey of the available English material. In the survey, one can see the marked changes that occurred within the period.

In Watt's intellectual biography, we briefly reviewed most of Watt's works and there emerged a general positive reaction to Watt as a scholar more sympathetic to Islam and Muslims than his predecessors and contemporaries. The general picture is that Watt has a different approach to that of Muir or Margoliouth. Even in the selection of themes and emphasis, Watt uses a more judicious methodology than Muir and Margoliouth.

As Muir's work contains much typical Christian missionary propaganda, and Margoliouth's is a slight improvement on Muir, Watt's can be seen as a more serious attempt at writing history. Despite evidence of Christian attitudes, forced conclusions and skilful imaginative reconstruction of events, Watt is the only one of the three who endeavours to detach himself as a historian.

One of Watt's greatest faults is in casting doubt on many of the classical traditions, attributing less credit to contemporary Islamic scholarship and relying often on his own conjectures. As pointed out, Watt claims that Muslim intellectuals have, from classical times, been living in intellectual isolation and have not studied other religions and cultures.[107] This view is, however, explicitly contradicted by a line of scholarship brought together by Tarīf Khālidī's recent account of Muslim historiography.[108]

Watt could be criticized as being out of touch regarding his view about the lack of modern Muslim critical thought (except Fazlur Rahman and Muhammad Arkoun).[109] The works of Ismā īl R. al-Fārūqī and the publications of the International Institute of Islamic Thought (IIIT) in Herndon (Virginia, USA) and many others belie Watt's position and betray his inability to keep abreast of such scholarship. Some might even argue that Watt respects Fazlur Rahman and Arkoun because, as 'Westernized' Muslim scholars their views are sometimes not wholly acceptable to many Muslim scholars.[110]

Watt's frequent readiness to question Muslim accounts makes him doubt Khadījah's age at the time of her marriage to Muḥammad and even that Jibrīl appeared to Muḥammad in Makkah.[111] Today, even without In-vitro Fertilization (IVF) it is not miraculous for a woman beyond the age of forty to give birth. As for the issue of Jibrīl's appearance, it is just not true that there is no mention of Jibrīl in the pre-Madīnan revelations. Jibrīl is certainly mentioned in *Sūrah al-Taḥrīm* (66: 4) a 'Makkan' *sūrah.*[112]

As we have noted earlier, Watt is a cautious historian and there is often evidence of this. He is prepared to take his Western contemporaries to task for what he sees as their unfairness in the application of critical scholarship to Muḥammad. He points out that Muḥammad received the worst press in the West of all historic personalities. He therefore rejects the dominant Western theory that the Qur'ān is Muḥammad's own composition.[113]

However, Watt is frequently self-contradictory. Shortly after rejecting the theory of the Qur'ān being Muḥammad's own work, he conveys the view that Muḥammad had a way of 'inducing' revelation. Even though he says that the topic is irrelevant to the theologian in assessment of the authenticity of the revelation, this does nothing to remove the charge that he accepts the argument.[114]

Zuntz points out the problems a theologian encounters when he assumes the role of a historian. As Zuntz said of Koch, one detects that the historian in Watt struggles with the theologian in him.[115] A typical example of this is where Watt refrains from analyzing a conception because, according to him, it is a sensitive matter in Muslim theology.[116] There is clear evidence of inconsistency here and Watt lays himself open to this accusation.

Another question mark about Watt's scholarship concerns his handling of the issue of the Satanic Verses, especially regarding his speculation about Muḥammad's motives. His tone is reminiscent of Muir and Margoliouth, whose scholarship Watt does not positively accept.[117] As for his views on the persecution suffered by the Muslims in Makkah, Arafat has dealt with this and we do not want to repeat the arguments here, except to say that Watt does not advance sound academic reasons for playing down the traditional sources.[118]

In fact, in general, Watt's emphasis on the Prophet's business acumen within the mercantile environment in Makkah tends to ignore much of the Prophet's religious personality.[119] Again, Guillaume warns of the danger of overplaying the economic aspect. Watt, however, often revisits this theme.[120] In an elaborate discussion sometimes bordering on the emotional, Zafar Ali Qureshi deals with the charge that Muḥammad was moved primarily by material rather than spiritual considerations.[121]

Watt's way of playing down the spiritual aspects of Muḥammad's life also comes up in his discussions on the battles that the Muslims took part in. He often assigns secular reasons for the outcome of such confrontations. On such issues, Watt is seen as a secular historian. For example, on the battle of Badr, he discounts the miraculous help. However, Watt, who accepts the Qur'ān as a source of history, does not state why he rejects the Qur'ānic reasons for the outcome of the battles.[122]

By entitling his first chapter on the Madīnan era 'The Provocation of the Quraysh', Watt makes the persecuted and 'exiled' Muslims appear as aggressors. While accepting that the killing of al-Ḥaḍramī was probably the *causa proxima* of the battle as Shiblī Nuʿmānī points out, it is necessary to look at the *causa remota* as well; that is events before the Nakhlah incident. If Watt had done that, Muḥammad would not have been portrayed as being provocative in his scouting of Makkah's environs.

The problem arises because of Watt's interpretation of the cardinal concept used in the text, ترصّدوا (*Taraṣṣadū*). His rejection of the meaning of this word as 'keep a watch', and insistence on translating it as 'lay in ambush', is not sound according to the available dictionaries. 'Lay in ambush' is indeed a forced interpretation of this concept.[123]

Regarding the emissaries the Prophet sent to various lands, Watt again allows speculation to overshadow the importance of this historical issue. He is of the opinion that the stories in the classical texts, of Muḥammad sending emissaries to the emperors of Byzantium and Persia, are false. His main argument is that these emperors were too powerful for Muḥammad to have attempted to approach them.[124] The rationale for this opinion is very weak in the light of Muḥammad's tremendous successes in Arabia; even without the religious consideration he might have felt confident that nothing could stand in his way. If the religious argument, of the universal consciousness of the Prophet's mission, is added then Watt's reasoning looks shallow.

We commend Watt's discussion of the Ḥudaibiyyah episode in fine detail, but it is strange that a scholar of his calibre should fail to discuss the lessons to be learnt from the Prophet's behaviour at Ḥudaibiyyah.[125] It is obvious that the Prophet showed true elements of faith, diplomacy, far-sightedness, patience and sincerity. However, Watt, like some of his predecessors, does not attempt to discuss any of these.

Watt's views about Muḥammad attempting to model Islam on Judaism, and failing that, turning against the Jews, is a repetition of some old theories.[126]

In his review of Watt's *Muhammad – Prophet and Statesman*, Tibawi comments on this as being part of the speculative theory.[127]

Watt's ideas form a prelude to the larger issue of Muḥammad's relationship with the Jews, and here the analysis turns rather scathing. The elaborate discussion on Muḥammad's intellectual and physical attacks on the Jews portrays the Prophet as aggressive and bad-tempered, who attempts to bring everybody under his power by fair means or foul.[128] One of the greatest problems in any modern work on the *Sīrah* is the pressure of anachronism where post-enlightenment criteria are used in judging pre-enlightenment attitudes. We see Watt's conclusions on the confrontations in Madīnah as anachronistic. He is unable to perceive the issue in the light of seventh-century Arabia. Even in modern times, the two World Wars and the recent Gulf War, not to mention the 'divinely sanctioned Crusades', should teach us how to handle the seventh-century confrontations in Madīnah. Whatever the situation, it is against fairness and objectivity to portray Muḥammad in the colours Watt has done.

Another inconsistency is detected in the application of principles. Watt himself questions European critique on Muḥammad's morality and points out the unfairness of applying modern European criteria to the seventh-century Arab prophet.[129] One wonders why he does not remember this in his criticism of Muḥammad's dealings with the Jews.

In his general assessment of the Prophet's personality, one sees a different Watt. He seems to defend Muḥammad against what he considers irresponsible or misplaced attacks by some scholars.[130] Nevertheless, his lapses are again discernible in his concluding remarks in *Muhammad – Prophet and Statesman*, where he comments on Muḥammad's prophetic consciousness. He sees Muḥammad as possessing a creative imagination and, strangely, puts him in the same category as Adolf Hitler. He writes:

> In Adolf Hitler the creative imagination was well developed, and his ideas had a wide appeal, but it is usually held that he was neurotic and that those Germans who followed him most devotedly became infected by his neurosis. In Muhammad, I should hold, there was a welling up of the creative imagination, and the ideas thus produced are to a great extent true and sound. It does not follow, however, that all the Qur'ānic ideas are true and sound. In particular there is at least one point at which they seem to be unsound – the idea that 'revelation' or the product of the creative imagination is superior to normal human traditions as a source of bare historical fact.[131]

We have cited Watt's opinion in full, primarily to give a full view of his reasoning. In the rather propagandistic work of Ahmad Ghorab, this is held against Watt as one who distorts Islam.[132] Ghorab claims to have traced the source of Watt's opinion to the work of Karl Barth who was known to have whipped up anti-Nazi emotions by comparing Nazism with Islam. Ghorab quotes Barth:

> Where it [Nazism] meets with resistance, it can only crush and kill – with the might and right which belongs to Divinity! Islam of old as we know proceeded in this way. It is impossible to understand National Socialism unless we see it in fact as a new Islam, its myth as a new Allah, and Hitler as this new Allah's prophet.[133]

Despite the general tone of Ghorab's book, we do not have any reason to discount this opinion. The argument of coincidence could be too difficult to justify. Watt, as a seasoned theologian, should have avoided such comment.

It is probably true that he who tries to trace an age-long development must necessarily neglect much detail. Granting this, one cannot help feeling that despite some very positive and realistic arguments, historical reality and even correct detail are often lost in the intense haze of abstract speculation. Watt's works, unfortunately, end up being categorized in this way. His many speculative and generalized methods are often contradictory.

Of course, this does not mean that Watt is the same as his predecessors or even contemporaries. He certainly stands apart from Muir and Margoliouth and most, if not all, of his British colleagues in the field. His interest in Inter-Faith relations as far as Islam is concerned, his anxiety about anti-religious and anti-spiritual philosophies and his call to men of faith to rally round and defend spirituality, all point to a very positive attitude towards Islam. As we said earlier, we have examined his work taking a cue from his own statement that, 'The sincerest tribute to a scholar is to take his views seriously and criticize him frankly.'[134]

In the following section we remark on the methodology of studying religion, especially in the case where the researcher does not share the faith he is looking at.

Methodology in the Study of Religion

In scholarship, there are always demands for objectivity, impartiality and the cultivation of dispassionate attitudes. The researcher is under pressure to allow the text to speak for itself. However, one cannot approach the text with a *tabula rasa*. One's baggage, comprising manifold things and values, is bound to play a part in the analysis. The impossibility of completely dispassionate research therefore haunts every scholar. When such arguments are translated onto the field of religious studies, the problem becomes even more acute.

Muḥammad Mustafā al-Marāghī, Grand Shaykh of al-Azhar, deliberates on such issues in his Foreword to Haykal's work on the life of the Prophet.[135] He writes:

> To suspend all prejudices, to observe, to experiment, to compare, to deduct and to extrapolate are all easy words. But for man standing under an inheritance of heavy biological and mental burdens, struggling against an oppressive environment of home, village, school, city and country, suffering under the tremendous weight of conditioning by temperament, health, disease and passion – how could it be easy for him to apply the law.[136]

The central question is the attitude that one should develop in approaching a religion that one does not share. A.C. Bousquet has given a guide as to what to take into consideration when studying religion.

He advises that one should not approach a particular faith as if it is a fossil, some ancient museum piece of antiquarian interest, because that would be a valueless and meaningless exercise.[137] If a religion is studied in this way, the real essence of it would be lost. Even though a scientific attitude might be brought to bear, only the externals would be observed; the real core would be glossed over. Though the mundane manifestations might be studied the inner essence would be neglected. Symbols might be observed with curiosity and conclusions deduced from them, but the real values which make that particular religion tick would not be reached. In such an approach, the symbol is confused with the Reality which the symbol merely represents. Instead of the symbol becoming a means to an end, it becomes an end in itself.

In the study of Islam and certainly of the Prophet, this observation should be taken seriously, otherwise the real Muḥammad might be missed. Watt has appropriately observed that, 'There need be no unbridgeable gulf between Western scholarship and Islamic faith; . . .'[138] Indeed, the scientific method which is the bedrock of Western scholarship has been a boon to contemporary advancement in world scholarship because it has helped check the excessive emotions which usually characterize studies which are supposed to be objective. The scientific method enables the student to carefully assemble and verify data and leads to better accuracy in documentation of observed or verified facts.

However, as a human institution, it needs to be acknowledged that the scientific method is not limitless. It has its own constraints and drawbacks. Without this recognition, scholars would deify it and think of it as an 'Infallible Oracle'. The scientific method does not have the ultimate ability to probe all things. And it is beyond these limits that the appropriate human faculties have to be marshalled. In the study of religion, this is crucial.

Ernst Benz of the University of Marburg (Germany), formerly director of the Klopstock Institute in Hamburg and of the Zeitschrift fur Religions – und Gestesgeschichte, notes one of the most pervasive obstacles in studying other religions. He says:

> One of the first difficulties to confront even an experienced inquirer into foreign religions is the fact that he more or less unconsciously takes his own point of view as normative for religion in general. This may be a banal statement, for the warning against this mistake is one of the most elementary rules in Inter-religious research. But it is nevertheless amazing to realise how difficult it is to avoid this pitfall.[139]

Once preconceived baggage is brought to bear on a study, the result is a sham. As one scholar put it: where this bias enters, pure scholarship leaves.

Looking at the question of truth and people's behaviour towards others who do not share their faith, Vroom notes that there is always a great deal of prejudice involved.[140] He notes that: 'Scholarly integrity demands that in an endeavour to acquire insight into the theme of religion and truth, philosophy of religion carried out from the perspectives other than that of Western (post) Christian culture [should] not be left out of consideration.'[141] This reminds us of Gibb's observation that in the case of Islam, it has to be studied from its own principles and standards.[142] Rodinson also acknowledges the extreme difficulty of remaining perfectly neutral, though he insists that every effort has to be made towards that end.[143]

Despite these disconcerting observations, we share the view that objectivity, impartiality and judicious application of the tools of modern scholarship are essential in the study of religion, and of Islam for that matter. This does not mean we have to continuously consider old ideas merely for their own sake. We agree with Watt and Rodinson that advancements in scholarship and the tremendous consciousness of Inter-Faith relations are good signs for the future where objectivity, fairness and justice, with which modern Western scholarship claims to be characterized, will be applied to the study of Islam.

Perhaps it needs to be acknowledged that in a world where geopolitical transformations and the impact of shifting paradigms seem to suggest that Islam should be seen as the new threat to the world, perhaps the optimism might be said to be over-rated.[144] However, this effort to arrive at a dispassionate and more judicious application of the ubiquitous 'scientific method' is a form of *Jihād* for all scholars, be they Muslims or not.

Notes

1. N. Daniel, *Islam and the West – The Making of an Image* (1960). (Revised Edition, Oxford: Oneworld Publications, 1993.) E. Said, *Orientalism – Western Conceptions of the Orient* (1978). (Reprinted with a new Afterword, 1995.)

2. Revised edition of *Islam and the West* (1993).

3. Reprint of *Orientalism* (1995).

4. *Konstantin den Store. Pax Romana: Pax Christina* (Copenhagen, 1952), p.74.

5. Koch was a professor of Theology at the University of Copenhagen.

6. See the review article 'The Theologian as Historian – Some Reflections Upon a New Book on Constantine the Great', *HJ*, Vol. 52 (October 1953–July 1954), pp.252–9, quotation on p.253. Zuntz was a senior lecturer in Hellenistic Greek at the University of Manchester.

7. *Ibid.*, p.259.

8. M. Rodinson, *Europe and the Mystique of Islam*, trans. from the French by R. Veinus (1988), p.117.

9. *Ibid.*

10. See his comments in *ibid.*, pp.131–3, footnote 3. J.D.J. Waardenburg has written a detailed article on Orientalists. See his 'Mustashrikūn', in *The Encyclopaedia of Islam*, New Edition, Vol. 7, pp.735–53.

11. 'Review of Edward Said's Other Work *Covering Islam*', *IQ*, Vol. 29, No. 1 (First Quarter, 1985), pp.52–60.

12. 'Orientalism and the Arab Elite', *IQ*, Vol. 26, No. 1 (First Quarter, 1982), (pp.3–15); see p.3.

13. 'Orientalism and its Critics', *BJMES*, Vol. 20, No. 2 (1993), pp.145–63.

14. *Ibid.*, p.148.

15. *Ibid.*, p.149.

16. *Ibid.*, p.158.

17. *Ibid.*, pp.160–1.

18. *MW*, Vol. 69, No. 2 (April 1979), pp.110–31.

19. *Ibid.*, pp.11–118.

20. *Ibid.*, p.118.

21. *Ibid.*, p.121.

22. Said, *Orientalism* (1995 reprint), p.329.

23. *Ibid.*, p.331.

24. *Ibid.*

25. *Ibid.*, p.333.

26. *Ibid.*

27. See Ch. 4.

28. Daniel, *Islam and the West*, p.11.

29. *Ibid.*, see p.13 and also Appendix 'A' which is on the imputation of idolatry to Islam.

30. *Ibid., passim,* and R.W. Southern, *Western Views on Islam, passim.*

31. *Islam and the West*, p.302.

32. *Ibid.*, pp.302–9.

33. *Ibid.*, p.307.

34. Thomas Carlyle, *On Heroes, Hero Worship and the Heroic in History* (1849). See also the edition with notes and Introduction by Michael K. Goldberg (Berkeley: University of California Press, 1993), esp. the Introduction and the notes on pp.257–79 on 'The Hero as Prophet'; and Watt, 'Carlyle on Muhammad', *HJ*, Vol. 52 (October 1954–July 1955), pp.247–54.

35. Daniel, *Islam and the West*, p.323.

36. Syed Naquib al-Attas, *Islam and Secularism* (1978).

37. *Islam and the West*, p.324.

38. *Hagarism – The Making of the Islamic World* (1977); see Ch. 4 for our comments on this book.

39. *Islam and the West*, p.325.

40. See his *Islamic Fundamentalism and Modernity* (1988).

41. *Islam and the West*, p.327.

42. *Ibid.* See also: Michael T. Shelly, *The Life and Thought of W.H.T. Gairdner, 1873–1928 – A Critical Evaluation of a Scholar-Missionary to Islam*, unpublished Ph.D thesis, Dept. of Theology, University of Birmingham (UK), (1988), esp. Ch. 3.

43. Jean M. Abd-el-Jalil, *Aspects Interieurs de l'Islam* (1949).

44. *Islam and the West*, pp.329–30.

45. *Ibid.*, p.330.

46. *Ibid.*, pp.330–1.

47. See *Mecca*. Such a position is problematic in Western enlightened scholarship though, where the scientific method does not necessarily accept a particular opinion just because it is supposed to be an orthodox view.

48. A. Hourani, *Europe and the Middle East* (1980), p.34.

49. *Islam and the West*, p.287.

50. See his Ph.D thesis, *Nineteenth Century Christian Views of Islam: Evidence by Six British Approaches,* submitted to the Dept. of Theology, University of Birmingham (1989), p.25. See also the published version of the thesis entitled *Victorian Images of Islam* (1992), p.14.

51. *Victorian Images*, p.109. For more analysis on Muir, his life and outlook on Islam and Muslims, see Ch. 5 of this work.

52. See Ch. 2, note 3.

53. Muir, *Life*, p.lxv.

54. *Ibid.*, p.li.

55. Syed Ahmad Khan, *The Life of Muhammad and Subjects Subsidiary Thereto* (London: Trubner, 1870). See also the 1979 reproduction, pp.311–12.

56. See: M.Z. Siddiqi, *Hadith Literature – Its Origin, Development and Special Features* (1993); M.M. al-Azami, *On Schacht's Origins of Muhammadan Jurisprudence* (1993), and *Studies in Early Ḥadith Literature* (1968); Ḥākim al-Nīṣabūrī, *al-Mustadrak alā al-Ṣaḥīḥayn* (1334–42 AH), and *Ma rifat Ulūm al-Hadīth* (1937); G.H.A. Juynboll, *The Authenticity of the Tradition Literature* (1969), and *Muslim Tradition – Studies in Chronology, Provenance and Authorship of Early Hadīth* (1983).

57. Muir, *Life*, see esp. pp.li–viii.

58. See his *Mahomet and Islam: A Sketch of the Prophet's Life from Original Sources and a Brief Outline of His Religion* (1895).

59. Muir, *Life*, see Ch. 3.

60. Sell, *Inspiration* (1930), p.64. See also Gairdner, *Inspiration – A Dialogue* (1909), p.47.

61. Gairdner, *Inspiration*, p.55.

62. See Muir, *Life*, pp.xcviii, 6–7, 19–20, 80–6 and Ch. 10.

63. *Ibid.*, see Ch. 7.

64. *Ibid.*, pp.lviii–lxx, 126–7. See also Daniel, *Islam and the West.*

65. Muir, *Life*, pp.178, 292 ff. It is arguable here whether polygamy as such is 'forbidden' in Christianity.

66. Bennet, *Victorian Images*, Introduction, p.14.

67. Compare Margoliouth's background in this chapter with Muir's. See *ibid.*

68. See the comments from the *DNB* cited above in footnotes 4 and 5 of Ch. 3.

69. See above, 'Margoliouth's Intellectual Biography', in Ch. 3.

70. See above, Ch. 3, p.56.

71. Margoliouth, *Mohammed*, p.vii.

72. *Ibid.*, p.2.

73. See above, Ch. 3, p.59.

74. See above, Ch. 3, p.62.

75. Margoliouth, *Mohammed*, p.216. See our comments in *ibid.*

76. See above, Ch. 3, p.62. Cf. his article on 'Muhammad' in *Encyclopaedia of Religion and Ethics.*

77. See his discussion on Muḥammad's prophethood, in *Mohammed*, p.86 ff.

78. See above, Ch. 3, p.65.

79. Daniel, *Islam and the West*, esp. Appendix 'A' devoted to 'Imputation of Idolatry to Islam', and *passim*, and see above, Ch. 3, p.68.

80. See R. Allen Brown (ed.), *Proceedings of the Battle Conference of Anglo-Norman Studies* (1979), pp.75–83.

81. *Ibid.*, p.82.

82. See above, Ch. 3, p.73. Note his controversy with Foster on the 'Is Islam a Christian Heresy' issue.

83. See, for example, *Mohammed*, p.149 ff.

84. See our argument above, Ch. 3, p.78.

85. See above, Ch. 3, p.83. See also Khalil S. Samir and Jorgen S. Nielsen: *Christian Arabic Apologetics During the Abbasid Period 750–1258* (1994), esp. Hugh Goddard's 'The Persistence of Medieval Themes in Modern Christian-Muslim Discussion in Egypt', Ch. 10.

86. *Mohammed*, p.247 ff. and above, Ch. 3, p.91.

87. See his comments on the visit of the Christian Delegation of Najrān and also his talk at St. Aldate's Church, Oxford, above, Ch. 3, p.97.

88. See above, Ch. 3, p.106.

89. Daniel, *Islam and the West*, pp.210–12 and Rosalind Hill, 'Crusading Warfare', p.82.

90. See above, Ch. 5 – the discussion on 'Watt's Intellectual Biography' and 'The Choice of Watt'.

91. Review in *MW*, Vol. 44, No. 1 (January 1954), (pp.49–51), p.49.

92. *Ibid.* Cf. Watt, *Mecca*, pp.16–20.

93. See *Mecca*, pp.55–8. Cf. Guillaume's review, pp.49–50.

94. Guillaume's review, pp.50–1.

95. See *IQ*, Vol. 1, No. 3 (October 1954), pp.182–4.

96. *Ibid.*, p.182.

97. *Mecca*, Ch. 5, esp. pp.117–33.

98. Arafat's review, pp.183–4.

99. *Ibid.*, p.184. Cf. Watt, *Mecca*, p.121 (note: I.H. = Ibn Hishām).

100. Arafat's review, p.184.

101. *Muhammad – Prophet and Statesman* (1961); see the review in *IQ*, Vol. 6, No. 3/4 (July–October 1961), pp.127–8.

102. Tibawi's review, *ibid.*, p.127.

103. *Ibid.*

104. *Konstantin, op cit.*, footnote 4.

105. Watt, *Muhammad – Prophet and Statesman*, pp.218–21.

106. *Ibid.*, see pp.194–5.

107. Watt, 'Islamic Attitudes to Other Religions', *SM*, Vol. 42 (1993), pp.245–55.

108. Tarīf Khālidī, *Arabic Historical Thought in the Classical Age* (1994).

109. See Watt's article 'Islam and Peace', *SM*, Vol. 39, pp.167–78.

110. For example, see the opinion expressed on this by A. Qamaruddin in his review of Watt's *Islamic Fundamentalism and Modernity*, *IQ*, Vol. 35, No. 2 (2nd Quarter, 1991), pp.140–5.

111. See his *Mecca*, pp.38–52.

112. See also the Qur'ān: *Sūrahs* 81: 19–24; 16: 102; 70: 4; 78: 38; 97: 4; and *passim.*

113. Watt, *Mecca*, pp.52–3. This is why he is prepared to criticize his teacher R. Bell for holding this opinion. See Watt's *Bell's Introduction* in the Intellectual Biography.

114. *Mecca*, pp.57–8.

115. Zuntz, 'The Theologian as Historian'.

116. *Mecca*, p.83.

117. *Ibid.*, p.104 ff.

118. *Ibid.*, p.117 ff. Cf. Arafat's review of *Mecca*. See above.

119. *Mecca*, Ch. 1.

120. See above, the discussion on the Intellectual Biography where in many of Watt's papers this theme comes up.

121. Zafar Ali Qureshi, *Prophet Muhammad and His Western Critics – A Critique of W. Montgomery Watt and Others* (1992), 2 vols., see Ch. 5. See other parts of this book for some rather interesting points despite its general emotive tone.

122. *Medina*, Chs. I and II. For example, on pp.65–6, Watt carries a general thought that material motives were behind the Prophet's activities in Madīnah. Cf. Qur'ānic references to the battle of Badr, e.g, *Sūrahs* 3: 12–13, 121–7; 8: 5–19, 42–51; 18: 58.

123. *Medina*, p.7.

124. *Ibid.*, p.40 ff.

125. *Ibid.*, p.46 ff.

126. *Ibid.*, pp.198–208.

127. See Tibawi's review above. See also Mohammed Khalifa, *The Sublime Qur'an and Orientalism* (1983), esp. Ch. 7.

128. Watt, *Medina*, p.205 ff.

129. *Ibid.*, pp.324–34.

130. See esp. Watt, *ibid.*, and *Muhammad – Prophet and Statesman*, pp.229–40.

131. Watt, *Muhammad – Prophet and Statesman*, pp.229–40.

132. *Subverting Islam – The Role of Orientalist Centres* (1994), pp.21–2

133. *Ibid.*, p.22, see footnote 7. Cf. Karl Barth, *The Church and the Political Problem of Our Day* (1939), p.40.

134. *Bell's Introduction*, p.v.

135. See Fārūqī's translation.

136. *Ibid.*, p.xxvii.

137. A.C. Bousquet, *Comparative Religion – A Short Outline* (1958 reprint). See esp. Ch. 1.

138. *Mecca*, p.x.

139. See his paper 'Obstacles to Understanding Other Religions', in Moses Jung et al. (eds.), *Relations Among Religions Today – A Handbook of Policies and Principles* (Leiden: E.J. Brill, 1963), pp.101–4; quotation on p.101.

140. Hendrik M. Vroom, *Religions and the Truth – Philosophical Reflections and Perceptions*, trans. from the Dutch by J.W. Rebel (1989). See esp. pp.22–5, 370–2.

141. See his *Mohammedanism*, p.vi.

142. *Ibid.*, p.24.

143. See his *Europe and the Mystique of Islam*, esp. pp.xii–xiv. See also the concluding sections of the book.

144. See, for example, J.L. Esposito, *The Islamic Threat – Myth or Reality?* (1992); Judith Miller, 'The Challenge of Radical Islam', *Foreign Affairs*, Vol. 72, No. 2 (Spring 1993) pp.43–56. (Miller characterizes Islam as anti-Western, Anti-American and Anti-Israel.); S. Huntington, 'The Clash of Civilizations', *Foreign Affairs*, Vol. 72, No. 3 (Summer 1993), pp.22–49. (The post-Huntington reverberations are being felt around the world.); J. Hippler and A. Lueg (eds.), *The Next Threat – Western Perceptions of Islam*, trans. by Laila Freise (1995). See esp. Lueg's paper on 'Perceptions of Islam in Western Debate' and Ch. 6 – 'The Islamic Threat and Western Foreign Policy', by Hippler.

Bibliography

BOOKS

Abd-el-Jalil, J.M., *Aspects Interieurs de l'Islam*, Paris, 1949.

Addison, J.T., *The Christian Approach to the Moslem*, New York: Columbia University Press, 1942.

Ahmad, B., *Muhammad and the Jews – A Re-examination*, New Delhi: Vikas, 1979.

Ahmad, F., *Propheten Muhammad*, Kuwait: Scientific Research House, 1979.

Ahsan, M.M. and Kidwai, A.R. (eds.), *Sacrilege Versus Civility: Muslim Perspectives on The Satanic Verses Affair*, Leicester: The Islamic Foundation, 1991.

ʿAlī, M.C., *A Critical Examination of the Popular Jihād*, Calcutta: Thacker, Spink & Co., 1885.

Ali, S.A., *The Spirit of Islam*, London, 1896, Calcutta, 1902.

Andrae, T., *Mohammed – The Man and His Faith*, London: Allen & Unwin, 1936.

Anees, M.A. and Athar, A., *Guide to Sira and Hadith Literature in Western Languages*, London and New York: Mansell Publishing Ltd., 1986.

Archer, J.C., *Mystical Elements in Mohammed*, New Haven, Connecticut: Yale University Press, 1924.

Aristotle, *Ethics*.

Arnold, T.W., *The Preaching of Islam*, London: Archibald, Constable & Co., 1896 and 1913.

Asad, M., *Islam at the Crossroads*, Lahore: Arafat Publications, 1975 (Reprint).

Asaf, H. et al. (eds.), *Orientalism, Islam and the Islamists*, Brattleboro, Vermont: Amana Books, 1984.

Attas, S.N. al-, *Islam and Secularism*, Kuala Lumpur (Malaysia): ABIM, 1978.

Azad, A.K., *The Tarjumān al-Qur'ān*, ed. and trans. by A. Latīf, London: Asia Publishing House, 1967.

Azami, M.M. al-, *On Schacht's Origins of Muhammadan Jurisprudence*, Cambridge: The Islamic Texts Society, 1993.

———, *Studies in Early Ḥadith Literature*, Beirut, al-Maktab al-Islāmī, 1968.

———, *Studies in Hadith Methodology and Literature*, Indianapolis: American Trust Publications, 1977.

Azmeh, A. al-, *Ibn Khaldun in Modern Scholarship: A Study of Orientalism*, London: Third World Centre, 1981.

———, *Islamic Studies and the European Imagination*, Inaugural Lecture, University of Exeter, 17 March 1986, University of Exeter, 1986.

ʿAzzām, A. al-R., *The Eternal Message of Muhammad*, trans. from the Arabic by C.E. Farah, London: The New English Library, 1965.

Barth, Karl, *The Church and the Political Problem of Our Day*, London: Hodder & Stoughton, 1939.

Becker, C.H., *Islamstudien*, Leipzig, Verlag Quelle und Meyer, 1924.

Bell, R., *Introduction to the Qur'ān*, Edinburgh: Edinburgh University Press, 1953.

———, *The Origins of Islam in its Christian Environment*, London, 1926.

Bell, R., *The Qur'ān – Translated with a Critical Rearrangement of the Sūrahs*, 2 vols. Edinburgh: T. & T. Clark, 1937–39.

Bennet, C., *Nineteenth Century Christian Views of Islam: Evidence by Six British Approaches*, Ph.D. Thesis, Dept. of Theology, University of Birmingham (UK), 1989.

———, *Victorian Images of Islam*, London: Grey Seal Books, 1992.

Blachère, R., *Le Probleme de Mahomet, Essai de Biographie Critique du Fondateur de l'Islam*, Paris: Presses Universitaires de France, 1952.

Bodley, R.V.C., *The Messenger: The Life of Mohammed*, New York: Doubleday & Co., 1946.

Bosworth, C.E., *Al-Maqrizi's 'Book of Contention and Strife Concerning the Relations between Banu Umayya and the Banu Hashim'*, trans. into English, with an introduction and commentary, Manchester: Manchester University Press, 1980.

Boulainvilliers, H.C. de, *Vie de Mahomet*, London, 1730.

Bousquet, A.C., *Comparative Religion – A Short Outline*, Hammondsworth (Middlesex, UK): Penguin Books, 1958 reprint.

Bowker, J., *The Religious Imagination and the Sense of God*, Oxford: Clarendon Press, 1978.

Brown, R.A. (ed.), *Proceedings of the Battle Conference of Anglo-Norman Studies*, Ipswich (UK): The Boydell Press, 1979.

Buhl, P.W., *Das Leben Muhammeds*, German trans. by H.H. Schaeder, Heidelburg, Quelle und Meyer, 1930.

Burton, R., *The City of the Saints Across the Rocky Mountains to California*, New York: Knopf, 1861, 1963 reprint.

Caetani, L ., *Annali dell' Islam*, Vol. 1, Milano: Ulrich Hoepli, 1905–26.

Carlyle, T., *On Heroes, Hero Worship and the Heroic in History*, New York: John Wiley, 1849.

Carr, E.H., *What is History?*, London: Penguin, 1985.

Cave, S., *An Introduction to the Study of Some Living Religions of the East*, London, 1962.

Chew, S.C., *The Crescent and the Rose: Islam and England During the Renaissance*, New York: Oxford University Press, 1937.

Clive, J., *Macaulay: The Shaping of the Historian*, New York: Knopf, 1973.

Cook, M., *Muhammad*, Oxford: Oxford University Press, 1983.

Cragg, K., *Muhammad and the Christian – A Question of Response*, London: Darton, Longman & Todd, 1984.

———, *Readings in the Qur'ān*, London: Collins, 1988.

Crone, P., *Meccan Trade and the Rise of Islam*, Princeton, NJ: Princeton University Press, 1987.

Crone, P. and Cook, M., *Hagarism – The Making of the Islamic World*, Cambridge: Cambridge University Press, 1977.

Daniel, N., *The Arabs and Medieval Europe*, 2nd. edition, London and New York: Longman, Beirut: Librarie du Liban, 1979.

———, *Heroes and Saracens: An Interpretation of the Chansons de Geste*, Edinburgh: Edinburgh University Press, 1984.

———, *Islam and the West – The Making of an Image*, Edinburgh: Edinburgh University Press, rev. edition, Oxford: Oneworld Publications, 1993.

Davenport, J., *An Apology for Mohammed and the Koran*, London: John Davy & Sons, 1869.

Dermenghem, E., *The Life of Mahomet*, trans. by A. Yorke, London: Longman, 1930.

———, *Muhammad and the Islamic Tradition*, trans. by J.M. Watt, New York: Harper & Brothers, 1958 (reprint).

Doi, A.R.I., *Nigerian Muslim Names – Their Meaning and Significance*, Ahmedabad (India): Muslim Publishing House, 1978.

Draycott, G.M., *Mahomet – The Founder of Islam*, London: Martin Secker, 1915.

Durant, W., *The Age of Faith: A History of Medieval Civilization – Christian, Islamic, Judaic – from Constantine to Dante: AD 315–1300*, New York: Simon & Schuster, 1950.

Esposito, J.L., *The Islamic Threat – Myth or Reality?*, New York and Oxford: Oxford University Press, 1992.

Farishta, G. de Z., *The Law and Philosophy of Zakat*, Vol. 1, ed. A.Z. Abbasī, Damascus: Jāmi' al-Huqūq Mahfūzah al-Mu'lafah, 1960.

Fārūqī, N.A., *Early Muslim Historiography: A Study of Early Transmitters of Arab History from the Rise of Islam to the End of the Umayyad Period, 612–750 AD*, Delhi: Idarah Adbiyat-i-Delhi, 1978.

Fazl, M.A., *The Life of Muhammad*, Calcutta: Manoranjan Banerji, 1910.

———, *Mohammad at the Bar of the Twentieth Century*, 1929.

——— (ed.), *Mr. Godfrey Higgins' Apology for Mohamed*, Allahabad: Allahabad Reform Society, 1929.

Ferro, M., *The Use and Abuse of History and How the Past is Taught*, London: Routledge & Kegan Paul, 1984.

Flannery, Austin (ed.), *Vatican Council II – The Conciliar and Post Conciliar Documents*, Bombay: Society of St. Paul, 1991.

Franch, R.S. de, *Raymond Lulle: Docteur des Missions Avec un Choix de Texts Traduits et Annotes*, Schweiz: Nouvelle Revue de Science Missionnaire, 1954.

Gabrieli, F., *Muhammad and the Conquests of Islam*, trans. from the Italian by Virginia Luling and Rosamund Linelli, London: Weidenfeld & Nicolson, 1968.

Gairdner, W.H.T., *Inspiration – A Dialogue*, London: Christian Literature Society, 1909.

Gaudeul, J.M., *Encounters and Clashes – Islam and Christianity in History*, I and II Texts, Rome: Pontifico Instituto di Studi Arabi e Islamici, 1984.

Gauhar, A. (ed.), *The Challenge of Islam*, London: Islamic Council of Europe, 1978.

Geertz, C., *The Interpretation of Cultures*, London: Hutchinson & Co., 1975.

Geiger, A., *Was Hat Mohammed Aus dem Judentume Aufgenommen?*, Leipzig, 1902 (Neudruck, 1971).

Gibb, H.A.R., *Mohammedanism – An Historical Survey*, Oxford: Oxford University Press, 1949.

Gibb, H.A.R. and Kramers, J.H., *The Shorter Encyclopaedia of Islam*, Leiden: E.J. Brill, 1953.

Gibbon, E., *The Decline and Fall of the Roman Empire*, London Methuen, 1925.

———, *Life of Mahomet*, Boston: Houghton Mifflin & Co., 1859.

Ghorab, A., *Subverting Islam – The Role of Orientalist Centres*, London: Minerva Press, 1994.

Glubb, J.B., *The Life and Times of Muhammad*, London: Hodder & Stoughton, 1970.

Goiten, S.D., *Jews and Arabs: Their Contacts Through the Ages*, New York: Schocken Books Inc., 1955.

Goldston, R., *The Sword of the Prophet: A History of the Arab World from the Time of Muhammad to the Present Day*, New York: Dial Press, 1979.

Goldziher, I., *Mohammad and Islam*, trans. by K.C. Seelye, New Haven, Connecticut: Yale University Press, 1917.

Graham, G.F.I., *The Life and Work of Syed Ahmad Khan*, Edinburgh: W. Blackwood, 1885, 2nd rev. edition, London: Hodder & Stoughton, 1909.

Grimwood-Jones, Diana (ed.), *Arab Islamic Bibliography*, Sussex (UK): Harvester Press, 1977.

Guillaume, A., *Islam*, Harmondsworth (Middlesex, UK): Penguin Books, 1954.

Guillaume, A., *The Life of Muhammad – Translation of Ibn Isḥāq's Sīrat Rasūl Allāh*, Oxford: Oxford University Press, 1955 and Karachi: Oxford University Press, 1978.

———, *New Light on the Life of Muhammad*, Journal of Semitic Studies Monograph No. 1, Manchester: Manchester University Press, n.d.

Gutmann, J. (ed.), *The Image and the World: Confrontations in Judaism, Christianity and Islam*, Missoula, Montana: Scholar's Press, 1977.

Hamidullah, M., *The First Written Constitution in the World*, 3rd. edition, Lahore: Shaikh Muhammad Ashraf, 1981.

Hastings, J. (ed.), *Encyclopaedia of Religion and Ethics*, Vol. 8, Edinburgh: T. & T. Clark, 1915.

Haykal, M.H., *The Life of Muhammad*, trans. from the 8th edition by Ismāʿil R. al-Fārūqī, Indianapolis: North American Trust Publications, 1976.

Hebbo, A., *Die Fremdworter in der Arabischen Propheten Biographie des Ibn Hischām*, Frankfurt: A.M. Lang, 1984.

Hippler, J. and Lueg, A. (eds.), *The Next Threat – Western Perceptions of Islam*, trans. by L. Freise, London: Pluto Press and Amsterdam: The Transnational Institute, 1995.

Hitti, P.K., *Islam and the West*, Princeton, NJ: Princeton University Press, 1962.

Hopkins, J., *Nicholas of Cusa's Pace Fidei and Cribratio Alkorani*, Minneapolis: The Arthur J. Banning Press, 1994.

Hourani, A., *Europe and the Middle East*, London: Macmillan, 1980.

———, *Islam in European Thought*, Cambridge: Cambridge University Press, 1991.

Hovannisian, R.G. and Vryonis, S. (eds.), *Islam's Understanding of Itself*, Eighth Giorgio Levi Della Vida Conference, May 1–3, 1981, California: Undena, 1983.

Howe, E.D., *The History of Mormonism*, New York: Painsville, 1834.

Hurgronje, C.S., *Mohammedanism: Lectures on Its Origin, Its Religious and Political Growth, and Its Present State*, New York: Putnam's, 1916.

Hussain, S.S., *Misconceptions About Prophet Muhammad*, Karachi: Educational Press, 1976.

Ibn Rushd, *Jihād in Mediaeval and Modern Islam – The Chapter on Jihād from Averroes' Legal Handbook 'Bidāyat al-Mudjtahid' and The Treatise 'Korān and Fighting' by the Late Shaykh al-Azhar, Mahmud Shaltut*, trans. and annotated by R. Peters, Leiden: E.J. Brill, 1977.

Ipema, P, *The Islamic Interpretation of Duncan B. Macdonald, Samuel M. Zwemer, A. Kenneth Cragg and Wilfred Cantwell-Smith: An Analytical Comparison and Evaluation*, unpublished Ph.D. Thesis, The Hartford Seminary Foundation, 1971.

Iqbal, A., *Diplomacy in Islam: An Essay on the Art of Negotiation as Conceived and Developed by the Prophet of Islam*, Lahore: Institute of Islamic Culture, 1965.

Iqbal, M., *Six Lectures on the Reconstruction of Religious Thought in Islam*, Lahore: Shaikh Muhammad Ashraf, 1982 reprint.

Irving, W., *Life of Mahomet*, London: J.M. Dent & Sons, 1849, reprint 1944.

Jameelah, M., *Islam and Orientalism*, Lahore: Muhammad Yusuf Khan, 1971.

Jeffery, A., *The Foreign Vocabulary of the Qur'an*, Baroda, 1938.

Juynboll, G.H.A., *The Authenticity of the Tradition Literature: Discussions in Modern Egypt*, Leiden: E.J. Brill, 1969.

———, *Muslim Tradition – Studies in Chronology, Provenance and Authorship of Early Hadīth*, Cambridge: Cambridge University Press, 1983.

Kabbānī, R., *Europe's Myths of Orient (Devide and Rule)*, London: Macmillan, 1986.

Kamali, M.H., *Principles of Islamic Jurisprudence*, rev. edition, Cambridge: The Islamic Texts Society, 1991.

Katsh, A.I., *Judaism and the Koran*, New York: A.S. Barnes, 1962.

Kedar, B., *Crusade and Mission: European Approaches Toward the Muslims*, Princeton, NJ: Princeton University Press, 1984.

Kennedy, H., *The Prophet and the Age of the Caliphates*, London and New York: Longman, 1986.

Kerr, M.H. (ed.), *Islamic Studies: A Tradition and its Problems*, Seventh Giorgio Levi Della Vida Conference, Malibu, California: Undena, 1980.

Khālidī, T., *Arabic Historical Thought in the Classical Age*, Cambridge: Cambridge University Press, 1994.

———, *Islamic Historiography: The Histories of Mas'ūdī*, Albany, NY: State University of New York Press, 1975.

Khalifa, M., *The Sublime Qur'an and Orientalism*, London and New York: Longman, 1983.

Khalīfah, A.H., *The Prophet and His Message*, Lahore: Institute of Islamic Culture, 1972.

Khan, S.A., *The Life of Muhammad and Subjects Subsidiary Thereto*, Lahore: Premier Books, 1979.

———, *A Series of Essays on the Life of Mohammed*, London: Trubner & Co., 1870.

Khattak, M.K., *Islam, the Holy Prophet and Non-Muslim World*, Lahore: Sind Sagar Academy, 1976.

Kister, M.J., *Studies in Jāhiliyya and Early Islam* (reprint of articles), London: Variorum, 1980.

Kritzeck, J., *Peter the Venerable and Islam*, Princeton, NJ: Princeton University Press, 1964.

Kurdī, A.A., *The Islamic State: A Study Based on the Islamic Holy Constitution*, London and New York: Mansell, 1984.

Lammens, H., *Islam – Beliefs and Institutions*, trans. from the French by E. Denison Ross, London: Methuen, 1929.

Lane, E.W., *An Arabic Lexicon*, Beirut, Lebanon: Librarie du Liban, 1968.

Lane-Poole, S., *Selections from the Qur'an and Hadith*, Lahore: Sind Sagar Academy, 1882 (1975 reprint).

Leff, G., *History and Social Theology*, Alabama: University of Alabama Press, 1969.

Leitner, G.W., *Muhammadanism*, Woking, 1889.

Lewis, B., *History – Remembered, Recorded, Invented*, Princeton, NJ: Princeton University Press, 1975.

———, *Islam from the Prophet Muhammad to the Capture of Constantinople*, 2 vols., ed. and trans., London: Macmillan, 1976.

———, *The Middle East and the West*, New York and London: Harper Torchbooks and Harper & Row, 1966.

Lings, M., *Muhammad – His Life Based on the Earliest Sources*, London: Islamic Texts Society and George Allen & Unwin, 1983.

Locke, J., *A Discourse on Miracles*, London, 1768.

Lukacs, J., *Historical Consciousness or the Remembered Past*, New York: Harper & Row, 1968.

MacDonald, D.B., *Aspects of Islam*, New York: Macmillan, 1911.

———, *The Religious Attitude and Life in Islam*, Chicago: University of Chicago Press, 1909.

McWilliam, H.O.A., *Muhammad and the World of Islam: Illustrated from Contemporary Sources*, London: Longman, 1977.

Mahmūd, A.H., *The Creed of Islam*, London: World of Islam Festival Trust, 1978.

Mālik, F.H., *Wives of the Prophet*, Lahore: Shaikh Muhammad Ashraf, 1966.

Margoliouth, D.S., *Lectures on Arab Historians*, Calcutta: University of Calcutta, 1930.

———, *Mohammed*, London and Glasgow: Blackie & Son Ltd., 1939.

———, *Mohammed and the Rise of Islam*, New York and London: G.P. Putnam, The Knickerbocker Press, 1905.

———, *Mohammedanism*, London: Williams & Norgate, 1911.

———, *The Relations Between Arabs and Israelites Prior to the Rise of Islam*, The Schweich Lectures 1921, London: The British Academy, Oxford University Press, 1924.

Martin, R.C. (ed.), *Approaches to Islam in Religious Studies*, Tucson: University of Arizona Press, 1985.

Masood, M., *Islam, the Holy Prophet and Non-Muslim World*, Lahore: Sind Sagar Academy, 1976.

Mawdūdī, S.A.A., *Tafhīm al-Qur'ān* (Urdu); *The Meaning of the Qur'ān* (English version), Lahore: Islamic Publications (Pvt.) Ltd. In 16 volumes. The first seven volumes were translated by Chaudhury Muhammad Akbar and edited by A.A. Kamal; remaining volumes were translated by A.A. Kamal. Vol. I published in 1967 and Vol. XVI published in 1988.

The Revised English version is translated and edited by Zafar Ishaq Ansari, under the title *Towards Understanding the Qur'ān*, Leicester: The Islamic Foundation. Vol. I appeared in 1988 and Vol. V in 1995 (translation is continuing).

Miles, G.H., *Muhammed. The Arabian Prophet – A Tragedy in Five Acts*, Boston: Phillips, Sampson & Co., 1850.

Moinuddin, H., *The Charter of the Islamic Conference and Legal Framework of Economic Co-operation Among its Member States*, Oxford: Clarendon Press, 1987.

Muir, W., *Addresses*, North West Provinces, Simla: Gut Press, 1876.

———, *Annals of the Early Caliphate*, London: Smith, Elder & Co., 1883.

Muir, W., *The Apology of Al-Kindy* (second ed.), London: Society for Promoting Christian Knowledge, 1887.

———, *Beacon of Truth*, trans., London: Religious Truths Society, 1894.

———, *The Caliphate, Its Rise, Decline and Fall*, London: Religious Tract Society, 1891, rev. Edinburgh: T.H. Weir, John Grant, 1924.

———, *The Coran: Its Composition and Teaching*, London: Society for Promoting Christian Knowledge, 1877.

———, *The Early Caliphate and the Rise of Islam*, London: Smith, Elder & Co., 1881.

———, *The Life of Mohammed from Original Sources*, London: Smith, Elder & Co., 1858–61.

———, *Mahomet and Islam: A Sketch of the Prophet's Life from Original Sources and a Brief Outline of His Religion*, London: Religious Tract Society, 1884.

———, *The Mohammedan Controversy; Biographies of Mohammed; Springer on Tradition; the Indian Liturgy and the Psalter*, Edinburgh: T. & T. Clark, 1897.

———, *The Sources of Islam*, trans., Edinburgh: T. & T. Clark, 1901.

———, *Sweet First Fruits*, London: Religious Truth Society, 1893.

———, *The Testimony Borne by the Coran to the Jewish and Christian Scriptures*, Agra: Agra Tract Society, 1860.

Nadwī, A.H.A., *Islamic Concept of Prophethood*, trans. by M. Ahmad, Lucknow (India): Academy of Islamic Research and Publications, 1976.

———, *Islamic Studies, Orientalists and Muslim Scholars*, trans. by A. Mohiuddīn, Lucknow: Academy of Islamic Research and Publications, 1983.

———, *Muhammad Rasulallah – The Life of the Prophet Muhammad,* trans. from Urdu by M. Ahmad, Lucknow: Academy of Islamic Research and Publications, 1979.

Nadwī, S.M., *An Early History of the Prophet of Islam*, Lahore: Shaikh Muhammad Ashraf, 1968.

Nadwī, S.S., *Muhammad – The Ideal Prophet*, trans. by M. Ahmad, Lucknow (India): Academy of Islamic Research and Publications, 1981.

Naff, T. and Roger, O. (eds.), *Studies in Eighteenth Century Islamic History*, London and Amsterdam: Feffer & Simmons, 1977.

Naṣr, S.H., *Muhammad: Man of Allah*, London: Muhammadi Trust, 1982.

Niazī, K., *Islam and the West*, Lahore: Shaikh Muhammad Ashraf, 1976.

Nicholson, R.A., *A Literary History of the Arabs*, Cambridge: Cambridge University Press, 1953.

Niṣabūrī, H. al-, *Maʿrifat ʿUlūm al-Ḥadīth*, Cairo, 1937.

———, *al-Mustadrak ʿalā al-Ṣaḥīḥayn*, Hyderabad, 1334–42 AH.

Nuʿmānī, S., *Sīrat an-Nabī (The Life of the Prophet, peace be upon him)*, 2 vols., Delhi: Idarāh-i-Adabi yat-i Delhi, 1979, rpt. 1983.

Ockley, S., *The History of the Saracens*, 5th edition, London, Henry G. Bohn, 1848.

O'Leary, de L., *Arabic Thought and its Place in History*, London: Routledge & Kegan Paul, 1954.

Padwick, C.E., *Muslim Devotions – A Study of Prayer Manuals in Common Use*, London: Society for Promoting Christian Knowledge, 1936.

Pailin, D.A., *Attitudes to Other Religions – Comparative Religion in Seventeenth and Eighteenth Century Britain*, Manchester, 1984.

Palmer, S.J., *Mormons and Muslims – Spiritual Foundations and Modern Manifestations*, Conference Papers, Utah: Bringham Young University, 1985.

P'Bitek, O, *African Religions in Western Scholarship*, Kampala, Nairobi, Dar es Salaam: East African Literature Bureau, n.d.

Peters, F.E., *Muhammad and the Origins of Islam*, Albany: State University of New York Press, 1994.

Pike, E.R., *Mohammed – Prophet and the Religion of Islam*, London: Weidenfeld & Nicolson, 1968.

Pike, R., *Encyclopaedia of Religion and Religions*, London: George Allen & Unwin, 1951.

Prideaux, H., *The True Nature of Imposture Fully Displayed in the Life of Mahomet*, 8th edition, London, 1723.

Qastallānī, I., *Mawahib Laduniyyah*, with commentary of Zarqani, 8 vols., Cairo, 1278.

Qureshi, S.A., *Letters of the Holy Prophet*, Karachi: International Islamic Publishers, 1983.

Qureshi, Z.A., *Prophet Muhammad and His Western Critics – A Critique of W. Montgomery Watt and Others*, 2 vols., Lahore: Idarah Maʿarif Islami, 1992.

Qutb, Sayyid, *Fī Ẓilāl al-Qur'ān*, Vol. IV, Beirut, Dār al-Shurūq, 1982.

Rahmān, A., *Muhammad as a Military Leader*, London: Muslim Schools Trust, 1980.

Rahman, F, *Islam*, 2nd. edition, Minneapolis and Chicago: Bibliotheca Islamica, 1979.

———, *Islamic Methodology in History*, Karachi: Central Institute of Islamic Research, 1965.

———, *Major Themes of the Qur'an*, Chicago: Bibliotheca Islamica, 1980.

———, *Prophecy in Islam: Philosophy and Orthodoxy*, London: George Allen & Unwin, 1958.

Rahnema, Z., *Payambar: The Messenger*, trans. from the Persian by L.P. Elwell-Sutton, 2 vols., reprint, Texas: The Zahra Trust, 1982.

Raleigh, Sir W., *The Life and Death of Mahomet*, London, 1637.

Rasūl, G.M., *The Origins and Development of Muslim Historiography*, Lahore: Shaikh Muhammad Ashraf, 1968.

Reland, A., *De Religione Mohammedica*, Utrecht, 1717.

Ridā, M.R., *The Revelation to Muhammad*, trans. from Arabic by A.-S. Sharāfuddīn, Part 1, second rev. edition, Bhiwandī (India): Ad-Dārul-Qayyimah, 1960.

Robertson, J.M., *A Short History of Christianity*, London: Watts & Co., 1902.

Rodinson, M., *Europe and the Mystique of Islam*, trans. from the French by Roger Veinus, London: I.B. Tauris, 1988.

———, *Mohammed*, trans. from the French by A. Carter, London: The Penguin Press, 1971.

Rogers, M., *The Spread of Islam*, Oxford: Elsevier-Phaidon, 1976.

Rosenthal, F., *A History of Muslim Historiography*, Leiden: E.J. Brill, 1952.

Rotter, G., *Ibn Hisham, 'Abd al-Mālik, Das Leben des Propheten Aus dem – Arabishen Ubertragen und Bearbeitet*, Tubingen, Basel: Erdmann, 1976.

Royster, J.E., *The Meaning of Muhammad for Muslims: A Phenomenological Study of Recurrent Images of the Prophet*, Ph.D. Thesis, Hartford, Connecticut: The Hartford Seminary Foundation, 1970.

Ṣābiq, as-S., *Fiqh-us-Sunnah*, Vol. 3, Indianapolis: American Trust Publications, 1986.

Sage, C.M., *Paul Albar of Cordoba: Studies on His Life and Writings*, Washington, DC: Catholic University of America Press, 1943.

Sahas, D.J., *John of Damascus on Islam, the 'Heresy of the Ishmaelites'*, Leiden: E.J. Brill, 1972.

Said, E.W., *Covering Islam: How the Media and the Experts Determine How We See the Rest of the World,* New York: Pantheon Books, 1981.

———, *Orientalism – Western Conceptions of the Orient,* London: Routledge & Kegan Paul, 1978. (Reprinted with a new Afterword, London: Penguin, 1995.)

Samir, K.S. and Nielsen, J.S., *Christian Arabic Apologetics During the Abbasid Period 750–1258,* Leiden: E.J. Brill, 1994.

Saunder, J.J., *A History of Medieval Islam,* London: Routledge & Kegan Paul, 1964.

Schacht, J., *The Origins of Muhammadan Jurisprudence,* Oxford, 1950.

Schacht, J. and Bosworth, C.E. (eds.), *The Legacy of Islam,* Oxford, 1974.

Schimmel, A., *And Muhammad is His Messenger – The Veneration of the Prophet in Islamic Piety,* Chapel Hill, North Carolina: University of North Carolina Press, 1985.

Scott, S.P., *History of the Moorish Empire in Europe,* Vol. 1, Philadelphia, 1904.

Seferta, Y.H.R., *The Concept of Religious Authority According to Tafsīr al-Manār and Other Writings of Muhammad Abduh and Rashīd Ridhā and its Bearing upon their Critique of Christianity and Judaism,* unpublished Ph.D. Thesis, Dept. of Theology, University of Birmingham (UK), 1984.

Seguy, M.-R., *The Miraculous Journey of Mahomet. Mir'āj Nāmeh,* Paris: Bibliotheque Nationale, 1977.

Sell, E., *Inspiration,* Madras (India), SPCK, 1930.

Shabo, A.M., *An Evaluative Study of the Bahīra Story in the Muslim and Christian Traditions,* unpublished MA Thesis, Dept. of Theology, University of Birmingham (UK), 1984.

Shelly, M.T., *The Life and Thought of W.H.T. Gairdner, 1873–1928 – A Critical Evaluation of a Scholar-Missionary to Islam,* unpublished Ph.D. Thesis, Dept. of Theology, University of Birmingham (UK), 1988.

Siddiqi, M.Z., *Hadith Literature – Its Origin, Development and Special Features*, Calcutta: Calcutta University Press, 1991; Cambridge: The Islamic Texts Society, 1993.

Simon, R., *Meccan Trade and Islam – Problems of Origin and Structure*, trans. by F. Sos, Budapest: A Kademiai Kiado, 1989.

Singer, I. (ed.), *The Jewish Encyclopaedia*, Vol. 8, New York and London: Funk & Wagnalls, 1904.

Smith, B.P., *Islam in English Literature*, second edition, Delmar, NY: Caravan Books, 1977.

Smith, R.B., *Muhammed and Muhammedanism*, London, Smith Elder, 1874.

Smith, W.C., *Islam in Modern History*, Princeton, NJ: Princeton University Press, 1977.

Sourdel, D., *Medieval Islam*, trans. by J.M. Watt, London: Routledge & Kegan Paul, 1983.

Southern, R.W., *Western Views of Islam in the Middle Ages*, Cambridge (Mass.): Harvard University Press, 1962.

Sprenger, A., *The Life of Mohammad from Original Sources*, Allahabad: Presbyterian Mission Press, 1851.

Stephen, L. and Sidney, Lee (eds.), *The Dictionary of National Biography – From the Earliest Times to 1900*, Vol. 12, London: Oxford University Press, 1921–22.

Store, K. den, *Pax Romana: Pax Christina*, Copenhagen, 1952.

Swartz, M.L. (ed.), *Studies on Islam*, New York and Oxford: Oxford University Press, 1981.

Tabari, A., *The Book of Religion and Empire*, trans. by A. Mingana, Manchester: Manchester University Press, 1922.

Taymiyyah, A. Ibn A. al-H. Ibn, *A Muslim Theologian's Response to Christianity: Ibn Taymiyya's al-Jawāb al-Sahīh*, ed. and trans. by T.F. Michel, Delmar, NY: Caravan Books, 1984.

Temkin, O., *The Falling Sickness*, second edition, Baltimore: Johns Hopkins University Press, 1971.

Torrey, C.C., *The Jewish Foundation of Islam*, New York: KTAV Publishing House, 1967.

Toynbee, A.J., *The World and the West*, London: The BBC Reith Lectures, 1954.

———, *Civilization on Trial*, London: Oxford University Press, 1948.

Troll, C.W., *Sayyid Ahmad Khan: A Reinterpretation of Muslim Theology*, New Delhi: Vikas Publishing House Pvt. Ltd., 1978.

Von Grunebaum, G.E., *Islam and Medieval Hellenism: Social and Cultural Perspectives*, ed. and Foreword by D.S. Wilson, London: Variorum Reprints, 1976.

Von Kramer, A. (ed.), *History of Muhammad's Campaigns by Aboo Abdallah Mohammad Omar Al-Wāqidy*, 1856.

Vroom, H.M., *Religions and the Truth – Philosophical Reflections and Perceptions*, trans. from the Dutch by J.W. Rebel, Grand Rapids (Michigan): William B. Eerdmans, 1989.

Wansbrough J., *Qur'anic Studies, Sources and Methods of Scriptural Interpretation*, Oxford University Press, 1977.

Watt, W.M., *Bell's Introduction to the Qur'ān*, Edinburgh: Edinburgh University Press, 1970.

———, *Early Islam – Collected Articles*, Edinburgh: Edinburgh University Press, 1990.

———, *Freewill and Predestination in Early Islam*, London, Luzac, 1948.

———, *The Influence of Islam on Medieval Europe*, Edinburgh: Edinburgh University Press, 1972.

———, *Islam and Christianity Today: A Contribution to Dialogue*, London: Routledge & Kegan Paul, 1983.

———, *Islamic Creeds – A Selection*, Edinburgh: Edinburgh University Press, 1994.

Watt, W.M., *Islamic Fundamentalism and Modernity*, London and New York: Routledge, 1988.

———, *Islamic Philosophy and Theology*, Edinburgh: Edinburgh University Press, 1962.

———, *Islamic Political Thought*, Edinburgh: Edinburgh University Press, 1968.

———, *The Meccan Prophet in the Qur'ān*, Edinburgh: Edinburgh University Press, 1987.

———, *Muhammad at Mecca*, Oxford: Clarendon Press, 1953.

———, *Muhammad at Medina*, Oxford: Oxford University Press, 1956.

———, *Muhammad – Prophet and Statesman*, Oxford: Clarendon Press, 1961.

———, *Muhammad's Mecca – History in the Qur'ān*, Edinburgh: Edinburgh University Press, 1988.

———, *Muslim-Christian Encounters: Perceptions and Misconceptions*, London: Routledge, 1991.

———, *Truth in the Religions – A Sociological and Psychological Approach*, Edinburgh: Edinburgh University Press, 1968.

———, *What is Islam?*, London and Harrow: Longmans, Green & Co. and Beirut: Librarie du Liban, 1968.

Weiss, B.G. and Green, A.H., *A Survey of Arab History*, Cairo: The American University of Cairo Press, 1985.

Wellhausen, J., *Muhammad and the Jews of Madina* with an Excursus *Muhammad's Constitution of Madina*, trans. and ed. by W. Behn, Freisburg im Breisgau: Klaus Schwarz Verlag, 1975.

Wessels, A., *A Modern Arabic Biography of Muhammad: A Critical Study of Muhammad Husayn Haykal's Hayat Muhammad*, Leiden: E.J. Brill, 1972.

White, J., *A Comparison of Mahometanism and Christianity: Bampton Lecture*, London: F.C. & J. Rivington, 1811.

White, J., *Sermons Preached Before the University of Oxford in the Year 1784*, Oxford, 1784.

Wickham-Legg, L.G. (ed.), *The Dictionary of National Biography 1931–1940*, London: Oxford University Press, 1949.

Widengren, G., *The Ascension of the Apostle and the Heavenly Book*, Uppsala, Sweden: A-B Lundequistski Bokhandeln, 1950.

———, *Muhammad, The Apostle of God and His Ascension (King and Saviour V)*, Uppsala: Almqvist & Wiksell, Bokrychien Aktiebolag, 1955.

Wilson, J.C., *Muhammad's Prophetic Office as Portrayed in the Qur'ān*, unpublished Ph.D. Thesis, Edinburgh University, 1949.

Wollaston, A.N., *Muhammad – His Life and Doctrines with Accounts of His Immediate Successors*, London: John Murray, 1904.

Yusuf, S.M., *An Essay on the Sunnah – Its Importance, Transmission, Development and Revision*, Lahore: Institute of Islamic Culture, 1977.

Zaydān, J., *Umayyads and Abbāsids: Being the Fourth Part of Jurji Zaydān's History of Islamic Civilization*, trans. by D.S. Margoliouth, London: Darf, 1987.

ARTICLES

Abdel-Malek, A., 'Orientalism in Crises', *Diogenes*, (1963), p.44.

Abdīn, al-T. Z. al-, 'The Political Significance of the Constitution of Medina', in *Arabian and Islamic Studies*, edited R. Bidwell and G.R. Smith (London: Longman, 1983), pp.146–52.

Abū Zahra, S.M., 'An Analytical Study of Dr. Schacht's Illusions', *Journal of Islamic Studies*, Cairo, Vol. 1, No. 1 (1968), pp.24–44.

Adams, C.J., 'Authority of the Prophetic Hadith in the Eyes of Some Modern Muslims', in *Essays on Islamic Civilization*

Presented to Niyazi Berkes, ed. D.P. Little (Leiden: E.J. Brill, 1976), pp.25–47.

Adivar, A., 'A Turkish Account of Orientalism', *Muslim World*, 43 (1953), pp.266–82.

Adolf, Helen, 'Christendom and Islam in the Middle Ages: New Light on "Grail Stone" and "Hidden Host" ', *Speculum*, 32 (1957), pp.103–15.

Aḥmad, I., 'Wāqidī as a Traditionist', *Islamic Studies*, Vol. 18, No. 3 (1979), pp.243–53.

Aḥmad, K., 'The Significance of the Hijra', *Islamic Literature*, Vol. 17, No. 9 (1971), pp.21–8.

Aḥmad, M., 'Was Muhammad Illiterate?', *Islam and the Modern Age*, Vol. 8, No. 2 (1977), pp.1–15.

Aḥmad, N., 'A Scottish Orientalist (J.B. Gilchrist) and His Works', *Libri*, 28 (1978), pp.196–204.

Ahsan, M.M., 'Orientalism and the Study of Islam in the West: A Select Bibliography', *Muslim World Book Review*, Vol. 1, No. 4 (1981), pp.51–60.

———, 'The Qur'ān and the Orientalists – A Note on the Authenticity of the So-Called Satanic Verses', *Islamic Quarterly*, Vol. 24, No. 3/4 (1980), pp.89–95.

———, 'Review of Norman Daniel's *Islam and the West – The Making of an Image*', *Muslim World Book Review*, Vol. 1, No. 3 (Spring 1981), p.53.

———, 'Review of Prof. A.L. Tibāwī's "Second Critique of English-Speaking Orientalists and their Approach to Islam and the Arabs" ', *Muslim World Book Review*, Vol. 1, No. 3 (Spring 1981), pp.18–20.

Akkād, A.M. el-, 'The Seal of the Prophets', *Majallat al-Azhar*, 32v (1960–61), pp.5–9.

Algar, H., 'The Problem of Orientalists', *Islamic Literature*, Vol. 17, No. 2 (1971), pp.31–42.

ʿĀlī, B., 'Sociological Study of Muhammad', *Voice of Islam* (Karachi), Vol. 20, No. 9 (1972), pp.501–11.

ʿAlī, Farrukh B., 'Al-Hudaybiya: An Alternative Version', *The Muslim World*, Vol. 71 (1981), pp.47–62.

Alleaume, G., 'L'Orientaliste Dans se Miroir de la Litterature Arabe', *British Society for Middle Eastern Studies Bulletin*, Vol. 9, No. 1 (1982), pp.5–13.

Alphandery, P., 'Mahomet-Anti Christ das le Moyen Age Latin', in *Melanges Harturig Derenbourg (1844–1908) Recueil de Travaux d'erudition Dedies a la Memoire d'hartwig Derenbourg par ses Amis et ses eleves* (Paris: Ernest Levoux, 1909), pp.261–77.

Alvervy, M.T. d', 'Deux Traductions Latines du Coran au Moyen Age', *Archives d'Histoire Doctinale et Litteraire du Moyen Age*, Paris, (1946–8).

Alvervy, M.T. d' and Vajda, G., 'Marc de Tolede, Traducteur d'Ibn Tumart', *Al-Andalus*, Vol. 16, fasc. 1 and 2; Vol. 17, fasc. 1 (1951–2).

Alwaye, A.M.M., 'The Significance of "The Night Journey and the Ascent" ', *Majallat al-Azhar*, 41 (September 1969), pp.5–10.

———, 'The Miraculous Journey of the Prophet from Mecca to Jerusalem', *Majallat al-Azhar*, Vol. 47, No. 5 (1975), pp.1–5.

———, 'Al-Mirʿāj, The Ascent of the Prophet', *Majallat al-Azhar*, Vol. 45, No. 3 (1973), pp.1–11; Vol. 45, No. 4 (1973), pp.1–5.

Ananikian, M.H., '*Tahrif* or the Alteration of the Bible According to the Muslems' *The Muslim World*, Vol. 14 (1924), pp.61–84.

Anawati, G.C., 'Dialogue with Gustav E. Von Grunebaum', *International Journal of Middle Eastern Studies*, 7 (1976), pp.123–8.

Ancona, A.D., 'La Legenda Di Maometto in Occidente', *Ciornale Storico di Litteatura Italiana*, 13 (1889), pp.199–281.

Andrae, T., 'Die Person Muhammaeds in Lehre und Glauben Seiner Gemeinde', (Stockholm: P.A. Norstedit & Soner, 1918), pp.28–39 and 52 ff.

———, 'Muhammad's Doctrine of Revelation' (trans. by A. Jeffrey), *The Muslim World*, Vol. 23, No. 2 (1933), pp.252–71.

Angawi, S., 'Review of Watt's *Muhammad's Mecca*', *Journal of Islamic Studies*, Vol. 3, No. 2 (July 1992), pp.240–3.

Anon, 'Professor Margoliouth's "Life of Mohammed" ', *The Muslim World*, Vol. 2, No. 3 (July 1912), p.311.

Anouar, A.M., 'Orientalism in Crisis', *Diogenes*, 44 (1959), pp.103–40.

Ansari, A.S.B., 'Review of Watt's *What is Islam?*', *Hamdard Islamicus*, Vol. 4, No. 3 (Autumn 1981), pp.91–7.

Arafat, W., 'A Controversial Incident in the Life of Hassan b. Thābit', *Bulletin of the School of Oriental and African Studies*, 17 (1955), pp.197–205.

———, 'Early Critics of the Authenticity of the Poetry of the Sīra', *Bulletin of the School of Oriental and African Studies*, 21, Pt. 3 (1958), pp.453–63.

———, 'The Elegies on the Prophet in Their Historical Perspective', *Journal of the Royal Asiatic Society* (1967), pp.15–21.

———, 'Review of Watt's *Mecca*', *Islamic Quarterly*, Vol. 1, No. 3 (October 1954), pp.182–4.

———, 'New Light on the Story of Banu Qurayzah and the Jews of Madīna', *Journal of the Royal Asiatic Society* (1976), pp.100–7.

Aslam, Q.M., 'A Note on the Psychological Analysis of Religious Experience in the Light of a Tradition of the Prophet', *Islamic Culture*, 8 (1934), pp.387–92.

Ayād, M.K., 'The Beginning of Muslim Historical Research' (trans. from the German and annotated by M.S. Khān), *Islamic Studies*, Vol. 17, No. 1 (1978), pp.1–26.

Azīz, A., 'Trends in the Political Thought of Medieval Muslim India', *Studia Islamica*, 17 (1963), pp.121–30.

Azīz, Z., 'Review of Watt's *Islam and Christianity*', *The Islamic Guardian*, Vol. 5, No. 2 (April-June 1984), pp.18–28.

Baldwin, M.W., 'Western Attitudes Towards Islam', *Catholic Historical Review*, 28 (1942), pp.403–11.

Bausani, A., 'Islam as an Essential Part of Western Culture', in *Studies on Islam: A Symposium on Islamic Studies Organized in Cooperation with the Academia dei Lincei in Rome, Amsterdam, 18–19 October, 1973*, Amsterdam and London: North Holland Publishing Company, 1974, pp.19–36.

Bell, R., 'The Development of Mohammed's Personality', *The Muslim World*, Vol. 4, No. 4 (October 1914), pp.353–64.

———, 'Mohammed's Call', *The Muslim World*, Vol. 24, No. 1 (1934), pp.13–19.

———, 'Muhammad and Previous Messengers', *The Muslim World*, Vol. 24, No. 4 (1934), pp.330–40.

———, 'Muhammad's Visions', *The Muslim World*, Vol. 24, No. 2 (April 1934), pp.145–54.

Benaboud, M., 'Orientalism and the Arab Elite', *Islamic Quarterly*, Vol. 26, No. 1 (First Quarter 1982), pp.3–15.

———, 'Orientalism on the Revelation of the Prophet: The Cases of W. Montgomery Watt, Maxime Rodinson and Duncan Black MacDonald' (Review Article), *American Journal of Islamic Social Sciences*, 3 (December 1986), pp.309–26.

Bennabī, M., 'Islam in History and Society', *Islamic Studies*, 18 (1979), pp.33–47, 281–97; 19 (1980), pp.29–48.

Benz, E., 'Obstacles to Understanding Other Religions', in *Relations Among Religions Today – A Handbook of Policies and*

Principles, ed. Moses Jung et al. (Leiden: E.J. Brill, 1963), pp.101–4.

Berenson, B., 'Mohammad: Was He an Imposter?', *Harvard Monthly*, 4 (April 1887), pp.48–63.

Biecher, J.E., 'Christian Humanism Confronts Islam: Sifting the Qur'ān with Nicholas of Cusa', *JECS*, 13 (1976), pp.1–14.

Bignani-Odier, J. and Della Vida, M.-G.L., 'Une Version Latine de l'Apocalypse Syro-Arabe de Serge-Bahirā', *Melanges d'Archeologie et d'Histoire* (Ecole Fr. de Rome), Tome 62 (Paris, 1950).

Bijlefeld, W.A., 'A Prophet and More than a Prophet?', *The Muslim World*, Vol. 59, No. 1 (January 1969), pp.1–28.

Boase, A.W., 'Review of Cook's *Muhammad*', *Muslim World Book Review*, Vol. 4, No. 3 (1984), pp.6–7.

Bohnstedt, J.W., 'The Infidel Scourge of God: The Turkish Menace as Seen by German Pamphleteers of the Reformation Era', *Transactions of the American Philosophical Society held at Philadelphia for Promoting Useful Knowledge*, New Series, Vol. 58, Part 9 (1968).

Bosworth, C.E., 'A Dramatisation of the Prophet Muhammad's Life: Heri de Bornier's "Mahomet" ', *Numen, International Review of the History of Religions*, 17 (1970), pp.105–17.

Bouvat, L. and Reby, J., 'Le Prophete Mohammed en Europe: Legende et Literature', *Revue du Monde de Musulman*, 9 (1909), pp.264–72.

Braumann, M.M., 'The Origin of the Principle of ʿIsmah: Muhammad's "immunity from sin" ', *Museon*, 88 (1975), pp.221–5.

Brohi, A.K., 'Seerat-un-Nabī in Contemporary Perspective', *Voice of Islam* (Karachi), Vol. 20, No. 9 (1972), pp.455–73.

Broomfield, G.W., 'The Psychology of Mohammed', *The Muslim World*, Vol. 16, No. 1 (1926), pp.37–58.

Brown, L.E., 'The Patriarch Timothy and the Caliph al-Mahdī', *The Muslim World*, Vol. 21 (1931), pp.38–45.

Bryan, J., 'Mohammed's Controversy with Jews and Christians', *The Muslim World*, Vol. 9, No. 4 (1919), pp.383–415.

Buaben, J.M., 'Review of Watt's *Muhammad's Mecca*', *Islam and Christian-Muslim Relations*, Vol. 1, No. 2 (December 1990), pp.286–9.

Buhl, F.P.W., 'The Character of Muhammad as a Prophet', *The Muslim World*, Vol. 1, No. 4 (1911), pp.356–64.

Caetani, L., 'The Development of Muhammad's Personality' (trans. by R.F. McNeile), *The Muslim World*, 4 (1914), p.3.

Caillet, E., 'Blaise Pascal on Mohammed', *The Muslim World*, 36 (1946), pp.100–6.

Cambier, G., 'Une Copie de la Vita Mahumeti au British Museum' (MS Add. 24.199), *Rev. Moyen Age Latin*, 19 (1963), pp.171–6.

Childers, E., 'The Western Image of Arabs', in *Nederlands-Arabische Kring 1955–1965: Eight Studies Marking its First Decade* (Leiden: E.J. Brill, 1966), pp.29–46.

Charfi, A.M., 'Christianity in the Qur'ān Commentary of Ṭabarī', *Islamo Christiana*, Vol. 6 (1980), pp.105–48.

Clarke, J.F., 'Mohammed and His Place in Universal History', *Dublin University Magazine*, 18 (1873), pp.460–86.

Colonna, F.. 'A Critique of Orientalism or a Critique of Scripturalism?', *Review of Middle Eastern Studies*, 2 (1976), pp.23–33.

Crabites, P., 'Mohammed as Champion of Women', *Nineteenth Century*, 96 (July 1924), pp.137–45.

Cutler, A. 'The Ninth-Century Spanish Martyrs' Movement and the Origin of Western Christian Missions to the Muslims', *The Muslim World*, 55 (1965), pp.321–39.

Daniel, N., 'The Critical Approach to Arab Society in the Middle Ages', *Annales Islamologiques*, Vol. 17 (1981), pp.31–52.

———, 'Learned and Popular Attitudes to the Arabs in the Middle Ages', *Journal of the Royal Asiatic Society* (1977), pp.41–52.

Denny, F.M., 'Ummah in the Constitution of Maḍīnah', *Journal of Near Eastern Studies*, 36 (1977), pp.39–47.

Dodd, C., 'A Critique of Orientalism: A Review', *British Society for Middle Eastern Studies*, Vol. 6, No. 2 (1979), pp.85–95.

Donner, F.M.G., 'Mecca's Food Supply and Muhammad's Boycott', *Journal of Economic and Social History of the Orient*, 20 (1977), pp.249–66.

———, 'Muhammad's Political Consolidation in Arabia up to the Conquest of Mecca: A Reassessment', *The Muslim World*, 69 (1979), pp.229–47.

Duri, A.A., 'Al-Zuhrī: A Study on the Beginnings of History Writings in Islam', *Bulletin of the School of Oriental and African Studies*, 19 (1957), pp.1–12.

Eaton, H.G., 'Review of Edward Said's Other Work *Covering Islam*', *Islamic Quarterly*, Vol. 29, No. 1 (First Quarter 1985), pp.52–60.

Ehlert, T., 'Muhammad', *The Encyclopaedia of Islam*, New Edition, Vol. VII, C.E. Bosworth et al. (eds.), (Leiden and New York, E.J. Brill, 1993), pp.735–53.

Escovitz, J.H., 'Orientalists and Orientalism in the Writings of Muhammad Kurd 'Ali', *International Journal of Middle Eastern Studies*, 15 (1983), pp.95–109.

Fārūqī, I.R. al-, 'The Essence of Religious Experience in Islam', *Numen, International Review of the History of Religions*, Vol. 20, No. 95 (1973).

———, 'Towards a Historiography of Pre-Hijrah Islam', *Islamic Studies*, Vol. 1, No. 2 (1962), pp.65–87.

Fārūqī, N.A., 'Some Methodological Aspects of the Early Muslim Historiography', *Islam and the Modern Age*, Vol. 6, No. 1 (1975), pp.88–98.

Fischel, W.J., 'Ibn Khaldun's Use of Historical Sources', *Studia Islamica*, 14 (1961), pp.109–19.

Foster, F.H., 'An Autobiography of Mohammed', *The Muslim World*, Vol. 26, No. 2 (April 1936), pp.130–52.

———, 'Reply to Professor Margoliouth's Article, January 1933', *The Muslim World*, Vol. 23, No. 2 (April 1933), p.198.

Freemon, F.R., 'A Differential Diagnosis of the Inspirational Spells of Mohammed the Prophet of Islam', *Epilepsia*, 17 (1976), pp.423–7.

Fueck, J., 'The Originality of the Arabian Prophet', in *Studies on Islam* (trans. and ed. M.L. Swartz), (New York: Oxford University Press, 1981), pp.3–22.

Gabrieli, F., 'Apology for Orientalism', *Diogenes*, 50 (1965), pp.128–36.

Gairdner, W.H.T., 'Mohammed Without Camouflage', *The Muslim World*, Vol. 9, No. 1 (1919), pp.25–7.

Gardet, L., 'Le Prophete', *Table Ronde*, 126 (1958), pp.11–26.

Gaudeul, J.M., 'Learning from Polemics', I and II, *Encounter*, No. 75 (May 1981), pp.1–28; No. 80 (December 1981), pp.1–26.

Gaulmer, J., 'Orientalisme et Humanisme', *Orient*, 2 (1957), pp.7–13.

Gibb, H.A.R., 'Pre-Islamic Monotheism in Arabia', *Hartford Theological Review*, 55 (1962), pp.269–80.

Gil, Moshe, 'The Constitution of Medina: A Reconsideration', *Israel Oriental Studies*, 4 (1974), pp.44–66.

Goiten, S.D., 'Muhammed's Inspirations by Judaism?', *Journal of Jewish Studies*, Vol. 9, No. 3–4 (1958), pp.149–62.

———, 'Who Were Mohammed's Main Teachers?', *Tabriz*, 23 (1951–52), pp.146–59.

Goldfeld, I., 'The Illiterate Prophet (Nabi Ummi): An Enquiry into the Development of a Dogma in Islamic Tradition', *Der Islam*, 57 (1980), pp.58–67.

Grafflin, D., 'The Attack on Orientalism', *Journal of Asian Studies*, 42 (1982–83), pp.607–8.

Green, A.H., 'The Muhammad-Joseph Smith Comparison: Subjective Metaphor, or a Sociology of Prophethood', in *Mormons and Muslims – Spiritual Foundations and Modern Manifestations,* ed. Spencer J. Palmer (Conference Papers), (Utah, Bringham Young University, 1985).

Guillaume, A., 'The Biography of the Prophet in Recent Research', *Islamic Quarterly*, Vol. 1, No. 1 (1954), pp.5–11.

———, 'A Note on the Sira of Ibn Ishaq', *Bulletin of the School of Oriental and African Studies*, 18 (1956), pp.1–4.

———, 'Review of Watt's *Mecca*', *The Muslim World*, Vol. 44, No. 1 (January 1954), pp.49–51.

Haddawy, H., 'Early Steps Towards Modern Orientalism', *URM* (1983), pp.18–23.

Halliday, F., 'Orientalism and its Critics', *British Journal of Middle Eastern Studies*, Vol. 20, No. 2 (1993), pp.145–63.

Hamīd, A. and ʿAlī, A. al-R., 'The Mohammed of the Newspapers', *The Muslim World*, 18 (1928), pp.167–72.

Hamidullah, M., 'Discovery of Another Original Letter of the Prophet', *Islamic Culture*, Vol. 16, No. 3 (1942), pp.339–42.

———, 'Life of the Holy Prophet: New Light on Some Old Problems', *Islamic Order*, Vol. 1, No. 2 (1979), pp.84–94.

———, 'Muhammad Ibn Isḥāq (the Biographer of the Holy Prophet)', *Journal of Pakistan Historical Society*, 15 (1967), pp.77–100.

———, 'Muhammad the Prophet of God', *Cultures*, Vol. 7, No. 4 (1980), pp.25–38.

Hamidullah, M., 'Review of Cragg's *The Call of the Minaret*', *Islamic Quarterly*, Vol. 3, No. 4 (January 1957), pp.245–9.

———, 'Two Christians of Pre-Islamic Mecca, 'Uthman Ibn al-Huwairith and Waraqah Ibn Naufal', *Journal of Pakistan Historical Society*, 6 (1958), pp.97–103.

Hammershaimb, E., 'The Religious and Political Development of Muhammad', *The Muslim World*, Vol. 39, No. 2 (1949), pp.126–35; Vol. 39, No. 3 (1949), pp.195–207.

Henniger, J., 'Pre-Islamic Bedouin Religion', in *Studies on Islam*, (trans. and ed. M.L. Swartz), (New York: Oxford University Press), 1981, pp.86–98.

Hermansen, M.K., 'Kenneth Cragg's, *Muhammad and the Christian*', *American Journal of Islamic Social Sciences*, Vol. 2, No. 1 (July 1985), pp.130–1.

Hess, A.C., 'Consensus or Conflict: The Dilemma of Islamic Historians. A Review Article', *American Historical Review*, 81 (1976), pp.788–99.

Hillenbrand, C., 'Some Medieval Islamic Approaches to Some Material: The Evidence of a 12th Century Chronicle' (Ta'rīkh Mayya fāriqīn wa-Amīd of Ibn al-Azrāq al-Fāriqī), *Oriens*, 27–28 (1981), pp.197–225.

Hingora, Q.I., 'The Prophet's Struggles Before His Hijrah', *Islamic Literature*, Vol.17, No. 9 (1971), pp.5–19.

Hirschfeld, H., 'Historical and Legendary Controversies Between Muhammad and the Rabbis', *Jewish Quarterly Review*, 10 (1897–98), pp.100–16.

Hoffman-Ladd, V.J., Review of Watt's *Islamic Fundamentalism and Modernity*', *International Journal of Middle Eastern Studies*, Vol. 23, No. 3 (August 1991), pp.414–17.

Horovitz, J., 'The Earliest Biographies of the Prophet and Their Authors', *Islamic Culture*, Vol. 1 (October 1927), pp.535–59; Vol. 2 (1928), pp.22–50, 164–82, 495–526.

Hossain, M., 'Review of Watt's *Muslim-Christian Encounters*', *Journal of Islamic Studies*, Vol. 3, No. 2 (July 1992), pp.257–8.

Hourani, G.F., 'Ethical Presuppositions of the Qur'ān', *The Muslim World*, Vol. 70 (1980), pp.1–28.

Howard, E., '*Mohammed: The Rise of Islam* by D.S. Margoliouth' (Book Review), *The Church Missionary Intelligencer*, Vol. 57 (July 1906), pp.545–6.

Huntington, S., 'The Clash of Civilizations', *Foreign Affairs*, Vol. 72, No. 3 (Summer 1993), pp.22–49.

Idrīs, H.R., 'Reflexions Sur Ibn Isḥāq', *Studia Islamica*, 17 (1962), pp.23–35.

Inalcik, H., 'The Study of History in Islamic Countries', *Middle East Journal*, 7 (1953), pp.451–5.

Inayatullah, S., 'Personalia', *Islamic Culture*, Vol. 11, No. 4 (October 1937), pp.534–6.

Irving, T.B., 'The Rushdie Confrontation – A Clash in Values', *Islamic Order Quarterly*, Vol. 2, No. 3 (3rd. Quarter, 1989), pp.43–51.

———, 'Terms and Concepts – Problems in Translating the Qur'ān', in *Islamic Perspectives – Studies in Honour of Mawlānā Abul A'lā Mawdūdī*, ed. K. Aḥmad and Z.I. Anṣārī (Leicester, The Islamic Foundation, 1979), pp.121–34.

Issawi, C., 'The Historical Role of Muhammad', *The Muslim World*, Vol. 40, No. 2 (1950), pp.85–95.

Jabur, S. al-, 'The Prophet's Letter to the Byzantine Emperor Heraclius', *Hamdard Islamicus*, Vol. 1, No. 3 (1978), pp.36–50.

Jalīlī, A.H., 'L'Orientalisme et l'esprit de notre temps', *Proceedings of the 27th International Congress of Orientalists* (1967/1971), pp.231–2.

Jeffery, A., 'David Samuel Margoliouth', *The Muslim World*, Vol. 30, No.3 (July 1940), p.295.

———, 'The Quest of the Historical Mohammed', *The Moslem World*, Vol. 16, No. 4 (October 1926), pp.327–48.

Jenkinson, E.J., 'Did Mohammed Know Slavonic Enoch?', *The Muslim World*, 21 (1931), pp.24–8.

Jomier, J., 'Prophetisme Biblique et Prophetisme Coranique. Rassemblances et Differences', *Revue Thomiste*, 77 (1977), pp.600–9.

Jones, J.M.B., 'The Chronology of Maghāzī: A Textual Survey', *Bulletin of the School of Oriental and African Studies*, 19 (1957), pp.245–80.

———, 'Ibn Isḥāq and al-Wāqidī', *Bulletin of the School of Oriental and African Studies*, Vol. 22, No. 1 (1959), pp.41–51.

Jones, M., 'The Conventional Saracen of the Song of Geste', *Speculum*, 17 (1942), p.202.

Karmi, H., 'The Prophet Muhammad and the Spirit of Compromise', *Islamic Quarterly*, 8 (1964), pp.89–94.

Kerr, D.A., 'The Prophet Muhammad in Christian Theological Perspective: A Discussion Paper', Centre for the Study of Islam and Christian-Muslim Relations, Birmingham, (1982).

Khalīl, I., 'Maqālāt Sīrat Nabawī Awr Mustashriqīn Montgomery Watt Kā Afkār Kā Tanqīdī Jā'izah' (Urdu), *Sīrat Nabawī Awr Mustashriqīn* (August 1987), pp.90–141.

Khan, M.A.M., 'A Critical Study of the Poetry of the Prophet's Time and its Authenticity as the Source of Sira', *Islamic Culture*, Vol. 38, No. 4 (1964), pp.249–87.

———, 'Life of the Prophet at Mecca as Reflected in Contemporary Poetry', *Islamic Culture*, 42 (1968), pp.75–91.

Khan, M.S., 'Arabic Historiography by Francesco Gabrieli: Notes and Commentary', *Islamic Studies*, Vol. 19, No. 1 (1980), pp.49–74.

Khoury, P., 'Jean Damascene et l'Islam', *Proche Orient Chretien*, 7 (1957), pp.44–63; 8 (1958), pp.313–39.

Kister, M.J., 'Al-Hira: Some Notes on its Relations with Arabia', *AREA*, Vol. 15 (June 1968), pp.143–69.

Kister, M.J., 'At-Tahannuth: An Enquiry into the Meaning of a Term', *Bulletin of the School of Oriental and African Studies*, Vol. 31, No. 2 (1968), pp.223–36.

Laroui, A., 'For a Methodology of Islamic Studies. Islam Seen by G. Von Grunebaum', *Diogenes*, 83 (1973), pp.12–39.

Latham, J.D., 'Review of Watt's *The Influence of Islam on Medieval Europe*', *Islamic Quarterly*, Vol. 17, No. 3–4 (July–December 1973), pp.191–2.

Latīf, S.A., 'Was the Prophet of Islam Unlettered?' *Islamic Literature*, Vol. 12, No. 6 (1966), pp.51–62.

Lewis, B., 'Gibbon on Muhammad', *Daedalus*, 105 (1976), pp.89–101.

———, 'Some English Travellers in the East', *Middle Eastern Studies*, 4 (1968), pp.296–315.

———, 'The Use of Muslim Historians of Non-Muslim Sources', in *Historians of the Middle East*, ed. B. Lewis and P.M. Holt (Oxford: Oxford University Press, 1962), pp.180–91.

Librande, L., 'Technical Terms in Hadith Study', *The Muslim World*, 72 (1982), pp.34–50.

Little, D.P., 'Three Arab Critiques of Orientalism', *The Muslim World*, Vol. 69, No. 2 (April 1979), pp.110–31.

Lull, R., 'Disputatio Raymundi Christiani et Hamar Saraceni', *in Beati Raymundi Lulli Opera Omnia*, ed. I. Salzinger, pp.1721 ff.

Luther, M., 'On the War Against the Turks' (trans. by C.M. Jacobs), in *Luther's Works Vol. 46, The Christian in Society III*, ed. R.C. Schultz (Philadelphia: Fortress Press, 1967).

Lyall, C.J., 'Obituary of Sir William Muir', *Journal of the Royal Asiatic Society* (1905), p.876.

———, 'The Words "Hanif" and "Muslim" ', *Journal of the Royal Asiatic Society*, Vol. 35 (1903), pp.771–84.

Majul, C.A., 'A Landmark of Importance in History (the Hejira)', *Cultures*, Vol. 7, No. 4 (1980), pp.39–48.

Makdīsī, G., 'Interaction Between Islam and the West', *Revue des Etudes Islamiques*, 44 (1976), pp.287–309.

Margoliouth, D.S., 'Is Islam a Christian Heresy?', *The Muslim World*, Vol. 23, No. 1 (January 1933), pp.6–15.

———, 'On the Origin and Import of the Names Muslim and Hanīf', in *Journal of the Royal Asiatic Society*, Vol. 35 (July 1903), pp.467–93.

———, 'The Origins of Arabic Poetry', *Journal of the Royal Asiatic Society*, Vol. 57 (1925), pp.417–49.

———, 'The Relics of the Prophet Mohammed', *The Muslim World*, Vol. 27, No. 1 (1937), pp.20–7.

Miller, J., 'The Challenge of Radical Islam', *Foreign Affairs*, Vol. 72, No. 2 (Spring 1993), pp.43–56.

Miller, R., 'Islam and the West', *Theology*, 83 (1980), pp.119–22.

Miller, W.A., 'A Note on Islam and the West', *Theology*, Vol. 84, No. 697 (January 1981), pp.35–40.

Moharram, B.M.L., 'War Moḥammed Epileptiker?', *Beilage Zur Allgemeinen Zeitung*, 3 (1902), pp.368–71, 380–2.

Moinul, H.S., 'Prophet Muhammad: The Advent of a New Religio-Social Order', *Journal of Pakistan Historical Society*, 20 (1972), pp.1–33.

Mourād, M., 'La Critique Historique Occidentale et les Biographies Arabes de Prophete', in *Les Arabet et L'Occident* (Geneva: Labor et Fides, Paris: Publs. Orientalistes de France, 1982), pp.95–110.

Muir, W., 'The Belief of Mahomet in His Own Inspiration', *Calcutta Review*, 23 (1854), pp.313–31.

———, 'The Birth and Childhood of Mahomet', *Calcutta Review*, 22 (1854), pp.360–78.

———, 'The "Church of Islam" at Liverpool', *The Church Missionary Intelligencer* (1892), pp.413–17.

Muir, W., 'The Coptic Church in Sudan and Nubia', *The Church Missionary Intelligencer* (1899), pp.260–4.

———, 'The Life of Mahomet, from His Youth to His Fortieth Year', *Calcutta Review*, 23 (1854), pp.66–95.

Munro, D.C., 'The Western Attitude Towards Islam During the Period of the Crusades', *Speculum*, 6 (1931), pp.329–43.

Murad, K., 'Watt's *What is Islam?*', *Muslim World Book Review*, Vol. 1, No. 3 (Spring 1981), pp.3–9.

Nadwi, S.A.H.H., 'The Critique of the Anti-Ḥadīth Movement', *Voice of Islam* (Karachi), Vol. 10, No. 6 (1962).

Nadwi, S.M., 'Belief in Qurān and Disbelief in Ḥadīth: Can They Go Together?', *Islamic Literature*, Vol. 17, No. 3 (1971), pp.13–17.

Naqvi, S.A.R., 'Prophet Muhammad's Image in Western Enlightened Scholarship', *Islamic Studies*, Vol. 20, No. 2 (Summer 1981), pp.137–51.

Nawāb, A.R.K., 'The Play "Mahomet" in England', *Asiatic Quarterly Review* (2nd Series), 12 (January 1891), pp.195–205.

Newby, G.D., 'An Example of Coptic Literary Influence on Ibn Ishaq's Sirah', *Journal of Near Eastern Studies*, 31 (1972), pp.22–8.

Nielsen, J.S., 'Review of Watt's *Islamic Fundamentalism*', *New Community*, Vol. 15, No. 4 (July 1989), pp.639–40.

———, 'Review of Watt's *Muslim-Christian Encounters*', *New Community*, Vol. 18, No. 2 (January 1992), pp.342–3.

Nieuwenhuijze, C.A.O. Van, 'The Prophetic Function in Islam: An Analytic Approach', *Correspondance d'Orient: Etudes*, 3 (1963), pp.99–119.

Norris, H.T., 'Review of Cook's *Muhammad*', *Bulletin of the School of Oriental and African Studies*, Vol. 48, Pt. 1 (1985), p.131.

Nowaihī, M. al-, 'Towards a Re-Evaluation of Muhammad's Prophet and Man', *The Muslim World*, 60 (1970), pp.300–13.

Palmer, E.H., 'Muhammad and Muhammedanism', *Quarterly Review* (1877), pp.205–37.

Papathanassiou, A.N., 'Christian Missions in Pre-Islamic South Arabia', *Theologica*, Vol. 65, Issue 'A' (1994), pp.133–40.

Paret, R., 'Recent European Research on the Life and Works of the Prophet Muhammad', *Journal of the Pakistan Historical Society*, Vol. 6, No. 2 (1958), pp.81–96.

———, 'Revelation and Tradition in Islam', in *We Believe in One God*, ed. A. Schimmel and A. Falaturi (London, 1979), pp.27–34.

Perkins, J.H., 'Was Mohammed an Imposter or an Enthusiast?', *The North American Review*, 64 (October 1846), pp.496–513.

Pickthall, M., 'Review of *Mohammed: The Man and His Faith*', *Islamic Culture*, Vol. 11, No. 1 (January 1937), pp.150–4.

Plesser, M., 'Muhammed's Clandestine 'Umra in the Du'l-Qa'da 8 H. and Sura 17,1', *Rivistadegli Studi Orientali*, 32 (1957), pp.525–30.

Polk, W.R., 'Islam and the West – Sir Hamilton Gibb Between Orientalism and History', *International Journal of Middle Eastern Studies*, 6 (1975), pp.131–9.

Porter, J.E., 'Muhammad's Journey to Heaven', *Numen, International Review of the History of Religions*, 21 (1974), pp.64–80.

Qamaruddin, A., 'Review of Watt's *Islamic Fundamentalism*', *Islamic Quarterly*, Vol. 35, No. 2 (2nd Quarter, 1991), pp.140–5.

Qarā'ī, A.Q., 'Review of Watt's *Islam and Christianity Today*', *Al-Tawhid*, Vol. 11, No. 3 (April–June 1985), pp.136–76.

Qureishi, Z.A., 'Prophet Mohammad and His Western Critics', *Islamic Literature*, Vol. 14, No. 3 (1968), pp.5–12.

Rahman, F., 'Approaches to Islam in Religious Studies: Review Essay', in *Approaches to Islam in Religious Studies*, ed. R.C. Martin (Tucson: The University of Arizona Press, 1985).

———, 'Divine Revelation and the Prophet', *Hamdard Islamicus*, Vol. 1, No. 2 (1978), pp.66–72.

Rahman, F., 'Islam's Attitude Towards Judaism', *The Muslim World*, 72 (1982), pp.1–13.

———, 'The Religious Situation of Mecca from the Eve of Islam upto the Hijrah', *Islamic Studies*, 16 (1977), pp.289–301.

Raisanen, H., 'The Portrait of Jesus in the Qur'ān: Reflections of a Biblical Scholar', *The Muslim World*, Vol. 70, No. 2 (April 1980), pp.122–33.

Rao, R., 'Mohammed the Prophet', *Islam and the Modern Age*, Vol. 9 (February 1978), pp.67–85.

———, 'Muḥammad', *Al-Serat*, (Selected Articles 1975–83), (London: Muhammadi Trust, 1983), pp.17–30.

Rauf, M.A., 'A Muslim Response to the "Pre-Islamic Period of Sīrat al-Nabī" ', *The Muslim World*, 62 (1972), pp.42–8.

———, 'Outsiders' Interpretations of Islam: A Muslim's Point of View', in *Approaches to Islam in Religious Studies*, ed. R.C. Martin (Tucson: The University of Arizona Press, 1985), pp.179–88.

Reeves, M.E., 'History and Prophecy in Medieval Thought', *Medievalia Et Humanistica* (New Series), No. 5 (1974), pp.51–75.

Ringreen, H., 'Islam in Western Research', *Islamic Literature*, Vol. 8, No. 5–6 (1956), pp.91–4.

Rippin, A., 'Literary Analysis of Qur'ān, Tafsīr and Sīra. The Methodologies of John Wansbrough', in *Approaches to Islam in Religious Studies*, ed. R.C. Martin (Tucson: The University of Arizona Press, 1985), pp.151–63.

———, 'Review of Watt's *Early Islam*', *Bulletin of the School of Oriental and African Studies,* Vol. 55, Pt. 1 (1992), pp.195–6.

Rizvi, K., 'The Status of the Poet in Jahiliyya', *Hamdard Islamicus*, Vol. 6, No. 2 (Summer 1983), pp.97–110.

Robson, J., 'Ibn Isḥāq's Use of the Isnād', *Bulletin of the John Rylands Library*, Vol. 38, No. 2 (1956), pp.449–65.

———, 'Review of Guillaume's Translation of Ibn Isḥāq's

Sīrat Rasūl Allāh', *The Muslim World*, Vol. 46, No. 3 (July 1956), pp.272–3.

Rodinson, M., 'A Critical Survey of Modern Studies on Muhammad', in *Studies on Islam*, ed. and trans. Merlin L. Swartz (New York and Oxford: Oxford University Press, 1981), pp.23–85.

———, 'The Life of Muhammad and the Sociological Problem of the Beginnings of Islam', *Diogenes*, 20 (1957), pp.28–51.

Rofe, H., 'How Revelations Came to the Prophets', *Islamic Literature*, Vol. 6, No. 8 (1954), pp.471–6.

Rosenthal, F., 'The Influence of the Biblical Tradition on Muslim Historiography', in *Historians of the Middle East*, ed. B. Lewis and P.M. Holt (Oxford: Oxford University Press, 1962), pp.35–45.

Royster, J.E., 'Muhammad as Teacher and Exemplar', *The Muslim World*, 68 (1978), pp.235–58.

———, 'The Study of Muhammad: A Survey of Approaches from the Perspective of the History and Phenomenology of Religion', *The Muslim World*, 62 (1972), pp.49–70.

Saʿadeh, M.R., 'Why not Canonize Muhammad?', *The Muslim World*, 27 (1937), pp.294–7.

Sabah, R. al-, 'Inferno XXVIII: The Figure of Muhammad', *Yale Italian Studies*, Vol. 1, No. 2 (1977), pp.147–61.

Saunders, J.J., 'Mohammed in Europe: A Note on Western Interpretations of the Life of the Prophet', *History*, 39 (1954), pp.14–25.

Savory, R.M., 'Christendom vs. Islam: 14 Centuries of Interaction and Coexistence', in *Introduction to Islamic Civilization*, ed. R.M. Savory (Cambridge, 1976), pp.127–35.

Schaar, S., 'Orientalism at the Service of Imperialism. A Review Article of Edward Said's *Orientalism*', *Race and Class*, 21 (1979), pp.67–80.

Schimmel, A., 'The Place of the Prophet of Islam in Iqbal's Thought', *Islamic Studies*, Vol. 1, No. 2 (1962), pp.65–87.

———, 'The Prophet Muhammad as a Centre of Muslim Life and Thought', in *We Believe in One God*, ed. A. Schimmel and A. Falaturi (London, 1979), pp.35–61.

Sellheim, R., 'Prophet, Chalif und Geschichte. Die Muhammed Biographie des Ibn Ishaq', *Oriens*, 18–19 (1965–6), pp.33–91.

Serjeant, R.B., 'The Constitution of Medina', *Islamic Quarterly*, 8 (1964), pp.3–16.

———, 'Review of Guillaume's Translation of Ibn Isḥāq's Sīrat Rasūl Allāh', *Bulletin of the School of Oriental and African Studies*, 21, Pt. 1 (1958), pp.1–14.

———, 'The Sunnah Jāmiʿah, Pacts with the Yathrib Jews and the Tahrīm of Yathrib: Analysis and Translation of the Documents Comprised in the So Called "Constitution of Madīna" ', *Bulletin of the School of Oriental and African Studies*, 41 (1978), pp.1–42.

Shamsi, F.A., 'The Date of Hijrah', *Islamic Studies*, Vol. 23, No. 4 (Winter 1984), pp.289–324.

Sharma, A., 'The Significance of the Alleged Illiteracy of the Prophet', *Islam and the Modern Age*, Vol. 7, No. 4 (1976), pp.46–53.

Siddiqi, M., 'The Holy Prophet and the Orientalists', *Islamic Studies*, Vol. 19, No. 3 (Autumn 1980), pp.143–65.

Silverstein, T., 'Dante and the Legend of the Miʿrāj: The Problem of Islamic Influence on the Christian Literature of the Other World', *Journal of Near Eastern Studies*, 11 (1953), pp.89–110, 189–97.

Simon, G., 'Luther's Attitude Toward Islam', *The Muslim World*, 21 (July 1931), pp.257–62.

Sivan, E., 'Orientalism, Islam and Cultural Revolution', *Jerusalem Quarterly*, 5 (1977), pp.84–94.

Smith, H.P., 'Moslem and Christian Polemic', *Journal of Biblical Literature*, 45 (1926), pp.243–5.

Smith, S., 'Events in Arabia in the 6th Century A.D.', *Bulletin of the School of Oriental and African Studies*, Vol. 16, Pt. 3 (1954), pp.425–68.

Sourdel, D., 'Mahomet et les Etudes Muhammadiennes d'apres deux Publications Recentes', *Revue des Etudes Islamiques*, 31 (1963), pp.105–10.

Sprenger, A., 'Muhammad's Journey to Syria and Professor Fleisher's Opinion Thereon', *Journal of the Asiatic Society of Bengal* (New Series), 21 (1853), pp.576–92.

———, 'Notes on Alfred V. Kraemer's Edition of Wākidy's Campaigns', *Journal of the Asiatic Society of Bengal* (New Series), 25 (1856), pp.53–74, 199–220.

———, 'On the Earliest Biography of Mohammed', *Journal of the Asiatic Society of Bengal* (New Series), 20 (1851), pp.395–7.

———, 'On the Origins and Progress of Writing Down Facts Among Mussulmans', *Journal of the Asiatic Society of Bengal* (New Series), Vol. 25 (1856), pp.303–29, 375–81.

Staiger, E., 'Goethe's Mahomet', *Trivium*, 7 (1949), pp.187–99.

Tatlock, J.S.P., 'Mohammed and His Followers in Dante', *Modern Language Review*, 27 (1932), pp.186–95.

Thimme, H., 'Mormonism and Islam', *The Muslim World*, 24 (1934), pp.155–67.

Thomson, R.M., 'William of Malmesbury and Some Other Western Writers on Islam', *Medievalia Et Humanistica* (New Series), No. 6 (1975), pp.179–87.

Thomson, W., 'Muhammad, His Life and Person', *The Muslim World*, Vol. 34, No. 2 (1944), pp.96–137.

———, 'A New Life of Mohammed', *The Muslim World*, Vol. 36, No. 4 (1946), pp.344–51.

Tibawi, A.L., 'Aspects of the Early Muslim History', *Journal of the Middle Eastern Society*, 1 (1947), pp.23–34.

———, 'Christians Under Muhammad and His First Two Caliphs', *Islamic Quarterly*, 6 (1961), pp.30–46.

———, 'Ibn Isḥāq's Sīra, A Critique of Guillaume's Translation (*The Life of Muhammad*)', *Islamic Quarterly*, Vol. 3, No. 3 (October 1956), pp.196–214.

———, 'Review of Watt's *Islamic Political Thought*', *Islamic Quarterly*, Vol. 14, No. 1 (January–March 1970), pp.53–4.

———, 'Review of Watt's *Muhammad – Prophet and Statesman*', *Islamic Quarterly*, Vol. 6, No. 3/4 (July–October 1961), pp.127–8.

Togan, A.Z.V., 'The Concept of Critical Historiography in the Islamic World of the Middle Ages' (trans., notes and comments by M.S. Khan), *Islamic Studies*, Vol. 14, No. 3 (1975), pp.175–84; Vol. 16, No. 4 (1977), pp.303–26.

Vahiduddin, S., 'Richard Bell's Study of the Qur'an: A Critical Analysis', *Islamic Culture*, Vol. 30, No. 3 (July 1956), pp.263–72.

Valimamed, M.D., 'Review of Crone and Cook, *Hagarism – The Making of the Islamic World*', *Muslim World Book Review*, Vol. 1, No. 2 (Winter 1981), pp.64–6.

Van Ess, J., 'Tribute to William Montgomery Watt', in Welch and Cachia (eds.), *Islam – Past Influence* (Edinburgh: Edinburgh University Press, 1979), p.ix.

Voorhis, J.W., 'The Discussion of a Christian and a Saracen', *The Muslim World*, 25 (July 1935), pp.266–73.

———, 'John of Damascus on the Moslem Heresy', *The Muslim World*, 24 (1934), pp.391–8.

Waadenburg, J., 'Changes of Perspective in Islamic Studies Over the Last Decades', *Humanidra Islamica*, 1 (1973), pp.247–60.

———, 'Mustashrikūn', *The Encyclopaedia of Islam*, New Edition, Vol. 7, C.E. Bosworth et al. (eds.), (Leiden and New York: E.J. Brill, 1993), pp.735–53.

Waltz, J., 'Muhammad and Islam in St. Thomas Aquinas', *The Muslim World*, Vol. 66, No. 2 (1976), pp.81–95.

———, 'The Significance of the Voluntary Martyrs of Ninth Century Cordoba', *The Muslim World*, 60 (1970), pp.143–59, 226–36.

Warner, M., 'The Question of Faith: Orientalism, Christianity and Islam', in *Orientalist: De la Croix to Matisse*, ed. M.A. Stevens (London: Royal Academy, Weidenfeld & Nicolson, 1984), pp.32–9.

Watt, W.M., 'Allamah Shiblī's Sīrat al-Nabī; II: Life at Makkah', *Journal of Pakistan Historical Society*, 15 (1967), pp.130–61; 201–32, 273–304.

———, 'Carlyle on Muhammad', *The Hibbert Journal*, Vol. 52 (October 1954–July 1955), pp.247–54.

———, 'The Christianity Criticized in the Qur'ān', *The Muslim World*, Vol. 57, No. 3 (July 1967), pp.197–201.

———, 'The Condemnation of the Jews of Banū Qurayzah', *The Muslim World*, Vol. 42 (1952), pp.160–71.

———, 'Conditions of Membership of the Islamic Community', *Studia Islamica*, Vol. 21 (1964), pp.5–12.

———, 'Economic and Social Aspects of the Origin of Islam', *Islamic Quarterly*, Vol. 1, No. 2 (July 1954), pp.90–103.

———, 'The Expedition of al-Hudaibiyya Reconsidered', *Hamdard Islamicus*, Vol. 8, No. 1 (Spring 1985), pp.3–6.

———, 'Gaps in Our Knowledge of the Background of Muhammad's Life', in *Proceedings of 23rd International Congress of Orientalists*, ed. D. Sinor (London: Royal Asiatic Society, 1954), pp.345–6.

———, 'A Great Muslim Mystic', *Studia Missionalia*, Vol. 35 (1986), pp.161–78.

———, 'His Name is Ahmad', *The Muslim World*, Vol. 43, No. 2 (1953), pp.110–17.

Watt, W.M., 'Ideal Factors in the Origin of Islam', *Islamic Quarterly*, Vol. 2, No. 3 (October 1955), pp.160–74.

———, 'Islam and Peace', *Studia Missionalia*, Vol. 39 (1989), pp.167–78.

———, 'Islamic Attitudes to Other Religions', *Studia Missionalia*, Vol. 42 (1993), pp.245–55.

———, 'Islamic Fundamentalism', *Studia Missionalia*, Vol. 41 (1992), pp.241–52.

———, 'The Materials Used by Ibn Isḥāq', in B. Lewis and P.M. Holt: *Historians of the Middle East* (Oxford: Oxford University Press, 1962), pp.23–34.

———, 'Muhammad's Contribution in the Field of Ultimate Reality and Meaning', *Ultimate Reality and Meaning*, 5 (1982), pp.26–38.

———, 'Muhammad as the Founder of Islam', *Studia Missionalia*, Vol. 33 (1984), pp.227–49.

———, 'Pre-Islamic Arabian Religion in the Qur'ān', *Islamic Studies*, 15 (1976), pp.73–9.

———, 'Prophet Muhammad's Image in Western Enlightened Scholarship' (A paper read at the National Seerat Conference held in Islamabad, 19–20th January 1981), *Islamic Studies*, Vol. 20, No. 2 (Summer 1981), pp.137–51.

———, 'Review of Daniel's *Islam in the West*', *The Hibbert Journal*, 59 (October 1960–July 1961), pp.209–12.

———, 'Review of Padwick's *Muslim Devotions*', *The Hibbert Journal*, 59 (October 1960–July 1961), pp.385–6.

———, 'Secular Historians and the Study of Muhammad', *Hamdard Islamicus*, Vol. 1, No. 3 (1978), pp.51–3.

———, 'The Sociologist and the Prophet: Reflections on the Origin of Islam', in *Arshi Presentation Volume*, Presented to Imtiaz Ali Khan Arabi on His Sixty-First Birthday, December 8, 1965, pp.29–36.

Watt, W.M., 'Thoughts on Islamic Unity', *Islamic Quarterly*, Vol. 3, No. 3 (October 1956), pp.188–95.

———, 'Thoughts on Muslim-Christian Dialogue', *The Muslim World*, Vol. 57, No. 1 (January 1967), pp.19–23.

———, 'The Use of the Word "Allah" in English', *The Muslim World*, Vol. 43, No. 3 (July 1953), pp.245–7.

———, 'Western Historical Scholarship and the Prophet of Islam', in *Message of the Prophet*, a series of articles presented at the First International Congress on Seerat, Islamabad, 1976, pp.68–75 and *Al-Seerat*, Vol. 2, No. 2 (1976), pp.3–7.

———, 'Women in Early Islam', *Studia Missionalia*, Vol. 40 (1991), pp.161–73.

Waugh, E., 'Following the Beloved: Muhammad as Model in the Ṣūfī Tradition', in *The Biographical Process: Studies in the History and Psychology of Religion*, ed. R.E. Reynolds and D. Capps (The Hague: Mouton, 1976), pp.63–85.

——, 'The Popular Muhammad: Models in the Interpretation of an Islamic Paradigm', in *Approaches to Islam in Religious Studies*, ed. R.C. Martin (Tucson: The University of Arizona Press, 1985), pp.41–58.

Weir, T.H., 'Was Mohammed Sincere?', *The Muslim World*, Vol. 8, No. 4 (1918), pp.352–8.

Wendell, C., 'The Pre-Islamic Period of Sīrat al-Nabī', *The Muslim World*, 62 (1972), pp.12–41.

Wessels, A., 'Modern Biographies of the Life of the Prophet Muhammad in Arabic', *Islamic Culture*, Vol. 49, No. 2 (April 1975), pp.99–105.

Zaki, Y., 'The Concept of Revelation in Islam', *Islamic Quarterly*, 27 (1983), pp.72–82.

Zuesse, E.M., 'The Degeneration Paradigm in the Western Study of World Religions', *Journal of Ecumenical Studies*, Vol. 13, No. 1 (1976), pp.15–35.

Zuntz, G., 'The Theologian as Historian – Some Reflections Upon a New Book on Constantine the Great', *The Hibbert Journal*, Vol. 52 (October 1953–July 1954), pp.252–9.

Zwemer, S.M., 'The Character of Muhammad', *The Muslim World*, Vol. 1, No. 4 (1911), pp.253–5.

———, 'The Illiterate Prophet: Could Mohammed Read and Write?', *The Muslim World*, Vol. 11, No. 4 (1921), pp.344–63.

———, 'Karl Gottlieb Pfander 1841–1941', *The Muslim World*, 31 (1941), pp.217–26.

———, 'Return to the Old Qibla', *The Muslim World*, Vol. 27, No. 1 (1937), pp.13–19.

———, 'Tor Andrae's *Mohammed*', *The Muslim World*, Vol. 26, No. 3 (July 1936), pp.217–21.

Index